ECO-TOURISM, ENVIRONMENTAL PROBLEMS AND SUSTAINABLE DEVELOPMENT

ENV BOOKS SERIES

ECO-TOURISM ENVIRONMENTAL PROBLEMS AND SUSTAINABLE DEVELOPMENT

Editors

Dr. Soubam Premchandra Singh
Manager
Operation Centre at United Register System Certification Ltd.
Noida (UP) (India)

Dr. Ashok K. Rathoure
GM-Consultancy
Eco Group of Companies, New Civil Road
Surat (Gujarat) (India)

&

Dr. Pawan Kumar 'Bharti'
Society for Environment, Health Awareness of
Nutrition & Toxicology (SEHAT)
B-225/5D, Top Floor, Subhash Gali
Road No. 7, Block B, Ashok Nagar
Shahdara, Delhi -110 093
(India)

Associate Editor

Dr. Alka Chauhan
Society for Environment, Health Awareness of
Nutrition & Toxicology (SEHAT)
B-225/5D, Top Floor, Subhash Gali
Road No. 7, Block B, Ashok Nagar
Shahdara, Delhi -110 093
(India)

DPH

**DISCOVERY PUBLISHING HOUSE PVT. LTD.
INDIA**

Published by:
Namit Wasan

DISCOVERY PUBLISHING HOUSE PVT. LTD.
4383/4B, Ansari Road, Darya Ganj
New Delhi-110 002 (India)
Phone : +91-11-23279245, 43596064-65
Fax : +91-11-23253475
E-mail : discoverypublishinghouse@gmail.com
namitwasan9@gmail.com
sales@discoverypublishinggroup.com
web : www.discoverypublishinggroup.com

First Edition: **2018**

ISBN: 978-93-86841-57-5

Eco-tourism, Environmental Problems and Sustainable Development

© **Editors**

All rights reserved. No part of this publication should be reproduced, stored in a retrieval system, or transmitted in any form or by any means: electronic, mechanical, photocopying, recording or otherwise, without the prior written permission of the author and the publisher.

This book has been published in good faith that the material provided by authors/editors is original. Every effort is made to ensure accuracy of material, but the publisher and printer will not be held responsible for any inadvertent error(s). In case of any dispute, all legal matters are to be settled under Delhi jurisdiction only.

ENV Books Series, India

Calls descriptive and error free chapters for upcoming volumes of books on various environmental issues. Send your manuscripts to envbooks@gmail.com

Founding Editor (Editor-in-Chief)

Dr. Pawan Kumar 'Bharti'

Society for Environment, Health, Awareness of
Nutrition & Toxicology (SEHAT-India)
1775, Sohanganj, Near Clock Tower, Delhi-7, (India)
E-mail:*gurupawanbharti@rediffmail.com*

Other Important Titles by Editor-in-Chief:

1. **Advances in Biotechnology and Ecological Sciences**
   Bharti, P.K., Chauhan, A. and Ray, J. (eds.)
   (ISBN: 978-93-5056-358-8).

2. **Advances in Agriculture and Ecology**
   Bharti, P.K.; Chauhan, A. and Ezeaku Peter Ikemefuna (eds.)
   (ISBN: 978-93-5056-362-5).

3. **Agriculture and Environmental Biotechnology**
   Bharti, P.K. and Chauhan, A. (eds.)
   (ISBN: 978-93-5056-479-0).

4. **Agriculture Crops and Food Security**
   Bharti, P.K., and Chauhan, A. (eds.)
   (ISBN: 978-93-5056-881-1)

5. **Agriculture Development and Sustainable Environment**
   Ray, J. and Bharti, P.K. (eds.)
   (ISBN: 978-93-5056-759-3).

6. **Agriculture Ecology and Environment**
   Bharti, P.K. and Olubukola O. Babalola (eds.)
   (ISBN: 978-93-5056-480-6).

7. **Agriculture Ecology, Sustainable Development and Agribusiness Management**
   Mehta Piyush; Sharma Pankaj; and 'Bharti' P.K. (eds.)
   (ISBN: 978-93-5056-851-4).

8. **Agriculture, Environment and Nano-science**
   Bharti, Pawan K. (ed.)
   (ISBN: 978-93-5056-760-5).

9. **Agriculture Production and Climate Change**
   Khalid, Monowar Alam; Bharti, P.K. and Chauhan, Alka (eds.)
   (ISBN: 978-93-86841-54-4).

10. **Agricultural Practices and Crop Disease Control**
    Chauhan Alka and Sharma Anubhuti (eds.)
    (ISBN: 978-93-5056-859-0).
11. **Agro-biodiversity:** *Conservation and Sustainable Development*
    Sharma, Pankaj; Singh, Narayan; and Bharti, P.K. (eds.)
    (ISBN: 978-93-505-782-1).
12. **Agro-forestry and Climate Change**
    Bharti, Pawan K. and Singh, Narayan (eds.)
    (ISBN: 978-93-5056-514-8).
13. **Agro-forestry and Sustainable Agriculture**
    Sharma, Pankaj; Bharti, P.K. (eds.)
    (ISBN: 978-93-5056-786-9).
14. **Air Pollution and Ecosystem Health**
    Swami Abhishek and Bharti, P.K. (eds.)
    (ISBN: 978-93-5056-877-4).
15. **Analytical Techniques in Chemical and Biological Sciences**
    Mala, Deep & 'Bharti', P.K. (eds.)
    (ISBN: 978-93-86841-59-9).
16. **Aquaculture and Fisheries Environment**
    Gupta, S.K. and Pawan K. Bharti (eds.)
    (ISBN: 978-93-5056-408-0).
17. **Aquatic Biodiversity and Pollution**
    Bharti, P.K.; Chauhan, A. and Kaoud, H.A.H. (eds.)
    (ISBN: 978-93-5056-359-5).
18. **Aquatic Ecology and Biotechnology**
    Bharti, P.K. and Zaki, M.S.A. (eds.)
    (ISBN: 978-93-5056-451-6).
19. **Aquatic Environment and Toxicology**
    Bharti, Pawan K. (ed.)
    (ISBN: 978-93-5056-236-9).
20. **Biodiversity, Biotechnology and Environmental Conservation**
    Bharti, P.K. and Bhandari, G. (eds.)
    (ISBN: 978-93-5056-750-0).
21. **Biodiversity, Biotechnology & Pollution Control**
    Bharti, P.K., and Chauhan, A. (eds.)
    (ISBN: 978-93-5056-887-3)
22. **Biodiversity of Aquatic Ecosystem:** *Significance, Threat and Conservation*
    Bharti, P.K. and Kaoud, H.A.H. (eds.)
    (ISBN: 978-93-5056-297-0).
23. **Biological Diversity and Ecology**
    Arya, M.K.; Bharti, P.K. and Ritesh Joshi (eds.)
    (ISBN: 978-93-5056-785-2).

24. **Bioremediation and Microbial Biotechnology**
    Gupta, Sandeep; and Bharti, P.K. (eds.)
    (ISBN: 978-93-5056-783-8).
25. **Biotechnological Approaches and Water Ecosystem**
    Zaki, M.S.A.; and Bharti, P.K. (eds.)
    (ISBN: 978-93-5056-779-1).
26. **Biotechnology, Agro-ecology and Environment**
    Chauhan, Avnish and Bharti, P.K. (eds.)
    (ISBN: 978-93-5056-757-9).
27. **Biotechnology and Environmental Management**
    Arya Arun; Maheswari Raaz K., & Bharti, P.K (eds.)
    (ISBN: 978-93-5056-862-0).
28. **Clean Technologies and Environmental Protection**
    Chauhan, A.; Sharma, S. and Bharti, P.K. (eds.)
    (ISBN: 978-93-5056-731-9).
29. **Climate Change and Agriculture**
    Bharti, P.K. and Chauhan, Avnish (eds.)
    (ISBN: 978-93-5056-148-5).
30. **Climate Change and Biodiversity**
    Bharti, P.K. and Chauhan, Avnish (eds.)
    (ISBN: 978-93-5056-360-1).
31. **Climate Change, Disaster Management and Environment**
    Chauhan, Alka; Bharti, P.K. (eds.)
    (ISBN: 978-93-5056-784-5).
32. **Conservation and Cultivation of Medicinal Plants**
    Bharti, P.K. and Singh Narayan (eds.)
    (ISBN: 978-93-5056-740-1).
33. **Crop Irrigation and Farming System**
    Chauhan, Alka and P.K. Bharti (eds.)
    (ISBN: 978-93-86841-40-7).
34. **Crop Productivity and Plant Disease Management**
    Chauhan, Alka; Bharti, P.K. and Sadana, Deepti (eds.)
    (ISBN: 978-93-5056-791-3).
35. **Eco-toxicology and Eco-technology**
    Bharti, P.K. and Zaki, M. (eds.)
    (ISBN: 978-93-5056-313-7).
36. **Energy Technologies for Clean Environment**
    Bharti, Chhavi Kumar and Bharti, P.K. (Eds.)
    (ISBN: 978-93-86841-22-3).
37. **Environmental Biotechnology and Application**
    Bharti, P.K. and Chauhan, Avnish (eds.)
    (ISBN: 978-93-5056-262-8).

38. **Environmental Conservation and Biotechnology**
    Chauhan, A. and P.K. Bharti (eds.)
    (ISBN: 978-93-5056-512-4).
39. **Environmental Economics and Sustainability**
    José G. Vargas-Hernández; Khalid Alam Monowar and Bharti, P.K. (eds.)
    (ISBN: 978-93-86841-37-7).
40. **Environmental Health and Problems**
    Bharti, P.K. and Gajananda, Kh. (eds.)
    (ISBN: 978-93-5056-263-5).
41. **Environmental Pollution and Biodiversity**
    Bharti, P.K.; Chauhan, Avnish and Kumar, P. (eds.)
    (ISBN: 978-93-5056-149-2).
42. **E-waste and Environmental Issues**
    Bhalla, R., and Bharti, P.K. (eds.)
    (ISBN: 978-93-5056-886-6)
43. **Experiments on Enhancement of Agricultural Yield**
    Chauhan, Alka and P.K. Bharti (eds.)
    (ISBN: 978-93-86841-50-6).
44. **Farming Techniques and Crop Production**
    Chauhan Alka; Sharma Anubhuti; Ray Jaswant and 'Bharti' P.K. (eds.)
    (ISBN: 978-93-5056-855-2).
45. **Faunal Biodiversity and Biotechnology**
    Sethi, V. Kumar; Bharti, P.K. (eds.)
    (ISBN: 978-93-86841-44-5).
46. **Fisheries and Toxicology**
    Zaki, M.S.A.; Bharti, P.K. and Chauhan, A. (eds.)
    (ISBN: 978-93-5056-452-3).
47. **Fish Habitat and Aquaculture**
    Bharti, P.K.; Gupta Kr. Sanjay (eds.)
    (ISBN: 978-93-5056-744-9).
48. **Forest and Biodiversity Conservation**
    Chauhan Alka; Bharti, P.K. (eds.)
    (ISBN: 978-93-5056-873-6).
49. **Food Processing, Management and Nanotechnology**
    Chauhan, Avnish; Bharti, P.K. (eds.)
    (ISBN: 978-93-5056-796-8).
50. **Food Technology and Research Advancement**
    Chauhan, Avnish; Bharti, P.K. (eds.)
    (ISBN: 978-93-86841-49-0).

51. **Freshwater Ecosystem and Xenobiotics**
    Bharti, P.K.; Zaki, M. and Chauhan, A. (eds.)
    (ISBN: 978-93-5056-299-4).
52. **Geospatial Technology and Ecosystem Assessment**
    'Bharti' Chhavi Kumar; Chauhan, Alka & Bharti, P.K. (eds.)
    (ISBN: 978-93-86841-36-0).
53. **Geospatial Technology and Water Management**
    Chauhan, Alka; Bharti, P.K. (eds.)
    (ISBN: 978-93-5056-885-9).
54. **Heavy Metals and Metalloids in Biosphere:** *Impacts & Assessment*
    Chauhan, Avnish, Gupta, Sandeep; and Bharti, P.K. (eds.)
    (ISBN: 978-93-5056-860-6).
55. **Heavy Metals and Pesticides in Environment**
    'Bharti', P.K.; Bhalla, Resham; Chauhan, Abhishek & Mala, Deep (eds.)
    (ISBN: 978-93-86841-60-5).
56. **Land Reclamation, Soil Quality and Agriculture**
    Bharti, P.K., and Chauhan, A. (ed.)
    (ISBN: 978-93-5056-882-8).
57. **Limnology and Aquatic Science**
    Sharma, S., and Bharti, P.K. (eds.)
    (ISBN: 978-93-5056-735-7).
58. **Medicinal and Nutritional Values of Plants**
    Chauhan, Alka; Bharti, P.K. (eds.)
    (ISBN: 978-93-5056-883-5).
59. **Medicinal Plants:** *Distribution, Utilization and Significance*
    Sharma, P.; Bharti, P.K. and Narayan Singh (eds.)
    (ISBN: 978-93-5056-734-0).
60. **Microbial Applications and Environment**
    Bharti, Pawan K. (ed.)
    (ISBN: 978-93-5056-515-5).
61. **Microbial Ecology and Habitat**
    Bharti, Pawan K. (ed.)
    (ISBN: 978-93-5056-514-8).
62. **Microbial Environment and Bioremediation**
    Chauhan Alka; K. Rathoure Ashok; and K Maheshwari Raaz (eds.)
    (ISBN: 978-93-5056-856-9).
63. **Microbiological and Pharmacological Aspects of Biodiversity**
    Sharma, P., Sharma, N.G.; Sharma, P., and Bharti, P.K. (ed.)
    (ISBN: 978-93-5056-878-1).
64. **Natural Ecosystem and Climate Change**
    Bharti, P.K., and Kh. Gajananda (ed.)
    (ISBN: 978-93-5056-745-6).

65. **Nutraceuticals and Pharmaceuticals from Medicinal Plants**
    Bharti, P.K., Khan, M.M. Abid Ali and Rathoure, Ashok Kumar (ed.)
    (ISBN: 978-93-86841-55-1).
66. **Organic Farming and Bio-fertilizers**
    Sethi, Vinaya Kumar; and Bharti, P.K. (eds.)
    (ISBN: 978-93-86841-23-0).
67. **Pest Management and Agro-Techniques**
    Biswas, Asim; Bharti, P.K., Chauhan, Avnish (eds.)
    (ISBN: 978-93-5056-794-4).
68. **Physical and Chemical Analysis of Environment**
    Mala, Deep; Bharti', P.K. & Bhalla, Resham (eds.)
    (ISBN: 978-93-86841-61-2).
69. **Plant Biomass and Energy Solutions**
    'Bharti', P.K.; 'Bharti' Chhavi Kumar; Rastogi, Amit and Chauhan, Alka (eds.)
    (ISBN: 978-93-86841-62-9)
70. **Plant Biotechnology and Industrial Applications**
    Chauhan, A., and Bharti, P.K. (ed.)
    (ISBN: 978-93-5056-884-2).
71. **Plant Disease Management:** *Control & Elimination Strategies*
    Chauhan, A., and Bharti, P.K. (ed.)
    (ISBN: 978-93-86841-41-4).
72. **Plant Response to Environmental Stress**
    Chauhan, Alka; 'Bharti', P.K. and Chauhan, Avnish (eds.)
    (ISBN: 978-93-86841-58-2).
73. **Pollution, Plant Health and Biotechnology**
    'Bharti', P.K.; Rathoure, Ashok Kumar; Tripathi, Rashmi (eds.)
    (ISBN: 978-93-86841-63-6).
74. **Prakriti me Aushadhi** (*in Hindi*)
    Singh, J.R.; Bharti, P.K. and Bharti, B.
    (ISBN: 978-93-5056-200-0).
75. **Production of Fruits and Vegetables:** *Technologies and Challenges*
    Chauhan, Avnish; Bharti, P.K. and Chauhan, Alka (ed.)
    (ISBN: 978-93-86841-25-4).
76. **Seed Technology, Plant Growth and Cropping System**
    Tyagi, P.K. and Bharti, P.K. (eds.)
    (ISBN: 978-93-5056-738-8).
77. **Seed Treatment, Plant Health and Agro-technology**
    Chauhan, A. and Bharti, P.K. (eds.)
    (ISBN: 978-93-5056-810-1).

78. **Soil Characteristics and Agro-ecology**
    Avnish Chauhan and Bharti, P.K. (eds.)
    (ISBN: 978-93-5056-758-6).
79. **Soil Contamination and Conservation**
    Ezeaku, P.I. and Bharti, P.K. (eds.)
    (ISBN: 978-93-5056-737-1).
80. **Soil Quality and Contamination**
    Bharti, P.K. and Chauhan, Avnish (eds.)
    (ISBN: 978-93-5056-361-8).
81. **Stress Tolerance and Plant Productivity**
    Kumar, Prasann; 'Bharti', P.K (eds.)
    (ISBN: 978-93-86841-56-8).
82. **Sustainable Aquaculture Management**
    Gupta, S.K.; Bharti, P.K (eds.)
    (ISBN: 978-93-5056-797-5).
83. **Waste Disposal and Management**
    Bharti, P.K.; Tabassum, B. and Bajaj, P. (eds.)
    (ISBN: 978-93-5056-729-6).
84. **Waste Generation and Utilization**
    Bajaj Priya; Tabassum, B., and Bharti, P.K. (eds.)
    (ISBN: 978-93-5056-792-0).
85. **Waste Management and Environmental Health**
    Tabassum, B., Bajaj Priya, and Bharti, P.K. (eds.)
    (ISBN: 978-93-5056-777-7).
86. **Water Resources:** *Mapping Monitoring and Management*
    Tyagi, P.K., Chauhan, Avnish and Bharti, P.K. (eds.)
    (ISBN: 978-93-5056-861-3).
87. **Water Resources and Agriculture**
    Bharti, P.K. and Ezeaku Peter Ikemefuna (eds.)
    (ISBN: 978-93-5056-481-3).
88. **Waste Resources Management:** *Monitoring and Assessment*
    Gupta, Sandeep and Bharti, P.K. (eds.)
    (ISBN: 978-93-5056-799-9).

Preface

Environmental issues are harmful effects of human activity on the biophysical environment. Environmental protection is a practice of protecting the natural environment on individual, organizational or governmental levels, for the benefit of both the environment and humans. Environmentalism, a social and environmental movement, addresses environmental issues through advocacy, education and activism.

Sustainability is the key to prevent or reduce the effect of environmental issues. There is now clear scientific evidence that humanity is living unsustainably, and that an unprecedented collective effort is needed to return human use of natural resources to within sustainable limits. For humans to live sustainably, the Earth's natural resources must be used at a rate at which they can be replenished.

The life support system on this planet consists of air, water, land, flora and fauna. Normally these are mutually interconnected and also interdependent. The activities of man constitute one single factor, which often disrupt the intricate balance among the foregoing constituents of the life support system. In his eagerness to urbanize and industrialize, man has not only destroyed plant cover built up meticulously by nature over millions of years, but also polluted air, water and land, so much so that development has become synonymous with deforestation and desertification and progressed with pollution.

Developmental activities carry with them the seeds of environmental damage, assisted and abetted by both needs and greed of man. Activities such as manufacturing, processing, transportation and consumption not only deplete the stock of natural resources but also add stress to the environmental system by accumulating the stock of wastes. The productivity of the economic system, however, depends on the supply and quality of natural and environmental resources. While water, soil, air, forest and fisheries resources are productive assets, the pollution of water, air, atmosphere and noise are the by-products of economic development.

The present book updates the subject content of ecotourism, environmental problems and solutions like water pollution and treatment, wood degradation and preservation technique, surfactant fate, biodiversity conservation, ecology, biotechnology, agriculture and sustainable development.

Thanks are due to publisher and contributors from various institutions and universities.

The book will be helpful for the researchers, academia working in the field of ecotourism, environmental problems and solutions, ecology, biotechnology, agriculture and sustainable development.

–Editors
(envbooks@gmail.com)

Contents

Preface

1. Introduction — 1-5
2. Residents' Satisfaction to Ecotourism Impacts and their Attitudes and Opinions towards Ecotourism Plans and Development in Kodagu, Karnataka, India — 6-25
   Nichola A. Ramchurjee and Charles V. Ramchurjee
3. Socio-environmental Survey of Mainpat
   An Important Ecotourism Hamlet of Chhattisgarh, India — 26-55
   Chandrahas Singh and Nandkumar Singh
4. Rural Entrepreneurship
   An Economic Development Paradigm through Entrepreneurial Potential Assessment of Beekeepers — 56-88
   Esakkimuthu M and Kameswari VLV
5. Ecological Status Around Pindara Jetty in Kalyanpur Taluka of Devbhumi Dwarka in the State Gujarat — 89-122
   Ashok Kumar Rathoure
6. Impact of Poor Environmental Sanitation in Shuwarin Kiyawa Local Government Area Jigawa State, Nigeria — 123-140
   Mustapha Bashir Kazaure
7. Management Practices in *Litopenaeus Vannamei* Farming in Coastal Purba Medinipur, West Bengal and Life and Works of a Great Fishery Scientist — 141-153
   Subrato Ghosh and Himadri Chandra
8. An Overview on Biomedical and Biodental Waste Management — 154-184
   Sheela Kumar Gujjari; Pragyan Mohanty; Anil Kumar Gujjari
9. Photo Degradation of Surfactants towards Pollution Free Society and Environment — 185-212
   Swati Sharma; Rashmi Sharma; Arun Kumar Sharma

10.	**A Review on Adsorbent Nature of Graphene/Metal Oxide Composites for Water Remediation Technology** *Rabinarayan Panigrahi; Dr. Ranjan Kumar Pradhan* *Dr. Manas Ranjan Senapati*	213-225
11.	**Present Status and Future Strategies of Wood Preservation Industry** *Bandana Dhiman and Bhupender Dutt*	226-245
12.	**Application of Biotechnological Tools for Characterization and Management of Seed Borne Diseases** *Richa Chauhan*	246-255
13.	**Role of Agriculture in National Development with Special Reference to India** *Prasann Kumar*	256-271
	Index	273-279

Eco-tourism, Environmental Problems and Sustainable Development
Edited by: Dr. Soubam Premchandra Singh; Dr. Ashok K. Rathoure
  Dr. Pawan Kumar 'Bharti'
ISBN: 978-93-86841-57-5
Edition: 2018
Published by: Discovery Publishing House Pvt. Ltd., New Delhi (India)

Introduction

Eco-tourism is a form of tourism involving visiting fragile, pristine, and relatively undisturbed natural areas, intended as a low-impact and often small scale alternative to standard commercial mass tourism. It means responsible travel to natural areas conserving the environment and improving the well-being of the local people. Its purpose may be to educate the traveler, to provide funds for ecological conservation, to directly benefit the economic development and political empowerment of local communities, or to foster respect for different cultures and for human rights. Since the 1980s, eco-tourism has been considered a critical endeavor by environmentalists, so that future generations may experience destinations relatively untouched by human intervention. Several university programs use this description as the working definition of eco-tourism.

Generally, eco-tourism deals with interaction with biotic components of the natural environments. Eco-tourism focuses on socially responsible travel, personal growth, and environmental sustainability. Eco-tourism typically involves travel to destinations where flora, fauna, and cultural heritage are the primary attractions. Eco-tourism is intended to offer tourists an insight into the impact of human beings on the environment and to foster a greater appreciation of our natural habitats.

Responsible eco-tourism programs include those that minimize the negative aspects of conventional tourism on the environment and enhance the cultural integrity of local people. Therefore, in addition to evaluating environmental and cultural factors, an integral part of eco-tourism is the promotion of recycling, energy efficiency, water conservation, and creation of economic opportunities for local communities. For these reasons, eco-tourism often appeals to advocates of environmental and social responsibility.

The term 'eco-tourism', like 'sustainable tourism', is considered by many to be an oxymoron. Like most forms of tourism, eco-tourism generally depends on air transportation, which contributes to global climate change. Additionally, the overall effect of sustainable tourism is negative where like eco-tourism philanthropic aspirations mask hard-nosed immediate self-interest. An ecotourist is different from a tourist in the sense that, he or she is mindful of his environment, in most cases contributing to the sustainability of such surroundings.

Eco-tourism is a responsible tourism which conserves the environment and sustains the well being of local people. It:

- Builds environmental awareness
- Provides direct financial benefits for conservation
- Provides financial benefits and empowerment for local people
- Respects local culture
- Supports human rights and democratic movements such as:
- Conservation of biological diversity and cultural diversity through ecosystem protection
- Promotion of sustainable use of biodiversity, by providing jobs to local populations
- Sharing of all socio-economic benefits with local communities and indigenous peoples by having their informed consent and participation in the management of eco-tourism enterprises
- Tourism to unspoiled natural resources, with minimal impact on the environment being a primary concern.
- Minimization of tourism's own environmental impact
- Affordability and lack of waste in the form of luxury
- Local culture, flora, and fauna being the main attractions
- Local people, who benefit from this form of tourism economically, and often more than mass tourism

The Nature Conservancy adopts the definition articulated by the World Conservation Union (IUCN):

"Environmentally responsible travel to natural areas, in order to enjoy and appreciate nature (and accompanying cultural features, both past and present) that promote conservation, have a low visitor impact and provide for beneficially active socio-economic involvement of local peoples."

Most tourism in natural areas today is not eco-tourism and is not, therefore, sustainable. Eco-tourism is distinguished by its emphasis on conservation, education, traveler responsibility and active community participation. Specifically, eco-tourism possesses the following characteristics:

- Conscientious, low-impact visitor behavior
- Sensitivity towards, and appreciation of, local cultures and biodiversity
- Support for local conservation efforts
- Sustainable benefits to local communities
- Local participation in decision-making
- Educational components for both the traveler and local communities

Environmental issues are harmful effects of human activity on the biophysical environment. Environmental protection is a practice of protecting the natural environment on individual, organizational or governmental levels, for the benefit of both the environment and humans. Environmentalism, a social and environmental movement, addresses environmental issues through advocacy, education and activism.

The carbon dioxide equivalent of greenhouse gases (GHG) in the atmosphere has already exceeded 400 parts per million (NOAA) (with total "long-term" GHG exceeding 455 parts per million) (Intergovernmental Panel on Climate Change Report). This level is considered a tipping point. "The amount of greenhouse gas in the atmosphere is already above the threshold that can potentially cause dangerous climate change. We are already at risk of many areas of pollution ... It's not next year or next decade, it's now." The UN Office for the Coordination of Humanitarian Affairs (OCHA) has stated "Climate change is not just a distant future threat. It is the main driver behind rising humanitarian needs and we are seeing its impact. The number of people affected and the damages inflicted by extreme weather has been unprecedented.

Sustainability is the key to prevent or reduce the effect of environmental issues. There is now clear scientific evidence that humanity is living unsustainably, and that an unprecedented collective effort is needed to return human use of natural resources to within sustainable limits. For humans to live sustainably, the Earth's natural resources must be used at a rate at which they can be replenished (and by limiting global warming).

Concerns for the environment have prompted the formation of green parties, political parties that seek to address environmental issues. Initially these were formed in Australia, New Zealand and Germany but are now present in many other countries.

Sustainable development is the organizing principle for meeting human development goals while at the same time sustaining the ability of natural systems to provide the natural resources and ecosystem services upon which the economy and society depend. The desirable end result is a state of society where living and conditions and resource use continue to meet human needs without undermining the integrity and stability of the natural systems.

While the modern concept of sustainable development is derived mostly from the 1987 Brundtland Report, it is also rooted in earlier ideas about sustainable forest management and twentieth century environmental concerns. As the concept developed, it has shifted to focus more on economic development, social development and environmental protection for future generations. It has been suggested that "the term 'sustainability' should be viewed as humanity's target goal of human-ecosystem equilibrium (homeostasis), while 'sustainable development' refers to the holistic approach and temporal processes that lead us to the end point of sustainability".

The concept of sustainable development has been—and still is—subject to criticism. What, exactly, is to be sustained in sustainable development? It has been argued that there is no such thing as a sustainable use of a non-renewable resource, since any positive rate of exploitation will eventually lead to the exhaustion of Earth's finite stock; this perspective renders the Industrial Revolution as a whole unsustainable.

Sustainability can be defined as the practice of maintaining processes of productivity indefinitely—natural or human made—by replacing resources used with resources of equal or greater value without degrading or endangering natural biotic systems. Sustainable development ties together concern for the carrying capacity of natural systems with the social, political, and economic challenges faced by humanity. Sustainability science is the study of the concepts of sustainable development and environmental science. There is an additional focus on the present generations' responsibility to regenerate, maintain and improve planetary resources for use by future generations.

The ecological stability of human settlements is part of the relationship between humans and their natural, social and built environments. Also termed human ecology, this broadens the focus of sustainable development to include the domain of human health. Fundamental human needs such as the availability and quality of air, water, food and shelter are also the ecological foundations for sustainable development; addressing public health risk through investments in ecosystem services can be a powerful and transformative force for sustainable development which, in this sense, extends to all species.

Environmental sustainability concerns the natural environment and how it endures and remains diverse and productive. Since natural resources are derived from the environment, the state of air, water, and the climate are of particular concern. The IPCC Fifth Assessment Report outlines current knowledge about scientific, technical and socio-economic information concerning climate change, and lists options for adaptation and mitigation. Environmental sustainability requires society to design activities to meet human needs while preserving the life support systems of the planet. This, for example, entails using water sustainably, utilizing renewable energy, and sustainable material supplies (e.g. harvesting wood from forests at a rate that maintains the biomass and biodiversity).

REFERENCES

https://en.wikipedia.org/wiki/Ecotourism
https://www.nature.org/greenliving/what-is-ecotourism.xml
http://www.ecotourism.org/what-is-ecotourism
https://en.wikipedia.org/wiki/Environmental_issue
https://en.wikipedia.org/wiki/List_of_environmental_issues
https://en.wikipedia.org/wiki/Sustainable_development

Pages: 6-25

Eco-tourism, Environmental Problems and Sustainable Development
Edited by: Dr. Soubam Premchandra Singh; Dr. Ashok K. Rathoure
Dr. Pawan Kumar 'Bharti'
ISBN: 978-93-86841-57-5
Edition: 2018
Published by: Discovery Publishing House Pvt. Ltd., New Delhi (India)

Residents' Satisfaction to Eco-tourism Impacts and their Attitudes and Opinions towards Eco-tourism Plans and Development in Kodagu, Karnataka, India

Nichola A. Ramchurjee*
Charles V. Ramchurjee

ABSTRACT

Eco-tourism strives to be not only a conservation mechanism and an economic development tool, but also a development process that seeks to remain harmonious with local cultural and social needs. The purpose of this paper is to explore residents' satisfaction to eco-tourism plans and development. It also examines how the attitudes and opinions of the standards of living affect the eco-tourism impacts. This study takes Kodagu, Karnataka India as a case study and emplys the questionnaire method. The result show that residents overall satisfaction with the current eco-tourism planning and management is high. The study further reveal that residents' satisfaction towards economic, social, cultural and environmental impacts affect their support of the eco-tourism plans and development in the area. The majority of the residents are positively satisfied and are willing to support future eco-tourism plans and development thus raising their standards of living.

Key words: eco-tourism plans and development, eco-tourism, satisfaction, attitudes, opinion, environmental impacts, economic impacts, social impacts, cultural impacts, management, Kodagu Karnataka, economic development tool.

Department in Environmental Science, University of Mysore - 570 006 (Karnataka) (India)
Corresponding Author: Nichola A. Ramchurjee
Full Postal Address: 655 East 233rdStreet, Apt #A7, Bronx, N.Y. 10466, New York, USA

INTRODUCTION

In recent decades, the tourism industry has increased its global GDP contribution and it has continued to grow, although important differences exist across countries. As a result of this expansion, there is growing interest in the study of the impact of tourism development on surrounding environments. It is essential to take into account the satisfaction and attitudes of local residents when designing tourism development policies (Allen, Long, Perdue & Kieselbach, 1988; Ap, 1992; Diedrich & García-Buades, 2009; Gursoy, Jurowski & Uysal, 2002; Ritchie & Inkari, 2006) and the attitudes and opinions of the local residents (Ramchurjee & Suresha, 2013).

With a view to involving local residents in tourism policies, it is essential that residents have a positive attitude towards tourism development in their community. Long term planning in tourism is associated with the reactions of local residents to it. Tourism can develop and grow when local residents have a positive attitude toward it and when they see their role in the process of the tourism development. However, when this is not the case, unsatisfied, apathetic or unhappy residents will ultimately transmit their feelings to tourists, who, in turn, are likely to be reluctant to visit destinations where they feel unwelcome (Fridgen, 1991; Royo & Ruiz, 2009). Moreover, the local residents will be unwilling to work in the tourism industry, there will be fewer entrepreneurial and innovative initiatives, and resident-tourist interactions will also very likely be negative (Pearce, 1998; Díaz & Gutiérrez, 2010). In short, given that resident behaviour is an essential aspect of the tourism product, the ultimate goal is to understand and subsequently manage residents' attitudes and seek support for the area's tourism development model (Akis, Peristianis& Warner, 1996; Díaz & Gutiérrez, 2010).

An approach to the concept of attitudeis that of "a mental and neural state of readiness, organized through experience, exerting a directive and dynamic influence upon the individual's response to all objects and situations with which it is related" (Allport, 1935). According to Summers, 1982 attitude has also been defined as a process that leads an individual to behave in a particular manner with respect to an object or stimulus. Attitudes are not innate, but are acquired over time through a learning process influenced by external and internal factors (i.e., family, social groups, experience, personality, etc.).

Tourism is not only a powerful social and economic force but also a factor in the physical environment as well. It has the power to improve the environment, provide funds for conservation, preserve culture and history, to set sustainable use limits and to protect natural attractions. Eco-tourism potentially provides a sustainable approach to development (Okech, 2009). In this scope, eco-tourism is a form of natural resource-based tourism that is educational, low-impact, non-consumptive, and locally oriented: local people must control the industry andreceive the bulk of the benefits to ensure sustainable development (di Cesare, D'Angelo and Rech, 2010). Eco-tourism comes with a definitional promise to promote responsible travel to natural areas, to make a positive contribution to environmental conservation and to enhance the well-being of local communities (Angelica, Zambrano, Broadbent and Durham 2010; Honey, 2008); therefore, eco-tourism focuses on the local culture of a certain region (area) as well as the natural beauty, the geological structure, the natural vegetation and the fauna (Masberg and Morales, 1999), and is a tourism type which includes the subjects of conservation of natural areas, education, economic gain, qualified tourism and participation of local people (BenzerKilic, 2006). Eco-tourism offers benefits for local residents, conservation support, low-scale development, low visitor numbers and educational experiences (Nepal, 2002). Eco-tourism has attracted increasing attention in recentyears, not only as an alternative to mass tourism, but as a means of economic development and environmental conservation (Schaller, 2010). Researchers have considered eco-tourism as a solution for decreasing environmental and socio-economic problems and as a sustainable development tool in ecologically sensitive areas. Eco-tourism is an important instrument used forcontribution to preservation of the natural landscape and offers a solution to the poverty problem commonplace in underdeveloped regions. In addition, it produces a structure utility for the economic development and political progress of the local population, providing a resource for training of the visitors and for preservation (Barkin, 1996; Gregory, 2005; Robert and Santos, 2005; Williams and Ferguson, 2005; Açiksöz, Görmüs, and Karadeniz, 2010). In this scope, in order to be successful at and sustain eco-tourism activities which local people and natural environment are at the center, first it is needed to know better the values of the people and the social environment. This demonstrates that in opening an area to eco-tourism it definitely requires to begin with local organization and local people education (May, 1991). As Drumm and Moore (2002) suggest, a good planning depends on active participation of relevant groups. Since local people would be the group that would affect and would be affected mostly by eco-tourism, provision of theirpower and participation would be crucial. In many studies conducted recently, too, how the developments experienced in the tourism were perceived by the local people have been analyzed and attitudes of local people towards effects of tourism have been examined (Kuvan and Akan, 2005; Ko and Stewart, 2002; Yoon, Gursoy, and Chen, 2001; Teye, Sönmez, and Sirakaya, 2002; Bertan, 2010; Kiper and Arslan, 2007; Kiper, Özdemir, and Basaran, 2009; Mohammadi, Khalifah, and Hosseini, 2010).

ECONOMIC IMPACTS OF ECO-TOURISM

Many studies have suggested that a majority of residents view tourism as a tool for economic development that support towards tourism activities as an economic development strategy. As Horn and Simmons (2002) noted, the economic importance of tourism plays a role in determining residents' attitudes. Economic impacts are easier to research in a local community because of the small size and generally visible impacts on national economic growth. It can be also an essential component for community development (Ashe, 2005). Undoubtedly tourism plays an important role in (a) the economic development of nations by stimulating the development of basic infrastructure, (b) contributing to the growth of domestic industries that supply the tourism industry, (c) attracting foreign investment especially in hotels, and (d) facilitating transfer of technology (Upchurch &Teivane, 2000).

Residents are more likely to view tourism as a tool to reduce unemployment since tourism activities create new opportunities for employment and it further increases revenue to individual, community and government (Gursoy, Jurowski, & Uysal, 2002; Gursoy & Rutherford, 2004; Keogh, 1990; Walpole & Goodwin, 2001). Sharma (2004) states tourism creates employment opportunities in both developed and developing countries; however, the tourism impacts and implications of this employment are different in developed and developing countries (Sharma, 2004, p. 44). Tourism can have positive economic effects on local economies, and a visible impact on national economic growth. It can be also an essential component for community development (Ashe, 2005). The economic impacts of tourism are, therefore, generally perceived positively by the residents (Tatoglu, Erdal, Ozgur, & Azakli, 2000). Due to these positive effects, many communities have seen tourism as a promising opportunity for reducing problems of their communities (Andriotis, 2005). Local residents do see new business opportunities in tourism and are motivated to explore them. Almost all studies reported that there is a positive relationship between economic benefits and attitudes towards tourism development (Davis, Allen, & Cosenza, 1988; Perdue, Long, & Allen, 1990).

SOCIAL AND CULTURAL IMPACTS OF ECO-TOURISM

Residents' perceptions of social and cultural impacts of tourism development have been studied extensively. However, the findings of these studies have produced different results. Although economic benefits are often assumed to largely improve the quality of life of residents, sociocultural factors may not always be as positive (Andereck *et al.*, 2005). The sociocultural impacts of tourism can be more difficult to assess as they are more of a subjective or qualitative measure of impacts on a destination in contrast to quantitative economic measurement (Mason, 2003). The sociocultural impacts of tourism needed careful consideration, as impacts can either influence a community either positively or negatively. Influxes of tourists bring diverse values to the community and influence behaviors and family life (Kreag, 2001). Tourism can be influential in increasing a community's access to knowledge as well as new language skills and learning. It is important in giving community confidence and identity (Smith & Robinson, 2006).

Tourism also is a powerful agent for social and cultural change (Ivanovic, 2009). It promotes the local community's interest in expanding their education and knowledge while seeking to provide better tourist services (Nyaupane, Morais, & Dowler, 2006). Tourism also can play a role in revitalizing community culture and traditions and enhancing a sense of community in local heritage (Godfrey and Clarke 2000, p. 26). Tourism has been linked with increased awareness of other cultures, practices, behaviors, values and heritage. It helps local communities and visiting tourists gain a better knowledge of each other's languages through interaction (Singh *et al.* 2003). According to Puczko and Ratz (2005) tourism brings changes to the traditional way of life and family relations to the local residents, it also affects the nature and functioning of the local society's structures and have many predictable problems. On the other hand, there is the emergence of new jobs, old towns, facilities and places are revitalized and social life of the local residents significantly improves by learning about other cultures and languages. Local residents do see new business opportunities in tourism and are motivated to explore them. At the same time, they know that some negative physical, cultural, social and economic impacts will emerge. The most complex problems that accompany tourism development, resides in the relationship and communication between tourists and local residents.

Most researchers reported that residents view tourism as providing social and cultural benefits to host community (Besculides, Lee, & McCormick, 2002; Gursoy & Rutherford, 2004; Sirakaya, Teye, & Sonmez, 2002). However, few of them reported that residents tend to perceive social and cultural impacts of tourism development negatively (Johnson, Snepenger, & Akis, 1994; Jurowski, Uysal, & Williams, 1997; Perdue, Long, & Allen, 1987; Tosun, 2002). There are negative social and cultural impacts on the host community such as changes in family structure due to the adaptation practices to suit tourists' need (Dyer *et al.*, 2007). Researchers who examined the relationship between perception of negative social impacts and support for tourism development showed that there is a negative relationship between negativesocial impacts and residents' perceptions of tourism development (Gursoy, Jurowski, & Uysal, 2002; Sirakaya, Teye, & Sonmez, 2002).

ENVIRONMENTAL IMPACTS OF ECO-TOURISM

Most of the tourism-related literature on residents' attitudes to environmental issues have centered on residents' perceptions on the impact of tourism on the environment (Nicholas *et al.*, 2009). In other ways, much of the literature on the environmental impacts of tourism has been focused in the context of developed countries while there has been virtually no effort to explore these impacts in other countries (Colantonio & Potter, 2006). The environmental impacts of tourism on community can take the form of both the quality of the physical environment and access to these resources in which positive environmental impacts of tourism on a community include increased awareness of the environment and measures to protect the natural resources, the establishment of national parks or wildlife preserves, the preservation of historical buildings and monuments, as well as improved roads and other public facilities (Liu *et al.*, 1987; Mason, 2003). Conversely, negative environmental impacts that are frequently highlighted include littering, overcrowding, traffic congestion, as well as pollution of water and soil along with the deterioration of natural resources as a result of the constructions of tourism services, such as erections of hotels (Liu *et al.*, 1987; Mason, 2003). Information about residents' attitudes towards the environment is of particular importance for the sustainability of protected areas and indigenous communities (Nicholas *et al.*, 2009).

In reference to the environment, Liu *et al.* (1987) analyze local resident perceptions of the potential negative impacts of tourism as a function that is directly dependent on the ratio between the number of tourists and the number of residents. Thus, growing pressure from tourism (with a higher ratio of tourists per resident, for instance) heightens perceptions of the environmentalproblems that tourism causes for the community, such as the congestion of cities, tourist centers and nature reserves, noise, waste generation and pollution, the destruction of the local flora and fauna, and urban pressure. This in turn generates stronger criticism of tourism, with a growing public awareness among the population of the environmental problems that it brings about and a subsequent increase in opposition to tourism development.

Environmental knowledge affects level of impacts to be accepted by host community. This is related to assertion that environmental knowledge is negatively correlated with the acceptance (Furman, 1998; Van Liere & D unlap, 1980) and environmental concern is negatively correlated with the acceptance of negative impacts (Floyd, Jang, & Noe, 1997). When local community has lower knowledge than those who are more educated in this field, they tend to accept greater impacts. This is due to lack of environmental knowledge makes them unable to realize the impacts perceived. As suggested in literatures, environmental impacts are justified by individual economic gains, when there is an economic benefit from tourism activities, the revenue earned is his or hers. However, when the negative environmental impacts are divided over all fellow residents the net individual benefit is higher than the environmental costs; as a result they will ignore the consequences on environment (Husbands, 1989; Lankford & Howard, 1994; Walpole & Goodwin, 2001).

METHOD

This study explored the residents' attitudes and opinions towards the eco-tourism impacts in the local communities of Kodagu, Karnataka India. This study is based on both quanitative and qualititative methodologies to investigate the local residents' attitudes and opinions towards eco-tourism impacts. The research study used the survey questionnaire mthod. The questionnaires were distributed from door-to-door, this method was chosen because of its higher response rate than other methods (Andereck and Nickerson, 1997). The self-administered questionnaire was also chosen chosen because it is "less time-consuming" and "less expensive" (Sekaran, 2000). The questionnaire was structured on a five-point Likert scale, in which the respondents can express themselves. Each statement was represented the scale with 5=strongly agree to 1=strongly disagree. The items for the residents attitudes and opinions towards eco-tourism impacts were taken from my ppretvious study (Ramchurjee & Suresha, 2013). The questionnaire was designed to gather demographic information on respondents such as gender, age, education and occupation. The rationale behind gathering this information, was to determine whether the local residents' satisfaction towards eco-tourism impacts were influenced economic impacts, social impacts, cultural impacts and environmental impacts. The other sections collected data on the local residents' standards of living and their attitudes and opinions on the current eco-tourism plans and development occurring in Kodagu.

STUDY AREA

Kodagu is an administrative district in Karnataka, India. Before 1956, it was a separate administrative state, (*Chisholm,* 1911). After 1956, the state was merged with Mysore State. It occupies an area of 4,102 square kilometres (1,584 sq mi) (Government of India, 2011) in the Western Ghats of southwestern Karnataka. The district is bordered by Dakshina Kannada district to the northwest, Hassan district to the north, Mysore district to the east, Kasaragod district in west and Kannur district of Kerala to the southwest, and Wayanad district of Kerala to the south. It is a hilly district, with the lowest elevation at 120 metres (390 ft) above sea-level. The highest peak, Tadiandamol, rises to 1,750 metres (5,740 ft), with Pushpagiri, the second highest, at 1,715 metres (5,627 ft). The main river in Kodagu is the Kaveri (Cauvery), which originates at Talakaveri, located on the eastern side of the Western Ghats, and with its tributaries, drains the greater part of Kodagu. Agriculture is the most important factor that upholds the economy of Kodagu and the main crops cultivated in this region are rice and coffee. Coorg is rich in natural resources which included timber and spices. Madikeri (English: Mercara) is the headquarters of Kodagu.

TOURISM ON KODAGU

Kodagu is rated as one of the top hill station destinations in India. Some of the most popular tourist attractions in Kodagu include Talakaveri, Bhagamandala, Nisargadhama, Abbey Falls, Dubare, Nagarahole National Park, Iruppu Falls, and the Tibetan Buddhist Golden Temple.

Abbey falls – is a scenic waterfall. It is a big attraction for tourists and the movie industry. The best season to visit the fall is in the mnsoon season, about June to August or until the monsoon period ends.

Mallalli falls - is situated in Bettadahalli Gram Panchayat in the Somwarpet taluk. It can be seen as the river Kumaradhara gushing through the valley and falling into a gorge, with lush green mountains around.

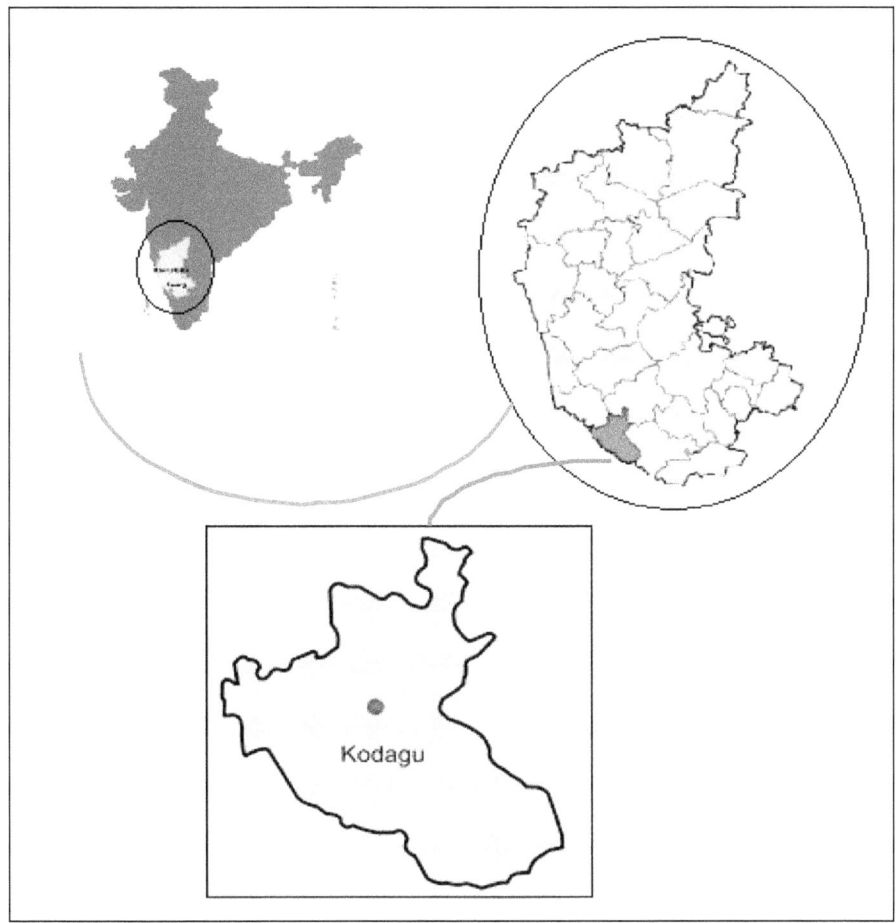

Fig. 2.1: Map of study site

Iruppu falls - is a sacred place called Iruppu in south Kodagu on the Brahmagiri range of hills. The river Lakshmana-tirtha flows nearby. Legend says that Lakshmana shot an arrow into the Brahmagiri hills and brought into being, the river Lakshmanatirtha. The river descends perpendicularly into a great cataract known as the Iruppu Falls. It is an important pilgrim point for many devotees, the temple is dedicated to Lord Ram and is visited by thousands of devotees from far and near on Shivaratri day

Nagarahole National Park - *Nagarhole* is a kannada word meaning "snake river" - which flows through the park. The park and animal life is part of the country's first "bio-sphere reserve". Many flora and fauna can be seen when visiting the National Park.

Pushpagiri Wildlife Sanctury - is located 30 km from Somwarpet towards KukkeSubramanya. The Wildlife Sanctury is suitable for trekkers who want to experience the wilderness of the Western Ghats. It is home to different kinds of wild species like elephants, deers, wild cats etc.

Madikeri - Madikeri is the capital of the Kodagu also known as Coorg. This place is known as the "Scotland of India". Millions of tourists come to this place to visit coffee plantations, lush green forests, misty hills and some breath taking views of other areas. Madikeri is also known for it's amazing climate. Madikeri also has a world record in the production of cardamom crop.

Madikeri Fort - This 19th century fort, is situated in the centre of Madikeri. It houses a Ganesha temple, a chapel, a district prison and a small museum. The fort offers a beautiful view of Madikeri. According to an official explanation board at the site, Mercara, the headquarters of Coorg or Kodagu district, was founded by Prince Mudduraja of the Haleri Dynasty in 1681 CE, and was named after him as Muddurajanakeri — which became "Muddukayray" and Madikeri over time. The British termed the place Mercara. Mudduraja built a mud fort and a palace inside the fort, in the last quarter of the 17th century. This fort was later rebuilt of granite masonry, after it was captured by the "Tiger of Mysore" Tipu Sultan. Tipu named it Jaffarabad. In 1790, Doddaveer Rajendra took possession of the fort, and in April 1834, the British took control of it. Built on an elevated area, the fort has been described as an "irregular hexagon" on plan, almost confirming to the shape of the hilltop. There are six circular bastions at the angles, the entrance on the east is intricate and circuitious and guarded by three successive gates.

Raja's Seat - According to legend, the Kings of Kodagu spent their evenings here. But what's unforgettable about Raja's seat is the spectacular sunset that one can enjoy from here. A sophisticated musical fountain is also located here. The best timings for viewing the sunset and the musical fountains are from 17:30 to 19:30 Hrs. however, it is not always possible to see the sunset when it is cloudy.

Bagamandala - Temple and river confluence - Bhagamandala is on the banks of the confluence of three rivers, Cauvery, Kannike and the sub terranianSujyoti, popularly known as "TriveniSangama". The famous Sri Bhagandeswara temple is located on the bank of the river. Pilgrims visiting Bhagamandala take bathes (or sprinkle water on your head) in the Triveni Sangama, confluence of rivers and worship at the temple complex.

Mandalpatti, View point - Mandalpatti viewpoint provides breath taking view of the nearby hills. The view point is about 1600 meters above sea-level.

Talakaveri/Talacauvery - Kaveri river which is one of the 7 sacred rivers of SaptaSindhus in the Hindu scriptures, originated at a place is called Talakaveri (head of Cauvery) in the Brahmagiri hills, at about 4,500 ft above sea level. This place is marked by a tirtha kundike or Brahma kundike (small spring/pond) from where the river emerges as a small perennial spring, but flows underground again to emerge a short distance away. Two temples, a Shiva temple and with a rare and ancient Shiva Linga, and another temple dedicated to Lord Ganesha are located on the banks of the river. This temple has a holy Ashwantha tree where, according to legend, the Trimurtis - Brahma, Vishnu and Mahesh gave darshan to sage Agastya.

Dubare Elephant Camp - this is mainly an elephant capturing and training camp at the edge of the Dubare forest, located on the banks of the Kaveri river. The largest land animal is captured here with the help of tamed elephants and local tribals - the Kurbas - and is held captive for upto 6 months in large teak wood cages. The tamed elephants attend to various jobs during the day and in the mornings they come to the river to bathe and to be scrubbed clean by their mahouts. Afterwards the mahout obliges eager tourists for elephant rides within the camp. In the mornings, all the elephants are offered a special treat of ladoos made of ragi and jaggery, each no smaller than a cannon ball.

RESULTS AND DISCUSSION

Profile of the Respondents

Table 2.1 shows the profile of the 158 respondents who took part in the survey. The majority of the respondents are aged 18-33 years old accounting for 81.6% of the survey. About 67.5% of the residents are employed either professionally, self-employed or as homemakers. Approximately 72.2% of the respondents have attended high school and continued to futher their studies to the university level earning a bachelor degrees. 20.9% of the local people in this survey have vocational/trade certifications. Many of the respondents (67.1%) between the ages 18-33are employed and holds a Bachelor's Degree or higher. Of the many variables studied, education has proven to be the most consistent in its relationship to levels of concern. Ramchurjee and Suresha (2014) indicates that there is a significant relationship between level of education and expressed environmental attitudes and opinions. Moreover, education is traditionally viewed as a function of the amount of schooling received (e.g., high school versus university levels of education).

Table 2.1: Profile of respondents

	Description	Percent
Gender	Male	67.1
	Female	32.9
	Total	100.0
Age	18-25	58.2
	26-33	23.4
	34-41	2.5
	42-49	9.5
	50-57	3.8
	58-65	2.5
	Total	100.0
Occupation	Student	28.5
	Professional	44.3
	Self-employed	17.1
	Homemaker	5.7
	Unemployed	1.3
	Others	3.2
	Total	100.0
Education	High school	7.0
	Pre-University	12.0
	University	22.2
	Post-Graduate Degree	38.0
	Vocational/trade qualification	20.9
	Total	100.0

AWARENESS OF THE RESPONDENTS TO STANDARDS OF LIVING AND ECO-TOURISM PLANS AND DEVELOPMENT

Figure 2.2 shows the awareness by gender of the residents of their Standards of living and eco-tourism plans and development occurring in Kodagu. It can be seen that males are more conscious and do take further interests in the impacts of eco-tourism affecting the lives of the residents. This maybe so, because males are the head of the households and would obviously give more attention to the current development of eco-tourism in the area.

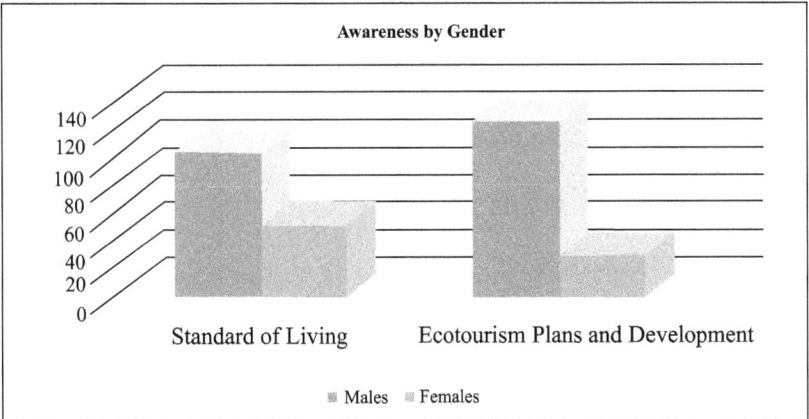

Fig. 2.2: Awareness of the standards of living and eco-tourism plans and development by gender

Figure 2.3 describes the occupation of the residents and their awareness of Standards of living and eco-tourism plans and development. It can be seen, that the local residents take interests in these plans because these concepts can lead to the residents being involved in the eco-tourism industry and earning supplemental income to help in the home.

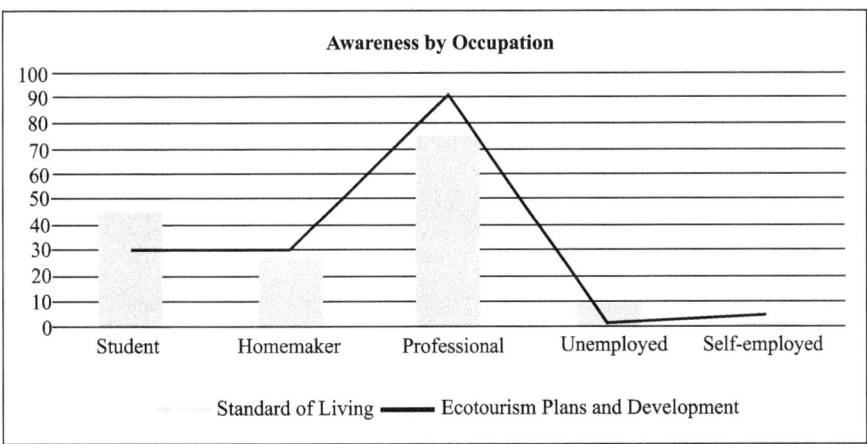

Fig. 2.3: Shows the awareness of standards of living and eco-tourism plans and development by occupation

Figure 2.4 explains that at all levels of education, Standards of living is the one aspect in which the residents are more concern about. This is directly due to the economic benefits the residents can gain through eco-tourism.

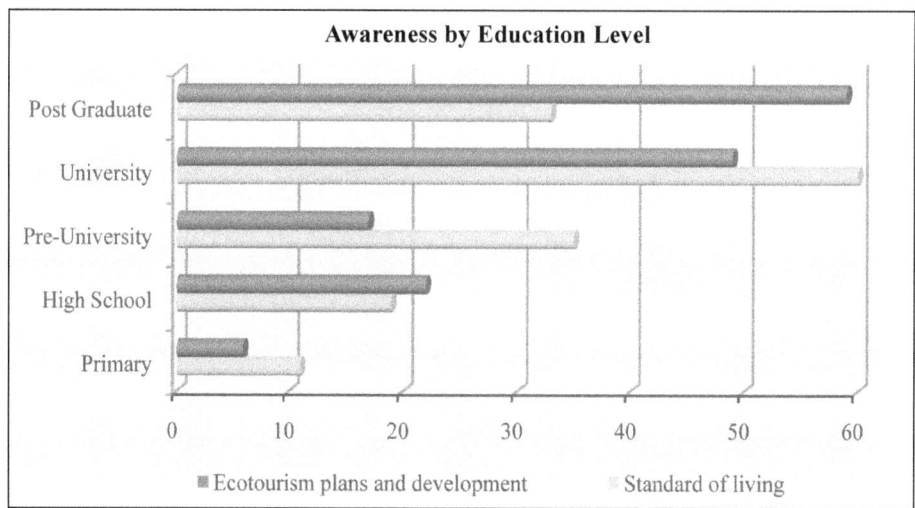

Fig. 2.4: Awareness of standards of living and eco-tourism plans and development by education levels

Table 2.2: Showing results for an Independent t-test Analysis

	Test	Equal Variances Assumed		Equal Variances not Assumed	
		Standards of Living	Eco-tourism Plans and Development	Standards of Living	Eco-tourism Plans and Development
Leven's test for Equality of Means	F	2.761	4.270		
	Sign.	0.099	0.837		
t-test for equality of Means	t	7.397	3.970	9.205	4.397
	df	156	156	0.433	0.319
Sig. (2-tailed)		0.000	0.000	0.000	0.019
Mean difference		0.568	0.612	0.568	0.612
Std. error difference		0.347	0.406	0.279	0.367
95% Confidence interval of the difference lower		1.882	0.810	2.006	0.485
95% Confidence interval of the difference upper		3.254	02.414	3.254	2.739

An independent t-test analysis was conducted to compare the effects of eco-tourism plans and development currently taking place on the Standards of living of the residents. Table 2.2 shows the t-test for Equality of Means.

Table 2.3: Significant difference in Standards and of living and Eco-tourism plans and development

	Means	Std. Deviation	Std. Error Mean
Standards of living	13.890	0.475	0.090
Eco-tourism plans and development	9.630	0.081	0.296

From table 2.3, it can be seen there was a significant difference in the value of Standards of living of the residents (mean=13.890, SD=0.475) and the manner in which Eco-tourism plans and development are being carried out (mean=9.630, SD=0.081).

Correlation between independent variables – Pearson product-moment correlation

Table 2.4: Correlation between independent variables

		Standards of Living	Eco-tourism Plans and Development	Economic Aspects	Social Aspects	Cultural Aspects	Environmental Aspects
Standards of living	Pearson Correlation	1	0.783**	0.925**	0.157*	0.123	0.525**
	Sig. (2-tailed)		0.000	0.000	0.049	0.024	0.000
Eco-tourism plans and development	Pearson Correlation	0.783**	1	0.674**	0.636**	0.503**	0.521**
	Sig. (2-tailed)	0.000		0.000	0.000	0.000	0.000
Economic Aspects	Pearson Correlation	0.925**	0.674**	1	0.125	0.198*	0.162*
	Sig. (2-tailed)	0.000	0.000		0.019	0.013	0.042
Social Aspects	Pearson Correlation	0.157*	0.636**	0.125	1	0.258**	0.129
	Sig. (2-tailed)	0.049	0.000	0.019		0.000	0.017
Cultural Aspects	Pearson Correlation	0.123	0.503**	0.198*	0.258**	1	-0.123**
	Sig. (2-tailed)	0.024	0.000	0.013	0.000		0.023
Environmental Aspects	Pearson Correlation	0.525**	0.521**	0.162*	0.129	-0.123	1
	Sig. (2-tailed)	0.000	0.000	0.042	0.017	0.023	

**: Correlation is significant at the 0.01 level (2-tailed)

The Pearson product moment correlation coefficient (or Pearson correlation coefficient, for short) is a measure of the strength of a linear association between two variables and is denoted by r. Basically, a Pearson product-moment correlation attempts to draw a line of best fit through the data of two variables, and the Pearson correlation coefficient, r, indicates how far away all these data points are to this line of best fit (i.e., how well the data points fit this new model/line of best fit).

The Pearson correlation coefficient, r, can take a range of values from +1 to -1. A value of 0 indicates that there is no association between the two variables. A value greater than 0 indicates a positive association; that is, as the value of one variable increases, so does the value of the other variable. A value less than 0 indicates a negative association; that is, as the value of one variable increases, the value of the other variable decreases.

The stronger the association of the two variables, the closer the Pearson correlation coefficient, r, will be to either +1 or -1 depending on whether the relationship is positive or negative, respectively. Achieving a value of +1 or -1 means that all your data points are included on the line of best fit – there are no data points that show any variation away from this line. Values for r between +1 and -1 (for example, $r = 0.8$ or -0.4) indicate that there is variation around the line of best fit. The closer the value of r to 0 the greater the variation around the line of best fit. The Pearson product-moment correlation does not take into consideration whether a variable has been classified as a dependent or independent variable. It treats all variables equally. This is because the Pearson correlation coefficient makes no account of any theory behind why you chose the two variables to compare.

A Pearson product-moment correlation coefficient was computed to assess the relationship between the independent variables, Standards of living, Eco-tourism plans and development, Economic Aspects, Social Aspects, Cultural Aspects, and Environmental Aspects. Strong negative association was seen between Cultural Aspects and Environmental Aspects. The colleration coefficient is -0.123. This maybe due to the possible impacts when tourism brings changes in value systems/behaviors and threatening cultural identity and heritage. Changes often occur in community structure, collective traditional lifestyles, ceremonies and morality.

All other associations exhibited strong positive correlations. The strongest positive correlation was found between Standards of living and Economic Aspects, having a coefficient of 0.783. he next positive relationship was exhibited between Eco-tourism plans and development and Economic Aspects having a coefficient of 0.674. It can be seen that tourism expenditures generate income to the host economy and can stimulate the investments necessary to finance growth in other economic sectors. Tourism is one of the top five export categories for as many as 83% countries and is a main source of foreign exchange earnings for at least 38% of the countries. Tourism can generate job opportunites and induce local governments to infrastructures development and improvements improving the standards of living for the local people.

The next strong positive links was between Eco-tourism plans and development and Social Aspects with a coefficient of 0.636. Tourism has the potential to promote social development through employment creation, income redistribution and poverty alleviation. It can also strengthen communities, improve culture and traditions, and foster social exchanges between hosts and guests.

The correlations between Standards of living and Eco-tourism plans and development and Environmental Aspects shows the 5th and 6th highest positive associations. The coefficients are 0.525 and 0.521 respectively. The quality of the environment, both natural and man-made is essential to tourism. Tourism has the potential to create beneficial effects on the environment by contributing to environmental protection and conservation such as development of parks, and natural areas. It is a way to raise awareness of environmental and it can serve as a tool to finance protection of natural areas.

Eco-tourism plans and development and Cultural Aspects represents the 7th strong positive association with a coefficient of 0.503. Tourism can boost the preservation and tramission of cultural and historical traditions, which often contributes to the conservation and sustainable management of natural resources, the protection of local heritage, and renaissance cultures, cultural arts and crafts.

CONCLUSION

This study revealed that the residents of the Kodagu district assessed the eco-tourism impacts from both a negative and positive point of view. However, when eco-tourism impacts were compared in relations to their satisfaction, observations were strongly positive with regards to economic, social and cultural aspects, but negative with regards to environmental aspects. It can be seen, that the overall measurement of economic and social aspects were statistically significant. It reflects positive insights by the residents such as contributions to economic benefits, increase of social well being of the residents and the strengthening of positive cultural exchanges between the residents and tourists. There was generally positive relationship between the level of awareness of eco-tourism plans and development and the current level of eco-tourism impacts. This is seen when there is a gain through eco-tourism, the local residents' satisfaction in economic, social, culture and the environment increases and the residents' attitudes and opinions influences their overall satisfaction.

REFERENCES

Açiksöz, S. Görmüs, S. Karadeniz, N. (2010): Determination of Eco-tourism Potential in National Parks: Kure Mountains National Park, Kastamonu-Bartin, Turkey. *African J. Agric. Res.*, 5(8): 589-599.

Akis, S. Peristianis, N. Warner, J. (1996): Residents' Attitudes to Tourism Development: The Case of Cyprus. *Tourism Management*, 17, 481-494.

Allen, L.R. Long, P.T., Perdue, R.R. and Kieselbach, S. (1988): The Impact of Tourism Development on Residents' Perceptions of Community life. *Journal of Travel Research*, 26: 16-21.

Allport, G.W. (1935): Attitudes. In C. Murchison (Ed.), A Handbook of Social Psychology (pp. 798-844). New York: Clark Univ.

Andereck, K.L. Nickerson N.P. (1997): Community Tourism Attitude Assessment at the Local Level. In The Evolution of Tourism: Adapting to Change, Proceedings of the 28th Annual Travel and Tourism Research Association Conference. Lexington, KY: Travel and Tourism Research Association, 86-100.

Andereck, K. Valentine, K. Knopf, R. Vogt, C. (2005): Residents Perceptions of Community Tourism Impacts. *Annals of Tourism Research*, 32(4): 1056-1076.

Andriotis, K. (2005): Community Groups' Perceptions of and Preferences for Tourism Development: Evidence from Crete. *Journal of Hospitality & Tourism Research*, 29(1): 67-90.

Angelica, M. Zambrano, A. Broadbent, E.N. Durham, W.H. (2010): Social and Environmental Effects of Eco-tourism in the Osa Peninsula of Costa Rica: the Lapa Rios case. *J. Eco-tourism*. 9(1): 62-83.

Ap, J. (1992): Resident's Perceptions on Tourism Impacts. *Annals of Tourism Research* 19(4): 665-690.

Ashe, J.W. (2005): Tourism Investment as a Tool for Development and Poverty Reduction: the Experience in Small Island Developing States (SIDS). The Commonwealth Finance Ministers Meeting, 18-20 September, Barbados

Barkin, D. (1996): Eco-tourism: A Tool for Sustainable Development. Retriewed 16 June 2010 from: http://www. Planeta/96/0596 monarch.html

BenzerKiliç, N. (2006): The Assessment of the Natural and Cultural Resources of Bolu-GoynukWith the Eco-tourism Point of View. Ankara University Graduate School of Natural and Applied Sciences Department of Landscape Architecture, Ph.D. Thesis, 266.

Bertan S (2010). Relationship between Tourism Support and Tourism Impacts on Socio-cultural in Pamukkale. Int. J. Econ. Admin. Studies., 2(4): 83-91.

Besculides, A. Lee, M.E. McCormick, P.J. (2002): Resident's Perceptions of the Cultural Benefits of Tourism. *Annals of Tourism Research*, 29(2), 303-319.

Colantonio, A. Potter, R.B. (2006): Urban Tourism and Development in the Socilaist State: Havana during the "Special Period," *Humanities and Social Sciences Online*, xii + 256.

Chisholm, H. (ed.) (1911): "Coorg". Encyclopædia Britannica. 7 (11ᵗʰ ed.). Cambridge University Press. 91-92.

Di Cesare, F. D'Angelo, L. Rech, G. (2009): Films and Tourism: Understanding the Nature and Intensity of their Cause-effect Relationship. *Tourism Review International*, 13(2): 103-112.

Díaz, R. Gutiérrez, D. (2010): La actitud del residenteen el destinoturístico de Tenerife: evaluación y tendencia. PASOS: *Revista de Turismo y Patrimonio Cultural*, 8 (4), 431-444.

Diedrich, A. Garcý´a-Buades, E. (2008): Local Perceptions of Tourism as Indicators of Destination Decline. *Tourism Management*, 1-10.

Drumm, A. Moore, A. (2002): Eco-tourism Development, an Introduction Eco-tourism Planning. Vol. I. *The Nature Conservancy*, USA.

Dyer, P. Aberdeen, L. Schuler, S. (2007): Tourism Impacts on an Australian Indigenous Community. *Tourism Management*, 24: 83-95.

Floyd, M. Jang, H. Noe, F. (1997): The Relationship Between Environmental Concern and Acceptability of Environmental Impacts Among Visitors to Two US National Parks Settings. *Journal of Environment Management*, 51: 391-412.

Fridgen, J. (1991): Dimensions of Tourism. East Lansing, MI: American Hotel and Motel Association Educational Institute.

Furman, A. (1998: A Note on Environmental Concern in a Developing Country: Results from An Istanbul Survey. *Environment and Behaviour*, 30 (4): 520-534.

Godfre, K. Clarke, J.(2000): The Tourism Development Handbook: A Practical Approach to Planning and Marketing. London: Continuum.

Government of India. (2001): "Districts of India"Retrieved 11 January 2011.

Gregory, T. (2005): Conflict Between Global and Local Land use Values in Latvia's Gauja National Park. *Landscape Res*. 30: 413-30.

Gursoy, D. Jurowski, C. & Uysal, M. (2002): Resident Attitudes: A Structural Modeling Approach. *Annals of Tourism Research*, 29(1): 79-105.

Gursoy, D. Rutherford, G. (2004): Host Attitudes toward Tourism: An Improved Structural Model. *Annals of Tourism Research*, 31(3): 495-516.

Honey, M. (2008): Eco-tourism and Sustainable Development: Who Owns Paradise? (Washington, DC: Island Press).

Horn, C. Simmons, D. (2002): Community Adaptation to Tourism: Comparisons between Rotorua and Kaikoura, New Zealand. *Tourism Management*, 23: 133-143.

Husbands, W. (1989): Social Status and Perception of Tourism in Zambia, *Annals of Tourism Research*, 16: 237-253.

Ivanovic, M.(2009): Cultural Tourism. USA: Juta and Company Limited.

Johnson, J. Snepenger, D. Akis, S. (1994): Residents Perceptions of Tourism Development. *Annals of Tourism Research*, 21(3): 629-637.

Jurowski, C. Uysal, M. Williams, D. R. (1997): A Theoretical Analysis of Host Community Resident Reactions to Tourism. *Journal of Travel Research*, 36(2): 3-11.

Liu, J. Sheldon, P. Var, T. (1987): A Cross-national Approach to Determining Resident Perceptions of the Impact of Tourism on the Environment, *Annals of Tourism Research*, 14: 17-37.

Kiper, T. Arslan, M. (2007): The Expectations of the Local Community and Visitors from Tourism in Eural Areas: Case of Safranbolu–Yörükköyü Village. *Pakistan J apl. Sci.*, 7(17): 2544-2550.

Kiper, T. Özdemir, G. Basaran, B. (2009): Applicability of Agricultural Tourism and the Role of Women: A Case Study of SarköyMürefte. The International Conference of BENA Pollution Management and Environmental Protection (September 16-20, 2009), Book of Abstract, pp. 119, Tirana, Albinia.

Ko, D.W. Stewart, W.P. (2002): A Structural Equation Model of Residents' Attitudes for Tourism Development, *Tourism Management*, 23: 521- 530.

Kreag, D, (2001): The Impacts of Tourism: Minnesota Sea Grant Program.

Kuvan, Y. Akan, P. (2005): Residents' Attitudes toward General and Forest-related Impacts of Tourism: The Case of Belek, Antalya, *Tourism Management*, 26: 691-706.

Lankford, S.V. Howard. D.R. (1994): Developing a Tourism Impact Attitude Scale. *Annals of Tourism Research*, 21 (1): 121-39.

Masberg, B. Morales, N. (1999): A Case Analysis of Strategies in Eco-tourism Development. *Aquatic Ecosiysem Health and Management*, 2(3): 289-300.

Mason, P. (2003): Tourism Impacts, Planning and Management. Jordan Hill, Oxford: Butterworth–Heinemann.

May, M. (1991): Tourism, Environment and Development, *Tourism Management*, 12 (2): l12-118.

Mohammadi, M. Khalifah, Z. Hosseini, H. (2010): Local People Perceptions toward Social, Economic and Environmental Impacts of Tourism in Kermanshah (Iran). *Asian soc. sci.*, 6(11): 1911-2025.

Nepal, S.K. (2002): Mountain Eco-tourism and Sustainable Development, Ecology, Economics and Ethics. *Mountain Research and Development*, 22: 104-109.

Nicholas, L. Thapa, B. Ko, Y. (2009): Residents' Perspectives of a World Heritage site e the Pitons Management Area, St. Lucia. *Annals of Tourism Research*, 36(3): 390-412.

Nyaupane, P.Morais, B. Dowler, L.(2006): The Role of Community Involvement and Number/ Type of Visitors on Tourism Impacts: A Controlled Comparison of Annapurna, Nepal and Northwest Yunnan, China. *Tourism Management*, 27(6): 1373-1385.

Okech, R.N. (2009): Developing Urban Eco-tourism in Kenyan Cities: A Sustainable Approach, J. Ecol. Nat. Environ., 1(1): 001-006.

Pearce, P.L. (1998): The relationship between Resident and Tourists: The Research Literature and Management Directions. In W.F. Theobald (Ed.), Global Tourism (pp. 129-149). Oxford: Butterworth-Heinemman.

Perdue, R.R. Long, P.T. Allen, L.R. (1990): Residents Support for Tourism Development. *Annals of Tourism Research*, 17(4): 586-599.

Puczko, L. Ratz, T. (2000): Tourist and Resident Perceptions of the Physical Impacts of Tourism at Lake Balaton, Hungary: Issues for Sustainable Tourism Management. *Journal of Sustainable Tourism*, 8(6): 458-479.

Ramchurjee, N.A. Suresha, S. (2013): Eco-tourism in Bagalkot District, Karnataka, India: An Assessment of the Inhabitants' Awareness Level and Attitudes, *International Journal of Environmental Sciences*, 3(6): 2278-2290.

Ritchie, B.W. Inkari, M. (2006): 'Host Community Attitudes toward Tourism and Cultural Tourism Development: The Case of the Lewes District, Southern England', *International Journal of Tourism Research*, 8 (1): 27-44.

Robert, H. Santos, C. (2005): Tourists and Local Preferences towards Eco-tourism Development in the Maya Biosphere Reserve, Guatamala. *Environ. Dev. Sustainability*, 7: 303-318.

Royo, M. Ruiz, M.E. (2009): Actitud del residentehacia el turismo y el visitante: factoresdeterminantesen el turismo y excursionismo rural-cultural. *Cuadernos de Turismo*, 23, 217-236.

Schaller, D. (2010): Indigenous Eco-tourism and Sustainable Development: The Case of Río Blanco, Ecuador. http://www.eduweb.com/schaller/RioBlancoSummary.html Accessed: 23.08.2010.

Sharma, K. (2004): Tourism and Economic Development, Sarup & Sons.

Singh, S. Timothy, J. Dowling, K. (Eds.) (2003): Tourism in Destination Communities. Cambridge, USA: CABI publishing.

Sirakaya, E. Teye, V. Sonmez, S. (2002) Understanding Residents Support for Tourism Development in the Central Region of Ghana. *Journal of Travel Research*, 41(1): 57-67.

Smith, K. Robinson, M. (Eds.) (2006): Cultural Tourism in a Changing World: Politics, Participation, and (Re) Presentation. United Kingdom: Channel View Publications Ltd.

Summers, G.F. (1982): Medición de actitudes. Ciudad de Mexico: Editorial Trillas.

Tatoðlu, A.P.E. Erdal, A.P.F. Özgür, A.P.H. Azakli, A.P.S. (2000): Resident Perceptions of the Impact of Tourism in a Turkish Resort Town. *Challenges for Business Administrators in the New Millennium*, 2: 745-755.

Tey.e V. Sönmez, S.F. Sirakaya, E. (2002): Residents' Attitudes toward Tourism Development, *Annals of Tourism Research*, 29 (3): 668-688.

Tosun, C. (2002): Host Perceptions of Impacts: A Comparative Tourism Study. *Annals of Tourism Research*, 29(1): 231-253.

Upchurch, R.S. Teivane, U. (2000): Resident Perceptions of Tourism Development in Riga, Latvia. *Tourism Management*, 21: 499-507.

Van Liere, K. Dunlap, R. (1980): The Social Bases of Environmental Concern: A Review of Hypotheses, Explanations and Emprical Evidence. *Pubilc Opinion Quaterly*, 44: 181-197.

Walpole, M. Goodwin, H. (2001): Local Attitudes towards Conservation and Tourism Around Komodo National Park, Indonesia. *Environmental Conservation*, 28: 160-166.

William, C. Ferguson, M. (2005): Recovery from Crisis: Strategic Alternatives for Leisure and Tourism Providers based within a Rural Economy. *Inter. J. Public Sector Manage*. 18: 350-66.

Yoon, Y. Gursoy, D. Chen, J.S. (2001): Validating a Tourism Development Theory with Structural Equation Modelling, *Tourism Management*, 22: 363-372.

Pages: 26-55
Eco-tourism, Environmental Problems and Sustainable Development
Edited by: Dr. Soubam Premchandra Singh; Dr. Ashok K. Rathoure
Dr. Pawan Kumar 'Bharti'
ISBN: 978-93-86841-57-5
Edition: 2018
Published by: Discovery Publishing House Pvt. Ltd., New Delhi (India)

Socio-environmental Survey of Mainpat
An Important Eco-tourism Hamlet of Chhattisgarh, India

Chandrahas Singh
Nandkumar Singh

INTRODUCTION

Eco-tourism is entirely a new approach in tourism. Eco-tourism is a preserving travel to natural areas to appreciate the cultural and natural history of the environment without hampering the integrity of the ecosystem. It helps in creating economic opportunities that make conservation and protection of natural resources advantageous to the local people. The word 'eco-tourism' has been coined relatively recently and there remains no consensus about its meaning. Eco-tourism is a niche market for environmentally aware tourists who are interested in observing nature' (Wheat, 1994). Elman put it bluntly as 'a tour advertised as environmentally friendly can be just as suspect as many of the products tarred up with green packaging at your grocery store' (Wight, 1994), making no distinction between nature tourism and eco-tourism. Others have also used eco-tourism and nature tourism synonymously (Lindberg1991; Aylward and Freedman, 1992).

Relationship between Eco-tourism and Sustainable Tourism

Eco-tourism basically deals with nature based tourism, and is aimed "to conserve the environment and improves the well-being of local people". On the other hand, sustainable tourism includes all segments of tourism, and has same function to perform as of eco-tourism – to conserve the resources and increase the local cultural and traditional value.

Department of Environmental Science, University Teaching Departments (UTD), Sarguja University, Ambikapur - 497 001 (Chhattisgarh) (India)

Table 3.1: Definitions of eco-tourism

Source	Definition
Conservation International (Ziffer, 1989).	A form of tourism inspired primarily by the natural history of an area, including its indigenous cultures. The ecotourist visits relatively undeveloped areas in the spirit of appreciation, participation and sensitivity. The ecotourist practices a non-consumptive use of wildlife and natural resources and contributes to the visited areas through labor or financial means aimed at directly benefiting the conservation of the site and the economic well-being of the local residents.
World Conservation Union (Brandon, 1996)	Environmentally responsible travel and visitation to relatively undisturbed natural areas, in order to enjoy and appreciate nature that promotes conservation, has low negative visitor impact, and provides for beneficially active socio-economic involvement of local populations.
Martha Honey (Honey, 1999, 25).	Travel to fragile, pristine, and usually protected areas that strive to below impact and (usually) small scale. It helps educate the traveler; provides funds for conservation; directly benefits the economic development and political empowerment of local communities; and fosters respect for different cultures and for human rights.
International Eco-tourism Society (2004)	Responsible travel to natural areas that conserves the environment and sustains the well-being of local people.

Though the goals of eco-tourism and sustainable tourism are much similar, but the latter is broader and conceals within itself many aspects and categories of tourism.

Eco-tourism in India

India is a mega-biodiversity rich country. She presents a unique combination of almost all landform features across the globe. The peninsular nation is bordered by water bodies on all three sides while mighty Himalayas border the north of the subcontinent. There are several ways to enjoy Mother Nature in most pristine way. The few places such as the Himalayan Region, Kerala, the northeast India, Andaman & Nicobar Islands and the Lakshadweep islands are some of the places where you can enjoy the treasured wealth of the Mother Nature. *Thenmala* in Kerala is the first planned eco-tourism destination in India created to cater to the eco-tourists and nature lovers. India is one of those rare countries, which has a wonderful blend of all the resources essential to make it as a golden star on the tourism map of the world. Eco-tourism in the Indian context has significant implications for nature and culture conservation, rural livelihoods and conservation education.(ATREE 2006). The main objective of the tourism policy in India is to position tourism as a major engine of economic growth and harness its direct and multiplier effect on employment and poverty eradication in a sustainable manner by active participation of all segments of the society Apart from marketing and promotion, the focus of tourism development plans is also on integrated development of tourism infrastructure and facilities through effective partnership with various stakeholders. (ARMTGI 2016).

It was only after the 1980's tourism activity gained momentum in India. In India tourism and its development in an organised manner has received attention over 45 years only. The significant development that took place was setting up of the Indian Tourism Development Corporation (ITDC) in 1966 to promote India as a tourist destination and the Tourism Finance Corporation (TFC) in 1989 to finance tourism projects. Altogether, 21 Government-run hotel management and catering technology institutes and 14 food craft institutes were also established for imparting specialized training in hoteliering. The Ministry of Tourism is the nodal agency for the development and promotion of tourism in India and catering. In the year 1986, Tourism has been declared as 'Tourism Industry' by the Government of India (GOI). On March 4, 1993, the United Nations Statistical Commission adopted WTO's (World Tourism Organisation's) recommendations on tourism. The Ministry of Tourism has the specific agenda to promote tourism in the country in a responsible and sustainable manner and as per this mandate promotion of eco-tourism assumes larger importance.

Eco-tourism has been broadly defined as tourism which is ecologically sustainable. The concept of ecological sustainability explains the environmental carrying capacity of a given area.

The general principal of eco-tourism guiding the initiatives of the Ministry is as under:

(a) The local community should be involved leading to the overall economic development of the area.

(b) The likely conflicts between resource use for eco-tourism and the livelihood of local inhabitants should be identified and attempts made to minimize the same.

(c) The type and scale of eco-tourism development should be compatible with the environment and socio-cultural characteristics of the local community.

(d) It should be planned as a part of the overall area development strategy, guided by an integrated land-use plan avoiding inter-sectoral conflicts and ensuring sectoral integration, associated with commensurate expansion of public services.

However, India's tourism infrastructure is barely keeping pace with the industry increase and problems are evident in the accommodation, transport and personnel sectors. In addition, India has real problems with environmental pollution and tourist pressures causing substantial damages to its natural treasures (Gadgil and Guha, 1994), wildlife (Bolton, 1994). The case of sustainable development has already been put Before India (Roy, Tisdell and Sen, 1995).

Eco-tourism Places in Chhattisgarh

Chhattisgarh, the 26th state of the Indian Union, is located in the central part of India and was formed on 1st November, 2000. Chhattisgarh is famous for its enchantingly beautiful natural landscapes, rich cultural heritage and unique tribal populations. The Chhattisgarh region is known as a great repository of biological diversity. The unique combination of rich cultural heritage and biological diversity makes Chhattisgarh an ideal eco-tourism destination with immense potentials for the growth eco-tourism the region. The Indian Govt. is actively collaborating with the local officials of the state to realize the full potential of eco tourism growth of the region in order to make. In addition, Chhattisgarh has also formulated several ecological plans and working in the direction to become the country's first bio-fuel self reliant state. And to achieve this goal the green state has devised a plan to plant over 100 million saplings of *Jatropa Carcass* (locally known as *Ratanjot*). Chhattisgarh is also unique in its wildlife population and has three National Parks (Indravati National Park, Gurughasidas National Park, and Kanger Ghati National Park) and eleven wildlife Sanctuaries Badalkhol (Jashpur), Tamorpigla (Surajpur), Sitanadee (Dhamtari), Achanakmar (Mungeli), Gomarda (Raigarh), Baranwapara (Mahasamund), Semarsot

(Balrampur), Bhairamgarh (Bijapur), Pamed (Bijapur), Udayantee (Gariyabandh), Bhoramdev (Kavardha) housing some of the rare wildlife and bird species. With so much of variety for eco tourism, Chhattisgarh promises to be an ideal holiday destination for nature lovers, wildlife enthusiasts and also for those who want to discover the unique tribal life of the region. Chhattisgarh has identified some regions with a very high potentiality for eco-tourism. The green state has launched an eco-tourism project covering three potential tourist tracks such as Raipur Turturia Sirpur, Bilaspur Achanakmar and Jagdalpur Kanger Valley National Park. In addition, a number of herbal gardens and natural health resorts such as in Mainpat in Surguja district of Northern Chhattisgarh have been created with increased local participation. The use of ethno medicine, which has been practiced by aboriginal tribes since centuries, predating even Ayurveda, is also being promoted in Chhattisgarh. The major eco-tourism attractions, which are getting prime attention in Chhattisgarh, include the protection and development of the wildlife areas, camping grounds and trekking facilities. With so many initiatives, Chhattisgarh is destined to become the most favorite eco-tourism destination in India.

Important Eco-tourism Places in Sarguja District

Sarguja District lies in the northern part of Chhattisgarh and historically it was a princely state. According to mythological scripts, Lord Rama had visited Sarguja during his 14 years of exile into the forests. Sarguja is surrounding by various states such as Jharkhand, Uttar Pradesh, Orissa and Madhya Pradesh. Sarguja has a geographical spread of over 22,237 km^2; most of the terrain of the district is hilly and forest. Sarguja is also known for high tribe population, diverse culture, karma dance, beautiful waterfalls.

1. Mahamaya temple: This temple was eradicated by Kalchuri dynasty's king named Raja Rattan Singh in 1050 A.D. The main goddess of this temple is Goddess Durga.
2. Ramgarh forest Hill: At this place Sita vengra and Jogi named two main popular caves are there. These natural caves were found in year 1848 by Clone Aalsi.
3. *Thinthini pathher:* If this rock is hit by any hard thing then is produces the sound like a metal. This sound is being taken as the sound of God.
4. Devgargh: At these main seeing sites like Gouri Shankar mandir, Shaili shiv mandir, Golfi math, and archaeological statues are the natural beauties of this place.
5. Maheshpur: A village of Ambikapur tahsil, Udaipur is situated on the bank of the Rihand amidst calm and quict scenic beauty the archaeology of this place may date back to a very early age.
6. Mainpat- Popularly known as *'Shimla of Chhattisgarh'.*

This study would attempt to understand the emergence of Mainpat as an important eco-tourism hamlet of Chhattisgarh, India with the following objectives in consideration.

Objective
- To assess the current status of Mainpat as an eco-tourism destination of Surguja, Chhattisgarh.
- To identify and analyze the socio-environmental factors that contribute in making Mainpat as a popular eco-tourism destination
- To propose a comprehensive strategy for sustainable management of Mainpat.

Need of the Study:
- Eco-tourism is important from a socio-economic as well as ecological perspective.
- Eco-tourism experiences are aimed at helping people to foster an appreciation of the environment, the conservation of wildlife, plants and resources, and respect and understanding of native peoples.
- The field is socially important because it provides a way for people to travel responsibly, and to learn about and respect the people and society.
- Eco-tourism is economically vital since it contributes to the livelihood generation of the people directly or indirectly associated with the trade in turn helping in holistic development of the region.
- Eco-tourism projects which are well-run can help to conserve natural resources, and can be an incentive for local people to preserve their resources, rather than exploit them.

REVIEW LITERATURE

In this chapter an attempt has been made to review the work done on "Socio-environmental survey of Mainpat: an important eco-tourism hamlet of Chhattisgarh, India" as follows:

Buchsbaum (2004) critically examine the impacts and challenges of eco-tourism;analyze the potential of eco-tourism as a strategy for sustainable development. He conclusively suggests that Eco-tourism has more promisefor achieving sustainability than alternative types of land use such as agriculture, cattlegrazing, logging, or mass tourism.In order to increase the likelihoodthat eco-tourism achieves goals of sustainable development in Costa Rica, all of the key actors must to begin to take more proactive measures in order to ensure that eco-tourism is carefully planned and implemented. Eco-tourism must account for social, economic and environmental implications, in order to succeed. A much more balanced and integrated approach, founded on the guiding principles of sustainable development, is essential to maximize the benefits and minimize the negative impacts of eco-tourism in Costa Rica.

Anitha V. & Muraleedharan P.K. (2006) in their study on" Economic valuation of eco-tourism development of recreational site in the natural forest of southern western ghats", states that eco-tourism is a direct consumptive benefit, which is highly under priced. This tourism sector has certain crucial environmental implications because it depends upon natural endowments for its existence. As deforestation accelerates, there has been a surge of interest in high profile uses such as plantation forestry and tourism. With increasing urbanization and media focus on wildlife and natural ecosystems, eco-tourism could be a viable alternative for sustainable management of the forests. The study attempts to estimate the economic potential of eco-tourism in Athirappily-Vazhachal, southern Western Ghats and suggest suitable strategies and action plan. The Central Government with the introduction of eco-tourism policy and guidelines as part of new tourism policy (2002) paid special attention on traditional picnic spots ofnatural forests. Eco-tourism is one of the key sectors for India in the service sector negotiations under General Agreement on Trade in Services (GATS) in the WTO. The support of the local communities is indispensable for the successful development of tourism in Athirappily-Vazhachal. The resident perception in this regard based on social and environmental priorities among different choices indicates tourism (93%) and conservation of biodiversity (72.86%) as occupying the largest support. The positive impacts of tourism in Athirappily-Vazhachal measured through employment and income multipliers highlighted that labour intensive investment in tourism will ensure employment security. The study results highlighted that a 1 percent change in the visitor flow will lead to 4.7 per cent change in the level of employment. The strategies for sustainable tourism in Athirappily-Vazhachal recreation sites focuses on the Pro-Poor Tourism strategy as laid down in World summit on sustainable tourism (2002) giving due weightage the to economic benefits, non-economic benefits and policy reform in the area with special reference to the poor. The study further recommends a site-specific programme *"One Tourist One Rupee Ten trees Program"* towards action plan for ensuring environmental and economic security in the eco-tourism based economy.

Edwards R. (2010) in his study on "The Role of Conservation Research and Education Centers in Growing Nature-Based Tourism"concludes that there are increasing numbers of private (nonprofit and for-profit) centers that carry out conservation research and education in locations of environmental concern. Such centers generate revenue streams that directly support conservation programs and also sustain surrounding human communities.

Dixit S.K. and Narula V.K. (2010) in his study on "Eco-tourism in Madhav National Park: Visitors perspectives on Environmental Impact " discusses that eco-tourism potentially provides a sustainable approach to tourism development in India. However, to realize this potential the adverse effects of visitor activity and associated infrastructure on the natural environment and the tourism experience must be identified to guide management actions and thus to sustain the resources on which eco-tourism ultimately depends. This study, conducted in Madhav National Park in Shivpuri, M.P., India, reports one of the first efforts to identify the impacts of eco-tourism in India from the perspective of visitors. This study, with its sociopolitical approach, contributes to a greater understanding of the implications of the ecotourists experience for eco-tourism management in India.

Ramchurjee N.A. (2013) in his study on "Eco-tourism in Balkot district, Karnataka, India explores the scope to which the local residents of the Bagalkot district have positive attitudes and awareness towards eco-tourism impact of sustainable development. The investigation was based on three primary factors, namely social and cultural impacts, level of awareness towards eco-tourism and empowerment of the local community. The study revealed that the residents showed a high degree of awareness and sensitivity regarding the socio-cultural issues. They are in need of training and education related to eco-tourism in order to improve their lifestyles, economy and resource management. Their involvement in eco-tourism programs would be a potential strategy to promote and support sustainable development in the area.

Joshi V.M.(2014) in his study on "Eco-Tourism – A Key to Protect the Biodiversity in Maharashtra", attempts to find out significance of eco-tourism in protection of biodiversity in Maharashtra. A detailed study is needed to investigate the pressure and negative impact on biodiversity in India. Adoption of eco-tourism on the grounds of environment carrying capacity will lead to sustainable tourism development and this is the need of the hour.

Rai R.K. and Rai B.S. (2015) in his study on "Conservation of Crocodylus palustris in Kotmi Sonar of Janjgir - Chamapa (C.G.) India", crocodile. Highlights the conservation efforts by Government of Chhattisgarh in conservation of crocodiles which is has been categorized as a vulnerable species in the Red List of IUCN and is placed under schedule 1 of the Wild Life Protection Act, 1972. The physicochemical conditions of Munda pond provide an optimal conditions for, growth and vital activities for this species, Crocodylus palustris. The population of Crocodylus palustris is gradually increasing up to 378. The establishment of incubation centre, artificial hatchery and other technical facilities helps in the increasing population of *Crocodylus palustris*.The potentialities of Crocodile Park showed explored from point of view of knowledge, research activities and eco-tourism as well.

Bhattacharya S. *et al.* (2015) Eco-tourism aspects surveys on the topography, demography, agriculture, livestock, water management, education, culture, health, waste management, transport, biodiversity, human animal conflict were done in this area. Medicinal plant diversity was studied in the village area and Biodiversity of Senchal Wildlife Sanctuary was documented by visiting the forest areas.

STUDY AREA

Mainpat is a small hamlet in the Sarguja district in the northern part of the state of Chhattisgarh, India. Lying about 45 kilometres (28 mi) by road from Ambikapur, the hill station features the Tiger Point Waterfall, Fish Point waterfall, Jaljali, Buddhist Monastery and Mehta Point (Tourism *Surguja District Government*) apart from host of other adventurous and exciting places of tourist interest. The place displays an exquisite natural beauty with pristine landscapes and mighty waterfalls breaking across the hills and lush green forests. The romantic dawn and dusk is very enchanting and soothing to the busy souls away from the hustles and bustles of daily urban life and filled with soulful music of nature. Manipat is said to be the best honey moon destination as well. In Surguja, 'Pat' is ascribed to a 'plateau' region. Mainpat is on a plateau with the area surrounded by jungles. The place has beautiful hill slopes, jungles, waterfalls and is a unexploited hill station. There is a Tibetan settlement that offers an excellent opportunity for interaction with them. In fact, Mainpat is also known as 'Mini Tibet' because of the settlements (Chhattisgarh Tourism Board). The products of this place are very famous such as woolen clothes or handicrafts. One can enjoy dishes like *thupka, momos, bamboo rice* etc. specialty of Tibetan food. At this place one can feel cold even during hot summer days. So, the place is also popularly termed as *'Shimla of Chhattisgarh'*. The altitude of the place is 1075 m ASL with dense forest. Mainpat consists of 24 villages with population of 25,000 approx. It is considered to be one of the emerging eco-tourism hotbeds of Chhattisgarh.

Place To Visit in Mainpat:

- **Dhakpo Monastery:** This is a Gelug monastery and unlike all other monasteries, this monastery is small.
- **Fish Point:** This waterfall is near the Tibetan camp number 6. This is a beautiful place and a must see place. The place got its name from a particular kind of fish found in the place.
- **Tiger Point:** This is another waterfall near the Tibetan camp number six and a good place for picnics. There are steps leading to the falls. The other waterfalls are *Sarbhanja* and King's Waterfall. Tiger Point is also the gateway to Mainpat.
- **Tibet Refugee Camp:** There are four Tibetan camps located in the region which houses the Tibetan refugees since many years.
- **Mehta Point and Parpatia:** These two points present excellent view of the region with mighty Sal trees dotting the entire landscape.

- **Jaljali:** This is the most exciting and ecologically unique place where the ground shakes as one walks or jumps around. Probably, this place is one of its kind in the world.

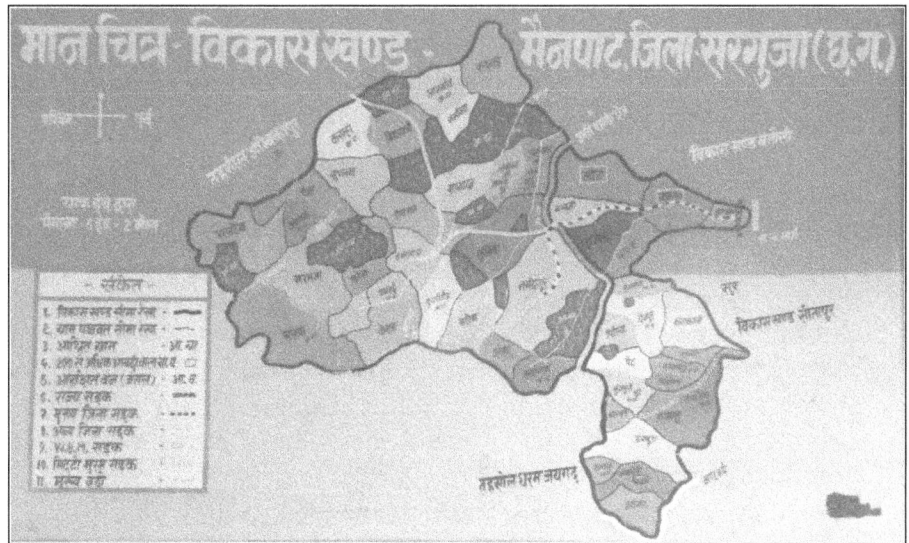

Fig. 3.1: Map of the Mainpat as displayed in Kamleshwarpur block office, Mainpat

History

The cluster of villages was traditionally home to the Yadavs and tribes including the Manjhi. The major livelihood of these tribes includes pastoralism and animal husbandry. Tibetan refugees have settled in this place since 1962. The population of the Tibetans in this place is approximately around 1825.

Geography

Geographical area is 45, 466 hectare. It lies between 22°45′ north latitude and 83°18′ east longitude. Agriculture land area is around 19, 450 hectare, irrigated agriculture land area is 1350 hectares.

The high-lands of Surguja district have peculiar 'pat formations' – highlands with small tablelands. Mainpat forms an ideal definition of a 'pat'. The soil of the Mainpat can be broadly classified into four major types: red and yellow soils, alluvial soils, laterite soils, and medium blue soils. Red and yellow soils are derived from the parent rocks of the Gondwana System including sedimentary rocks. They are formed *in-situ* from the erosion of such rocks caused by rain.

The red color is due to wide diffusion of iron while hydration of ferric oxide results in a yellow color in the soil. This soil is of lighter texture and has a porous and friable structure. Soluble salt is found in small quantities. Lime, kankar and free kankar are totally absent. These soils are poor in potash, nitrogen, humus and carbonate and differ greatly in consistency, color, depth and fertility The colour of the soil is not uniform but varies from yellow to grey. Laterite soils are well developed on the summits of the plateau regions of Mainpat blocks. In winters temperature dips to below 2 °C (35.6 °F) and in summers it rises above 35 °C (95 °F)

MATERIAL AND METHODOLOGIES

The investigation entitled "Socio-environmental survey of Mainpat: an important eco-tourism hamlet of Chhattisgarh, India" was conducted during 2016-17. The details on site and methodology adopted used are given below:

1. Primary Data Collection by the help of Focused Group Discussion, Questionnaire based surveys, Personal Interviews, Random Rural Appraisal (RRA) and Participatory Rural Appraisal (PRA).
2. Secondary Data Collection from Government Reports, Research Centers, Panchayat Registers, Hotel Registers, available documentation in tourist places.
3. Sample Surveys from tourist destinations of the study area.
4. Photographic Documentation.

Some General Information of Mainpat (Data collection Block office Mainpat)

- Establishment of Mainpat block: 01/04/1964.
- Geographical area: 45466 Hectare.
- Population: 76573 = 38703(M), 37870(F).
- Number of Courtyard Shelter Center: 218, Main Center -159, Mini Center- 59.
- Number of Village Panchayat : 39, Revenue village- 46.
- Number of Educational institution: Primary School- 142, Medill School -71, Higher Secondary School- 04, Hostel -09, Hermitage (ashram) School- 08, High School-07.
- Number of Primary Health Center:
  1. Narmadapur
  2. Kamleshwarpur
  3. Vandana.
- Number of Deputy Health Center: 22
- Number of Veterinary Hospital: 2 (Kamleshwarpur & Narmadapur)
- Number of Veterinary Store: 3 (Mharanipur,Vandana & Rajapur)
- Number of Bank: 4 (Central Bank Narmadapur, SBI Kamleshwarpur, Chhattisgarh Gramin Bank Kamleshwarpur, District Government Center Bank Kamleshwarpur

- District Panchayat President: Mrs. Pati Ekka
- District Panchayat Vice President: Mr. Atal Bihari Yadav
- Lok Sabha Area : Sarguja, Assembly Area : Sitapur.
- Number of resort: 2 (Anmol & Saila resort kamleshwarpur).

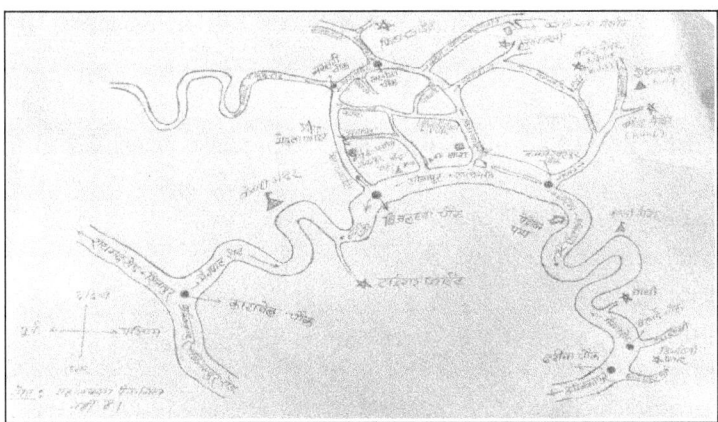

Fig. 3.2: Study area route map

Agricultures

Advanced farming techniques have created wonders for the potato farmers of the hilly Mainpat region during the Kharif season in Surguja district of Chhattisgarh. Kharif season paddyand maize also cropping here, after harvesting kharif crop, then cropping Ravi crop like a mustard and tau. The Indira Gandhi Agricultural University (IGAU) has opened a Research Centre at Mainpat. Scientists are producing high quality potato seeds here and Strawberry plant distributing it among the famers. Interestingly, the Tibetan Refugees are growing potatoes in these villages in the traditional agricultural mode.

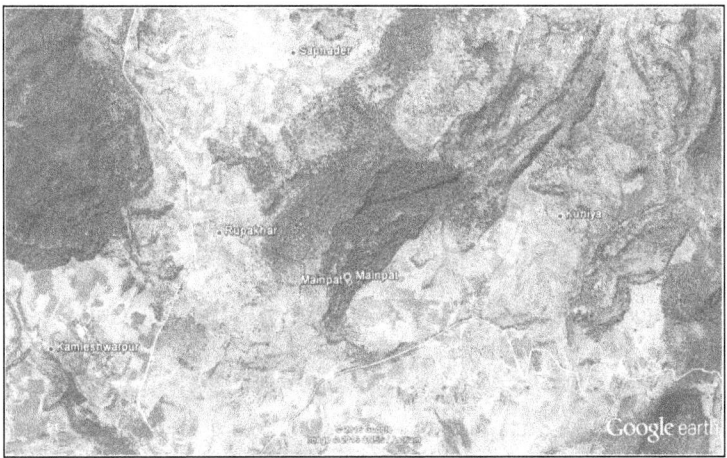

Fig. 3.3: Map of Mainpat

Land

The land has been classified into 6 categories. About 41.67% of the total area is actually developed to agriculture while about 5.70% remains under fallow land. Again about 11.44% of the land may be brought under cultivation by improving the techniques and reclamation of the marginal area. About 1.27% is barren and uncultured while 33.09% is in the form of forest, 6.83% land is developed to building, road etc.

Soil

Soil of Mainpat Sarguja district can be broadly classified in four major classes:

- Red and yellow soils.
- Alluvial soils.
- Literate soils.
- Medium blue soils.

Method of Data Collection

The Study is based both on primary and secondary data. The primary data for the study was collected by conducting Surveys among the tourists with the help of structured questionnaires and interview schedules. The Department of Tourism, Non-Governmental organizations, Hotels, Travel Agencies and Tour operators, Universities and College Libraries etc. were visited and relevant information's were collected. Secondary data were also obtained from sources like Government publications, Government departments, etc and other agencies in the field of tourism.

The study followed the following steps:

- **Interviews** – This was the main method of data collection administered to the government and to local community representatives. An interview guideline was prepared containing detailed list of questions and checklist for every department/official being interviewed. Data collected from interviews was documented through notes taken by the interviewers rather than through tape or video recordings as the latter would not have been appropriate with several government officials.
- **Focus group discussions** – In order to collective perspectives from local community members, focus group consultations were organized. A discussion guideline was prepared for the conducting the discussions. Data from the focus group discussions has been documented in writing and through audio visuals.
- **Field observation** – Field observation has been another important instrument for collecting qualitative data, especially for socio-cultural and environmental impacts of tourism activity. At each field site, a considerable amount of time was spent at different locations to observe

tourist behavior, interaction of tourists with local people and the impacts of such interaction. Data recorded through field observation was immediately documented.

- **Participant observation** – Here, members of the research team went as tourists to different sites to observe tourist behavior, and to get first-hand experience of how local community members viewed and interacted with tourists. Observations were documented through field notes.

RESULT AND DISCUSSION

1. Population Structure

At Mainpat, there are 38,703 Males and 37,870 Females with total population of 76,573 people. The census report of 2011 was collected from Maimpat Block Office. The census data is represented Male and female ratio and literate illiterate ratios are shown in table 3.2 and SC, ST, And General Population profile of Mainpat table 3.3.

Table 3.2: Population Census data (2011) of Mainpat

Total Population	No. of Males	No. of Females	No. of Literates (Male)	No. of Literates (Female)	No. of Illiterates (Male)	No. of Illiterates (Female)
76573	38703(51%)	37870(49%)	24383	16284	14320	21585

Source: C.G. Census (2011).

Table 3.3: SC, ST, and general population profile of Mainpat

Block	Total Population	% of SC Population	% of ST Population	% of Genral Population
Manipat	76573	2.80%	79.20%	18.00%

Source: C.G. Census (2011)

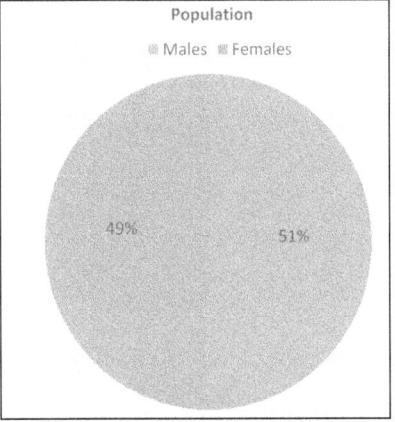

Fig. 3.4: Male and female population in Mainpat
Source: C.G. Census (2011)

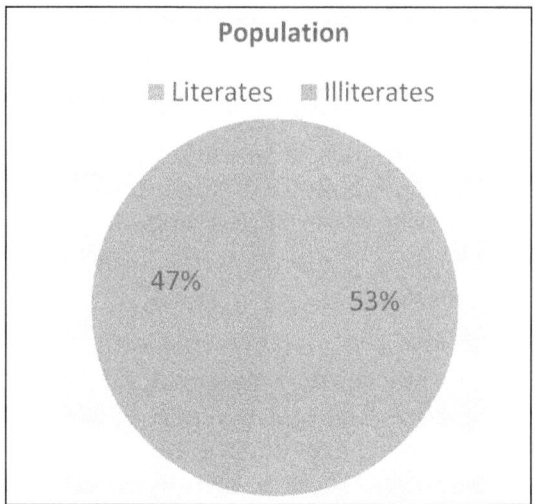

Fig. 3.5: Literates and illiterates population in Mainpat
Source: C.G. Census (2011)

2. Monthly footfall rate of visitors at Tiger point

Main pat block the maximum number of tourists monthly footfall rate of visitors at Tiger point during December to March however medium in November, April and May and minimum in June, July, August and September. It can be supported from the visitor's data record collected from the Tourist office at (Tiger Point) which shows that the maximum number 9555 visitors recorded in January followed by 8011 in February, 7950 in December, 7000 in March, 3360 in November, 2900 in April, 1000 in May, 700 in June, 506 in October, 700 in June, 500 in July, 556 in August and minimum of 400 visitors in September (Figure 3.6). The decrease in visitors during May to October is mainly due to bad weather such rain, storms etc.

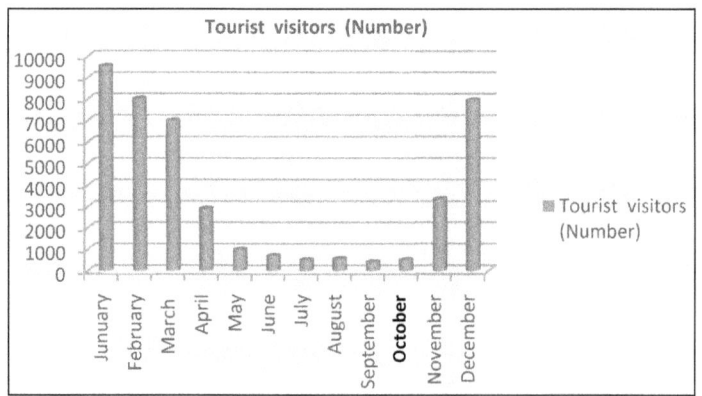

Fig. 3.6: Monthly footfall rate of visitors at tiger point
Source: Tiger point visitor's centre

3. Monthly footfall rate of visitors at Jaljali point

Main pat block the maximum number of tourists monthly footfall rate of visitors at Jaljali Point during December to March however medium in November, April and May and minimum in June, July, August and September. It can be supported from the visitor's data record collected from the Tourist office at (Jaljali Point) which shows that the maximum number 9006 visitors recorded in January followed by 8000 in February, 7900 in December, 7044 in March, 3360 in November, 2807 in April, 912 in May, 664 in June, 466 in October, 436 in July, 556 in August and minimum of 395 visitors in September (Fig. 3.7). The decrease in visitors during May to October is mainly due to bad weather such rain, storms etc.

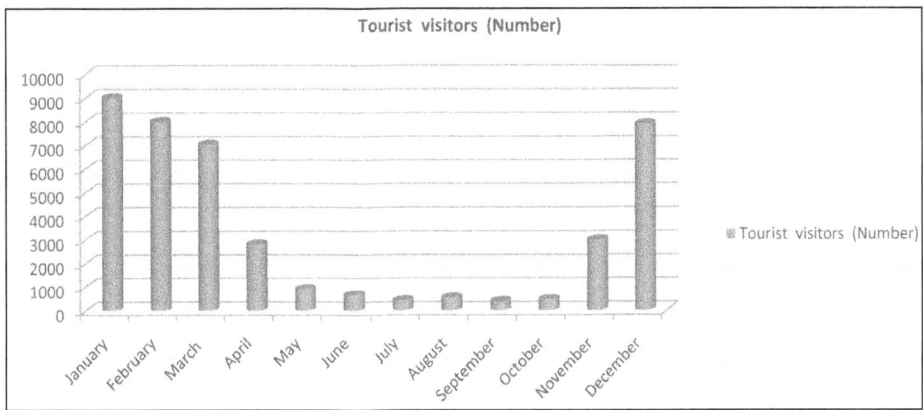

Fig. 3.7: Monthly footfall rate of visitors at Jaljali point

Source: Jaljli point visitor's center

4. Mainpat tourist response on information source

(n=100 respondents during December January: the months of highest footfall)

According to tourist respondents the information about the eco-tourism places was acquired in Main pat block as maximum from friends and relatives in destination Buddha temple (56%), Tiger Point (57%) and Jaljali magical land (85%) as 56%, 57% and 85% followed Media- Print/Digital as 29%, 25% and 05%, Government Tourist Office 11%, 12% and 05%, and Chhattisgarh Tourism Development Board Website as 4%, 6% and 5% respectively. However in destination Mehta point and Fish point the maximum is reported from friends and reletives as 49% and 47% each followed by Media- Print/Digital as 25% and 30%, government tourists office as 20% and 19% and Chhattisgarh Tourism Development Board Website as 5%. In Tiger point the maximum is reported from friends as 30% followed by relatives as 28%, media as 25%, government tourists office as 12% and Chhattisgarh Tourism Development Board Website as

5% (Figure 3.8). The response from the tourist shows that the information regarding the eco-tourism spots in the Mainpat blocks are not sufficient hence some arrangement for advertisement and popularizing the destinations especially websites should be commenced in order to give more information about the tourism destinations.

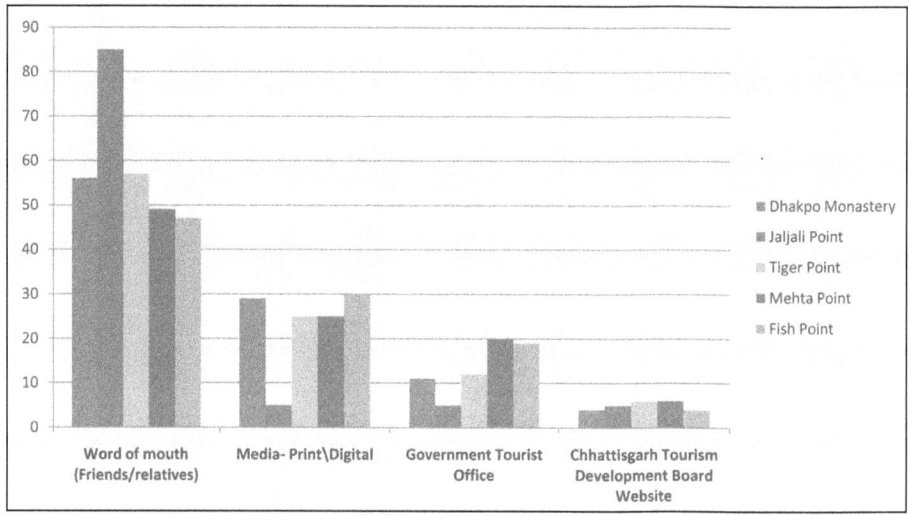

Fig. 3.8: Mainpat Tourist response on information source

5. Mainpat Tourist response on their travel motive

According to tourist respondents in the Main pat block the travel motive of the tourist registered maximum from Religious reasons in destination Dhakpo Monastery (27%), Tiger Point (21%) and Jaljali magical land (25%) as 27%, 21% and 25% followed Recreation as 15%, 30% and 27%, Eco-tourism 14%, 23% and 21%, Documentation (Photo/Video-graphy) as 20%, 30% and 14%, Family visits as 23%, 23% and 15% and Adventure Tourism as 12%, 22% and 25% respectively. However in destination Mehta point and Fish point the maximum is reported from Religious reasons as 20% and 21% each followed by Recreation as 24% and 20%, Eco-tourism as 22% and 19%, Documentation (Photo/Video-graphy) as 25% and 20%, Family visits as 21% and 25% and Adventure Tourism as 21% and 12% (Figure 3.9).

6. Satisfaction Ranking Report Card of different tourist destinations of Mainpat: (n=100)

As an eco-tourism destination, the following principal parameters are considered in the Satisfaction Ranking such as; Accommodation, Fooding, Maintenance of tourist places, Weather, Local Culture and Accessibility and Miscellaneous facilities. The tourist's response for satisfaction ranking (0-5 score) in Mainpat is found to be between 0 to 4 among the various tourist sites recorded during the scope and duration of our study.

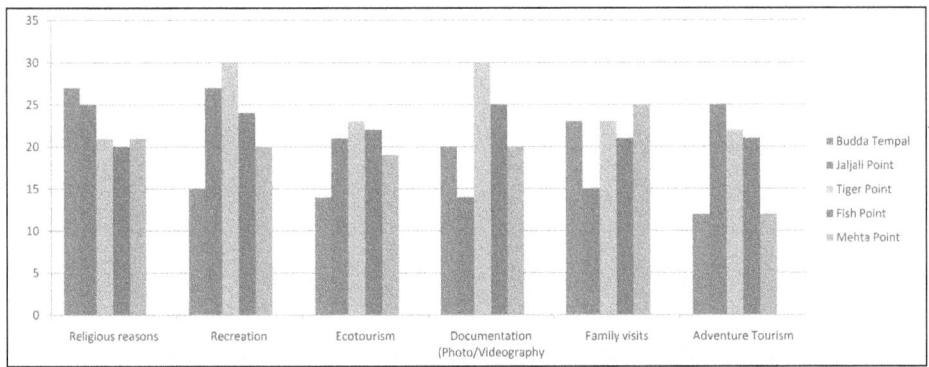

Fig. 3.9: Mainpat tourist response on their travel motive
Source: Individual Interviewed from the various sites
of tourist interest in Mainpat, Surguja (C.G.)

The recorded values are divided into specific categories such as; Low (< 1), Medium (1 to 3) and High (> 4). The high ranking sites of Mainpat are Jaljali point, Buddha temple and Tiger point. The factors considered are maintenance of tourist places and preservation of local culture. Mainpat ranks medium if Weather and Accommodation facilities are considered while ranks very low in fooding facilities. Accessibility of the tourist sites within Mainpat and the Miscellaneous facilities are recorded low to medium in almost every sites. (Figure 3.10).

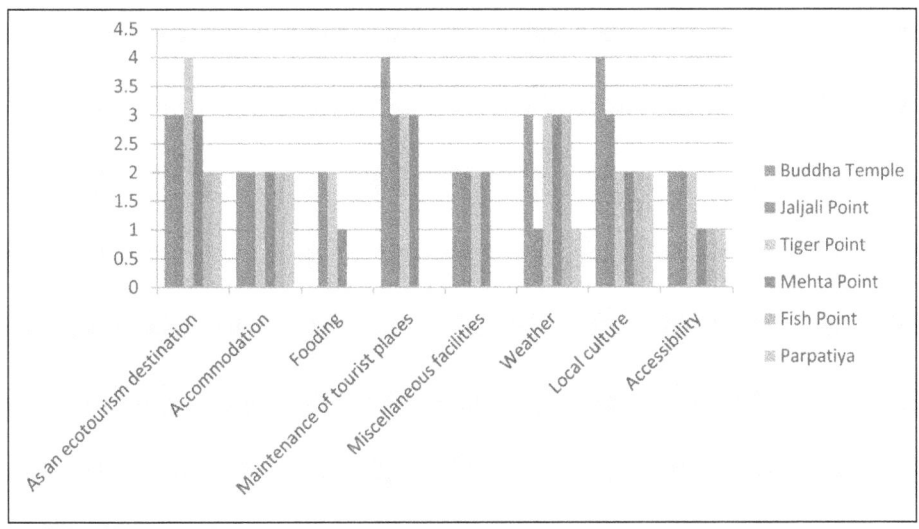

Fig. 3.10: Mainpat Tourist response on
satisfaction ranking (Individual Interviewed %)

7. Seasonal Tourist Inflow in Mainpat during a calendar year (2016-17)

During winter season, Mainpat records maximum tourist inflow amounting to 82%, medium flow of about 60% stays during autumn season. (13.67% and 23.75%) tourist inflow is recorded during summer and rainy seasons respectively during a calendar year. (Figure 3.11).

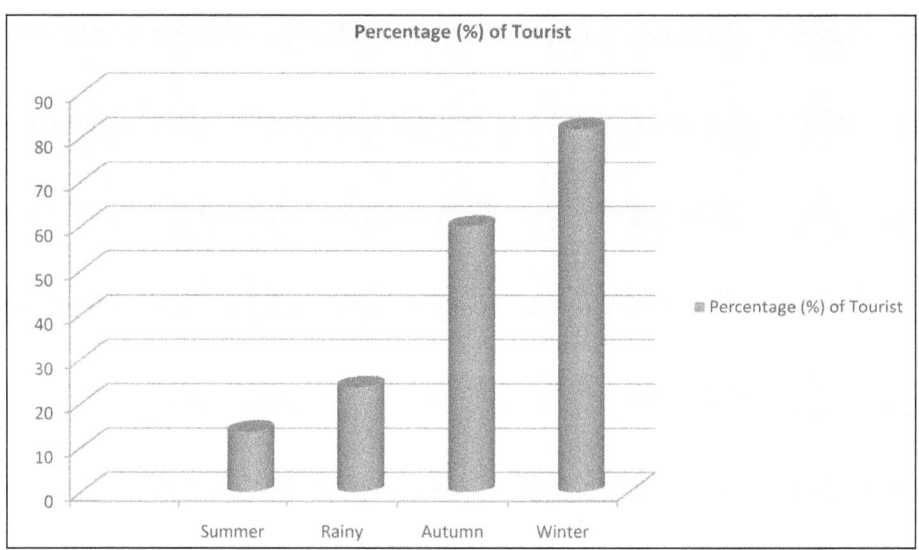

Fig. 3.11: Season wise tourist stay percentage (%) in Mainpat

8. Major plant species recorded in the study area:

Table 3.4

S.No.	Common Name	Botanical Name	Family
(1)	(2)	(3)	(4)
1.	Sal	*Shorea robusta*	Dipterocarpaceae
2.	Aam	*Mangifera indica*	Anacardiaceae
3.	Dhawada	*Anogeissus latifolia*	Combrataceae
4.	Bel	*Aegle marmelos*	Rutaceae
5.	Kadamb	*Anthocephalus cadamba*	Rubiaceae
6.	Neem	*Azadirachta indica*	Meliaceae
7.	Bamboo	*Bambusa arundinaceae*	Gramineaceae
8.	Kachnar	*Bauhinia variegate*	Fabaceae
9.	Samel	*Bombax ceiba*	Bombaceae
8.	Chironjee	*Buchania lanzan*	Anacardiaceae
9.	Kusum	*Carthamus tinctorius*	Compositae

(Table Contd...)

(1)	(2)	(3)	(4)
10.	Nimbu	*Citrus medica*	Rutaceae
11.	Neilgiri	*Eucalyptus grandis*	Myrtaceae
12.	Gulmohar	*Delonix regia*	Fabaceae
13.	Sisham	*Dalbergia sisso*	Fabaceae
14.	Tendu	*Diospyrus melanoxylon*	Ebenaceae
15.	Munga	*Erythrinia indica*	Fabaceae
16.	Jamun	*Eugenia jombolana*	Myrtaceae
17.	Bargad	*Ficus bengalensis*	Moraceae
18.	Pipal	*Ficus religiosa*	Moraceae
19.	Pakri	Ficus infectoria	Moraceae
20.	Khamer	*Gmelina arborea*	Lamiaceae
21.	Litchi	*Litchi chinensis*	Sapindaceae
22.	Maida	*Litsea chinensis*	Lauraceae
23.	Mahua	*Maduca indica*	Sapotaceae
24.	Mulberry	*Morus alba*	Moraceae
25.	Karanj	*Pongamia pinnata*	Fabaceae
26.	Guava	*Psidium guyava*	Myrtaceae
27.	Ashoka	*Saraca indica*	Fabaceae
28.	Ashoka	*Saraca indica*	Fabaceae
29.	Bhelwa	*Semecarpus anacardium*	Anacardiaceae
30.	Sagwan	*Tectona grandis*	Verbenaceae
31.	Ber	*Zizyphus mauritiana*	Rhamnaceae
32.	Imli	*Tamarindus indica*	Fabaceae

9. **Major animal species recorded in the study area**

Table 3.5

S.No.	Common Name	Scientific Name	Family
1.	Monkey	*Macaca mulatta*	Cercopithecidae
2.	Rabbits	*Lepus nigricollis*	Leporids
3.	Fox	*Vulpes bengalensis*	Canidae
4.	Bear	*Melursus ursinus*	Ursidae
5.	Palm squirrel	*Funambulus palmarum*	Sciuridae
6.	Chameleon	*Chamaeleo zeylanicus*	Chamaeleonidae
7.	Langur	*Semnopithecus entellus*	Cercopithecidae

10. **Annual Household Income in Mainpat**

According to the respondents in Mainpat block the maximum 36% have aannual household income between 0.5-1.0 lacs followed by 0.25-0.50 lacs, 1.00-2.00 lacs, 2.00-3.00 lacs and less than 0.25 lacs as 32%, 12%, 12% and 8% respectively (Figure 3.12).

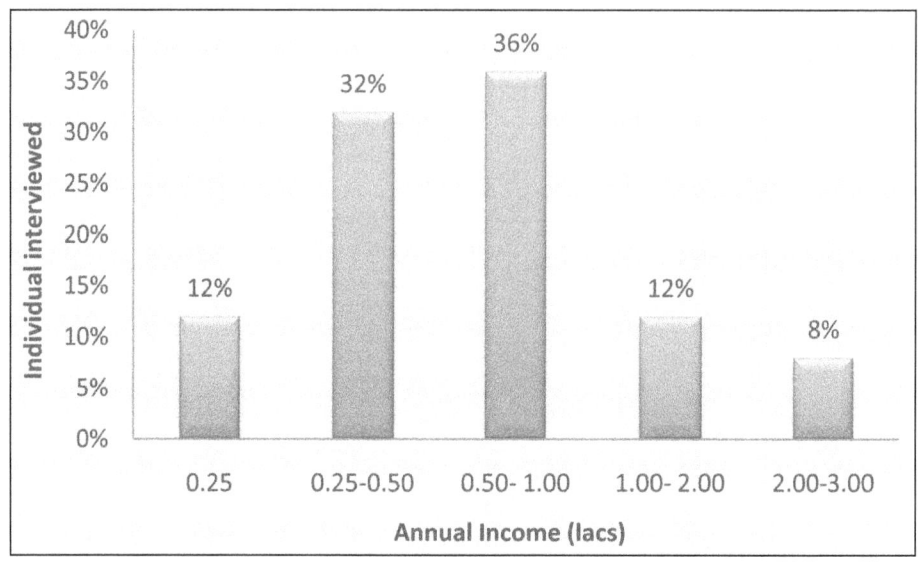

Fig. 3.12: Annual household incomes in Mainpat

11. Major Government and Nongovernment site in mainpat

Resorts

Saila Resort: The resort is the property of Chhattisgarh Tourism Board, situated at Kamleshwarpur, near Police Station at Mainpat, Dist: Surguja. The resort has 22 rooms in a cottage pattern having AC in every room and 29 beds used as dormitory.

Fig. 3.13: Saila resort Mainpat

- Anmol Resort

Fig. 3.14: Anmol resort Mainpat

- Potato Research Center

The chief minister of Chhattisgarh Dr. Raman Singh opening potato research center. The research centre would be proved useful in promoting potato cultivation in a scientific method. Under the guidance of this centre, farmers of the state would be successful in increasing more potato production and extension of potato cultivation area, he added.

The chief minister dedicated the streetlight extension work from Kamleshwar Chowk to Motel costing Rs. 28 lakh to the people.

Fig. 3.15: Potato research center Mainpat

In-charge and chief scientist of the Potato Research Centre Dr. RK Mishra. The centre would operate from Barima in Mainpat, with the establishment of the centre, potato farmers of Sarguja, Korea, Surajpur, Balrampur, Jashpur and Raigarh districts will get direct benefit.

The Kharif season, the climate of these hilly areas was favourable for potato production, but a study conducted in the last 10 years showed that because of infected seed and unscientific method of cultivation the potato production area has shrunken from 10,000 hectare to 1,000 hectare. At present, the research centre will exhibit hybrid quality potato seeds like Khyati, Pukhraj and Flysona from Shimla in 15-acre land of tribal farmers. The farmers will be imparted training and provide scientific information time to time. The state government and the Indira Gandhi Agriculture University have prepared a work plan for research in fruit varieties cultivated in winter season.

DISCUSSIONS

The present study entitled "Socio-environmental survey of Mainpat: an important eco-tourism hamlet of Chhattisgarh, India" was carried out in Sarguja University, Ambikapur C.G. during the year 2016-2017. The entire study is summarized in this section under the following heads.

- Demography of the study site
- Status of eco-tourism management and development in study site.
- To assess the future prospects of eco-tourism in study site

Demography of Study Site

The blocks, Mainpat total population of 76573. The total Villages in Main pat Block are 46. The highest percentage Scheduled Tribe is 79.80% followed by General SC. The maximum annual household income lies between 0.5-1.0 lacs. The Literacy level among the population of the Mainpat are as 53% and 43%, literates and illiterates.

Status of Eco-tourism Management and Development in Study Site

According to the primary data collected from the local respondents and secondary data sources like Internet, articles, review papers etc., the popular and famous eco-tourism places in Mainpat Block are Tiger point which is at height of 1080 MSL, Mehta point which is located in the area called Pharphatia at a height of 1085 MSL and Fish point which is located at the bank of river Machchri. Jaljali magical land is one of the most popular tourist place of interest in Mainpat.

In Main pat block the maximum number of tourist visit during December to March however medium in November, April and May and minimum in July, August and September. The information source regarding the eco-tourism spots in the blocks are not sufficient hence some arrangement for advertisement and popularizing the destinations especially websites should be commenced in order to give more information about the tourism destinations.

In the Main pat block the travel motive of the tourist registered maximum to have fun and entertained and visit friends & relatives.

The tourist respondents in the Main pat discussed some problems and suggested the following:

- Frequent conveyance (Bus facility) from major towns (Ambikapur and Sitapur) and Ambikapur Railway station is to be arranged.
- Day-wise Conducted tour package facilities are to be introduced by the Goverment of Chhattisgarh.
- Auto-rickshaw facility for travel to nearby spots.
- Guide facility especially for foreign tourist/ visitors having language problem with local residents.
- Hotel/Lodge facility with restaurant services.
- Proper site maintenance and conservation.
- Protection from criminal activities.
- Currency exchange facilities
- ATM problems.

To Assess the Future Prospects of Eco-tourism in Study Site

To assess the future prospects of eco-tourism in the study site is done by potentiality determination. It is done by processes of ranking method in which Tourist demand of an area was assessed through the preference or choice of tourist towards various components of its unique attractions (background tourism resources). The Demand Component were Wild life, Scenery and natural landscape, Art and handicraft Boating/Rafting Native life and culture Flora and Fauna Angling/Fishing Adventure sports Local Dance and festivals Antique exhibition Nightlife entertainment Trekking and Research.

The percentage of tourist preferring each category of attraction is considered as an index to judge the significance of that category. From the analysis it is found that 3 destinations belong to high moderate potential category (Buddha Temple and Jal jali), (1) destination belong to low moderate potential category (Tiger point) and (2) destinations belongs to low moderate potential category (Mehta point and Fish point).

CONCLUSION AND RECOMMENDATIONS

Eco-tourism is a new concept in tourism. It is a purposeful travel to natural areas to understand the cultural and natural history of environment, taking care not to alter the integrity of the ecosystem, while producing economic opportunities that make conservation of natural resources beneficial to local people. The growing recognition among tourists that natural environment needs protection and conservation, promoted the concept of eco-tourism. The study reaches the conclusion that among the present eco-tourism destinations Mainpat is popular and can be considered to have very high potential, followed by Jal jali, Buddha Temple which come under category high moderate potential, Tiger point under low moderate potential category and Mehta point and Fish point under low moderate potential category.

Hence according to the tourist respondents and personal suggestion, in order to succeed an eco-tourism must be economically viable as a business, conserve the natural environment and provide tangible benefits to the local people. The eco-tourism structure must be improvedto direct more money into local communities and provides a promising opportunity. Any form of tourism that does not reduce the availability of resources and does not inhibit future travelers from enjoying the same experience. Although ecotourists claim to be educationally sophisticated and environmentally concerned, they rarely understand the ecological consequences of their visits and how their day-today activities append physical impacts on the environment hence some checks in form of fine should be introduced.

The suggestions given below can rectify these problems up to a certain extend. Eco-tourism is a very good exploitation area for Mainpat Sarguja

Suggestions
1. There should be more awareness about the eco-tourism destinations in Mainpat by the tourism department through broachers, pamphlets, media advertisements etc.
2. More websites should be commenced in order to give more information about the tourism destinations.
3. More activities have to be introduced and performed by the government to promote eco-tourism.
4. Sanitation facilities should be increased and improved by the authorities in order to provide better facilities to the visitors.
5. More infrastructural facilities like roads, railways, hospitals, hotels etc have to be provided at the eco-tourism destinations.
6. The transportation facilities to the eco-tourism destinations should be increased.
7. Locals should be allowed to participate in the activities of the tourism departments in order to get better support from them.
8. Shopping facilities of the eco-tourism destinations must be increased and indigenous products have to be popularised.
9. Shows like musical fountain, laser show etc must be made technological and should be showed at all times.

10. Instead of making the eco-tourism destinations as 'holiday spots', it must be changed to 'learning spots'.
11. Hotels at the eco-tourism destinations should be establish and should be able to provide local food, local entertainments etc.
12. Cultural programmers should be introduced at the eco-tourism destinations as a medium of cultural exchange.
13. Professionalism in hospitality management should be enforced.
14. Good gardening system should be introduced at the tourism destinations in order to give better environment.
15. The female penetration in the eco-tourism destinations should be increased.
16. Serious research on the ecological diversity at the eco-tourism destinations should be given proper importance.
17. Introduce proper enforcement of rules at the tourism destinations with the help of police and similar agencies.
18. Visit-Information centers' must be established to provide every kind of information such as giving proper direction on safe travelling, secure lodging, arrange proper guidance, saving from exploitation and providing legal assistance.
19. New ways and means must be introduced to promote health tourism.
20. Sufficient funds must be made available from the Government for eco-tourism purpose.

PHOTOS GALLERY

REFERENCES

(ATREE 2006): White Paper on Eco-Tourism Policy (Draft) Center for Conservation Governance and Policy Ashoka Trust for Research in Ecology and the Environment (ATREE).

(ARMTGI 2016): Annual Report: Ministry of Tourism Government of India.

Anitha V. and Muraleedharan P.K. (2006). Economic Valuation of Eco-tourism Development of Recreational site in the Natural Forest of Southern Western Ghats.

Abraham S. (2015). The Relevance of Wetland Conservation in Kerala. International Journal of Biology Studies.

Aylward, B. and Freedman S. (1992), Eco-tourism in Global Biodiversity (B.Groombridge, ed.), Chapman and Hall. London.

Bhattacharya S., Ghosh G., Banerjee t., Goswami S., And Das P. (2015). Socio-environmental Survey of an Ecologically Important Hamlet of Darjeeling District, West Bengal, India. Department of Environmental Studies, Rabindra Bharati University, Kolkata. International Letters of Natural Sciences Vol. 33 (2015) pp. 51-72.

Brandon, K. (1996). Eco-tourism and Conservation: A Review of Key Issues. Washington, DC: The World Bank.

Bolton, R.N. and Drew, J.H. (1994), "A Multistage Model of Customers' Assessment of Service. Chhattisgarh Tourism Board, cgtourism.choice.gov.in

Buchsbaum B. D.(2004). Eco-tourism and Sustainable Development in Costa Rica. Major Paper Submitted to Virginia Polytechnic Institute and State University.

Daily Pioneer. 25 December. 2013. Retrieved 14 April 2014. "Chhattisgarh plans Mainpat Carnival".

Dixit S.K. and Narula V.K. (2010). Eco-tourism in Madhav National Park: Visitors Perspectives on Environmental Impact. South Asian Jounral of Tourism and Heritage, Vol. 3, No. 2.

Edwards R. (2010). The Role of Conservation Research and Education Centers in Growing Nature-based Tourism. Great Plains Research 20 (Spring): pp. 51-70.

Gadgil and Guha (1994). "Development and Forest Ecology Changes". pp: 101-136.

Honey, M. (1999). Eco-tourism and Sustainable Development. Who Owns Paradise? Island Press, Washington D.C.

Joshi V.M. (2014). Eco-tourism – A Key to Protect the Biodiversity in Maharashtra. International Journal of Innovative Research in Science, Engineering and Technology (An ISO 3297: 2007 Certified Organization) Vol. 3.

International Eco-tourism Society. International Eco-tourism Society website, accessed on February, 26, 2004. Available: www.eco-tourism.org

Lindberg, K. (1991). Policies for Maximizing Nature Tourism's Ecological and Economic Benefits. Washington: World Resources Institute London: Pitman

Mainpat Hill Station, www.echhattisgarh.in

Ramchurjee N.A. (2013). Eco-tourism in Balkot District, Karnataka, India: An Assessment of the Inhabitants Awareness Level and Attitude. International Journal of Environmental Sciences Vol. 03, No. 6.

Rai R.K. and Rai B.S. (2015). Conservation of Crocodylus Palustris in Kotmi Sonar of Janjgir - Chamapa (C.G.) India. IOSR Journal of Environmental Science, Toxicology and Food Technology (IOSR-JESTFT) e-ISSN: 2319-2402,p- ISSN: 2319-2399. Volume. 1 Issue. 3, PP. 24-29.

Roy, K.C., Sen., R.K. and Tisdell, C.A. (1995). *Economic Development and Environment: A Case Study of India*, Calcutta: Oxford India Paperback, Oxford University Press, xvi + 164. [ISBN 019 563431 4]

Wheat, S. (1994). Taming Tourism. C and graphical Magazine Vol. 66: pp: 16-19.

Wight, P. (1994). Tourism: Ethics or Eco-Sell? *Journal of Travel Research* 3 (1): 3-49.

Ziffer, K. (1989) Eco-tourism: The Uneasy Alliance. Washington D.C., Conservation International.

Pages: 56-88
Eco-tourism, Environmental Problems and Sustainable Development
Edited by: Dr. Soubam Premchandra Singh; Dr. Ashok K. Rathoure
Dr. Pawan Kumar 'Bharti'
ISBN: 978-93-86841-57-5
Edition: 2018
Published by: Discovery Publishing House Pvt. Ltd., New Delhi (India)

Rural Entrepreneurship
An Economic Development Paradigm through Entrepreneurial Potential Assessment of Beekeepers

Esakkimuthu M*
Kameswari VLV

ABSTRACT

Development of any nation depends primarily on the role played by entrepreneurs and entrepreneurship development among rural people is increasingly being recognized as a means of overall development of rural community. Micro and small enterprises play an important role in creating employment opportunities, resource utilization, income generation and promoting change in a gradual and peaceful manner. The crisis in Indian agriculture continues to be alarming consequent to the liberalization of trade and globalization of market economy. The challenges to Indian agricultural extension system in the aftermath of this deepening crisis in the agricultural sector have led to the experimentation of varied extension approaches to suit the emerging situation. The most important approach prevailing in the Indian context is the market-led extension approach. Globally, there will be enough food to feed the World population, which will touch 8.3 billion in 2030. At the same time, about hundred million people in developing countries will remain hungry. In rural India context, beekeeping were prosperous growth can be achieving sustainable value chain. Beekeeping is an important agrienterprise. But, India's contribution

---

* Kerala Agricultural University, KAU Main Campus, KAU P.O. Vellanikkara, NH - 47, Thrissur, Kerala - 680 656 (India)
Govind Ballabh Pant University of Agriculture and Technology (India)

to the global production is very meagre. Among Indian states, Tamil Nadu is the second largest producer of honey. Several Non-Governmental Organisations, cooperative societies, and State Agricultural Universities are promoting beekeeping as an important agri-enterprise in the state. To assess the entrepreneurial potentials and adoption of various recommended scientific practices in beekeeping the research study was conducted with 213 respondents based on simple random sampling in Kanniyakumari district of Tamil Nadu, India.

Key words: Agri-entrepreneurship, rural, development, beekeeping, Tamil Nadu.

INTRODUCTION

India is an agrarian country. Over 58% of India's population is supported by agriculture. Even while India's industrial and service sectors are growing by leaps and bounds, growth rate of agriculture is below 2%. However, in the long run, growth of other sectors is invariably linked to the fortunes of agriculture due to intricate forward and backward linkages. Hence, India's economic status continues to be determined by agriculture sector, and the situation is not likely to change in the foreseeable future.

The country recorded impressive achievements in agriculture during three decades since the onset of Green Revolution in late sixties. This enabled the country to overcome widespread hunger and starvation, achieve self-sufficiency in food, reduce poverty and bring economic transformation to millions of rural families. The situation, however, started taking a downturn in the mid-nineties with slowdown in growth rate of output, which then resulted in stagnation or even decline in farmers' income leading to agrarian distress. Over the years, this has been turning more and more serious. Agriculture now supports 58% of the population, as against 75% at the time of independence. During the same period, the contribution of agriculture and allied sectors to the Gross Domestic Product (GDP) has fallen from 61 to 19%. As of today, India supports 16.8% of World's population on 4.2% of World's water and 2.3% of land resources and per capita availability of resources is about 4 to 6 times less as compared to the world average. This will decrease further due to increasing demographic pressure and consequent diversion of the land for non-agricultural uses.

Around 51% of India's geographical area is already under cultivation as compared to 11% of the world average. The present cropping intensity of 136% has registered an increase of only 25% since independence. Further, rainfed drylands constitute 65% of the total net sown area. There is also an unprecedented degradation of land (107 million ha) and groundwater resources, and also fall in the rate of growth of total factor productivity. Natural resource base of agriculture, which provides for sustainable production, is either shrinking or degrading leading to adverse affects on production capacity. However, demand from the sector is rising rapidly due increase in population and per capita income and growing demand from industry sector. There is, thus, an urgent need to identify the problems confronting agriculture sector, restore its vitality and put it back on high growth trajectory. The deceleration needs to be arrested and agricultural productivity has to be doubled by 2050 to meet the growing demands of the population.

Agricultural Land holding Pattern in India

Last four decades has witnessed a sharp decline in the average size of operational land holdings in India. The average size of operational land holdings has reduced by half from 2.28 ha in 1970-71 to 1.16 ha in 2012-13. Consequently, the number of land holdings in marginal and small categories have increased by 56 million and 11 million respectively, during the same period. This is an indication of the immense population pressure on the limited land resources available for cultivation. The size of the land holding has implications for investments in agriculture, its productivity, farm mechanization and farm incomes. Increasing number of small and marginal holdings render farming a challenging task. This calls for innovative solutions in terms of production, marketing and access to various markets.

State-wise analysis of average land holding size reveals a declining trend all states, except Nagaland and Punjab. However, the intensity of reduction varies across states. In Bihar and Kerala, the average size of holding fell by more than three times during the last four decades, whereas in Andhra Pradesh, Karnataka, Madhya Pradesh and Maharashtra, it was reduced by more than two times. During the same period, the average land holding size increased in the marginal farmer category in Himachal Pradesh, Odisha, Punjab and West Bengal. This needs to be probed further as it confronts the logic of increasing fragmentation of land consequent to population pressure on it. In the small farmer category, the average size of holding has increased in Odisha, Punjab and West Bengal. In the large farmer category (more than 10ha.), the average size of holdings has increased in the states of Arunachal Pradesh, Assam, Gujarat, Haryana, Kerala, Odisha, Tamil Nadu and West Bengal between 1970-71 and 2012-13 (Government of India, 2013).

Small and marginal holders face several problems in agriculture like small and fragmented land holdings, shortage of good quality seeds, problem of irrigation, lack of mechanization, inadequate storage facilities, scarcity of capital, absence of marketing network, lack of value addition technology, non-availability of quality inputs, lack of timely credit, etc These factors make agriculture economically unviable for small holders. While their farm sizes may be small, marginal and small farmers contribute significantly towards both diversification and food security. It has also been pointed out that small holdings are equal or better than large holdings, but that it is not enough to compensate for the disadvantages faced by small holders. Hence, the economic viability of marginal and small farmers is crucial for livelihood in rural areas and the entire country. However, small scale agriculture can be made profitable through product diversification and entrepreneurship. There is an urgent need to nurture small holders and turn them into agripreneurs, who are not just farmers, but are also thinkers, risk takers and innovators. Agro-based industries provide an excellent opportunity to farmers for local entrepreneurship and employment generation thus improving their socio-economic conditions. Small scale enterprises play an important role in employment creation, resource utilization, income generation and in promoting change in a gradual and peaceful manner. In rural India, there is tremendous scope for agri-enterprises such as mushroom cultivation, lac culture, horticultural seedling production, sericulture, ornamental plants production and paddy cum pisiculture, etc. which can not only increase the farmers income but also help in diversification. Beekeeping is such remunerative agri-enterprise.

Entrepreneurship and Economic Development

"India lives in villages and its true spirit lives in rural areas". These words of the Father of the Nation, Mahatma Gandhi, are very much relevant even in the New Millennium. Gandhiji was not in favor of heavy and large industries. He reasoned that while large-scale industries can increase production, they cannot provide employment to millions of poor rural Indians. According to him, the crying need of India was production by masses through rural entrepreneurship and not mass production by heavy industries. The advantages of rural entrepreneurship are, therefore, very clear. Firstly, it can produce self-employment opportunities to millions and thus, reduce unemployment. Secondly, it can augment employment avenues for people in backward and rural areas and bring in balanced regional development to alleviate poverty.

Entrepreneurship development among rural people is increasingly being recognized as a means of overall development of rural community. One way of fostering regional development on the basis of entrepreneurship is to motivate and encourage people in the area to start their own entrepreneurial careers. The development of any nation depends primarily on the important role played by entrepreneurs. Hence, the part played by entrepreneurs is of vital importance in a developing country like India.

In India, after independence, the government decided to pursue the path of state sponsored and planned economic development. As a part of this strategy, individuals or group enterprise and initiatives were encouraged, assisted, guided and regulated by the state in various ways, so that their activities can have visible impact in the form of economic transformation along the lines considered appropriate and desirable by the state. The idea behind this was that persons who have no financial resources or managerial background could be induced to start small enterprises, which would be effective tools for widening the entrepreneurial base in the country. Micro, small and medium enterprises play important role in employment creation, resource utilization, and income generation and in promoting change in a gradual and peaceful manner. In this endeavor, behavior of the individual has been highlighted as a major contributing factor and, therefore, supply of entrepreneurs is being recognized as critical to development process.

In the present era, it is being realized that entrepreneurship contributes to development of a country in several ways, viz. assembling and harnessing various inputs, bearing risks, innovating and imitating technologies to reduce the cost and increase quality and quantity of goods and services, expanding the horizons of market and coordinating and managing the manufacturing unit at various levels. In fact, the rapid economic development of a country crucially depends upon the number and abilities of entrepreneurs.

After independence, conscious efforts were made towards economic and social transformation. India followed socialistic pattern of development policy within the framework of five-year plan. Accordingly, government concentrated on the development of infrastructure for industrial and agricultural development. Thus, it was during late sixties that the small-sector began to be recognized as an instrument for tapping entrepreneurial potential of the country's human resources. In the initial stages, the government envisaged a promotional package to facilitate setting up of entrepreneurial units. This package consisted of financial assistance and incentives, infrastructural facilities technical and managerial guidance through a network of a number of support organizations of central, state and local government organizations

But the insufficient progress of this sector, however, made the policy planners realize that facilities and incentives were necessary but not sufficient in itself to ensure adequate entrepreneurial response all together. In fact, entrepreneurial growth required focus on human resource development more than anything else. Entrepreneurs are key persons of any country for promoting economic growth and technological change. The appearance of their activities, i.e. the development of entrepreneurship is directly related to the socio-economic development of the society. This does not mean that individual or group enterprise and initiative did not have any role to play; but that these will be assisted, guided and regulated by the state in various ways, so that their activities can come to some results in the form of economic transformation along the lines considered appropriate and desirable by the state. The idea behind this was that the persons who have no financial resources or managerial background could be induced to take small-scale industries and thus, small industries could be effective tools for widening the entrepreneurial base in the country.

Entrepreneurship Development Programmes in India

About 80% of the World's population is living in economically undeveloped countries of Asia, Africa and South America. After gaining independence, many of these underdeveloped nations embarked on a planned and systematic path towards development. In India, the development strategy has gone through the phases of community development, technological development and lastly development with equity. Despite six decades of development efforts, there is a huge gap between urban and rural areas and haves and have-nots, and nowhere is this gap more glaring than the growing chasm between small and large farmers in rural India. All the development efforts of the government were unable to significantly improve the conditions of agricultural labourers and small and marginal farmers. Taking note of this, the Government of India has undertaken several steps to implement special projects for small and marginal farmers and agricultural labourers and bring an improvement in their socio-economic status.

One of the most pressing problems in many of the developing countries is large scale unemployment, especially in rural areas. Hence, the basic aim of all development initiatives is to provide people with jobs, so as to increase their economic condition. The Government of India and the state governments have launched several schemes employment generation schemes whose main focus is entrepreneurship development. Self-employment through entrepreneurship development is being promoted through many schemes by different government departments. Besides an array of programmes that promote setting up of village and small-scale enterprises, there are special schemes for scheduled castes and tribes. The current strategy for promotion of self-employment and entrepreneurship in rural areas largely relies on formation of self-help groups to empower rural communities and enable them to take up income generation activities. Some of the important entrepreneurship development initiatives in India are:

Integrated Rural Development Programme (IRDP)

This program was introduced in 1978 by the Government of India about 2,300 blocks of the country. In 1980's the program covered all the blocks of the country. It was sponsored on the basis of 50:50 by central and state government. The core objective of the program was to provide self employment opportunities to poor rural households and to raise the income generating capacity of target group. The target beneficiaries were small and marginal farmers, agricultural labourers, families of SC/ST (Scheduled Caste & Scheduled Tribes). Under this scheme, the beneficiaries were provided with productive assets and inputs by the government through financial assistance in terms of subsidy, advanced credit facilities by the nationalized credit institutions. The needy families were selected based on Below Poverty Line (annual income less than Rs.11,000/-) criteria. TRYSEM was initiated subsequently to provide skills to the targeted beneficiaries.

Training of Rural Youth for Self-Employment (TRYSEM)

This program was initiated in 1979. The main objective of the program was to provide vocational training to rural youth living below poverty line for ensuring self-employment. A provision was made under this program that at least 30 percent of beneficiaries should be women and it aimed at promoting self-employment among rural women by providing skill training in vocations which are acceptable to the beneficiaries. The major trades under TRYSEM were tailoring, printing and binding, basket making, radio repair, electrical works, pump repair, carpentry, blacksmith, production of mushroom, honey processing, cultivation of medicinal herbs and plants, poultry farming, fruit plants nursery, processing of fruits and vegetables, sericulture, installation of biogas plants, etc. It also provided facilities like scholarship to the young boys and girls, loan from commercial banks, guidance and consultancy related to the small scale industries.

Development of Women and Children in Rural Areas (DWCRA)

This program is a sub-scheme of IRDP and was launched by the Department of Women and Child Development, Government of India in 1982. This program was launched following evaluation of IRD where it was noticed that the benefits were not flowing to women in adequate measure. It aimed at empowering rural women by starting self-employment ventures and articulating their needs and demands through formation of self help groups. This program was introduced in 50 districts on a pilot scale basis

Scheme for Training and Employment Programme (STEP)

This program was initiated in the year 1987 to train women living below poverty line in the fields of sericulture, rural and small industry, handicraft, handloom work, agriculture and animal husbandry, etc. Under this program 2.65 lakh women had received benefits till 1996.

Swarnajayanti Gram Swarozgar Yojana (SGSY)

On 1 April 1999, IRDP and allied programmes, including the Million Wells Scheme (MWS), were merged into a single programme known as Swarnajayanti Gram Swarozgar Yojana (SGSY). The SGSY is conceived as a holistic programme of micro enterprise development in rural areas with emphasis on organising the rural poor into self-help groups, capacity-building, planning of activity clusters, infrastructure support, technology, credit and marketing linkages. It aimed to promote a network of agencies, namely, the District Rural Development Agencies (DRDA), line departments of state governments, banks, NGOs and Panchayati Raj Institutions (PRI) for implementation of the programme. Under this program, 50 per cent of the self-help groups must be formed exclusively by women and that 50 per cent of the benefits should flow to SCs and STs. There is also a provision for disabled beneficiaries. The programme is credit driven and subsidy is back-ended. The credit and subsidy ratio is pegged at 3:1. The subsidy is fixed at 30 per cent of the project cost subject to a maximum of Rs. 7,500 per individual beneficiary for those in the general category and 50 per cent of the project cost subject to a maximum of Rs. 10,000 in the case of SCs/STs. In the case of group projects, the subsidy is 50 per cent of the project cost subject to a ceiling of Rs. 1.25 lakh. Funds under the scheme are shared between the Centre and State Governments in the ratio of 75:25.

Concept of Entrepreneur and Entrepreneurship

According to Encyclopedia Britannica, an entrepreneur is an individual responsible for the operation of business, including the choice of a product, the mobilization of the necessary capital, decisions on product prices and quantities, the employment of the labor and expanding or reducing the productive facilities.

The word "entrepreneur" appeared for the first time in French lexicon. In the early 16th century, the term entrepreneur was used to refer to men engaged in military expeditions. Around 17th century, the term took a different meaning and was used to refer to architects and contractors of public works. Later, an entrepreneur was seen as a person who specializes in taking judgmental decisions about the coordination of scarce resources. Entrepreneurship as a concept gathered prominence in economic literature mainly through the writings of Cantillon (1734), who gave the concept some analytical treatment and assigned an economic role to the entrepreneur by emphasizing on 'risk' as a prominent entrepreneurial function.

According to Webber (1930), entrepreneurs are the product of particular social conditions in which they live and it is the society which shapes the personality of individuals as entrepreneurs. Gordon (1961) stated that an entrepreneur was not simply innovators, but people with the will to act, to assume risks and to bring about change through the organization of human efforts. Hagen (1962) conceptualizes an entrepreneur as a creative problem solver interested in things that are in practical and technological realm. Further he emphasized that most entrepreneurial activities do not involve innovative techniques to any considerable degree but rather involve coping with the method of doing business and of combining inputs quite similar to those combinations already in existence.

According to Schumpeter (1970), an entrepreneur is an innovative agent, who introduces something new into the economy – a new method of production, a new product, a new source of material or new markets. An entrepreneur's function is to revolutionize the pattern of production by exploiting an invention or introducing an untried technological possibility for producing a new commodity. An entrepreneur is primarily concerned with changes in the formula of production over which he has full control. He has a definite ability to create something new to prove its worth. The basic concept of entrepreneurship connotes effectiveness or an urge to take risk in the face of uncertainties.

Kirzner (1979) defines entrepreneur as performing various functional roles as risk taker, decision maker, organizer or coordinator, innovator, employer of factors of production, gap seeker and input completer, arbitrager. According to him, entrepreneur being alert to economic opportunities uses information advantages for his own profits.

The term 'entrepreneurship' is commonly associated with the term 'entrepreneur'. Entrepreneurship refers to a set of activities performed by an entrepreneur. Thus many scholars believe that an entrepreneur precedes entrepreneurship. Entrepreneurship is the process of identifying opportunities in the market place, marshalling the resources required to pursue these opportunities and investing the resources to exploit the opportunities for long term gains. It involves creating wealth by bringing together resources in new ways to start and operate an enterprise. The term, however, has been used in different ways by various scholars.

According to Schumpeter (1970) entrepreneurship is a function of group level pattern, managerial skill, leadership, an organizational building, high achievement, capable of completing inputs, socio-political and economic structure etc. Rao and Mehta (1978) described entrepreneurship as a creative and innovative response to the environment. Such response can take place in any field of social endeavor - business, industry, agriculture, education, social work and the like. Beginning new things or doing things that are already being done in a new way is, therefore, a simple definition of entrepreneurship. De (1981) concluded that entrepreneurship is a package of personality characteristics of entrepreneurs. The characteristics conventionally associated with entrepreneurship include leadership, innovativeness, risk taking and so on.

Drucker (1986) views entrepreneurship neither as a science nor an art. According to him, it is a practice and has a knowledge base. Knowledge in entrepreneurship is a means to an end. Entrepreneurship has also been described as a process undertaken by an entrepreneur to augment the business interest. Basically, it is an exercise involving innovation and creativity that will go towards establishing the enterprise. It is the propensity of mind to take calculated risks with confidence to achieve a pre-determined business or industrial objectives (Edvinraj, 2005). Thus, entrepreneurship is a purposeful activity indulged in by initiating and maintaining economic activities for the production and distribution of wealth. It has been recognized as an essential ingredient of economic development and an integral part of socio-economic transformation.

According to Gaikwad (2008) entrepreneurship connotes innovativeness, an urge to take risk in face of uncertainties, and intuition, i.e. the capacity of seeing things in a way which afterwards proves to be true. Spread of entrepreneurial activities in recent years has led to their classification based on area of work/ specialization. Market orientation of agriculture coupled with increase in post harvest ventures and agro based industries has led to a special type of entrepreneurs called agriprenurs or agricultural entrepreneurs. Joshi and Kapoor (1973) define farm entrepreneur as a person or a group of persons who organize and operate the business related or based on agriculture and is responsible for the results. He is pioneer in organizing and developing farm based activities. Haredero (1979) described an agricultural entrepreneur as a person who introduces changes which directly or indirectly lead to higher agricultural inputs. Bhattacharya (1983) observed that in South East Asian countries, efforts at developing agriculture have provided some areas of the countryside with better infrastructure in comparison to other areas (irrigation, communication and cooperative institutions). In this changed scenario, some farmers have responded better than other farmers with new enterprises. This group of farmers was known as agricultural entrepreneur. An agri-entrepreneur is a person who undertakes self employment opportunities in agriculture such as food processing and packaging, preservation of seasonal vegetables and fruits, seed processing and preservation, etc. In addition, opportunities fro entrepreneurship also exist through input procurement and distribution, hiring of implements and equipment, besides supply of inputs like bio-fertilizers, bio-pesticides, vermi-compost, soil amendments, etc.

Beekeeping in India

Small and marginal holdings constitute 80% of the total land holdings in India. They face several challenges which include lack of access to credit, technology, irrigation facilities, inputs and market. While their farm sizes may be small, marginal and small farmers contribute significantly towards both diversification and food security. It has also been pointed out that small holdings are equal or better than large holdings, but that it is not enough to compensate for the disadvantages faced by small holders. Hence, the economic viability of marginal and small farmers is crucial for livelihoods in rural areas and for the entire country. To improve agricultural productivity or income of the farmers, it is necessary to develop an entrepreneurial culture and organizational competencies among farmers. There is an urgent need to nurture local agripreneurs, who are not just farmers, but are also thinkers, risk takers and innovators. Agro-based industries provide an excellent opportunity to the farmers for local entrepreneurship and employment generation, thus improving their socio-economic conditions. In the rural India there is tremendous scope for agrienterprises such as mushroom cultivation, lack culture, horticultural seedling production, sericulture, ornamental plants production and paddy cum pisiculture, etc. which can not only increase the farmers income but also help in diversification.

Apiculture is an age old tradition in India but has the potential to develop as a prime agri-horticultural and forest based industry. Honey production is a lucrative business and it generates employment opportunities for farmers, farm women and rural youth. Apiculture is an economically profitable enterprise and can be a useful enterprise as it can add to the income and improve the economic condition of the farmers. There is enough scope for taking up beekeeping on a commercial scale. Beekeeping has a special advantage in India where majority of the farmers are small or marginal land holders and a large area is under horticultural crops.

The total global demand for honey is around one million tonnes. Germany is the world's largest consumer of honey and imports 90,000 tonnes of honey based products annually. China is the largest producer of honey and exports 80,000 tonnes annually. In comparison, India produces 27,000 tonnes of honey per year and exports 7,000 tonnes. Hence, there is an immense possibility for India to increase its export share, if more people take up bee keeping for honey production. Up to 1950s, apiculture was not taken as a serious venture in India. In 1956, Khadi and Village Industries Commission (KVIC) had taken interest in this field and formed Beekeeping Directorate. In 1962, KVIC established Central Bee Research and Training Institute (CBRTI) at Pune. Up to that period, only Indian bees (*Apis cerana indica*) were used for beekeeping. In 1962, Italian bees (*Apis mellifera*) were introduced in India.

Beekeeping has a long tradition in Tamil Nadu, which is the second largest producer of honey in India. Both natural and cultivated vegetation in Tamil Nadu provide immense scope and potential for development of beekeeping ventures. Beekeeping ventures in Tamil Nadu predate establishment of KVIC and serious efforts in this field were taken up since 1924. In 1924, Dr. Spencer Hatch, the Secretary of the Marthandam YMCA trained farmers in scientific beekeeping and also popularized Newton's hive box (a movable frame hive box) and honey extraction machine. Marthandam Beekeeping Society (MBS) was formed in 1937 for the collection and marketing of honey in the state. From 1957 onwards, KVIC has taken lead in collection and marketing aspects to promote the venture in the state. Tamil Nadu has greater scope for apiculture compared to other states in India due to large scale cultivation of horticultural crops. Beekeeping in Tamil Nadu is mainly aimed at producing honey and wax. But, it can be made more profitable by producing related products such as royal jelly, bee toxin, pollen and propolis, which have a very high demand in international markets.

Theories of Entrepreneurship

Various theories propounded by researchers indicate that the emergence of entrepreneurial activities is closely interlinked to economic, social, cultural, religious and psychological variables. Different scholars have developed various theories on entrepreneurship and these can be categorized as sociological, economic, cultural and psychological theories.

Sociological Theories of Entrepreneurship

Several scholars have explained the rise of entrepreneurs in terms of social factors like religious practices, norms, etc.

Webber (1947) propounded the theory of religious beliefs. According to him, entrepreneurship is a function of religious belief and religion shapes the entrepreneurial culture in any society. He emphasized that the entrepreneurial energies are exogenous supplied by means of religious belief. In his work *The Protestant Ethic and Spirit of Capitalism*, Weber states that Protestant Ethic encourages adventurous spirit, capitalism (economic system in which people have freedom to pursue economic activities and can own private enterprise) and glorifies entrepreneurial culture. According to Weber, the spirit of capitalism is intertwined with the motive of profit, resulting in creation of great number of business enterprises.

Hagen (1962) attempted to empirically determine measures that influenced entrepreneurial activity. He introduced the concept of 'withdrawal of status respect' – a complex psycho analytic variable. According to Hagen, following 'withdrawal of status respect', certain creative individuals reject traditional values and take up new roles and become entrepreneurs. His work describes the behavior pattern of individuals influenced by external stimulus, which in turn is responsible for entrepreneurship development.

Cochran (1974) reported the importance of society in shaping the entrepreneurial personality. According to him, the key ingredients to development of an entrepreneurial personality are role expectations, social sanctions and inter group relations in society. In addition, knowledge of environment, socio economic, cultural factors and support system are important factors.

Economic Theories of Entrepreneurship

According to this view, entrepreneurship and economic development are interdependent. Economic development takes place when a country's real national income increases over a period of time wherein the role of entrepreneurship is an integral part.

According to Knight (1921), entrepreneurs are a specialized group of persons who bear risk and deal with uncertainty. They are recipient of pure profit which is the reward for bearing the cost of uncertainty. Uncertainty, according to Knight, is a situation where the probability of alternative cannot be determined either by prior reasoning or by statistical inference. Business uncertainty can, however, be reduced by using the technique of consolidation in which individual instances are pooled and total uncertainty can be reduced. An entrepreneur willingly carries on those responsible activities which are neither insured nor salaried but guarantees interest to lender, wages to employees and rent to the landlord. However, the supply of entrepreneurship depends upon ability of the entrepreneur, willingness of the entrepreneur and the power to extend guarantee to others. Knight also identified social, economic and psychological factors which influence the supply of entrepreneur since entrepreneurial motivation and abilities are long-run problems.

Israel. M. Kirzner, the noted economist, put forth the theory of adjustment of price. According to him, the essential entrepreneurial element is the alertness to information rather than its possession alone. He contends that those entrepreneurs who have superior telescopic faculty keep themselves alert to confront any disequilibrium in the market through accumulating and using information.

Psychological Theory of Entrepreneurship

These theories try to explain entrepreneurship in terms of psychological characteristics of the individual. Most important among these is the theory given by David McCellend.

David McClelland was a psychological theorist and he proposed that every individual is driven to varying extents by one of three motivators; viz; achievement, power or affiliation. Affiliation is a strong desire to belong. People with high need for affiliation have a deep concern for relationships, strive to reduce uncertainty, and they love teamwork. They also tend to be less assertive, and tend be more dependent on others. Power refers to the ability to control and influence. People with high need for power try to win arguments, persuade and prevail. Achievement oriented people are driven to master complex challenges, to find solutions, overcome goals, and they love getting feedback on the level of success. Standards of excellence, precise goals and clear roles are what motivate these people. This results in a non-conscious concern for achieving excellence through individual effort. They usually set challenging goals for themselves, assume personal responsibility for accomplishment and take calculated risks for achieving these goals. They are very effective in leading task oriented groups and do well in entrepreneurial roles. According to McCellend, need for achievement is highest among entrepreneurs.

According to Schumpeter's psychological theory, entrepreneurship is a most likely to emerge when a society has sufficient supply of individuals possessing particular psychological characteristics. Schumpeter believed that entrepreneurs are primarily motivated by an atavistic will to power and establish a private kingdom. He also described the main characteristics of an entrepreneur as the capacity to see future trends, will to overcome fixed habits of thought and the capacity to withstand social opposition.

Conceptualisation of Entrepreneurial Potential

Literature on entrepreneurship development views an entrepreneur as a person who fulfils a role or a function in the economy. An impressive array of literature is available on their functions, qualities, and behaviour. Most of the theories on entrepreneurship highlight the contexts that give raise to entrepreneurship and highlight the role of economic, social and cultural factors in the process. In contrast, there are several psychological theories that link inherent characteristics of an individual and the likely manifestation of entrepreneurial ventures. Some models suggest that entrepreneurship is essentially an outcome of interaction between various components of which an entrepreneur is the prime mover or starting point.

According to Krueger and Brazeal (1994), the actual occurrence of an entrepreneurial activity requires a pre-existing preparedness to accept that opportunity. This "pre-existing preparedness" is the entrepreneurial potential. But that in itself is not sufficient to trigger an entrepreneurial venture. It has to be followed by something that precipitates the decision to start and continue an entrepreneurial venture (Shapero, 1982; Reynolds, 1992). Individuals with entrepreneurial potential often do not have any serious intention towards starting a business till the right conditions appear or occurrence of a trigger event. Till such time, their potential lies dormant. Hence, entrepreneurial potential can be viewed not only as a pre condition and contributory factor for an entrepreneurial event but exists temporally prior to it.

Delmar's (1996) model on entrepreneurship has four concepts; viz: business performance, entrepreneurial behaviour, the individual, and the environment. According to him, business performance (success) is determined by environment; i.e. market. It is also determined by the entrepreneurial behaviour (actions taken by the entrepreneur), which in turn is also affected by the environment. Besides these, an individual's i.e; entrepreneur's abilities and motivation also affect entrepreneurial behaviour.

This inherent ability may be defined as the entrepreneurial potential of an individual, which when combined with knowledge and requirements for a given task can give rise to successful entrepreneurial venture. Despite existence of a high entrepreneurial potential, a person may not become an entrepreneur as entrepreneurial activity does not occur in a vacuum. Instead, it is deeply embedded in a cultural and social context, human networks, and both social and economic conditions. In other words, high entrepreneurial potential does guarantee occurrence of entrepreneurial activity or its success. It merely increases the chances of both. There is a noteworthy distinction between those who would like to be entrepreneurs and those who actually become an entrepreneur. Entrepreneurial potential refers to an inclination, an openness, and a readiness to grasp a business opportunity: not necessarily a deliberate intention to become an entrepreneur.

The relationship between entrepreneurial potential and business performance is shown in (Figure 4.1). Business performance is influenced by entrepreneurial behavior, which refers to the manifest activities carried out by the entrepreneur. It is also influenced by the external environment which comprises of market, policies, etc. External environment also affects the entrepreneurial behavior i.e; the responses of an entrepreneur to various events and changes. However, it is important to recognize that external environment in turn is influenced by the larger socio-economic context. Both socio-economic context and environment determine motivation, which is a direct determinant of entrepreneurial behavior. Finally, entrepreneurial potential and motivation have a direct causal affect on entrepreneurial behaviour.

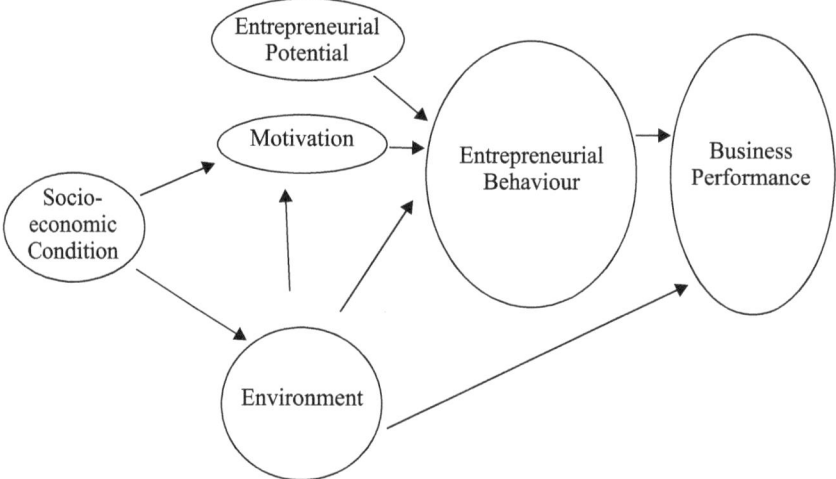

Fig. 4.1: Conceptual model of entrepreneurial potential

Generally, when the innate ability is supported by positive with socio-economic conditions, and high motivation, it leads to entrepreneurial behavior that is conducive for high business performance. Entrepreneurial potential is operationally defined as the extent to which an individual is capable of becoming an entrepreneur. It is a composite attribute and was studied in terms of five dimensions; viz; orientation concerning about innovativeness, economic motivation, need for achievement, risk taking ability and self-confidence. These dimensions were operationally defined as follows. (1) Innovativeness is the degree to which a beekeeper is likely to adopt new idea, practice or technology related to beekeeping earlier than other beekeepers in the same social system. (2) Economic motivation is defined as the occupational success in terms of profit maximization and the relative value placed by a farmer on economic ends. (3) Need for achievement is operationally defined as a beekeeper's desire for excellence and to attain a sense of personal accomplishment. 4) Risk taking ability refers to the degree to which a beekeeper is oriented towards taking risk and facing uncertainty while running the beekeeping enterprise. (5) Self-confidence is operationally defined as the degree of belief in one's own abilities in achieving the things one wishes.

Global gap between the rich and the poor is widening every day. In India, about 500 million people are dependent on agriculture. Large percentages among them have marginal and small holdings. While this is a strong disadvantage, this situation also opens up opportunities and possibilities for development of alternative income generating activities in agriculture and allied areas. The future progress and growth of agriculture sectors and economic well being of the farmers in the country will depend upon agripreneurial activities of farmers. Agripreneurial activities can play a significant role in the context of emphasis on eradication of poverty and employment generation of employment through diversification in the occupational opportunities available in the rural. Realizing this, governments and central and state level are taking up various initiatives to promote entrepreneurship among farmers and give a market ward orientation to agriculture.

Currently, promoting beekeeping among farmers as an agri-enterprise is one of the priority issues in the state of Tamil Nadu. The state has plenty of untapped human resources in rural areas whose potential, if properly utilized, can lead to development of the state. At present, a number of co-operative societies and NGOs are engaged in promoting beekeeping, honey collection and its marketing in the state. The National Horticultural Board (NHB) and State Horticultural Mission (SHM) are also playing a vital role in boosting apiculture in Tamil Nadu by providing training and inputs at subsidized rates to the beekeepers.

A look at the research trends reveals that, studies on entrepreneurship are mainly focused on assessing the entrepreneurial skills and entrepreneurial behavior. As such, very few studies are available on entrepreneurial potential and there is a huge gap in our understanding of how innate potential of a person interacts with conducive environmental factors to give rise to successful entrepreneurs. Even though some studies have been conducted in Tamil Nadu on adoption of beekeeping technologies, there are no studies on the extent to which beekeepers turn into entrepreneurs and on their entrepreneurial potential.

SUSTAINABLE BEEKEEPING PRACTICES IN INDIAN CONTEXT

For beekeeping to be sustainable, it must benefit bees and beekeepers. In recent years, as beekeepers realise that they are increasingly unable to arrest the decline in honey bee populations, some people have started to question the assumptions we have made about bees and our desire for products of the bee - honey and beeswax. "India lives in villages and its true spirit lives in rural areas". These words of the Father of the Nation, Mahatma Gandhi, are very much relevant even in the New Millennium. He was not in favor of heavy and large industries. He reasoned that while large-scale industries can increase production, they cannot provide employment to the millions of poor rural Indians. According to him, the crying need of India is production by masses through rural entrepreneurship and not mass production by heavy industries. The focus of rural entrepreneurship is, therefore, very clear. Firstly, it can produce self-employment opportunities, to the millions and thus, reduce unemployment. Secondly, it can augment employment avenues for others in backward areas and bring in balanced regional development to alleviate poverty.

(i) Sustainable biodiversity

Beekeeping does not attract much attention. It is easy to visit villages and not "see" beekeeping, unless actively looking for it. Beekeeping, however, is crucially important for agricultural well-being; it represents and symbolizes the natural biological interdependence that comes from insects, pollination and production of seed. Useful small-scale efforts to encourage beekeeping interventions can be found throughout the world, helping people to strengthen livelihoods and ensuring maintenance of habitat and biodiversity.

(ii) Environmental sustainability

It demands that ecosystems are not damaged beyond their capacity to maintain their own biological processes, functions, biodiversity and natural productivity. For humans, sustainability is the ability to meet the needs of the present without compromising the ability of future generations to meet their own needs. Beekeeping will be sustainable when interactions between humans and bees contribute positively to resilient and healthy populations of locally-adapted indigenous bees living in the wild and in the apiaries of beekeepers.

(iii) Bees-diligent pollinators

Pollination is necessary for all seed and fruit production by flowering plants. Transfer of pollen among flowers to allow their reproduction is a vital mechanism for maintaining life on earth. People harvest the seeds of some crops for food; examples are oilseed crops, nuts, legumes such as beans and peas, and cereals such as rice and maize. Other crops provide fruit that develops with the seed, for example citrus fruits, mangoes and tomatoes. Seed is required for the production of the next generation of crops and allows plant-breeding programmes to improve varieties.

Plant reproduction requires the transfer of pollen from the anthers, or male part of a flower, to the stigmas, or female part of a flower, either on the same plant or on a separate plant that may be some distance away. After thousands of years of evolution and adaptation to local environments, each plant species has specific requirements for this important transfer of pollen; many depend on foraging insects to transfer pollen among flowers. Many species of insects visit flowers to seek nectar or pollen; while doing so most will transfer a few pollen grains, thus contributing to pollination. Honeybees are highly efficient pollinating insects.

(iv) Honey value added products

Beeswax is the material that bees use to build their nests. It is produced by young honeybees that secrete it as a liquid from special wax glands. On contact with air, the wax hardens and forms scales, which appear as small flakes of wax on the underside of the bee. About one million wax scales make 1 kg of wax. Bees use the wax to build the well-known hexagonal cells that make up their comb, a very strong and efficient structure. Bees use the comb cells to store honey and pollen; the queen lays her eggs in them, and young bees develop in them. Beeswax is produced by all species of honeybees, although the waxes produced by different species have slightly different chemical and physical properties.

RESEARCH METHODOLOGY

Universe of the Study

Tamil Nadu state was one of the first of British settlements in India. The state is the successor to the old Madras Presidency, which covered the bulk of southern peninsula till 1901. The composite Madras State was later reorganised, and the present Tamil Nadu was formed in 1956. Tamil Nadu has a total geographical area of 1,30,058 sq.km with a population of 7,21,47,030 (Figure 4.2). The administrative units of state comprises of 32 districts, 76 revenue divisions, 226 taluks, 1,127 firkas, 16,564 revenue villages, 10 municipal corporations, 125 municipalities, 385 panchayat unions blocks, 561 town panchayats, 12,618 village panchayats, 39 lok sabha constituencies and 234 assembly constituencies (http://www.tn.gov.in).

Fig. 4.2: Map of Tamil Nadu

Agriculture is the major occupation of the people of Tamil Nadu. The total cultivated area in the state was 56.10 million hectares in 2013-14. The principal food crops include paddy, millets and pulses. Commercial crops include sugarcane, cotton, sunflower, coconut, cashew, chilli, gingelly and groundnut. Main plantation crops are tea, coffee, cardamom and rubber. Major forest produce include timber, sandalwood, pulp wood and fuel wood. Tamil Nadu occupies a premier position in the production and application of bio-fertilizers. Efforts are on to improve farming technologies so as to increase yield in low rainfall areas of the state. Annual food grain production in the year 2013-14 was 100.35 lakh mt.

Agriculture continues to be the most important sector of the state's economy, as 70 percent of the population is engaged in agriculture and allied activities for their livelihood. The state has a gross cropped area of around 63 lakh ha. The government policy and objectives have been to ensure increase in agricultural production in a sustainable manner so as to meet the food requirements of a growing population and raw material needs of agro based industries, thereby providing employment opportunities to the rural population. Tamil Nadu has all along been one of the states with a creditable performance in agricultural production and farmers have been relatively more responsive and receptive to changing technologies and market forces.

Locale of the Study

The study was conducted in Kanniyakumari district of Tamil Nadu state (Figure 4.3). This district was purposively selected for the study due to several reasons. Firstly, a large number of people in this district have taken up small scale agri-enterprises including beekeeping (Mahendran, 2004). Secondly, more than 70% of honey produced in Tamil Nadu comes from Kanniyakumari district alone (Chandy, 2009). Thirdly, the Marthandam Beekeeping Society, which is one of the oldest organizations involved in promoting beekeeping in the country, is also actively involved in the promotion of beekeeping venture in the district. It also has a State Agricultural University (Tamil Nadu Agricultural University) which is actively promoting beekeeping through Agriculture College and Research Institute, Killikulam. The University organizes training programs and other extension activities on a regular basis technical support to beekeepers in the district. Fourthly, Kanniyakumari district is unique as it receives both south-west and north-east monsoon because of which honey production can take place throughout the year. Lastly, this district produces a wide variety of horticultural crops, which is essential for beekeeping.

The area comprising the present Kanniakumari district was a part of the erstwhile Travancore state and was recognized as a separate district in the year 1956. Kanyakumari is the southern most district of Tamil Nadu. The district lies between 77° 15' and 77° 36' eastern longitudes and 8° 03' and 8° 35' northern latitudes. The district is bound by Tirunelveli District on the North and the east. The south eastern boundary is the Gulf of Mannar. On the south and the south west, it is bound by the Indian Ocean and the Arabian Sea. The state of Kerala forms the boundary in the west and north west.

The agro-climatic conditions of the district are suitable for growing a number of crops. However, there is distinct variation in the climatic conditions prevailing within the district. The south west monsoon period starts from the month of June and ends in September, while the north east monsoon period starts from October and ends in the middle of December.

Fig. 4.3: Map of Kanniyakumari

Selection of Blocks

Kanniyakumari district has nine blocks. After consultation with experts from the Marthandam Beekeeping Society and faculty members at Tamil Nadu Agricultural University all the nine blocks in Kanniyakumari district were taken for the study.

Selection of Villages

One village from each block, having maximum number of beekeepers, was purposively selected in the next stage of sampling.

Table 4.1: Sampling plan

S. No	Name of the District	Name of the Block	Name of the Village	Total Number of Beekeepers	Number of Beekeepers Selected
1.	Kanniyakumari	Agastheeswaram	Kulasekharapuram	56	28
2.		Thuckalay	Maruthakurichy	34	17
3.		Rajakkamangalam	Kesavarthanapuram	64	32
4.		Thovalai	Thovalai	48	24
5.		Kurunthancode	Thenkarai	38	19
6.		Thiruvattar	Pechiparai	66	33
7.		Killiyoor	Mathicode	54	27
8.		Munchirai	Panikulam	38	19
9.		Melpuram	Vilavancode	28	14
Total number	1	09	09	426	213

Selection of Respondents

List of total number of beekeepers in each village was taken from the Marthandam Beekeeping Society which is actively involved in promoting beekeeping in the district. Out of this, 50 per cent beekeepers were selected for study using simple random sampling.

Research Design

A research design is the arrangement of condition for collection and analysis of data in a manner that aims to combine relevance to research purpose with economy in procedure. Analytical research design was used to meet out the objectives set forth for the study.

Data Collection Tools and Techniques

A detailed structured interview schedule was used as a tool for data collection. Interview schedule consisting of open ended questions was developed for collecting data from the respondents. The interview schedule was prepared in English and was translated into Tamil before administering it to the respondents. The pilot test was conducted by the researcher to gain first hand information about various aspects to be studied, study area and to check the tool. Interview schedule was modified for final administration after pilot study.

Statistical Tools

Statistical analysis of quantitative data is an important aspect of research work, as it facilitates interpretation of the data. Data were analyzed in the light of objectives of the study and following statistical techniques were used.

(i) Percentage Analysis

Percentage values were calculated to make simple comparison. These were calculated by dividing the frequency of particular cell by total number of beekeepers and multiplying by 100.

$$P = (f/n) \times 100$$

Where, f = Frequency of particular cell; n= Total number of beekeepers; P= Percentage

(ii) Coefficient of Correlation

Coefficient of correlation is a number computed from a set of data and summarizes the extent to which variations in one variable go together with variation in other variable. It was used to find out the relationship between two variables. Karl Pearson's formula of coefficient of correlation given below was used to find the relationship between two variables.

$$r = \frac{Co\ v.\ (X_1 X_2)}{\sqrt{Var\ (X_1) Var\ (X_2)}}$$

Where,

r = Coefficient of correlation

X_1 and X_2 are the two variables

$Var(X_{1)} = 1/n \sum (X_1 - X_1)^2$

$Var(X_{2)} = 1/n \sum (X_2 - X_2)^2$

$Cov(X_1 X_2) = 1/n \sum (X_1 - x_1)(X_2 - x_2)$

RESULTS AND DISCUSSION

Profile and Communication Characteristics of Beekeepers

This section relates to the distribution of beekeepers with respect to the selected profile and communication characteristics of 213 beekeepers viz., age, educational status, land holding size, family size, annual income, extension agency contact, mass media exposure, credit orientation, trainings attended and extension participation towards beekeeping are as follows in the Table 4.2.

Table 4.2: Distribution of beekeepers based on their profile and communication characteristics

S.No.	Category	Variable
1.	Demographic	Age, education, family size
2.	Economic	Land holding size, annual income, credit orientation
3.	Extension and communication	Extension agency contact, extension participation, mass media exposure, training attended

From the above table 4.2 it was observed that, majority of the beekeepers had young and middle age group, high literacy rate, marginal land holding size, small family size, low annual income, medium level of extension agency contact, mass media exposure, credit orientation, extension participation and more than three training most of the beekeepers had undergone under Marthandam beekeeping society.

- The findings revealed that majority (43.19 per cent) of the respondents were up to 33 years in young age and an equal number of the respondents were middle age group of 34 - 48 years. The rest 13.62 per cent were above 48 years of old age.
- Out of the total respondents, maximum number of respondents (29.11 per cent) able to only read and write and an equal number were educated up to primary level. Further, 17.85 per cent respondents were educated up to middle school level, 12.67 per cent respondents who had high school level and 7.98 per cent of the respondents were illiterate. Only 3.28 per cent of the respondents were educated up to college level education.

- Among the total respondents, majority (92.49 per cent) of the respondents possessed the size of the land holding was less than one hectare followed by 7.05 per cent of the respondents who possessed the size of the land holding was one to two hectares. It was found that only 0.46 per cent beekeepers possessed land holding size of more than two hectares and none of them possessed land holding size of more than four hectares.
- The results showed that majority (60.09 per cent) of the respondents belonged to medium family size followed by 27.70 per cent respondents who belonged to small size family and 12.21 per cent respondents belonged to large size family.
- Majority (85.92 per cent) of the respondents had annual income of up to Rs. 50,000, 13.15 per cent of the respondents had annual income in the range of Rs. 50,001 to 1, 00, 000 and 0.93 per cent of the respondents earned more than Rs. 1, 00, 001 per annum.
- Among the respondents majority (59.62 per cent) of the respondents had a medium level of mass media exposure and 23.48 per cent of the respondents had a high level of mass media exposure. Only 16.90 per cent of the respondents had a low level of mass media exposure.
- The results revealed that majority (68.07 per cent) of the respondents had medium level of extension agency contact, 24.88 per cent of the respondents had low level of extension agency contact and 7.05 per cent of the respondents had high level of extension agency contact.
- Out of all the respondents, majority (80.28 per cent) of the respondents had medium level of extension participation, 12.20 per cent of the respondents had low level of extension participation and 7.52 per cent of the respondents had high level of extension participation.
- Among the respondents revealed that (69.95 per cent) of beekeepers had attended more than three trainings, 24.88 per cent had attended two trainings, 5. 17 per cent beekeepers had attended one training.
- The results showed that majority (80.75 per cent) of the respondents had medium level of credit orientation, 14.56 per cent of the respondents had high level of credit orientation and 4.69 per cent had low level of credit orientation.

Extent of Adoption of Scientific Beekeeping Technologies by Beekeepers
- A look from the results shows that majority (72.77 per cent) of the beekeepers had a high level of adoption of scientific beekeeping technologies, 27.33 per cent of the beekeepers had medium level of adoption and none of respondents had low level of adoption.
- From the results it was observed that majority (97.18 per cent) of the beekeepers had adopted artificial feeding of sugar solution to honey bees during lean season (April-June) and handling of beehive frames.

- A look at the results shows that 96.24 per cent of the respondents had adopted beehive inspection for predators at least once a week.
- The results revealed that vast majority (94.36 per cent) of the beekeepers had adopted placement of beehives near fruit/flowering plants.
- Use of sugarcane molasses/pine apple extract as feed for bees was adopted by 92.01 per cent of the beekeepers.
- The results revealed that application of formic acid near the beehives was adopted by 75.11 per cent.
- Keeping of honeybee box in the forest area/community land was adopted by 69.95 per cent beekeepers in the study area.
- The showed that placing of the bee box in the north-south direction was adopted by majority of the respondents (66.66 per cent).
- Extraction of other products apart from honey was adopted by majority i.e. 55. 39 per cent of the respondents.
- Use of mechanical honey extractor for extraction of honey was not adopted by 53.06 per cent of the respondents.
- Majority (85.45 per cent) of the respondents did not adopt production of other value added products from honey.
- It was found that heating of honey before bottling was not-adopted by majority (86.39 per cent) of the beekeepers.

Entrepreneurial Potential of Beekeepers

Entrepreneurial potential was conceptualised as a combination of five components viz; innovativeness, economic motivation, need for achievement, risk taking ability and self-confidence and is essential to succeed in beekeeping venture.

- The results showed that majority (84.51 per cent) of the beekeepers have high level of overall entrepreneurial potential, rest of the 15.49 per cent of the beekeepers have medium level of overall entrepreneurial potential and none of them have low level of overall entrepreneurial potential.
- Majority (98.12 per cent) of beekeepers had high level of risk taking ability, 1.88 per cent of the beekeepers had medium level of risk taking ability and none of beekeeper had the low level of risk taking ability had congregated.
- Out of the total number of respondents, majority (83. 57 per cent) of beekeepers had high level of economic motivation, 16.43 per cent of the beekeepers had low level of economic motivation and none of the beekeeper had low level of economic motivation.
- The results revealed that majority (63.38 per cent) of the beekeepers had high level of need for achievement and 36.62 per cent of beekeepers had medium level of need for achievement and none of the beekeeper had low level of need for achievement.

- It was found that majority (57.75 per cent) of the beekeepers had medium level of innovativeness and 42.25 per cent of the beekeepers had high level of innovativeness. None of the beekeeper had low level of innovativeness.
- From the results it was observed that, majority (88.26 per cent) of the beekeepers had medium level of self-confidence, 11.27 per cent of the beekeepers had low level of self-confidence and only 0.50 per cent had high level of self-confidence.

Relationship between Extent of Adoption of Scientific Beekeeping Technologies and Entrepreneurial Potential of Beekeepers

- Extent of adoption of scientific beekeeping technologies by the beekeepers had significant negative relationship with entrepreneurial potential of beekeepers.

Relationship between Socio-economic and Communication Characteristics of Beekeepers and their Entrepreneurial Potential

- It was observed that there is non-significant positive relationship between age and entrepreneurial potential of beekeepers.
- Results showed that there is a significant negative relationship between educational status and entrepreneurial potential of beekeepers.
- It was noticed that there is significant negative relationship between size of the land holding and entrepreneurial potential of beekeepers.
- It was observed that there is non-significant negative relationship between family size and entrepreneurial potential of the beekeepers.
- From the results it can be concluded that there is non-significant negative relationship between annual income and entrepreneurial potential of the beekeepers.
- It was revealed that there is non-significant negative relationship between mass media exposure and entrepreneurial potential of the beekeepers.
- The findings revealed that there is non-significant positive relationship between extension agency contact and entrepreneurial potential of the beekeepers.
- It was observed that there is non-significant negative relationship between extension participation and entrepreneurial potential of the beekeepers.
- It was observed that there is non-significant negative relationship between trainings attended and entrepreneurial potential of the beekeepers.
- A look at the results reveal that there is a non-significant negative relationship between credit orientation and entrepreneurial potential of the beekeepers.

Constraints Experienced by Beekeepers

This section relates to the distribution of beekeepers with respect to constraints perceived by the beekeepers with reference to the beekeeping enterprise are presented in Table 3 are as follows. In the present study, constraint is defined as the difficulties or problem faced by the beekeepers, which hinders the successful implementation of the scientific beekeeping practices. Based on the review of literature and discussion with University experts, farmers and Marthandam beekeeping society in sampling study area. The list of major 15 constraints was prepared and administered into beekeepers. Out of 15 constraints the first and foremost 5 constraints were perceived by most important constraints in beekeeping by the beekeepers of study area such as lack of technical-know how about disease management practice, absence of specific government schemes for beekeepers, no minimum price for honey and honey based products, lack of organized marketing network for the honey and honey product and absence of storage facilities at reasonable price etc. The procedure used for ranking the constraints is as follows. All the 15 constraints were translated into regional language of Tamil. Thereafter, beekeepers asked them to rank according to their experienced constraints. The perceived constraints were ranked according to their field difficulties with rank order of 1-15. The total score were worked out accordingly.

Table 4.3: Distribution of the respondents based on their constraints experienced by beekeepers

S.No.	Item	Rank
1.	Lack of technical-know how about disease management practice	I
2.	Absence of specific government schemes for beekeepers	II
3.	No minimum price for honey and honey based products	III
4.	Lack of organized marketing network for the honey and honey product	IV
5.	Absence of storage facilities at reasonable price	V
6.	Damage to colonies due to pest infestation	VI
7.	Absence of policy frame work	VII
8.	Lack of financial support	VIII
9.	Non-availability of equipments	IX
10.	Lack of group activity among the beneficiaries	X
11.	High price fluctuation	XI
12.	Lack of skill upgradation	XII
13.	High cost of honey filtering equipments	XIII
14.	Unsuitable agro-climatic conditions	XIV
15.	Non-availability of good quality bee box	XV

- A quick glance at Table 4.3 reveals that the most important constraint experienced by the beekeepers is the lack of technical-know how about disease management practice. The reason for this might be mostly loss of bee colonies due to Thai sac brood disease. This viral disease had destroyed ninety percent of the colonies is an outbreak during the early 1990s. The control measures for this disease is still not known completely. Destruction of the infected colonies is the only way to reduce the spread of disease.

- The second most important constraint experienced by the beekeepers is absence of specific government schemes for beekeepers. The reason for this might be due to the fact that, government is yet to consider beekeeping as a priority sector. It is seen as a subsidiary cottage industry. There is no more specific scheme planned for beekeeping the agricultural scheme. The commercial banks also sometimes quite reluctant to provide credit since beekeeping involves high amount of uncertainty.

- The third most important constraint experienced by the beekeepers is no minimum price for honey and honey based products. There is no more possibility for fixing the minimum amount of price for honey since beekeeping is still considered as a subsidiary occupation of the farmers and is included in the cottage industry group.

- The fourth most important constraint experienced by the beekeepers is lack of organized marketing network for the honey and honey product. This may be the government is not paying much attention to this enterprise. From the government side there is no more intervention in terms of marketing. Though, both governments (state as well as central government) are paying much more attention to agricultural, horticultural, commercial and cash crops but, this particular enterprise is least bothered by government.

- The fifth most important constraint experienced by the beekeepers is absence of storage facilities at reasonable price. As again, the government is offered for warehouse storage facility only for major agricultural commodities which include food grains, cotton, oilseeds, pulses etc but not honey. The core of this warehouse concept is when the farmers are producing huge amount of productivity in terms of cereals, pulses, oilseeds or whatever agricultural commodity obviously; they won't be fetch attractive remuneration. To avoiding this crisis, only the government established warehouse, through this agency the farmers are store their commodity upto getting good market price for their commodities. The organized marketing network, storage facilities also need to strengthen from the government side.

- Lack of insurance coverage to bee colonies was considered as the important constraint experienced by beekeepers. Unlike other enterprises in agriculture honeybee or bee-box not covered under insurance schemes.
- The next important constraint was the high cost of sugar. During the lean season honey bees are to be feed with sugar syrup or sugar solution which requires large quantities of sugar. High cost of sugar increase the cost of production. Government does not provide sugar at subsidized rates to beekeepers.
- Another important constraint is the high cost of transportation of honey bee colonies. Many of the beekeepers follow migratory beekeeping during the lean seasons. So, transferring of bee colonies during this season is quite cumbersome and transportation cost is also high.
- The next and foremost important constraint is lack of ability identify the pest and disease of honey bee. Since, honey bees live in colonies of thousands in number is very difficult to identify the incidence of pest and disease. Many beekeepers lack the technical know-how and expertise in this field. This may due to lack of adequate information regarding beekeeping.
- Delayed payment by the co-operative societies was also the major constraint faced by beekeepers. This may due to lack of organization in the co-operative societies. Delayed payment by the co-operative societies can also be substantiated by the lack of organized marketing channels which is considered as the next major constraint by the beekeepers. Since, honey production is dependent on the availability and flowering season of different crops, but its production and quality is not guaranteed. Therefore, arrangement for timely collection of honey and its sales network were not uniform and regular.
- Another constraint experienced by the beekeepers was the un-remunerative price for honey. The reason for this may be because the minimum price for honey is not yet fixed as apiary is considered as the cottage industry and as a subsidiary occupation of most of the farmers. The apiculturist were not treated on par with the agriculturists by government or other input agencies and so there is no possibility of fixing the minimum price.
- Lack of honey processing facilities was observed as the next constraint. Raw honey extracted from the bee hives needs processing to refine it so as to fetch a good price in the markets. Most of the farmers do the processing themselves or sell the honey as such fetching them low price. Since, the apiculturists are not an organized group and it is not in the priority sector, the government is not extending any facilities to beekeepers.

- Beekeepers practising migratory beekeeping had expressed safety to honeybee boxes as another constraint. Honeybee colonies have to be transferred from one place to another depending on the availability of nectar and pollen. Sometimes, the colonies are transferred to other areas were rubber is grown. Though theft of honey is not so common but if anything such happens the beekeepers cannot do much about it. Sometimes, when food is scarce the bee colonies may themselves leave the beehive boxes in search of food if artificial feeding is delayed.
- High cost of beehives and accessories was expressed as one of the constraint. Since, beekeeping is not considered in the priority sector, these inputs are not provided at a subsidized rate by the government unlike other fields of agriculture.
- Another constraint pointed out by the beekeepers was the non-availability of disease resistant bees. This is true because there is no indigenous strain resistant to diseases which are available. The strain which are available are exotic bees and are difficult to get from outside and the cost is also more.
- Inadequate extension support also expressed by beekeepers as a least constraint. This not considered as a major constraint because of the frequent training provided by Marthandam beekeeping society, Tamil Nadu Agricultural University, Krishi Vigyan Kendra, research station, non-governmental organization and other agencies involved in the development of this sector.

CONCLUSION

In a developing country like India which is largely dependent on agriculture, beekeeping can be an important agri-enterprise. While the current product of honey is low, it can be improved by encouraging farmers to take up beekeeping on a large scale and providing necessary training inputs. Currently, promoting beekeeping among farmers is one of the priority issues India. The country has plenty of untapped human resources in rural areas whose potential, if properly utilized, can definitely lead to development of the nation. At present, a number of co-operative societies and Non Governmental Organisations (NGOs) are engaged in beekeeping, honey collection and marketing in the state. The National Horticultural Board (NHB) and State Horticultural Mission (SHM) also play a vital role in boosting the apiculture industry in India by providing training and beekeeping inputs at subsidized rates to the beekeepers. If these problems are overcome means, beekeeping becomes more sustainable in Tamilnadu. Consumption and export can be take place at international level. The above discussed constraints will address means, it become economically viable venture for beekeepers.

REFERENCES

Bhattacharya, R. (1983): Women Entrepreneurship Development in India, *Global Institute of Management*, Bhubaneswar, pp: 42.

Cantillon, R. (1734): Development Banks and the New Entrepreneurship in India, *National Publishing House*, New Delhi, pp: 8.

Chandy. M. (2009): Self-employment for Rural Women, *Yojana*, 33(9): 24-28.

Cochran, T.(1974): The Entrepreneur in Economic Change, *In:* Entrepreneurship and Economic Development, Peter Kilby (ed.)., *Free Press*, New York, pp: 95-107.

De, D. (1981): Entrepreneurial Behaviour of Vegetable Growers, *M.Sc.,(Ag.) Thesis*, Banaras Hindu University, Varanasi, pp: 124.

Delmar, F. (1996): Entrepreneurship - Theory and Practice, *Lund University Press*, Europe, 27(3): 247-270.

Drucker, P. (1986): Innovation and Entrepreneurship, *Himalaya Publishing House*, Mumbai, pp: 547.

Edvinraj, S. (2005): Entrepreneurship Development, *Kisan World*, 28(6): 50-51.

Gaikwad, V.R. (2008): Socio-psychological Factors Influencing Industrial Entrepreneurship in Rural Areas - A Case Study in Tanakur Region of West Godavari District of Andhra Pradesh, *National Institute of Community Development Press*, Hyderabad, pp: 58-67.

Gordon, F.N. (1961): Foundation of Behavioural Research, *Holt Rinc Hart Winston International*, New York, pp: 645.

Government of India. (2013): Report of Rural Pulse on Agricultural Land holdings Pattern in India, pp: 12. (Available at www.Publication/Rural_Pulse_final142014.pdf. Accessed on 21.3.2015).

Hagen. (1962): The Theory of Social Change: How Economic Growth begins, *Tavista Publications*, London, pp: 263.

Heredero, J.M. (1979): Agricultural Entrepreneurship, *In:* Identification and Selection of Small Scale Entrepreneurs (*Eds.*, Rao, T.V. and Moulik, T.K.). ITIM, Ahmedabad, pp: 151-159.

Joshi and Kapoor. (1973): Study on Motivational Factors Influencing Acquisition of Farm Technology by Farmers, *Maharashtra Journal of Extension Education*, 19 (1): 186-189.

Kirzner. (1979): Rural Entrepreneurship: A Framework, *In:* Developing Entrepreneurship: A Handbook Learning System (Rao, T.V., and Pareek, U (*Eds.*,), New Delhi, pp: 58-66.

Knight, F.H. (1921): Risk, Uncertainty and Profit, *Houghton-Mifflin Co Press*, Boston, pp: 121.

Krueger, F.N., and Brazeal, V.(1994): Entrepreneurship: Theory and Practice, *In:* Entrepreneurial Potential and Potential Entrepreneurs, *Blackwell Publishing Ltd.*, New York, pp: 98-104.

Mahendran, S. (2004): Entrepreneurship Development in Agriculture, *Yojana*, 47(12): 19-20.

Rao and Mehta. (1978): Entrepreneurial Behaviour of Dairy Farmers in Prakasam District of Andhra Pradesh, *Indian Journal of Extension Education*, 39 (1&2): 69-73.

Reynolds, P.D. (1992): Sociology and Entrepreneurship-Concepts and Contributions, *In:* Entrepreneurship Theory and Practice, 16(2): 47-70.

Schumpeter, J.A. (1970): The Fundamental Phenomenon of Economic Development: Entrepreneurship and Economic Development, *Free Press*, New York, pp: 489.

Shapero. A. (1982): Social Dimensions of Entrepreneurship, *In:* The Encyclopedia of Entrepreneurship (Kent, C., Sexton, D., and Vesper, K. (*Eds.,*), *Englewood Cliffs*, Prentice Hall, New York, pp: 72-90.

Webber, M. (1947): Theory of Social and Economic Organization, (Trans A.M. Henderson and Talcott Parsons. (*Eds*), *Oxford University Press*, New York, pp: 561.

Webber. (1930): Business Enterprise in its Social Setting, *Mass Harvard University Press*, Cambridge, pp: 569.

www.tn.gov.in//tamilnadustate/consolidation, Pdf. 175p. Accessed on 4.5.2015.

Ecological Status Around Pindara Jetty in Kalyanpur Taluka of Devbhumi Dwarka in the State, Gujarat

Ashok Kumar Rathoure

SUMMARY

Pindara Jetty was in operation for handling mineral cargo since 1950 by Gujarat Maritime Board for handling of mineral cargo. The Pindara jetty has been notified on 18th July 1963 by Central Board of Revenue, Government of India under section 53 of Sea Customs Act 1878. For present chapter, the baseline study was conducted for the evaluation of the floral and faunal biodiversity of areanear Pindara jetty in Taluka Kalyanpur, Dist- Dwarka, Gujarat. The baseline ecological status (terrestrial and aquatic) has been presented in this chapter.

Key words: Marine National Park, Mangrove, Marine Sanctuary, DevBoomi Dwarka.

INTRODUCTION

Floristic and Faunistic pattern of the area was studied based on opportunistic survey (personal observation), inquiries from the local people and forest officials and secondary data. The study area falls under district: Devbhumi Dwarka, State: Gujarat. The bauxite export will be done at Pindara Jettty located at Virpur village in Kalyanpur Taluka of Devbhumi Dwarka. Pindara Jetty was in operation for handling mineral cargo since 1950 by Gujarat Maritime Board for handling of mineral cargo. The Pindara jetty has been notified on 18th July 1963 by Central Board of Revenue,

Government of India under section 53 of Sea Customs Act 1878. Pindara notified port limit is bordering from the other port limits of Salaiya in the east to Okha port limit in the west, to Pindara – Virpur village limits in the south and to 12 fathom (36.576 m) in the north. Out of the entire port limit only a small portion of jetty area of 0.81 hectares falls within the marine sanctuary and 3.68 hectares in eco sensitive zone which includes the existing roads leading to the Pindara Jetty. However, Pindara Jetty was notified on 18th July 1963 much earlier than notification of marine sanctuary notification in 1982 and eco sensitive zone of 1 km on 22nd August 2013.

STUDY AREA AND STUDY PERIOD

Study area: 326.53 sq km (10 km radii wrt Pindara jetty)

Core Zone: Projects site and 1 km radii wrt Pindara jetty.

Buffer Zone: 10 km radii wrt Pindara jetty.

Study Period: March to May 2017

Ground Thruthing: 22-24 May 2017

METHODOLOGY

List of vilages: Pindara Village, Mota Asota village, Mahadevia village, Mevasa village and Virpur village.

Data Collection and Literature

Mode of Data Collection	Parameters Monitored	Remarks
(1)	(2)	(3)
By Field Survey Hutto *et al.*, 1986; Welsh, 1987; Thommpson *et al.*, 1989; Welsh *et. al.*, 1991; Allen *et al.*, 1996; Misra, 2013.	For Floral diversity, Vegetation measurements: Tree, Shrub, Herbs, Grasses, Climbers Cultivated plants in the study area, Floristic composition of the study area, Medicinal plants of the study area, Status of the forest, their category in the study area, Rare and endangered flora in the study area. Endemic plants in the study area For Fauna in the study area: - Reptiles, - Amphibians, - Birds, - Fresh water fishes - Mammals, - Butterflies. Rare and Endangered fauna in the study area	Random survey, opportunistic observations, diurnal bird observation active search for reptiles, faunal habitat assessment, active search for microhabitat, scats, foot prints, animal call, pug marks, debarking sign, Nesting, Claws, Dung, etc. and information from local villagers. Bentham and Hooker, 1862-1883; Hunter, 1879; Dixit, 1984; Ghosh *et al.*, 2004; Lushington, 1915; Wilson and Reeder, 1993; BirdLife International, 2000; BirdLife International, 2004a, b; Wilson and Reeder, 2005; Bird Life International, 2010; Kumar and Srivastava, 2012; Kumar, 2013; Kumar *et al.*, 2013; Kumar and Aggarwal, 2013a,b). The status of individual species was assessed using the revised IUCN/SSC category system

(Contd...)

(1)	(2)	(3)
	Endemic fauna in the study area Wild life and their conservation importance in the study area.	(WCMC, 1988; IUCN, 1994; WCMC, 2000; IUCN, 2001, 2003, 2008, 2010. CPCB, 2000; 2007; Abhashi and Khan 2000.

Also, secondary data has been utilized from various pubished literatures for status of wildlife, bird, and floral species listed here for cross verification.

RESULTS AND DISCUSSION

Observations

Main crops of the study region are Bajra, Jowar, wheat & Tur etc. During survey natural flora of study region were found in degraded condition or under stress due to extensive industrialization. No distinct variation was observed in vegetation covered of study region. Vegetation near villages and along the road was represented by trees and shrubs. Dominant vegetation of a study area was bushes. Pindara bay is shallow in southern stretches having depths of 0-5 m below CD upto 10 km from the shore. Further north off Positra, maximum depths of 25 m are available. An island, Azad tapu is present in the eastern side of the Pindara bay. A creek is present in the vicinity of the proposed Pindara jetty. Sediment quality of the Pindara region indicates that the bed sediment is uncontaminated.

Quadrat at Pindara jetty

Discussion and Observation at Pindara jetty

Avicennia marina dominance at Pindara jetty

Stretch of Core Zone

Fig. 5.1: Photos showing pindara jetty and Core Zone Status

Red-naped ibis   Painted storks   Eurasian spoonbill

Lesser Whistling Duck   Black-headed ibis   Cormorant

Honey Bees   *Ficus benghalensis* (Oldest)   Tamarindus indica

Fig. 5.2: Floral and Faunal Biodiversity at Pindara Village

Coconut Plantation   Domesticated Goats   Domesticated Bulls

Fig. 5.3. Photos at Virpur Village

Blue Bull at Mahadeviya   Phoenix dactylifera (Khajur) at Mevasa   Shikra on Neem Tree at Mevasa

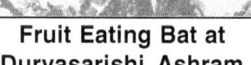

Fruit Eating Bat at Durvasarishi Ashram   Little Egret at Mahadeviya village   Sheep at Mota Asota

Fig. 5.4: Photos of Villages which comes under Buffer Zone

Table 5.1: List of trees in the study area

S. No.	Family and Scientific Name	Vernacular Name	Core	Buffer
(1)	(2)	(3)	(4)	(5)
1.	Fabaceae			
1/1	*Acacia nilotica*	Desi Baval	+	+
2/2	*Butea monosperma*	Khakhro	-	+
3/3	*Dalbergia sissoo*	Sissoo	-	+
4/4	*Pongomia pinnata*	Karanja	-	+
2.	Rutaceae			
5/1	*Aegle marmelos*	Bili	-	+
6/2	*Limonia acidissima*	Kothi	-	+

(Table Contd...)

(1)	(2)	(3)	(4)	(5)
4.	Cornaceae		+	
7/1	*Alangium salvifolium*	Ankol	-	+
5.	Meliaceae			
8/1	*Azadirachta indica*	Limdo	+	+
9/2	*Soymida febriguga*	Royno	-	+
6.	Combretaceae			
10/1	*Terminalia bellerica*	Baheda	-	+
11/2	*Terminalia arjuna*	Arjun	-	+
12/3	*Terminalia chebula*	Harde	-	+
13/4	*Terminalia catappa*	Badam	-	+
14/5	*Terminalia tomentosa*	Sadad	-	+
10.	Arecaceae			
15/1	*Phoenix sylvestris*	Khajuri	-	+
11.	Myrtaceae			
16/1	*Syzygium cumunii*	Jambudo		+
12.	Moraceae			
17/1	*Ficus carica*	Anjir	-	+
18/2	*Ficus hispida*	Bhoyumro	-	+
19/3	*Ficus bengalensis*	Vad	+	+
19/4	*Ficus racemosa*	Umero	-	+
19/5	*Ficus religiosa*	Pipdo	+	+
12.	Mimosaceae			
20/1	*Pithecellobium dulce*	Vilayati ambli	-	+
21/2	*Albizia odoratissima*	Kalo Shirish	-	+
22/3	*Albizia lebbeck*	Siras	-	+
23/4	*Prosopis cineraia*	Khijdo	-	+
13.	Caesalpiniaceae			
24/1	*Cassia fistula*	Garmalo	-	+
25/2	*Tamarindus indica*	Amli	-	+
26/3	*Bauhinia racemosa*	Apto	-	+
14.	Euphorbiaceae			
27/1	*Emblica officinalis*	Amla	-	+
28/2	*Bridelia retusa*	Asan	-	+
15.	Rubiaceae			
29/1	*Adina cordifolia*	Haldarvo	-	+
30/2	*Mitragyna parviflora*	Kalam	-	+
16.	Sapotaceae			
31/1	*Madhuca indica*	Mohwa	-	+
32/2	*Manilkara hexandra*	Khirni	-	+
17.	Verbenaceae			
33/1	*Gmelina arborea*	Savan	-	+
34/2	*Tectona grandis*	Sag	-	+

Table 5.2: List of shrub in the study area

S. No.	Family and Scientific Name	Vernacular Name	Core	Buffer
1.	**Asclepiadaceae**			
1/1	*Calotropis procera*	Akdo	+	+
2.	**Apocynaceae**			
2/1	*Carissa conjesta*	Karmada	-	+
3/2	*Holarrhena antidysenterica*	Kado	-	+
4/3	*Catharanthus pusillus*	Parvatirai	-	+
3.	**Rosaceae**			
5/1	*Rosa damascena*	Rose	-	+
4.	**Malvaceae**			
5/1	*Hibiscus rosa-sinensis*	Jasud	-	+
6/2	*Hibiscus vitifolius*	Van kapas	-	+
7/3	*Thespesia lampas*	Jungli bhindo	-	+
8/4	*Pavonia zeylanica*	Ambari	-	+
9/5	*Sida acuta*	Bala	-	+
10/6	*Sida ovata*	Dabi	-	+
5.	**Solanaceae**			
11/1	*Datura metel*	Dhanturo	-	+
6.	**Verbenaceae**			
12/1	*Lantana camara*	Lantana	-	+
7.	**Oleaceae**			
13/1	*Nyctanthes arbor-tristis*	Parijatak	-	+
8.	**Euphorbiaceae**			
14/1	*Riccinus communis*	Divelo (Erandi)	-	+
15/2	*Acalypha indica*	Vinchikanto		
9.	**Rhamnaceae**			
16/1	*Zizyphus mauritiana*	Bor	-	+
17/2	*Zizyphus galabrata*	Bor	-	+
18/3	*Zizyphus xylopyra*	Ghat Bor	-	+
19/4	*Zizyphus rugosa*	Toran	-	+
10.	**Acanthaceae**			
20/1	*Peristronphe bicalyculata*	Adhedo	-	+
21/2	*Adhatoda vasica*	Ardusi	-	+
22/3	*Dipteracanthus patulus*	Dhramandhrokali	-	+
11.	**Mimosaceae**			
23/1	*Prosopis juliflora*	Gando Baval	+	+

Table 5.3: **List of herbs in the study area**

S. No.	Family and Scientific Name	Vernacular Name	Core	Buffer
1.	Papaveraceae			
1/1	*Argemone mexicana*	Darudi	-	+
2.	Amaranthaceae			
2/1	*Aerva sanguinolenta*	Gorakhganjo	-	+
3/2	*Achyranthes aspera*	Anghedi	-	+
3.	Fabaceae			
4/1	*Arachis hypogea*	Magaphali	-	+
5/2	*Cassia tora*	Takla	+	+
6/3	*Trigonella foenum-graecum*	Methi	-	+
4.	Apocynaceae			
7/1	*Catharanthus roseus*	Sadaphuli	-	+
5.	Solanaceae			
8/1	*Capsicum annuum*	Marchi	-	+
9/2	*Datura metel*	Ganthovalo Dhanturo	-	+
6.	Apiaceae			
10/1	*Centella asiatica*	Khadabrahmi	-	+
7.	Malvaceae			
11/1	*Hibiscus lobatus*	Tali	-	+
8.	Lamiaceae			
13/1	*Ocimum sanctum*	Tulsi	-	+
9.	Phyllanthaceae			
14/1	*Phyllanthus fraternus*	Bhuiavali	-	+
10.	Poaceae			
15/1	*Andropogon pumilus*	Andropogon	-	+
16/2	*Arundinella pumila*	Bejariyun	-	+
17/3	*Pennisetum glaucum*	Bajra	-	+
18/4	*Setaria halepense*	Jangli-jowar	-	+
19/5	*Sorghum bicolor*	Jowar	-	+
20/6	*Triticum aestivum*	Wheat	-	+
11.	Liliaceae			
18/1	*Chlorophytum tuberosum*	Safedmusli	-	+

Table 5.4: List of Climbers in the Study Area

S. No.	Family and Scientific Name	Vernacular Name	Core	Buffer
1.	**Vitaceae**			
1/1	*Cissus repanda*	Gandovelo	-	+
2/2	*Cissus quadrangulare*	Hadsakal	-	+
3/3	*Cayratia auriculata*	Khat-Khatumbo	-	+
4/4	*Cayratia camosa*	Khatumbo	-	+
2.	**Nyctaginaceae**			
5/1	*Bougainvillea spectabilis*	Booganvel	-	+
3.	**Cucurbitaceae**			
6/1	*Cucurbita maxima*	Lal kolu	-	+
7/2	*Cucumis sativus*	Khira	-	+
8/3	*Coccinia grandis*	Tondla	-	+
9/4	*Momondica dioica*	Katwal	-	+
10/5	*Cucumis callosus*	Tarbucha	-	+
4.	**Menispermaceae**			
11/1	*Cissampelos pareira*	Abuta	-	+

Table 5.5: List of Twinner in the Study Area

S. No.	Family and Scientific Name	Vernacular Name	Core	Buffer
1.	**Asclepiadaceae**			
1/1	*Hemidesmus indicus*	Sariva	-	+
2/2	*Leptadenia reticulata*	Meethi dodi	-	+
3/3	*Ceropegia bulbosa*	Khadula	-	+
2.	**Asparagaceae**			
4/1	*Asparagus racemosus*	Shatavari	-	+
3.	**Minispermaceae**			
5/1	*Cocculus hirsutus*	Vasanvel	-	+
6/2	*Cyclea peltata*	Raj Patha	-	+

Table 5.6: List of Creeper in the Study Area

S. No.	Family and Scientific Name	Vernacular Name	Core	Buffer
1.	**Convolvulaceae**			
1/1	*Ipomoea aquatica*	Nali	-	+
2/2	*Ipomoea eriocarpa*	Maal ghanti	-	+
3/3	*Ipomoea pes-caprae*	Maryada-vel	-	+
2.	**Cucurbitaceae**			
4/1	*Luffa acutangula*	Galka	-	+
4/2	*Momordica charantia*	Karela	-	+

Table 5.7: List of Parasite in the Study Area

S. No.	Family and Scientific Name	Vernacular Name	Core	Buffer
1.	Convolvulaceae			
1/1	*Cuscuta chinensis*	Amarvel	-	+
2/2	*Cuscuta reflexa*	Akashvel	-	+

Table 5.8: Medicinally Important Plants Observed in the Study Area

S.No.	Scientific Name	Vernacular Name	Core	Buffer
1.	*Acacia nilotica*	Desi Baval	-	+
2.	*Azardirachta indica*	Limdo	-	+
3.	*Asparagus racemosus*	Shatavari	-	+
4.	Adhatoda vasica	Ardusi	-	+
5.	*Calotropis procera*	Akado	-	+
6.	*Cuscuta reflexa*	Akashvel	-	+
7.	*Datura metel*	Dhatura	-	+
8.	*Ficus bengalesis*	Vad	-	+
9.	*Ficus religiosa*	Paipal	-	+
10.	*Ocimum sanctum*	Tulsi	-	+
11.	*Catharanthus roseus*	Sadaphuli	-	+

Cultivated Plants in the Study Area

The prevalent cropping systems of this area are the cumulative results of past and present decisions by individuals; these decisions are usually based on experience, tradition, expected profit, personal preferences and resources, and so on. The crop occupying the highest percentage of the sown area of this region is taken as the major crop and all other possible alternative crops which are sown in this region either as substitutes of the base crop in the same season or as the crops which fit in the rotation in the subsequent season, are considered as minor crop.No any major/minor and vegetable crop in the core zone was observed during study period, but observed major/minor and vegetable crop in the buffer zone.

(a) **Major Crops in buffer zone:** *Arachis hypogaea* (Groundnut), *Zea mays* (Maize), *Sorghumbicolor* (Jowar) and *Pennisetum glaucum* (Bajra).

(b) **Minor crops in buffer zone:** *Triticum aestivum* (Wheat), *Cajanus cajan* (Tur), *Cicer arietinum* (Gram) and *Tagetes* (Marigold crop) for flower.

(c) **Major horticultural crops in buffer zone:** *Mangifera indica* (Kairi), *Manilkara zapota* (Chikku) and *Musa × paradisiaca* (Banana).

(d) **Major Vegetable corps:** The major vegetables grown in the study area (buffer zone) were: *Abelmoschus esculentus* (Bhinda), *Lagenaria siceraria* (Bottle gourd), *Luffa acutangula* (Gilka) and *Momordica charantia* (Bitter gourd)

(e) **Major Ornamental Plants:** Following is the list of ornamental plants in the study area (buffer zone) *Hibiscus rosa-sinensis* (China rose), *Ixora coccinea* (Red ixora), *Rosa* (Rose) and *Tagetes* (Marigold)

Status of the Forest, their Category in Study Area

MARINE NATIONAL PARK AND MARINE SANCTUARY ECO-SENSITIVE ZONE, JAMNAGAR

As per the S.O. 2561 (22.08.2013) Final ESZ Notification on Marine National Park and Marine Sanctuary, GujaratThe total area of 326.26 square kilometer around Marine National Park and Marine Sanctuary has been identified as eco-sensitive zone, of which 208.5818 square kilometer is the area towards landward side, 105.14 square kilometer towards sea and 12.5384 square kilometer is the area covered by rivers and the MarineSanctuary covers an area of 457.92 square kilometer and an area of 162.89 square kilometer as Marine National Park was notified in 1982. The entire southern coast ofthe Gulf in Jamnagar district is ringed by a cluster of 42 islands and many of them arefringed by coral reefs and mangrove vegetation; And whereas the high density and diversity in the Gulf of Kutch is due to the availability of different types of habitats like sandy, muddy, rocky, calcareous sea bed and coral beds and mangroves in the relatively sheltered waters of the Gulf and is defined as "portion of sea partially enclosed by sweep of coast and usually narrower at mouth than bay".

The flora of marine National Park mainly consists of mangroves and array of marine algae, including some commercially important species of *Agarophytes* and *Alginophytes* and the coastal line of the Gulf is fringed with luxuriant growth of *Avicennia, Rhizophora* and *Ceriops* species of mangroves and *Salvadora, Zizipus* and *Prosopis*are some of the terrestrial species found in that area.The Sanctuary has more than 70 sponge species, 37 species of hard coral and 24 species of soft coral, 150-200 species of fishes, 27 species of prawn, 30 species of crab, 200 species of mollusk, 3 species of sea turtle, 3 species of sea snake, 3 species of sea mammal, 94 species of aquatic bird and 78 species of terrestrial bird.The Central government had notified the area upto a length of one kilometer from the coastal boundary towards landward side, an area within 200 metre from the boundary of Marine National park and Sanctuary towards seaward side and 31 rivers flowing into the Gulf of Kachchh with their length varying from 0 to 5 kilometre and a width of 250 metre from the centre of the river on both sides of river from the boundary of the protected area of Marine National park and Marine Sanctuary in the state of Gujarat as the eco sensitive Zone.Towards landward side area of about 208.58 square kilometer including 36 villages adjoining Marine National Park and Sanctuary and the boundary of the ESZ from coastal boundary towards landward side extends up to a length of one Kilometre which include either whole or part of survey numbers upto this limit of one kilometer. The ESZ toward seaward constitute an area of 105.14 square kilometer and an area within 200 metre from boundary of Marine National Park and Sanctuary towards seaward side has been included in the said Zone. 31 Reivers which flow into the Gulf of Kachchh have been included in the ESZ. The ESZ is bounded by 22°55'31.33" N Latitude and 70°32'57.02" E Longitude towards east; 22°28'1.31" N and 69°3'33.77" E towards west; 22°56'14.26" N and 70°25'54.27" E towards North; 22°13'12.35" N and 69°17'43.97" E towards South.

The following activities are to be regulated in the Eco-sensitive Zone, namely:

1. **Management Plan for the Marine National Park and Marine Sanctuary Eco-sensitive Zone:**

    The Management plan shall be prepared by the State Government of Gujarat as per the State Town and Country Planning Act within a period of one year from the date of issue of the final notification. The Management plan shall be prepared in consultation with all concerned State Departments of Environment, Forest, Urban Development, Tourism, Municipal, Revenue and the Gujarat State pollution Control Board with a view to include therein various aspects of the environment and ecology.

    (i) The management Plan shall provide for restoration of denuded areas, conservation of existing water bodies, management of catchment areas, watershed management, groundwater management, soil and moistureconservation, needs of local community and such other aspects of the ecology and environment the need attention.

    (ii) The management plan should ensure that no restrictions are imposed on the existing legal land use pattern, as well as the legal infrastructure and activities and same would continue as before. However, the management plan would also factor in improvement of all infrastructure/activities to be more efficient and eco-friendly.

    (iii) The management plan shall demarcate all the existing revenue, revenue expansion areas, forests, green areas, horticultural areas, agricultural areas, orchards, natural springs, natural heritage sites and other environmentally and ecologically sensitive areas. No change of land use from green uses such as orchards, horticultural areas, agriculture, parks and other like places to non-green uses shall be permitted in the Management Plan.

    (iv) There shall be no reduction in Forest Zone, Green Zones and Agricultural Area, Mangrove Area and natural marine and other aquatic ecosystems.

(v) The Monitoring Committee oversee the proper execution of the Management Plan by all Departments and stakeholders as well. This Committee would also look into the grievances of people and find amicable solution of such grievances.

(vi) Adequate publicity shall be given to the provisions of the Management Plan.

(vii) Till the time the Eco-Sensitive Zone is finally notified, management plan prepared, approved by the Ministry and the Monitoring Committee is functional so as to ensure administration of the Eco-Sensitive Zone, all non-forestry developmental activities within the proposed boundary of the eco sensitive zone shall be referred to the Standing Committee of National Board of Wild Life (NBWL)

2. **Activity Prohibited in the Eco-sensitive Zone:** Commercial Mining, Setting of Saw Mills, Setting of industries causing pollution, Commercial use of firewood, Establishment of Major hydroelectric projects, Use of production of any hazardous substance, Undertaking activities related to tourism like over-flying the national park area by any aircraft, hot air ballons and activities related to coastal tourism, Discharge of untreated effluent and solid waste in natural water bodies or terrestrial area and Mechanised fishing including fishing by trawlers.

3. **Activity Regulated in the Eco-Sensitive Zone:** Felling of trees, Establishment of hotels and resorts, Drastic change of agriculture system, Commercial use of natural water resources including ground water harvesting, erection of electrical cables, Fencing of premises of hotels and lodges, Use of Polythene bags by shopkeepers, Widening of roads, Movement of vehicular traffic at night, Introduction of exotic species, Protection of hill slopes and rivers banks and coastal areas, Discharge of treated effluents in natural water bodies or terrestrial area, Air and vehicular pollution, Sign boards and hoardings, Salt work activities Sea water withdrawl and Erection of conveying systems and pipelines.

Proposed project area status: Only a small portion of jetty area of 0.81 hectares falls within the marine sanctuary and 3.68 hectares in eco sensitive zone which includes the existing roads leading to the Pindara Jetty. However, Pindara Jetty was notified on 18th July 1963 much earlier than notification of marine sanctuary notification in 1982 and eco sensitive zone of 1 km on 22nd August 2013.

Mangrove: Mangroves not only simply a type of specialised tree, but also an ecosystem that predominantly consists of mangrove trees. They have a remarkable ability to adapt and survive in their suffocating, saltladen environment. The mangrove (marine and terrestrial) encountered during study period in study area is enlisted in table below.

Table 5.9: List of Mangrove in the study area

S.No.	Scientific Name	Common Name	Family
Marine			
1.	*Avicennia marina*	Grey Mangrove	Acanthaceae
2.	*Avicennia officinalis*	Indian Mangrove	Acanthaceae
3.	*Avicennia alba*	–	Acanthaceae
Terrestrial			
4.	*Salvadora persica*	Toothbrush Tree	Salvadoraceae
5.	*Salvadora oleoides Decne*	Toothbrush Tree-Big	Salvadoraceae

Fig. 5.5: Marine National Park, Jamnagar near Durvasarishi Ashram at sea shore near Pindara village

Fig. 5.6: Marine National Park, Jamnagar near Mahadev Temple at sea shore near Mota Asota

Rare and Endangered Flora in the Study Area: The IUCN Red List is the world's most comprehensive inventory of the global conservation status of plant and animal species. It uses a set of criteria to evaluate the extinction risk of thousands of species and subspecies. These criteria are relevant to all species and all regions of the world. With its strong scientific base, the IUCN Red List is recognized as the most authoritative guide to the status of biological diversity. Out of 17000 species of higher plants known to occur in India, nearly 614 higher plant species were evaluated by IUCN. Among them 247 species are under threatened category (IUCN, 2008).

Among the enumerated flora in the study area, none of them were assigned any threat category by Red data book of Indian Plants (Jain and Sastry, 1984; Nayar and Sastry, 1987; 1988; 1990; Oldfield *et al.*, 1998; Kholia and Bhakuni, 2009) and Red list of threatened Vascular plants (IUCN, 2010).

Endemic Plants of the Study Area: De Candolle (1855), Swiss botanist, first used the concept of Endemic, which is defined as an area of a taxonomic unit, especially a species which has a restricted distribution or habitat, isolated from its surrounding region through geographical, ecological or temporal barriers. Out of 17000 species of known flowering plants of India nearly 5000 species are said to be endemic. Nearly 58 genera and 1932 taxa are found to be endemic to peninsular India (Nayar, 1980; Ahmedullah and Nayar, 1986; 1987; Jain 1992; Nayar, 1996; Vijaya Shankar *et al.*, 2005; Nautiyal *et al.*, 2009a,b; Shendage *et al.*, 2010).

Among recorded plant species none can be assigned the status of endemic plant of this region in core or buffer zone.

None of the rare and endangered floral species were recorded in study area during the field study.

Faunal Biodiversity of Study Area

Birds: The sighting of bird species was very less during the study period. The most commonly spotted bird species of this area were Cattle Egret, Intermediate Egret, Red-wattled Lapwing, Rock Pigeon, Eurasian Collared-Dove, Chestnut-headed Bee-eater, Bank Myna and Common Myna. Water birds are very common as creek and sea shore line is the major part falls under study area. The Indian Peafowl was observed which is listed as schedule – I as per IWPA, 1972 and others listed as schedule IV as per IWPA, 1972.

Systematic account of the birds in the study area with the status of occurrence is given in the Table below.

Table 5.10: Systematic Lists of Birds encountered in the Study Area

S.No.	Scientific Name	Local Name	Common Name	Schedule/IUCN	Status
(1)	(2)	(3)	(4)	(5)	(6)
1.	*Accipiter badius*	Shakro	Shikra	Schedule IV	R
2.	*Acridotheres ginginianus*	Ghoda kabar	Bank Myna	Schedule IV	R
3.	*Alauda gulgula*	Jad Agan	Oriental Sky Lark	Schedule IV	M
4.	*Amaurornis phoenicurus*	Safed chatari	White-breasted Water hen	Schedule IV	R
5.	*Aquila heliaca*	Shahi Garud	Imperial Eagle	Vulnerable	R
6.	*Ardeola grayii*	Khokhadbaglo	Indian pond heron	Schedule IV	R
7.	*Bubulcus ibis*	Dhorbaglo	Cattle Egret	Schedule IV	RM
8.	*Centropus sinensis*	Hoco	Crow-Pheasant	LC	R
9.	*Columba livia*	Kabutar	Blue Rock Pigeon	LC	R
10.	*Coracias benghalensis*	Deshi Neelkanth	Indian Roller	LC	R
11.	*Corvus splendens*	Kagdo	Crow	Schedule IV	R
12.	*Dicrurus macrocercus*	Kado kosi	Black drongo	LC	R
13.	*Egretta garzetta*	Baglo	Little Egret	Schedule IV	R
14.	*Elanus caeruleus*	Kapasi/Laudharo	Black-winged Kite	Schedule IV	R
15.	*Fulica atra*	Dasadi	Coot	Schedule IV	R
16.	*Grus grus*	Kunj	Common Crane	Schedule IV	R
17.	*Halcyon smyrnensis*	Moto Kalkalio	White-throated Kingfisher	Schedule IV	R
18.	*Lanius excubitor*	Dhori lefaddi	Great Grey Shrike	Schedule IV	RM
19.	*Merops leschenaulti*	Tarklo	Chestnut-headed Bee-eater	LC	R
20.	*Motacilla flava*	Pilo Divaliyo	Yellow Wagtail	Schedule IV	RM

(Table Contd....)

(1)	(2)	(3)	(4)	(5)	(6)
21.	Muscicapa striata	Nanu Chikyu	Spotted Flycatcher	Schedule IV	R
22.	Mycteria leucocephala	Dhonk	Painted Stork	Schedule IV	RM
23.	Nectarinia asiatica	Jambali Sunbird	Purple Sunbird	Schedule IV	R
24.	Passer domesticus	Chakli	House sparrow	LC	R
25.	Pavo cristatus	Mor	Indian Peafowl	Schedule I	R
26.	Phalacrocorax fuscicollis	Vichetkajio	Cormorant	Schedule IV	R
27.	Phalacrocorax niger	Nanokajio	Little Cormorant	Schedule IV	RM
28.	Philomachus pugnax	Tilio	Ruff	LC	R
29.	Phoenicopterus minor	Nano Surkabh	Lesser Flamingo	Schedule IV	RM
30.	Platalea leucorodia	Chamchichanch	Eurasian Spoonbill	Schedule IV	P
31.	Ploceus philippinus	Sugari	Baya weaver	Schedule IV	R
32.	Psittacula krameri	Popat	Rose-ringed Parakeet	Schedule IV	R
33.	Pseudibis papillosa	Kaadi	Red-naped ibis	Schedule IV	R
34.	Sternula albifrons	Nana vabagli	Little Tern	LC	R
35.	Streptopelia decaocto	Holdi	Eurasian Collared-Dove	Schedule IV	R
36.	Streptopelia orientaii	Holdi	Rufous TurtleDove	Schedule IV	RM
37.	Tachybaptus ruficollis	Dubki	Little Grebe	Schedule IV	R
38.	Throskiornismelanocephalus	Dhorikankansar	Black headed ibis	Schedule IV	M
39.	Turdoides caudatus	Lelu	Common Babbler	Schedule IV	R
40.	Vanellus indicus	Titodi	Lapwing	Schedule IV	R

Note: R-Resident, M- Migratory, RM – Resident & Migratory

Table 5.11: List of Birds in the Gulf

S. No. (1)	Common Name (2)	Scientific Name (3)	Status Habitat (4)
1.	**Podicipedidae**		
1/1	Great Crested Grebe	Podiceps cristatus	LM
2/2	Blacknecked Grebe	Podiceps nigricollis	M
2.	**Pelecanidae**		
3/1	White Pelican	Pelecanus onocrotalus	LM
4/2	Dalmatian Pelican	Pelecanus crispus	M
3.	**Phalacrocoracidae**		
5/1	Cormorant	Phalacrocorax carbo	LM
6/2	Indian Shag	Phalacrocorax fuscicolli	LM
7/3	Little Cormorant	Phalacrocorax niger	LM
8/4	Darter	Anhinga rufa	LM
4.	**Ardeidae**		
9/1	Grey Heron	Ardea cinerea	LM
10/2	Purple Heron	Ardea purpurea	LM
11/3	Little Green Heron	Ardeola striatus	LM
12/4	Pond Heron	Ardeola grayii	LM
13/5	Cattle Egret	Bubulcus ibis	-
14/6	Large Egret	Ardea alba	LM
15/7	Smaller Egret	Egretta intermedia	LM
16/8	Little Egret	Egretta garzetta	LM
17/9	Indian Reef Heron	Egretta gularis	LM
18/10	Night Heron	Nycticorax mycticorax	LM
5.	**Ciconiidae**		
19/1	Painted Stork	Mycteria leucocephala	LM
20/2	Blacknecked Stork	Ephippiorhynchus asiaficus	LM
6.	**Threskiornithidae**		
21/1	White Ibis	Threskiornis aethiopica	LM
22/2	Black Ibis	Pseudibis papillasa	-
23/3	Spoonbill	Platalea leucorodia	LM
7.	**Phoenicopteridae**		
24/1	Flamingo	Phoenicopterus roseus	LM
25/2	Lesser Flamingo	Phoenicopterus minor	LM
8.	**Anatidae**		
26/1	Ruddy Shel duck	Tadorna ferruginea	-

(Table Contd...)

(1)	(2)	(3)	(4)
27/2	Pintail	*Anas acuta*	M
28/3	Common Teal	*Anas crecca*	M
29/4	Spotbill Duck	*Anas poecilorhyncha*	LM
30/5	Shoveller	*Anas clypeata*	M
9.	**Accipitridae**		
31/1	Brahminy Kite	*Haliastur indus*	LM
32/2	Marsh Harrier	*Circus aeruginosus*	M
33/3	Osprey	*Pandian haliaetus*	M
10.	**Gruidae**		
34/1	Common Crane	*Grus grus*	M
35/2	Demoiselle Crane	*Anthropoides virgo*	M
11.	**Rallidae**		
36/1	Coot	*Fulica atra*	LM
12.	**Jacanidae**		
37/1	Pheasant - tailed Jacana	*Hydrophasianus chirurgus*	LM
13.	**Haematopodidae**		
38/1	Oystercatcher	*Haematopus stralegus*	M
14.	**Charadriidae**		
39/1	Redwattled Lapwing	*Vanellus indicus*	R
40/2	Grey Plover	*Pluvialis sugotarola*	M
41/3	Eastern Golden Plover	*Pluvialis dominica*	-
42/4	Large Sand Plover	*Charadrius leschenaultii*	M
43/5	Ringed Plover	*Charadrius hiaticula*	R
44/6	Kentish plover	*Charadrius alexandrinus*	R
45/7	Lesser Sand Plover	*Charadrius mongolus*	M
46/8	Whimbrel	*Numenius phaeopus*	M
47/9	Curlew	*Numenius arquata*	M
48/10	Blacktailed Godwit	*Limosa limosa*	M
49/11	Bartailed Godwit	*Limosa lapponica*	M
50/12	Spotted Redshank	*Tringa erythropus*	M
51/13	Common Redshank	*Tringa totanus*	M
52/14	Marsh Sandpiper	*Tringa stagnatilis*	M
53/15	Greenshank	*Tringa nebularia*	M
54/16	Green Sandpiper	*Tringa ochropus*	M
55/17	Wood Sandpiper	*Tringa glareola*	M
56/18	Terek Sandpiper	*Tringa terek*	M

(Table Contd...)

(1)	(2)	(3)	(4)
57/19	Common Sandpiper	*Tringa hypoleucos*	M
58/20	Turnstone	*Arenaria interpres*	M
59/21	Knot	*Calidris carutus*	-
60/22	Eastern Knot	*Calidris tenuirostris*	-
61/23	Sanderling	*Calidris alba*	-
62/24	Eastern Little Stint	*Calidris ruficollis*	-
63/25	Little Stint	*Calidris minuta*	M
64/26	Dunlin	*Calidris alpina*	M
65/27	Curlew-Sandpiper	*Calidris testacea*	M
66/28	Broadbilled Sandiper	*Limicola falcinellus*	M
67/29	Ruff and Reeve	*Philomachus pugnax*	M
68/30	Rednecked Phalarope	*Phalaropus lobatus*	M
15.	**Recurvirostidae**		
69/1	Blackwinged Stilt	*Himantopus himantopus*	R
70/2	Avocet	*Recurvirostra avosetta*	LM
16.	**Dromadidae**		
71/1	Crab Plover	*Dromas ardeola*	M
17.	**Burhinidae**		
72/1	Great Stone Plover	*Esacus magnirostris*	LM
18.	**Laridae**		
73/1	Herring Gull	*Larus argentatus*	M
19.	**Lesser Blackbacked**		
74/1	Gull	*Larus fuscus*	M
75/2	Blackheaded	*Larus ichthyaetus*	M
76/3	Brownheaded Gull	*Larus brunnicephalus*	M
77/4	Blackheaded Gull	*Larus ridibunds*	M
78/5	Slenderbilled Gull	*Larus genei*	M
79/6	Whiskered Tern	*Chiildonias hybrida*	M
80/7	Whitewinged Black	*Chiildonias leucopterus*	M
20.	**Tern**		
81/1	Gullbilled Tern	*Gelochelidon nilotica*	M
82/2	Caspian Tern	*Hdroprogne caspia*	LM
83/3	Common Tern	*Sterna hirunda*	M
84/4	Whitecheeked Tern	*Sterna repressa*	M
85/5	Brownwinged Tern	*Sterna anaethetus*	M
86/6	Little Tern	*Sterna albitrons*	M

(Table Contd...)

(1)	(2)	(3)	(4)
87/7	Saunders Little Tern	*Sterna saundersi*	LM
88/8	Large Crested Tern	*Sterna bergii*	M
89/9	Indian Lesser Crested Tern	*Sterna bengalenis*	M
90/10	Indian skimmer	*Rynchops albicollis*	LM
91/11	Sandwich Tern	*Sterna sandvicensis*	M
21.	**Alcedinidae**		
92/1	Common Kingfisher	*Alcedo atthis*	LM
93/2	Whitebreast	*Halcyon smyrnensisq*	LM
94/3	Blackcapped kingfisher	*Halcyon pileata*	M

R: Resident has been recorded breeding during the study.
LM: Local migrant, has not been recorded breeding during the study, but is known to nest within the state.
M: Migrant, does not breed in this area, spends the winter here and also sometimes the summer.
V: Not normally found in the area, one too few records only.
Source: Marine EIA for Bombay Mineral Limited by National Institute of Oceanography, 2017.

Migratory Pattern: Migration is the best studied of animal behaviours, yet few empirical studies have tested hypotheses explaining the ultimate causes of these cyclical annual movements. Fretwell's (1980) hypothesis predicts that if nest predation explains why many tropical birds migrate uphill to breed, then predation risk must be negatively associated with elevation. The proportion of nests depredated by different types of predators differed among elevations. In present study, total 90 bird species were recorded belongs to 21 family and almost are widespread resident species while Grey Heron was resident and winter visitor.

Herpetofauna: In amphibian group, the toads were sighted during the study period. The reptile, Common Garden Lizard, House Gecko and Fan-Throated Lizard, Common rat Snake and were observed in the region is given in the table below.

Table 5.12: List of Reptiles in the Study Area

S. No.	Scientific Name	Common Name	Schedule as per WPA 1972
1.	*Calotes versicolor*	Common garden lizard	Not listed
2.	*Calotes rouxi*	Roux's fores lizard	Not listed
3.	*Sitana ponticeriana*	Fan-throated lizard	Not listed
4.	*Chameleon zeylanicus*	Indian chameleon	Not listed
5.	*Naja naja*	Indian cobra	Schedule II
6.	*Hemidactylus flaviviridis*	House Gecko	Not listed
7.	*Daboia russelli*	Russell's viper	Schedule II
8.	*Bungarus caeruleus*	Common Indian Krait	Schedule IV
9.	*Xenochrophis piscator*	Checkered keelback	Schedule II
10.	*Echis carinatus*	Indian saw scaled viper	-

Table 5.13: Mammals in study area

S.No.	Common Name	Scientific Name	Status as per IWPA 1972/IUCN
1.	Five striped Palm Squirrel	*Funambulus pennantii*	Schedule IV
2.	Indian flying fox/Fruit bat	*Pteropus giganteus*	LC
3.	Indian Hare	*Lepus nigricollis*	Schedule IV
4.	Blue Bull	*Boselaphus tragocamelus*	Schedule III
5.	Small Asian mongoose	*Herpestes javanicus*	Schedule II

Fish was observed in the study area are listed in the Table below:

Table 5.14: List of Marine Fish

S.No.	Common Name	Scientific Name
1.	Pomfret	*Pampus Chinensis*
2.	Indian Prawn	*Penaus indicus*
3.	Blue Spot Grey Mullet	*Valamugil seheli*
4.	Grey Mullet	*Mugil cephalus*
5.	Mullet	*Mugil dussumieri*
6.	Indian Salmon	*Eleutheronema tetradactylum*
7.	Bombay Duck (Bumla)	*Horpodon neherius*
8.	Thread Fin	*Polynemus indicus*
9.	Mud Skipper	*Boleophthalmus*
10.	Hilsa shad	*Tenualosa ilisha*
11.	Jew fish	*Pseudoscioena sp.*
12.		*Pristopomas sp.**
13.		*Diacanthus sp.**

* Not seen directly

Domestic Animals: Camel, Bull, Buffalo, Sheep, Cow, Goat,*etc.*

Insects like Wasps, Honeybees and Signature spider was also recorded.

Rare and Endangered Fauna of Study Area: The IUCN Red List is the world's most comprehensive inventory of the global conservation status of plant and animal species. It uses a set of criteria to evaluate the extinction risk of thousands of species and subspecies. Among the birds in the study area, Pea fowl (*Pavo cristatus*) is included in schedule I of Wild life protection Act (1972), while many other birds are included in schedule IV. Among the reptiles, Indian Cobra (Naja naja), *Daboia russelli* (Russell's viper) and *Xenochrophis piscator* (Checkered keelback) is provided protection as per Schedule-II of Wild life Protection Act, (1972).

Endemic Fauna of the Study Area: None of the sighted animal species can be assigned endemic species category of the study area.

MARINE ENVIRONMENT STUDY BY NATIONAL INSTITUTE OF OCEANOGRAPHY (NIO)

The Gulf that opens to t he n orth-eastern Arabian Sea has channel d epths varying from 20 m at the head to 60 m in central areas of the outer Gulf. Within theGulf, though water depths of 25 m exist in the broad central portion upto a longitude 70° E, the actual fairway is obstructed by the presence of several shoals. The high tidal influx covers the low lying areas of a bout 1500 km^2 comprising networks of creeks and alluvial marshy tidal flats in the interior region. The creek system consists of three main creeks namely Nakti, Kandla and Hansthal and little Gulf of Kachchh interconnecting through many other big and small creeks. All along the coast, very few rivers drain into the Gulf and they carry only a small quantity of freshwater, except during brief monsoon. The southern shore of the Gulf has numerous islands and inlets covered with mangroves and surrounded by coral reefs. The northern shore is predominantly sandy or muddy confronted by numerous shoals.

Physical Processes: Tides in the Gulf are of mixed, predominantly semidiurnal type with a large diurnal inequality. The complex bathymetry, rugged bottom topography and undulations in the shoreline produce highly non-linear tidal interactions. The tidal front enters the Gulf from the west and due to shallow innerregions and narrowing cross-section, the tidal amplitude increases considerably, upst ream of Vadinar. The tidal elevations (m) along the southern Gulf are as follows:

Location	MHWS	MHWN	MLWN	MLWS	MSL
Okha	3.47	2.96	1.20	0.41	2.0
Sikka	5.38	4.35	1.74	0.71	3.0
Rozi	5.87	5.40	1.89	1.0	3.6
Kandla	6.66	5.17	1.81	0.78	3.9
Navlakhi	7.21	6.16	2.14	0.78	4.2

Thus, over the length of the Gulf the mean spring tidal range increases impressively from 3.47m at Okha to 7.21m at Navlakhi. The phase lag between Okha and Kandla is 2 h to 2 h 25 min while between Okha and Navlakhi it is 3 h to 3 h 20 min. Due to high tidal ranges in the inner regions, the vast mudflats and coastal low lands which get submerged during high tide are fully exposed during low tide.

Circulation in the Gulf is mainly controlled by the tidal flows and bathymetry though wind effect also prevails to some extent. The maximum surfaces currents are moderate (0.7-1.2 m/s) but increase considerably (2.0 - 2.5 m/s) in the central portion of the Gulf. The spring currents are 60 to 65 % stronger than the neap currents. The bottom currents are also periodic with a velocity normally 70 % of the surface currents.

Modelling of tides and currents in the Gulf indicate that (a) in the eastern half of the Gulf, the circulation favours an ett ransport towards Kandla (along the northern rim of the Gulf) with at endency to form a clockwise circulation, (b) in the western Gulf, the residual circulation presents anti-clockwise eddies of different sizes, except one clockwise eddy in the nor thern Gulf (off Mandvi), (c) the net transport from the open ocean into the Gulf is through the southern side of the mouth and the net outward transport is through the northern side, forming an anti-clockwise circulation in the western part, and (d) as the Gulf width suddenly drops at the mid-Gulf and coastal orientation changes abruptly thereafter, the water flow is deflected towards north and forms a dynamic barrier across Sikka-Mundra section that retards the flushing of the Gulf.

Water Quality: The general water quality of the Gulf in pre and post-monsoon seasons is compiled for different years. The annual variation of water temperature is between 20°C and 30°C though localised higher temperatures upto 35°C can result in isolated water pools formed in shallow intertidal depressions, during low tide. Vertical profiles of temperature and salinity reveal a nearly homogeneous water column with no vertical stratification due to intense tidal-driven turbulence mixing.

Suspended Solids are highly variable, spatially as well as temporally, and largely resulted from the dispersion of fine sediment from the bed and the intertidal mudflats, by tidal movements. Evidently, near shore shallow regions invariably sustain higher SS as compared to the central zones. The region between Okha and Sikka has high variable SS (4-308 mg/L) whereas the inner Gulf areas sustain markedly higher SS, even up to 700 mg/L. The pH range of the Gulf water is remarkably constant (8.0-8.3) though wide variations (7.6-8.8) are not iced sometimes. The evaporation exceeds precipitation leading to salinities markedly higher than that of the typical seawater. This is particularly evident in the inner Gulf where salinities as high as 40 psu commonly occur off Kandla and Navlakhi. Although the salinities decrease considerably for a brief period in some creeks of the Little Gulf of Kachchh under the influence of monsoonal runoff, the20impact of this decrease in the Gulf proper is small and salinities often exceed 36 psu at most of the locations.

The average DO is fairly high (35 mg/L) most of the times and the BOD is low (<0.1 - 6.3 mg/L) indicating good oxidising conditions. The nutrients (PO_4^{3-}–P, NO_3–N, NO_2–N, NH_4^+–N) are more or less uniformly distributed in the Okha-Sikka-Mundra segment and their concentrations indicate healthy natural waters. Their levels however are marginally high in the Kandla-Navlakhi segment. Infact, the network of creeks of the Little Gulf of Kachchh sustains high natural concentrations of nutrients perhaps due to high regeneration rates. As expected for a un-polluted coastal environment, the concentrations of PHC and phenols are low.

Sediment Quality

Central portion of the Gulf extending from the mouth to upstream of Sikka is rocky with sediments confined only to the margins. The nearshore sediment which consists of light gray silt and clay and fine sand with patches of coarse sand in-between, are poorly sorted with highly variable skewness. The major source of this sediment is considered to be the shore material and the load transported by the Indus River. The portion of sediment derived from the hinterland is considered to be small because of the low run-off. Moreover, the streams discharging in the Gulf (during brief monsoon season) are short with dams constructed on many of them.

The concentrations of heavy metals such as chromium, manganese, cobalt, nickel, copper, zinc, mercury and lead though variable, indicate natural background levels and there is no evidence of gross sediment contamination. The concentrations of PHC are also low though large quantities of petroleum crude and its products are handled at Vadinar, Sikka, Mundra and Kandla.

Marine Biodiversity: The Gulf abounds in marine wealth and is considered as one of the biologically richest marine habitat along the west coast of India.

The marine flora is highly varied and includes sand dune vegetation, mangroves, seagrasses, macrophytes and phytoplankton. In all 31 species of Chlorophyceae, 33 species of Phaeophyceae and 55 species of Rhodophyceae have been identified with the dominance of Phaeophyceae. The dominant species of sand dune flora are *Euphorbia caducifolia*, *E.neriifolia*, *Aloevera* sp, *Ephedra foliata*, *Urochodra setulosa*, *Sporobolus maderaspatenus*, *Eragrostis unioloides*, *Calotropis procera*, *Fimbristylis* sp, *Indigofera* sp and *Ipomoea pescaprae*. The common seagrasses found growing on the mud flats are *Halophila ovata*, *H.beccarii* and *Zostrea marina*.

The most common marine algal species are *Ulva fasciata*, *U. reticulata*, *Enteromorpha intenstinalis*, *Dictyota* sp, *Hypnea musciformis*, *Sargassum tennerimum*, *S.ilicifolium*, *Gracilaria corticata*, *Cystocera* sp, *Padina tetrastomatica*, *Corallina* sp, *Laurencia* sp, *Caulerpa racemosa*, *Bryopsis* sp, *Turbinaria* sp, *Ectocarpus* sp, *Acanthophora* sp, *Chondria* sp, and *Codium* sp.

The primary production of the water column as assessed from chlorophyll a concentration is generally high in the outer Gulf but decreases in the inner regions. Phytoplankton represents about 31 genera and 41 species. The major phytoplankton genera are Rhizosolenia, Synedra, Chaetoceros, Navicula, Nitzschia, Pleurosigma, Thalassiothrix, Biddulphia, Stauroneis, Coscinodiscus and Skeletonema. The Gulf also sustains good and variable zooplankton and benthic standing stock with diversity. The primary and secondary tropic levels offer congenial feeding grounds for prawns and fishes in the Gulf.

The vast intertidal zone of the Gulf is rich in biota. Sheltered bays, creeks and mud flats provide ideal sites form angrove vegetation over an estimated area of about 1066.9 km². The formations are of open scrubby type, with isolated and discontinuous distribution from Kandla-Navlakhi in the northeast to Jodia, Jamnagar, Sikka, Salaya and Okha in the southwest, as also at Pirotan, Positra, Dohlani and Dwarka. Vast stretches of mangroves also exist along the northern shore of the Gulf. The dominant species of mangroves are *Avicenniamarina var acutissima, A. officinalis, Bruguiera parviflora, B. gymnorphiza, Rhizophora mucronata, R. apiculata, Ageiceros corniculata, Ceriops tagal* and *Sonneratia apetata* alongwith the associated species of *Salicornia brachiata, Rosella Montana, Suaeda fruticosa, Artiplex stocksii* and *lichen.*

The marine fauna of the Gulf is rich, both in variety and abundance. Sponges having an array of colours are observed, both in the intertidal and subtidal biotopes. The common species of sponge is *Adocia sp*, associated with coral reef fauna. In sandy and silty mud shores, *Tetilla dactyloidea* (Carter) is common.

The most frequently encountered hydrozoans are *Sertularia sp* and *Plumularia sp*. The giant sea-anemone (*Stoichactis giganteum*) is a common sight inthe coral ecosystem. Sea anemones, belonging to *Anemonia, Bunodactis, Paracondylactis, Anthopleura* and *Metapeachia*, are wide spread. *Azoantharian, Gemmaria sp*, is found forming extensive hexagonal green mats in the coral pools. Another interesting actiniarian is the *Cerianthus sp* found in tubes in the soft mud.

One of the most interesting biotic features of the Gulf is the presence of living corals, thriving as patches, rather than reefs, either on the intertidal sand stones or on the surface of wave-cut, eroded shallow banks along the southern shore of the Gulf. The Gulf has 42 islands, 34 of wich have live corals. Siltation is the main causeaffecting the coral growth. The species diversity however is poor withidentification of 36 species of Scleractinian and 12 species of soft corals.

A number of polychaete worms, both sedentaria and errantia, with the dominant genera of Eurythoe, Terebella, Polynoe, Iphione and Nereis are rathercommon. A mongst a variety of sipunculid and echiuroid worms, the dominant species are *Dendrostromum sp, Asphidosiphon sp* and *Ikadella misakiensis* (Ikeda). The intertidal crustacean fauna is very rich and equally diverse with spider crab (*Hyas sp*) and furry crab (*Pillumnus sp*), as specialities.

Amongst the invertebrate component of the marine fauna of the Gulf, the molluscs have the highest representatives. As many as 92 species of bivalves, 55 species of gastropods, 3 species of cephalopods and 2 species each of scaphopods and amphineurans have been reported. The most no table members of the molluscan fauna are octopus, pearl oyster and a variety of chanks, including the sacred chank. *Pinna bicolar*, the bivalve is commonly noticed in the coral reef flat.

The echinoderm fauna, represented by 4 classes and 14 genera, have the commonest genera of Palmpsis, Astropecten, Asteria, Temnopleura and Holothuria. The subtidal benthic fauna of the Gulf is dominated by polychaetes, crustaceans, echinoderms, gastropods and bivalves, with an average biomass of 25 g/m².

The Gulf has a variety of exploitable species of finfishes and shellfishes. The sciaenids, polynemids, perches, eels, cat-fishes, elasmobranchs and prawns are commercially important groups with an average catch of 1.4 × 105 t/y. fishing grounds for Ghol, Karkara, Khaga, Dhoma, Magra and Musi exist in the Gulf.

The Gulf region offers plenty of facilities for feeding, breeding and shelter to a variety of birds. In the mangrove forests lining the islands and alongthe coast, the birds find a near perfect environment. In addition, they are well placed to reach their food supply *i.e.* the shoals of fish, squids, mud skippers and ot her animals, during low tide. All along the creeks and around islands, mangrove trees and mudflats are seen crowded with Grey Herons, Pond Herons, Painted Storks, Large and small Egrets, Darters, Cormorants, Flamingos, Lesser Flamingos, etcduring the periods of seasonal migration (November-March).

The large congregations of uncommon coastal waders such as Bar-tailed Godwit (*Limosa lapponica*), Sanderling (*Calidris alba*), Large Sand Plover (*Charadrius leschenaultii*), Eurasian Curlew (*Numenius arquata*), Eurasian Oystercatcher (*Haemotopus ostralegus*) and Crab Plover (*Dromas ardeola*) occur only in the Gulf. As per the Bird Life International Red Data List and IUCN 2002 Red Data Book, the MNP is home to several globally threatened species, such as Spot-billed Pelican (*Pelecanus philippensis*), Dalmatian Pelican (*P. crispus*), Greater Spotted Eagle (*Aquila clanga*), Indian Skimmer (*Rhynchops albicollis*), Black-necked Stork (*Ephippiorhynchus asiaticus*) and Pallas's Fishing Eagle (*Paliaeetus leucoryphus*). The Gulf region is also important for marine turtles and sea mammals.

Though a detailed systematic survey of biota is lacking, following number of species have been reported:

Flora/Fauna	Species (Nos.)
Algae	130
Molluscs	200
Sponges	70
Crabs	30
Corals	56
Birds	200
Fishes	200
Sea mammals	3
Sharks	8
Sea turtles	3
Prawns	27

Because of its high biogeographical importance and rich flora and fauna, several areas along the southern Gulf are notified under the Marine National Park (16,289 ha) and the Marine Sanctuary (29,503 ha).

Planktonic and Benthic Habitat

Survey was conducted for the study of planktonic and benthic habitat Study of biological status of any waterbody play an important role in assessing the causes of impact on water body and quality of the water. Here the biological parameter considered during EB survey are primary productivity, phytoplankton count, pigment Analysis, Zooplankton count, availability of benthic organism, fish and other micro habitat.

Table 5.15: List of intertidal algae of the Gulf

Name	Status*	Name	Status*	Name	Status*
(1)	(2)	(3)	(4)	(5)	(6)
Chlorophyceae		Phaeophyceae		Rhodophyceae	
Boodlea composita	C	Colpomenia sinuosa	C	Acanthophora delilei	C
Bryopsis indica	C	Cystoceira indica	C	A. specifera	R
B. plumose	C	Dictyota atomaria	C	Amphiroa fragilissima	R
B. ramulosa	C	D. bartayrisiana	R	Asparogopsis taxiformis	C
Caulerpa crassifolia	C	D. cervicornis	R	Botroycladia leptapoda	C
C. cupressoides	C	D. ciliolate	C	Calaglossa bombayance	R
C. racemosa	C	D. dichotoma	C	Ceramium sp.	C
C. scalpelliformis	C	D. divaricata	R	Champia indica	C
C. sertularioides	C	Dictyopteris australis	C	Chondria ornata	R
C. taxiformes	C	D. woodwardii	C	C.dasyphylla	R
C. verticillata	C	Ectocarpus sp.	C	Coelarthrum opuntia	C
Chaetomorpha indica	C	Hinskia mitchelle	C	Corallina officinalis	C
Chamaedoris auirculata	C	Hormophysa triquetra	R	Corynomorpha prismatica	R
Cladophora glomerata	C	Hydroclathrus clathratus	R	Cryptopleur sp.	R
C. prolifera	C	Iyengaria stellata	C	Dasya sp.	R
Codium decorticatum	R	Myriogloea sciurus	R	Desmia hornmanni	R
C. dwarkensis	C	Nemacystus decipiens	R	Gastroclonium iyengarii	R
C. elongatum	C	Padina gymnospora	R	Galaxaura oblongata	C

(Table Contd...)

(1)	(2)	(3)	(4)	(5)	(6)
Dictyosphaeria cavernosa	C	P. tetrastromatica	C	Gelidiella acerosa	C
Enteromorpha intenstinalis	C	Pocockiella sp.	C	Gelidiospsis gracilis	C
Halideda tuna	C	Rosenvingia intricata	R	Gigartina sp	R
Pseudobryopsis mucronata	R	Sargassum johnstonii	C	Gracilaria corticata	R
Spongomorpha sp.	C	S. tenerrimum	C	G. pygmaea	C
Udoea indica	C	S. plagiophyllum	R	Gastroclonium iyengarii	R
Ulva fasciata	C	S. swartzii	C	Galaxaura oblongata	C
U. lactuca	C	S. wisghtii	R	Gelidiella acerosa	C
U. reticulata	R	Spathoglossum asperum	R	Valonia utricularis	R
Valonia utricularis	R	S. variabile	C	Valloniopsis spachynema	R
Valloniopsis spachynema	R	Gelidiospsis gracilis	C	-	-
Stoechospermum marginatum	C	Gigartina sp	R	-	-
Spathoglossum asperum	R	Gracilaria corticata	R	-	-
S. variabile	C	G. pygmaea	C	-	-
Stoechospermum marginatum	C	G. verrucossa	R	-	-
Turbinaria ornata	R	Grateloupia inica	C	-	-
-	-	G. felicina	R	-	-
-	-	Haloplegma sp.	R	-	-
-	-	Halymenia floresia	R	-	-
-	-	H. porphyroides	C	-	-
-	-	H. venusta	C	-	-
-	-	Helminthocladia clayadosii	C	-	-
-	-	Heterosiphonia muelleri	C	-	-
-	-	Hypnea cervicornis	C	-	-
-	-	H. musciformis	C	-	-
-	-	Hypoglossum spathulatum	R	-	-
-	-	Laurencia papillosa	C	-	-
-	-	L. pedicularioides	C	-	-
-	-	Liagora cerenoides	R	-	-
-	-	Lophocladia lallemandi	R	-	-
-	-	Neurymenia fraxinifolia	R	-	-
-	-	Polysiphonia sp.	C	-	-
-	-	Rhodymenia australis	C	-	-
-	-	R. palmate	C	-	-
-	-	Scinaia indica	C	-	-

(Table Contd...)

(1)	(2)	(3)	(4)	(5)	(6)
-	-	*S. furcellata*	R	-	-
-	-	*Sebdenia polydactyla*	C	-	-
-	-	*Spyridia alternans*	C	-	-
-	-	*Soleria robusta*	C	-	-

Note: C=Common, R=Rare.
Soruce: NIO

Table 5.16: Distribution of corals in the Gulf

Species/Location	1	2	3	4	5	6	7	8	9	10	11	12	13	14	15
Esammocora digitata	-	-	-	-	-	-	-	+	-	-	-	-	-	-	-
Acropora humilis	-	-	+	+	-	-	+	+	-	-	-	-	-	-	-
A. squamosa	-	-	-	+	-	-	-	-	-	-	-	-	-	-	-
Montipora explanata	+	-	+	+	-	+	+	-	+	+	+	+	+	+	+
M. venosa	-	-	-	+	-	-	+	-	-	-	-	-	-	-	-
M. turgescons	-	-	-	-	-	-	+	-	-	-	-	-	-	-	-
M. hispida	+	+	-	+	+	-	+	+	+	+	+	-	-	-	+
M. foliosa	-	-	-	+	-	-	+	-	-	-	-	-	-	-	-
M. monasteriata	-	-	-	+	-	-	+	-	-	-	-	-	-	-	-
Coscinaraea monile	+	+	+	+	+	+	+	+	+	-	-	-	-	-	+
Siderastrea savignyana	+	-	-	-	-	-	-	-	-	-	-	-	-	-	-
Pseudosiderastrea tayami	+	-	-	-	-	-	+	+	+	+	+	+	+	+	+
Goniopora planulata	+	+	-	-	+	+	+	-	+	+	-	+	-	-	+
G. minor	-	-	-	+	-	-	+	-	-	-	-	-	-	-	+
G. nigra	+	+	-	+	+	+	+	-	-	+	-	-	-	-	+
Porites leutea	+	+	+	+	-	-	+	-	-	-	-	+	-	-	+
P. lichen	+	-	-	-	-	+	-	+	-	-	+	-	+	+
P. compressa	+	+	-	-	-	-	-	-	-	-	-	-	-	-	+
Favia speciosa	-	-	-	-	-	-	-	-	-	-	-	-	-	-	+
F. favus	+	+	+	+	+	+	+	+	+	+	+	+	+	+	+
Favites complanata	+	+	+	+	+	+	+	-	-	+	-	-	-	+	+
Species	1	2	3	4	5	6	7	8	9	10	11	12	13	14	15
F. melicerus	+	-	+	-	-	-	-	-	+	-	-	-	-	+	+
Goniastrea pectinata	+	+	+	+	+	+	+	-	+	+	-	+	+	+	+
Platygyra sinensis	+	+	+	+	-	-	-	-	-	+	-	-	-	+	+
Hydnophora exesa	+	+	+	+	-	-	-	-	-	+	-	+	-	-	+
Plesiastrea versipora	-	+	-	-	-	-	+	-	-	-	-	-	-	-	-
Leptastrea purpurea	-	-	-	-	-	-	-	-	-	-	Sikka point				
Cyphastrea serailia	+	+	+	+	+	+	+	+	+	-	-	+	+	+
Symphyllia radian	-	+	-	+	-	+	-	-	+	-	-	-	-	-	-

(Table Contd...)

Species/Location	1	2	3	4	5	6	7	8	9	10	11	12	13	14	15
Acanthastrea simplex	+	+	+	+	-	-	-	-	+	+	-	-	-	-	+
Mycedium elephantotus	-	-	-	+	-	-	-	-	-	-	-	-	-	-	-
Paracyathus stokesi	+	-	-	-	-	-	-	-	-	-	-	-	-	10	m
Polycyathus verrilli	+	-	+	-	-	-	+	-	-	-	-	-	-	-	-
Tubastraea aurea	+	+	+	+	+	-	-	-	+	+	-	-	-	-	-
Turbinaria crater	+	+	-	+	-	-	+	-	-	-	-	-	-	-	+
T.peltata	-	+	+	+	+	+	+	-	-	+	-	-	+	+	+

1 : Okha 2 : Dholio Gugar 3 : Dona
4 : Boria 5 : Mangunda 6 : Savaj
7 : Paga 8 : Manmarudi Langamarudi 9 : Ajad
10 : Bural reef 11 : Dhani 12 : Kalumbhar reef
13 : Narara reef 14 : Goose reef 15 : Pirotan island

Source: Marine EIA for Bombay Mineral Limited by National Institute of Oceanography, Goa, 2017

CONCLUSION

Study area comprise of sea shore and terestrial habitat. Spatial extent and distribution of vegetation types can be linked to the human induced changes and biodiversity characterisation. None of the sighted animal species can be assigned endemic species category of the study area. Some of the animal observed in the study area is protected under schedule I and II have to be protected and not disturbed at all, for the same, the conservation plan should be implemented for entire life of the project as per suggestions in conservation and from forest officials. An urgent need of Mangorve Management plan to implement by authority is recomonded for restoration of ecological balance of the area.

REFERENCES

Abbasi S.A. and Khan E.I. (2000).Greenbelts for Pollution Abatement (Concepts, Design, Applications). Discovery Publishing House New Delhi pp. 77

Ahmedullah M. and M.P. Nayar (1987). Endemic Plants of the Indian Region. Culcutta: Botanical Survey of India. 147 pp.

Ahmedullah M. and Nayar, M.P. (1986). Endemic Plants of the Indian Region. VoI. 1. Peninsular lndia. Bot. Surv. of India, Calcutta.

Allen L., Engeman R. and Krupa H. (1996) Evaluation of Three Relative Abundance Indices for Assessing Dingo E. Population. Wildlife Research. 23: 197-206.

Anderson T. (1867). An Enumeration of the Indian Species of Acanthaceae. Journal of Linnaean Society 9: 425-454.

APHA (1971). Standard Methods for the Examination of Water and Waste Water. American Public Health, Association, New York.

Batten SD, Clarke R, Flinkman J (2003). CPR Sampling: The Technical Background, Material and methods, Consistency and Comparability. Progress in Oceanography, 58, 193-215.

Bentham G. and Hooker J.D. (1862-1883). Genera Plantarum. L Reeve and Co., London.

BirdLife International (2000). Threatened Birds of the World. Lynx Edicions and BirdLife International, Barcelona and Cambridge, UK.

BirdLife International (2004a). Threatened Birds of the World 2004. CD-ROM. BirdLife International, Cambridge, UK.

BirdLife International (2004b). State of the World's Birds 2004-Indicators for our Changing World. BirdLife International, Cambridge, UK.

BirdLife International (2010). The BirdLife Checklist of the Birds of the World, with Conservation Status and Taxonomic Sources. Version 3. Available from http://www.birdlife.info/docs/SpcChecklist/Checklist_v3_June10.zip

Colebrook J.M. (1960). Continuous Plankton Records: Methods of Analysis, 1950-59. *Bulletins of Marine Ecology*, 5: 51-64.

CPCB (2000). Guidelines for Developing Green Belts, Central Pollution Control Board (CPCB), New Delhi, Programme Objective Series: PROBES/75/1999-2000, pp. 195.

CPCB, (2007). Phytoremediation of Particulate Matter from Ambient Environment through Dust Capturing Plant Species. Central Pollution Control Board (CPCB), New Delhi, 2007.

Dixit R.D. (1984). A Census of the Indian Pteridophytes. Flora of India Series 4. Botanical Survey of India, Howrah (Calcutta).

Edmondson WT (1974). A Simplified Method for Counting Phytoplankton. In: A Manual on Methods for Measuring Primary Production in Aquatic Environments (Ed. Vollenmeider RE) Balckwell Sci. Pub., Oxford, pp. 14-16.

Gamble J.S. (1924). The Flora of Presidency of Madras 2. Culcutta: Botanical Survey of India. 743 pp.

Ghosh S.R., Ghosh, B., Biswas, A. and Ghosh, R.K. (2004). The Pteridophytic Flora of Eastern India 1: 1-591. *In:* Flora of India Series 4, Botanical Survey of India, Kolkata.

Hunter W.W. (1879). Statlstlcal Account of Assani. Vol. II Trubner and Co.

HuttoD., Pletsechel S.M. and HendrickP. (1986). A Fixed Radius Point Count Method for Non-breeding Season use. The Auk. 103: 593-602.

IUCN (1994). IUCN Red List Categories. Prepared by the IUCN Species Survival Commission. IUCN, Gland, Switzerland.

IUCN (2001). IUCN Red List Categories and Criteria : Version 3.1. IUCN Species Survival Commission. IUCN, Gland, Switzerland and Cambridge, UK.

IUCN (2003). Guidelines for Application of IUCN Red List Criteria at Regional Levels: Version 3.0. IUCN Species Survival Commission. IUCN, Gland, Switzerland and Cambridge, UK.

IUCN (2008). Red List of Threatened Species. (www.iucnredlist.org).

IUCN (2010). Guidelines for Using the IUCN Red List Categories and Criteria, version 8.1 (August 2010), Prepared by the Standards and Petitions Subcommittee of the IUCN Species Survival Commission: on www. http://intranet.iucn.org/webfiles/doc/SSC/RedList/RedListGuidelines.pdf

Jain S. K. (1991). Dictionary of Indian Folk Medicine and Ethnobotany. Deep Publications, New Delhi.

Jain S.K. (1968). Medicinal Plants Nation Book Trust, New Delhi. Jain, S.K. 1983. Rare and Endangered Specles: Observation on Rare, Imperfectly known Endemic Plants. In the Sacred Groves of Western Maharashtra. Calcutta; Bot. Sur of India 169-178.

Jain S.K. (1992). The Problem of Endangered Species. Concepts, Problems and Solutions. *In:* Tropical Ecosystems: Ecolosv and Management (Eds. K.P.Singh and J.S. Singh.), Iiley Eastern iimited, New delhi. 69-80.

Jain S.K. and Rao R.K. (1983). An Assessment of Threatened Plants of India. Bot. Surv. of India. Calcutta.

Jain S.K. and Sastry A.R.K. (1980). Threatened Plants of India - A State of the Alf Report Bot. Surv. of India. New Delhi.

Jain S.K. and Sastry A.R.K. (1984). Safeguarding Plant Diversity in Threatened Natural Habitats. In Conservation of Threatened Natural Habitats. (Ed. Anthony V. Hall). African nat. Sci. Prog. Report. 92.

Kholia B.S. and Bhakuni K. (2009). Western Himalaya a New Range of Distribution for a Critically Endangered Fern, Dryopsis Manipurensis (Bedd.) Holttum et P.J. Edwards. Nelumbo, Bulletin of the Botanical Survey of India 51: 245-248.

Kumar Ashok (2013). Butterfly (Lepidoptera: Insecta) Diversity from Different Sites of Jhagadia, Ankleshwar, District-Bharuch, Gujarat, *Oct. Jour. Env. Res.* 1(1): 09-18.

Kumar Ashok (2014). Environmental Management Plan for Chemical Industries Especially Resin Manufacturing Unit, *Oct. Jour. Env. Res..* 2(3): 262-273.

Kumar Ashok and Aggarwal Savita Goyal (2013a). Ecology and Biodiversity Status of Sachin Gidc and its Surroundings with Special Reference to Conservation Measures for Indian Peafowl (Pavo cristatus) Schedule –I Bird species, *Oct. Jour. Env. Res.* 2(1): 82-100.

Kumar Ashok and Aggarwal Savita Goyal (2013b). Study of Common Property Resources (CPR) With Special Reference to Water and Biological Resources at Projected Area Near Village Ninat, Bardoli, District-Surat, *Oct. Jour. Env. Res.* 1(4): 319-331.

Kumar Ashok and Srivastava Meena (2012). Diversity of Medicinal Plants in Uttarakhand and their Conservation Strategy with Special Reference to Orchids, In: Proceeding of National Conference on Environemental Health: Challaneges and Management, Jan. 20-21, 2012, Organized by Pt. Deendayal Upadhyay Govt. PG College Rajajipuram, Lucknow. pp. 139-142.

Kumar Ashok, Srivastava Meena and Goyal Savita (2013). The Biodiversity at Sandi Bird Sanctuary, Hardoi with Special Reference to Migratory Birds. *Oct. Jour. Env. Res.* 1(3): 173-181.

Lackey J.B. (1938). The Manipulation and Counting of River Plankton and Changes in Some Organisms due to Formalin Preservation. US Public Health Reports 53: 2081-93.

Lushington A.W. (1915). Vernacular List of Trees, Shrubs and Woody Cl~rnbers of the Madras Presidency. Govt. Press, Madras.

Misra R. (2013). Ecology Workbook. Scientific Publishers. pp. 31-45.

Nautiyal DC, Sharma and SK, Pandit MK (2009). Notes on the Taxonomic History of Two Rare Species of Begonia (Begoniaceae) from Sikkim Himalaya and their Conservation. *Journal of Botanical Research Institute Texas* 3(2): 823-830.

Nayar M.P. (1980). Endemism and Patterns of Distribution of Endemic Genera (Angiosperms) in India. J. Econ. Tax. Bot. I: 99-110.

Nayar M.P. (1996). Hotspots of Endemic Plants of India, Nepal and Bhutan. Thiruvanathapuram: Tropical Botanical Garden and Research Institute. 204 pp.

Nayar MP and Sastry ARK (1987). Red Data Book of Indian Plants. Vol. I. Botanical Survey of India, Calcutta.

Nayar MP and Sastry ARK (1988). Red Data Book of Indian Plants. Vol. II. Botanical Survey of India, Calcutta.

Nayar MP and Sastry ARK (1990). Red Data Book of Indian Plants. Vol. III. Botanical Survey of India, Calcutta.

Ohasi H (1975). Flora of Eastern Himalaya, Third Report. University Museum of University of Tokyo Bulletin 8: 1-458

Oldfield, S., Lusty, C. and MacKinven, A. (1998). The World List of Threatened Trees. World Conservation Press, Cambridge.

Shendage S.M. and Yadav S.R. (2010). Revision of the Genus Barleria (Acanthaceae) in India. Rheedea 20(2): 81-230.

Thommpson F., Davidson I.D., O' DonnellI. J., Brazeau F. (1989). Use of Track Transects to measure the Relative Occurrence of Some Arboreal Mammals in Uncut Forest and Regeneration Stands. *Canadian Journal of Zoology*. 67: 1816-1823.

Vijaya Sankar, R., Ravikumar R. and N.M. Ganesh Babu (2005). On the Collection of a Peninsular Endemic, Barleria stocksii (Acanthaceae), after a Century. Zoo's Print 20: 1820.

Vollenweider R.A. (Ed). (1969). A Manual of Methods for Measuring Primary Production in Aquatic Environment. IBP Handbook No. 12, Blackwell Scientific Publications.

Welch F S. (1948). Limnological Methods. McGraw Hill Book Co Inc., New York.

WelshB., H.H., Jr. (1987). Monitoring herpetofauna in Woodlands of North Western California and South West Oregon: A Comparative Strategy. pp. 203-213.

Welsh C., H.H. Jr. and Lind A. (1991). The Structure of the Herpetofaunal Assemblage in the Douglas-fir/hardwood Forests of Northwestern California and South Western Oregon. pp: 395-411.

Wilson D.E. and Reeder D.M. (eds). (2005). Mammal Species of the World. A Taxonomic and Geographic Reference. Third Edition. Johns Hopkins University Press, Baltimore.

Wilson D.E. and Reeder, D.M. (eds). (1993). Mammal Species of the World a Taxonomic and Geographic Reference. Second Edition. Smithsonian Institution Press, Washington and London.

World Conservation Monitoring Centre (1988). The Conservation of Biological Diversity. WCMC., I.U.C.N., Cambridge, UK.

World Conservation Monitoring Centre (2000). Global Biodiversity: Earth's Living Resources in the 21st Century. *By*: Groombridge B. and Jenkins, M.D. World Conservation Press, Cambridge.

Eco-tourism, Environmental Problems and Sustainable Development
Edited by: Dr. Soubam Premchandra Singh; Dr. Ashok K. Rathoure
Dr. Pawan Kumar 'Bharti'
ISBN: 978-93-86841-57-5
Edition: 2018
Published by: Discovery Publishing House Pvt. Ltd., New Delhi (India)

Impact of Poor Environmental Sanitation in Shuwarin Kiyawa Local Government Area Jigawa State, Nigeria

Mustapha Bashir Kazaure

ABSTRACT

This research was conducted in shuwarin ward kiyawa local government on a topic titled "impact of poor environmental sanitation". This project comprises 100 questionnaires which were distributed to different respondent and retrieved, and the result was derived base on their opinions. This project contain five chapters; chapter one deals with the general introduction, statement of problem, purpose and objective of study, research question and research hypothesis, scope and delimitation, significant of the problem and definition of terms. The second chapter deals with relevant literature. From this chapter, different opinions of people were highlighted pertaining to environmental sanitation, scope of environmental sanitation, concept of poor environmental sanitation problem associated to poor environmental sanitation and hazards and pollution in the environment. The third chapter deals with the research methodology, method of data collection and analysis, sample size and sample techniques, scope and limitation of the study. The fourth chapter contains the data presentation, analysis and discussion and lastly chapter five deals with the summary, recommendation and conclusion. In addition the questionnaire method was adopted in the collection of data and it was analyzed that ignorance, poverty and lifestyle are the reason why most people neglect the practice of environmental sanitation, especially in shuwarin ward kiyawa local government jigawa state.

Department of Science Laboratory Technology, College of Science and Technology, Jigawa State Polytechnic Dutse, Nigeria.

INTRODUCTION
Background to the Study

Sanitation: is the hygiene means of promoting health through, prevention of human contact with hazard of waste as well as treatment and proper disposal of sewage or waste water. Hazard can be either physical, microbiological, biological or chemical agents of diseases waste that can cause health problems including human and animals excreta, solid waste domestic waste water (sewage or gray water) industrial waste and agricultural waste. Hygiene means of prevention can be by using engineering solution (e.g. sanitary sewers, sewage treatment surface run off management solid waste management, excreta management,) simple technology (e.g. pit latrines dry toilets urine, diverting dry toilets septic tanks) or even simple by behavior change in personal hygiene practices such as hand washing with soap.

Providing sanitation to people requires a system approach rather than only focusing on the toilets or waste water treatments plants self. (Raymond, ph *et al*, 2014) the experience of user, excreta, and waste water collection method, transportation or conveying of waste treatment, and are use or disposal all need to thoroughly considered (Campbell, h: *et al*, April 2013) the main objectives of a clean environment and breaking the cycle or life cycle of disease (WHO 2013)

Environmental sanitation: means the art of science of applying sanitary, biological and physical sciences principle and knowledge to improve and control the environmental and the factor there in for the perfection of health and welfare of public (www. Creg. LawsOrg.com)

Environment: natural environment concern passes all living and non living things occurring on natural on earth or same region there of it. It is environment that comprises the interaction of all living species. Climate whether and natural resources that affect human, survival and economic activities or is a physical surrounding or surface where by a man and animal all lives, it include all the condition effecting the life of an individual population. (WWW. Wikipedia. Com).Poor environmental sanitation: - sanitation activities aimed at improving or maintaining the basic environmental condition affecting the wellbeing of people this includes.

(i) Clean and safe water supply
(ii) Clean and safe cabinet air Efferent and industrial waste disposal.
(iii) Effluent and industrial waste disposal.
(iv) Protection of biological and chemical contaminant.
(v) Adequate housing in clean and safe surrounding also called environmental, hygiene (2006 web finance Inc).

Aims of the Study

To access the impact of poor environmental sanitation in Shuwarin.

Objectives of the Study

- To determine the impact of poor environmental sanitation
- To examine the problems that effect people on poor environmental sanitation.
- To identify the strategy that has been adopted in poor environmental sanitation in Shuwarin.

Justification of the Study

Over a years the poor environmental condition can has contribute significantly. To the height prevalence of communicable diseases in the country most of the diseases which includes, malaria, typhoid, diarrhea acute, repertory infection tuberculosis and helimentic infection account for a significant percentage of mobility and mortality rate.

Statement of the Problem

poor enviromental sanitation which has always been associated with african countries has significant negative effect on the national economy and that 49% of all reported sickness and injuries in sierra leone is related to poor sanitation, and lack of adquate sanitation is a major threat to the enviroment which include the degradation of the urban enviroment by the discriminant disposal of solid and liquid waste and the pollution of fresh water and lacks by unthreat human waste, the result being smaller contaminant fish catches.(mustapha,2007)

Scope and Delimination of the Study

This study on the impact of poor environmental sanitation will cover all the issue related to impact of poor environmental sanitation in "Kudanci" under shuwarin ward kiyawa local government Jigawa state.

Defination of some Terms

Impact: Is the measure of the tangible and intangible effects (consequences) of one thing or entity's action or influences up another.

Environment: Is the sum of total of all surrounding of a living organism including natural forces and other living things, which provide condition for the development and growth as well as of danger and damage or is a physical surrounding or surface where by a man and animals leave it includes all the condition affecting the life's of an individual populations.

Sanitation: Is the hygienic means of promoting health's through prevention of humans contact with hazards of waste as well as the treatment and proper disposal of sewage or waste water.

Environmental sanitation: This refers to the collection of actions of policies at improving or maintaining the standard of care environmental condition affecting the well being of then peoples.

LITERATURE REVIEW

Introduction

History of environmental health in Nigeria lies on the west coast of latitude and between 2 and 15 degree east longitude. It occupies approximately 923,768 square kilometers of land stretching from the gulf of guinea on the Atlantic coast in the south. To the fringes of Sahara desert in the north (Bala, 2004). The territorial boundaries are defined by the public of Niger and chad in the north, the Cameroon republic in the east and the republic of Benin in the west. The gulf of guinea delimits the southern boundary. By virtue of its regional extent, Nigeria encompasses multiple climate regimes and various ecological zones that influence the intensity of human activities and this has implications on west generation patterns, environmental degradations and populations. With an estimated population of about 170 million peoples, Nigeria has had a great leap in human population that has virtually doubled within 40years. This rapid population growth withoutcommensurate provision of infrastructures and services has to poor environmental sanitation characterized by increased urban slums, overstretched sanitary facilities, the generation of enormous waste and general reduction in the quality of life of the people. (Bala, 2004).

Over the years, the poor environmental sanitation condition has contributed significantly to the high prevalence of communicable diseases in the country. Most of the diseases which include; malaria, typhoid, diarrhea, acute respiratory infection, tuberculosis and helminthic infections account for a significant percentage of morbidity and mortality.Consequently despite increased efforts by various successive governments at improving public health and quality of life, basic health indicators have maintained poor since this sanitation related diseases still play a large role in creating ill health and poverty. Nigeria is committed to protecting and ensuring quality of environment that is adequate for good health and well-being for present and future generations. The Nigerian environment is richly endowed with abundant and diverse resources that are vital for the survival, health and quality of life of the populace. However, the efforts of first governments have achieved minimal success because of absence of an appropriate policy instruments to provide focus and direction for the planning and implementation of environmental sanitation programmed in the country. This and other gaps have necessities the call for a national environmental health policy that will adequatelyaddress the sanitations problems of the nation.

Scope of Environmental Sanitation

As is well-known, health is defined in the world health organization (WHO) constitution as "a state of complete physical, mental and social well-being and not merely absence of disease or infirmity." (WHO, 2014).

Also, according to the world health organization, "environmental health comprises those aspect of human health including quality of life, that are determined by physical, chemical, biological, social and psychosocial process in the environment. It also refers to the theories and practice of assessing, correcting, controlling and preventing those factors in the environment that can potentially adversely affect the of present and future generations." (Environmental defense 2004).

It is clear that this WHO definition of "health" and of "environmental health" are broad term. Yet having the full range of environmental issues on the table is important for a truly community based approach to environmental health. It is the community themselves who then help programme personnel to define the environmental health issues that are important, to decide which of this issues should be addressed, and to plan how to address these issues.

Concept of Environmental Sanitation

Environmental sanitation is an often misconstrued subject matter. The average man in the street and even those in government circle in the country understand it as no more than the routine evacuation of collected municipal solid waste. So long as there is less observed heaps of refuse, that is refuse is removed from the start, the average individuals feel satisfied with the state of the environment and those in governance may give themselves kudos without recourse to other critical factors in the environment that might be infringing on the well-being of the individual in the neighborhoods or the society at large. (Eli,2000) community environmental assessment workbook. By environmental law institute, Washington DC, USA page 1).

Sanitation in Colonial/Northern Nigeria

The roots of the contemporary sanitation crisis in Nigeria date from colonial times. Protected by stringentlyenforced segregations ordinances, the British did little to protect the health of Nigerians when they themselves did not stand to benefit and this neglect basic sanitation infrastructures has continued since independence. Both the colonial and contemporary environmental sanitation campaigns such as the fifth phase of the war against indiscipline, launched in Kano of (29 July, 1985) contain various characteristics of them so called "sanitation syndrome" namely, an incorrect analysis of the cause of sanitation problems, with the victims of poverty and exploitation being blamed for living in unsanitary environment and threatening public health; measures which are inadequate to protect the broad masses of the population primarily attributable to a lack of serious commitment to social justice rather than to the admittedly real shortage of funds; the use of the vocative metaphor of the "sanitation syndrome" to legitimate project which have little or nothing to do with the protective of health and the manipulation of environmental sanitation programmed by the ruling classes for their own benefits.(stock& Robert 1988).

Problem of Environmental Sanitation in Nigeria

It's like opening and old wound to raise catalogue of woes or raising dusts my attempts to enumerate the deplorable environmental sanitation situation in Nigeria as it is now, but was have no choice than to chronicle or highlight them to stimulate or provoke our action albeit satirically.

Practice are usually a policies. Hence to have a further discussion of sanitation practices, detailed understanding of the contemporary sanitation related policies are necessary starting from the pre-independence era, our country has had to grapple with environmental sanitation from the cantonment proclamation of GRA to the promulgation of public health act 1909 on environmental sanitation and building regulation of 1948.

Enforcement of environmental law largely the responsibility of environmental health officers. With thisin place the system is virtually collapsing in the following areas among numerousothers. Through this we shall be able to realize why and how everyday counts in sanitation matters. Sanitation counts on daily basis because in adequate sanitation is a major cause of disease worldwide and improving sanitation is known to have significant beneficial impact on heath in household and across communities.'

Out of the estimated population of Nigeria over 140 million, sanitation coverage in urban areas is about 70% in the rural areas 31% coverageranges as low as 10% to over 80% in some states. Only about 30%have access to improve sanitation and about 20% of the population use open defecation (WHO/UNICEF, 2003).

Nigerian populations generate refuse at the rate of 0.43kg/head/day and about 70-30% of it is organic in nature. Among other components, 15% accounts for plastics/nylon and about 1-2% is metal scrap (Sridhar, 2005).

It is common to find garbage glut in many of our countries from heaps and dumps being invaded by unprotected refuse pickers who seek out in living from wastes, stray animal also scatter the wastes to litter the environment. These illegal dumps serve as breeding around for disease vectors like mosquito while leached percolates the soil to contaminate ground water. Yes, everyday counts in environmental matter because the production of waste in general and domestic waste in particular in the most characteristic features of the development of our society this century. The quantity and composition of our waste are indicators of over habit as consumers and of our concern for the environment. (WHO, 2005), protection of the human environment. Retrieved September 12, 2009. From http://www.who.int.iphalen.

However, we must not forget that domestic refuse contain dangerous products such as solvents, batteries, paints, pesticides etc. the presence of what are called heavy metal is especially dangerous, these toxic elements build up in the earth and water from which they can enter the metabolism of living beings and threatening their existence. On daily basis, there squander behind the high level of consumption annoy most Nigerian resulting in heaps of refuse, most of which cannot be reintroduced into natures biogeochemical cycles. The more advanced the technology and the industrial civilization, the lager the various and categories of waste generated. Contamination also occurs when decomposition and recycling fail to take place. The challenged is to understand that over role in the biosphere is to manage natural resources that is to use and construct according to the very lows or spirit of the biosphere. The underlying premises must be the moderation and rationalization of our species relationship with it environment. (WHO,1971).Expert committee report of solid waste management, technical report series.(No. 125).

Depending on our administration of refuse and is over alimentary habits and consumption in general, we can increase or reduce the greenhouse effect, ozone layer depletion, global warming, urban heat island, acid precipitation. One can continue endlessly to catalogue all sorts of environmental sanitation problems that are springing up on daily basis. Food vendors are no more practicing personal and food contamination, adulteration and poisoning. We do not need to underrate this because more than 70% of the masses depend on vended food nowadays the water package industries aka "pure water" are not obeying the rules and regulations of sanitation food policy or no food policy. Generally, sanitation is a problem that people are often shy or unprepared to discuss, with household waste and its disposal being unpopular subject from local to the international level. (Environmental sanitation in environmental sanitation institute. Retrieved September 15, 2009 http://www.esi.org.in/sanitation.htm).

Consequencies of Poor Environmental Sanitation

Poor environmental sanitation which has always been associated with African countries has significant negativeeffects on the national economy and that 49% of all reported sickness and injuries in sierra Leone is related to poor sanitation, and lack of adequate sanitation is a major threat to the environment which includes the degradations of the urban environment by the discriminate disposal of solid and liquid waste and the pollution of fresh water and lakes by untreated human waste, the result being smaller contaminated fish catches.(Mustapha, 2007).

Many schools particularly rural schools had no latrines at all and of those with latrines most did not have separate latrine facilities for girls and boys. Lack of latrines especially separate latrines for girls was identified as the worst school experience for girls. This illustrate that the issue of poor sanitation is one of the special conditions which prevent girls from fuller participation and achievement in schools and to an extent force them out of school. Following the recent implementation of the policy for universal primary education, the ratio of pupils to latrines may now exceed and may encourage further drop out especially among adolescent girls. Morbidity figures available according to outpatient diagnoses shows that diarrhea, worm infection, eye infection and skin diseases accounted for 25.5% of all out patients visits to health, while malaria (another disease related to poor sanitation) accounted for further another 35.5% (i.e.a total of 59% of all outpatient visits are accounted by poor sanitation). Thelevel of nutritional stunting in the country is still among the worst rates of nutritional stunting in Africa and is partly attributed to the high incidence of diarrhea, an average of 5.2 episodes a year for children under five. By the end of April, many people had been taken ill with a total of more death due to poor sanitation diseases.

This gives a case fatality rate of 4.3%, causes identified for the diarrhea outbreak include overcrowding, lack of sanitary excreta disposal facilities, high water tables, lack of safe drinking water, poor food hygiene in markets (vender and purchases), and inadequate solid waste disposal. Along with a higher incidence of diarrhea, slum dwellers in swampy areas suffer a greater incidence of malaria special gender needs. Women and girls are the caretakers of the home changed with the responsibility of cooking(86%) water collection(70%), and fire wood collection(73%), child are(62%) and (88%) care for the sick and ideally.(Mustapha sesay 2007).

Women work an average of 15hours each day. No comparative figure is available for men, but it is estimated to be significantly lower. While 70-80% of the agricultural lab our force is female, only 79% of women cultivate their own land and only 30% have access to and control ovr the proceed, including the resources needed for sanitation services.

Twenty percent for formal sector employees are women and mostly in the lowest percentage in term of job. Sanitation affect men, women and children in different extents, but is generally worse for women simply because the problem of proximity for urination and defecation are especially acute for women and adolescent girls in urban areas and are heightened during menstruation. Further studies and gender analysis are required to determine the need of men, women, boys and girls and to determine the optimum course of strategy to involve the active participation of them all. (Mustapha, 2007).

Raising the profile of sanitation the national constitution state that it is the duty of verycitizen in the country to create and protect a clear and healthy environment. The first step in the process of improving sanitation in the country was to gather allexisting data on sanitation. Though there is a codify concept on sanitation, but how effective is that particular documents and how many.(Mustapha, 2007).

SierraLeoneare knowledgeable of that concept. Although those at the apex of the political cadre are saying that it is the most comprehensive statement on sanitation ever written in the country that covers the overall situation in the country, both past and present discuss the effects of poor sanitation and the reasons for its marginalization and calls for an accelerated national sanitation programme, yet many would love to be fortunate to peruse it and all fait with every bit containedtherein. the improvement of sanitationis a highly political process targeting all elected officials in the country starting with the president, who according to his political manifesto many years back included sanitation as part of his top priorities, moving down to the village level. Apparently it shouldb the intention of government to reach the center population by using a community based participatory approach, change the norms in regards to sanitation.(Mustapha, 2007).

The new approach to improving sanitation opine will build on the grass root, local government councils and development committees to plan and maintain their own sanitation improvementactivities and promote individuals action for change with the support of technocrats from all sectors including health, education and community development. The approach is based on the principles of empowering people to help themselves.

This process once inplace will start with participatory information collection leading to action plans also developed in a participatory manner.

The plans will provide peoples with increased knowledge (education) and increased understanding (free discussion), building on the collective wisdom, strength and best practices in the community around them. In urban centers pressure may need to be exerted on landlords and service standards. In rural areas, more emphasis may haveto be placed or deserving positive image for promoting sanitation within the contexts of the local traditions and beliefs. At the sametime specific efforts will be made to discourage negative taboos and beliefs.(Mustapha,2007).

Diseases Cause by Lack of Sanitation

Relevant diseases and condition caused by lack of sanitation and hygiene includes:

- Water borne diseases, which can contaminate drinking water.
- Diseasestransmitted by the fecal oral route.
- Infection with intestinal helminthic(worms) approximately two million people are infected with soil transmitted helminthes worldwide; they transmitted by eggs presence in human feces which in term contaminates soil in areas where sanitation is poor (zurbriigg c. 2014).
- Stunted grown in children
- Malnutrition particularly in child

The list of diseases that could be reduced with proper access to sanitation and hygiene practice is very long. For example in India 15 diseases have been listed which could be stumped out by improving sanitation (WHO and UNICEF).

1. Anemia, malnutrition
2. Ascariasis (a type of intestinal worm infection)
3. Camptylo bacteriosis
4. Cholera
5. Cyanobacteria toxins
6. Dengue
7. Japanese encephalitis (Je)
8. Leptospirosis
9. Malaria
10. Ring worm or tince (a type of intestinal worm infection)
11. Scabies
12. Schistosomiasis
13. Trachoma
14. Typhoid and paratyphoid enteric fever
15. Polio is another disease which is related to improper sanitation and hygiene.

Hazard Associated with Poor Environmental Sanitation

According to bologna king says an environmental hazard is a genericterm for any situation or state of events which poses a threat to the surrounding environment. Such a hazards generally consists of a chemical spill or dumping,but also of various emissions of pollutants or the leaching of pesticides and fertilizers into the surrounding environment.

Types of Environmental Hazard

- Chemical hazard
- Physical hazard
- Biological hazard
- Mechanical hazard
- Psychosocial hazard

Effect of Poor Environmental Sanitation

The effects of poor sanitation includes illness and diseases which in turn lead to reduction in productivity and poverty which is a cause of poor sanitation and a very large practiced of peoples defecates in the openon dry river beds, on railway tracks and many times directly in water. Untreated human excrete is human hazard, it may cause both soil and water pollution. Both the surface and ground water get polluted and it lead to diseases like cholera, typhoid, polio, meningitis, hepatitis and dysentery. Chadwick published a report in 1842 that was the first to detail that a lack of sanitation will lead to diseases for humans. (Chadwick 1842).

Effect of Environmental Problem

The environment is a delicate thing and the environmental problems, such global warming and water pollution are causing negative impact around the world. Many of the environmental problems being experienced are as a result of human contributions, such as excessive waste, pollution from industries and overpopulation. Meanwhile, the earth resources become or for the planets inhabitants. (kyra, 2007).

Global Warming

Global warming is common environmental buzz word used in reference to environmental problems. The phenomenon of global warming relates to gradual climate changes in the form of increased temperatures, longer heat waves and shortage clodpolls. Global warming, which is linked to the emission of greenhouse gases, affects the climate in a variety of ways, including a reduction in waterresources, the diminishing of certain ecosystem; glacial meltingand potential of plant and animal extinction.

Polluted Water

Water pollution is serious epidemic that directly affect the life of human, animal and plant. Consuming water that is saturated with waste can be toxic, but more and more bodies of water are in danger of becoming polluted due to things like oil spills, industrial plant and general sewage. Combine this with the fact that global warming and its raising temperature reduceswater availability because of the health impact of evaporation.

How to Handle Environmental Problem

Handling environmental problem often is a complex issue involving input from a variety of agencies and including the general public. Environmental problem of themselves are often complicated, especially when the sources of the issue is not easily identified. Often, an environmental problem does not exist in isolation. Rather, it can be part of a complicated environmental problem to people, most pollution is caused by human activities. Therefore, a solution may involve restrictions or cessation of certain activities; (chris, 2005).

- Identify the specific problem: - in order to solve an environmental problemsit must be clearly defined, this step will allow environmental managers and other agencies to develop an appropriate solutions.
- Creates a plan of action: - after identifying the problem, agencies and interestedparties can begin developing a plan for the solutions to the environmental problems. A plan create focus each party can have a clear role in its implementation.

- Perform initial testing: - testing provides a basilica and means to measure the sources or failure of solid and water testing, wildlife inventories and plant surveys.
- Look for a possible sources of the problems: - sometimes the sources of the environmental problem is evident, as in acidic mine drainage from an abandoned mine contaminating local water resources. Other times, the sources is not clear, as in n0n point source pollution (NSP) caused by runoff.
- Attempt to identify the causes by the process of elimination consider restricting access to the affected area to determine if human traffic is causing the issue. Sometimes, just reducing the environmentalpressures can allow the land to recover.
- Retest and resurvey affected sites: - as possible causes are eliminated, to find out if the effect is being mitigated. Recovery can occur slowly and not be readily visible. Testing can provide the necessary information.
- Investigate possible violations of environmental law: - if an industries is the source, for example, state or federal law may provide the took necessary to half the violator. Be aware that environmental issues can be cause by sources from the point of impact.
- Contact legislators to create laws and regulations, the clean water act (08 1972) for example does not have the provision with it to regulate sources such as agricultural runoff. Another concern is cost clean-up is often expensive requiring additional funding.
- Educate the general public about its effects on the environment: - many environmental issues grow into problems because ofthe failure of people to recognize their impact environmental problems causing by continually lettering or failure to recycle become greater over time.

Important of Environmental Sanitation
- Environmental sanitation can prevent illness on a population level. It can help to prevent the spread of diseases on a misuse scale.
- Environmental sanitation include solid waste management, water and waste water treatment, industrial waste treatment and noise and pollution control.
- Environmental sanitation is very important to keep people safe in their daily lives, and prevent diseases transmission. (www.wikipedia.com).

METHODOLOGY
Materials
Both questionnaire and face to face interview will be used to collect data from different respondents.

Study Area

SHUWARIN: Is a ward under Kiyawa local government located along kiyawa local government Jigawa state share boundaries with Dutse local government in which the village is located was created during military region of general Ibrahim Badamasi Babangida in 1889 and has the elevation of 429 meters and the localities latitude of 11°4656.2" (11.7823°) and longitude: 9°2428"(9.4678°) elevation of: 429 metres (1, 407 feet). Shuwarin ward, comprises of important comprise of important commercial area and made up of political peopleand obtain of ten village under it. Private schools, government school, as well as sources of education all located under it. In the study area, Compose a population of 5500 people living and interact together and they practices main religion of Islam with few numbers of Christian's practices. The main predominant occupation include these of the following high level of business, farming and fetty trading. Having different languages which include Hausa Fulani, Yoruba, Igala and Igbo.

Population of the Study

This research work is limited within Shuwarin area of kiyawa local government, which has the estimated population of over 5500 people of different genders according to 2006 general census.

Methods of Data Collection

Both open and close questionnaire where the use as method of data collection from different respondent. This help to gather the relevance information based on the research topic.

Methods of Data Analysis

This research project is going to determine impact of poor environmental sanitation using "Kudanci" area, under shuwarin ward kiyawa local government of Jigawa state, techniques use for expressing data is chi (x^2)

DISCUSSION AND ANALYSIS OF RESULT

This part discuss and analysis of result of the three hypotheses and formulated and tested as shown in the various table below:

Test of Hypothesis One

Ho: most people do not have knowledge on environmental sanitation.

Ha: the above statement is untrue.

Table 6.1: Knowledge attitude on environmental sanitation

Gender	Responders		Total
	Yes	No	
Male	45	25	70
Female	13	17	30
Total	58	42	100

From the appendix B, since X^2 cal. = 3.784 < X^2 tab. = 3.841 we accept the Ho (null) and conclude that most people do not know the broad concept of environmental sanitation.

Out of the questionnaire distributed to the respondents, 58 people's both male and female agreed with the statement, while 42 others both female and male do not agree with the statement (p<0.05).

Source: questionnaire

Test of Hypothesis Two

Ho: Majority of people do not aware that poor environmental sanitation can lead to disease transmission.

Ha: The above statement is untrue

Ho: P = 0

VS.

Ha: p ≠ 0

Table 6.2: Responses of people on whether poor environmental sanitation can lead to disease transmission

Gender	Responders		Total
	Yes	No	
Male	49	26	75
Female	12	13	25
Total	61	39	100

From the appendix C, since X^2 cal. = 2.367, X^2 tab. = 3.841. We accept Ho (null) and concluded that Majority of people do not aware that poor environmental sanitation can lead to disease transmission.

Out of 100 questionnaire distributed to the respondents 61 people both male and female agree with the statement, while 39 people both genders do not agreed to the statement (P<0.05).

Source: questionnaire

Text of Hypothesis Three

Ho: most of the diseases caused as a result of poor environmental sanitation include; cholera, malaria, typhoid etc.

Ha: the above statement is untrue.

Ho: P=0

VS.

Ha: P ≠ 0

Table 6.3: Disease present due to poor environmental sanitation

Gender	Responders		Total
	Yes	No	
Male	51	18	69
Female	19	12	31
Total	70	30	100

From the appendix D, since X^2 cal. = 1.622 < X^2 tab. = 3.841 we accept Ho (null) and conclude that most of the diseases are caused as result of poor environmental sanitation especially cholera, malaria, typhoid etc.

Out of 100 questionnaire distributed to the respondents, 70 people both male and female agreed with the statement, while 30 of the rest does not agreed with the statement (P<0.05).

Source: questionnaire.

APPENDIX B

Hypothesis I

Ho: most of the people do not have knowledge on environmental sanitation.

Ha: this statement is untrue.

Step II select the level of significance i.e., and degree of freedom

Deg. Freedom = 0.05 = 3.841 {r-1(c-1(1×1(1×1}

Step III let test statistic be = x^2 = (ad − bc)² M
$\qquad$ Klmn

Step IV state decision rule

Reject Ho if X^2cal > X^2 tab. = 3.841

Accept Ho if X^2cal < X^2 tab. = 3.841

Step V computes paired statistic

From table 6.1

X^2 = (ad − bc)²M
$\quad$ Klmn

X^2 = (45×17 − 25 × 13)2 × 100

70×30×58×42

X^2 = (765 − 325)² × 100

5115600

X^2 = (440)2 × 100

5115600

X^2 = 19360000

5115600

X^2 = 3.784

Step VI apply decision rule

Since X^2 cal. = 3.784 < X^2 tab. = 3.841 therefore we accept the null and conclude that most of the people do not have knowledge on environmental sanitation.

APPENDIX C

Hypothesis II

Ho: majority of people do not aware that poor environmental sanitation can lead to disease transmission.

Ha: the above statement is untrue.

Step II select the level of significance i.e., Alpha @ & degree of freedom

Df = 0.05 = 3.841 (r-1) (c-1) (1×1)(1×1) =1

Step III let test statistics be

$$X^2 = \frac{(ad - bc)^2 M}{Klmn}$$

Step IV state decision rule

Accept Ho if x^2 cal ≤ x^2 tab = 0.05 df 3.841

Reject Ho if x^2cal ≥ x^2 tab = 0.05 df 3.841

Step V computes paired statistic

From table 6.2

$$X^2 = \frac{(ad - bc)2 M}{Klmn}$$

$$X^2 = \frac{(49 \times 13 - 26 \times 12)^2\, 100}{75 \times 25 \times 61 \times 39}$$

$$X^2 = \frac{(637 - 312)^2\, 100}{4460625}$$

$$X^2 = \frac{(325)^2\, 100}{4460625}$$

$$X^2 = \frac{10562500}{4460625}$$

$$X^2 = 2.367$$

Step VI apply decision rule

Since x^2 = 2.367 < 0.05 df = 3.841.

Therefore we accept null hypothesis and concluded that majority of people do not aware that poor environmental sanitation can lead to disease transmission.

APPENDIX D
Hypothesis III

Ho: most of the diseases caused as a result of poor environmental sanitation include cholera, malaria, typhoid etc.

Ha: the above statement is untrue.

Step II select the level of significance i.e., Alpha @ & degree of freedom

Df=0.05 = 3.841 (r-1)(c-1)(1×1)(1×1) =1

Step III let test statistics be

$X^2 = (ad - bc)^2$ M
       Klmn

Step IV state decision rule

Accept Ho if x^2 cal ≤ x^2 tab = 0.05 df 3.841

Reject Ho if x^2cal ≥ x^2 tab = 0.05 df 3.841

Step V computes paired statistic

From table 6.3

$X^2 = (ad - bc)2$ M
       Klmn

$X^2 = (51×12 - 18×19)^2$ 100
69×31×70×30

$X^2 = (612 - 342)^2$ 100
4491900

$X^2 = (270)^2$ 100
4491900

$X^2 = 7290000$
4491900

$X^2 = 1.622$

Step VI apply decision rule

Since x^2 cal. = 1.622 < x^2 tab = 3.841 we therefore accept null hypothesis and concluded that most of the disease are caused as a result of poor environmental sanitation such as cholera, malaria, typhoid etc.

SUMMARY

This research is a case of study which attempt to justify the impact of poor environmental sanitation. A case study of cross sectional area of literate people in shuwarin ward kiyawa local government area of Jigawa state.

Conclusion

For the research, it was discover that the most of the respondents have or know little amount knowledge on environmental sanitation. This is result of adequate of health personal whose main responsibility is to create awareness among the people toward environmental health.

Also it was discover that some are educated enough and as a result they are practice and abide or comply by the instruction been given by the environmental health officer (EHO).

Recommendation

Base on the finding of this study, the following recommendation are hereby made:
1. The state government and local government should put more effort environmental sanitation and ensure effective and success health condition.
2. Inspection methods are those which promote and preserve environmental health.
3. The environment must be kept clean as well as human body to prevent establishment of pathogens and parasite.
4. The environment should involve or participate in matter relation to their health.
5. Employment of trained staff that help in creating awareness of people toward environmental sanitation.
6. Sanitation/inspection offer for monitoring environmental activities.

REFERENCES

Balan (2004) July.

Campbell, h (2013): April 20.

Char (1842): Solid Waste Effect of Human Development and Health.

W H O (2009): 111-health in Sub-Saharan African.

USEPA (2004) Waste Conversion and Utilization.

Environmental sanitationwww.oregonlaws.org.com.

Environmental Defense 2004

Environmental Sanitation in Environmental Sanitation Institute. Retrieved September 15, 2009.

http://www.esi.org.in/sanitation.htm

Eli {2000} Community Environmental Assessment Workbook. By Environmental Law Institute.

Washington DC, USA Page 1 Raymond, ph. *et al*, 2014.

Mustapha Esay' (2005). Information System in Municipal Waste Collection Resource, Conservation and Recycling, 54,123.

Robert Stock, (1988) "Glossary of Environment Statistics" 1997, UNSD 1997 unstats.un.org, Waste and Wastes Management and Unwanted or Unusable Materials which are Discarded after Primary use.

Sridhar, (2005) Report on the Environment Zamora No, M., molar, E., Grindlay, A. Rodriguez, M., Hurt Ado, a., and Calve, f. (2009). A Planning Scenario for the Application of Geographical.

WHO May, 2005, Protection of the Human Environment. Retrieved September 12, 2009. From http://www.who.int.iphalen.

WHO 1971. Expert Committee Report of Solid Waste Management, Technical Report Series. (No. 125).

Pages: 141-153

Eco-tourism, Environmental Problems and Sustainable Development
Edited by: Dr. Soubam Premchandra Singh; Dr. Ashok K. Rathoure
Dr. Pawan Kumar 'Bharti'
ISBN: 978-93-86841-57-5
Edition: 2018
Published by: Discovery Publishing House Pvt. Ltd., New Delhi (India)

Management Practices in *Litopenaeus Vannamei* Farming in Coastal Purba Medinipur, West Bengal and Life and Works of a Great Fishery Scientist

Subrato Ghosh
Himadri Chandra

ABSTRACT

Presently shrimp aquaculture in India is dominated by about 90% by *Litopenaeus vannamei*, a native of eastern Pacific Ocean. Commercial shrimp farming has been taken up in a big way in coastal belt of Purba Medinipur district in West Bengal. Since 2009, production and culture area of *Penaeus monodon* has gradually decreased while that of the substitute species *L. vannamei* has increased. Authors visited a well-equipped and newly-established *L. vannamei* farm comprising 17 grow-out ponds in Contai-I Development Block of this district on 26th September, 2017. Experiences gained about the farming practice of this newly-introduced species have been presented here. Towards the end, the illustrious career and contributions of renowned Indian fishery scientist 'Padmasree' Late Dr V.G. Jhingran has been presented.

Distinguishing Features of *L. vannamei*

The cultivable and economically-important penaeid shrimp *Litopenaeus (Penaeus) vannamei* (Boone, 1931), commonly known by the name white leg shrimp or Pacific white shrimp is a native of western Pacific coast, *i.e.*, of Mexico, and of Central and South America upto Peru. Its rostrum is moderately long with 7-10 dorsal and 2-4 ventral teeth, similar to the other

---

122/1V, Monohar Pukur Road, P.O. Kalighat, Kolkata - 700 026 (India)
* Vill. + P.O. Amarshi, PS Potashpur, Dist. Purba Medinipur, West Bengal (India)

economically-important species *Penaeus monodon* (rostrum armed with 7 or 8 dorsal and 3 ventral teeth), but body of *P. monodon* is reddish, carapace and abdomen transversely banded with alternative red and white, and has brown pleopods (walking legs); whereas the regular shell colour of farmed *Litopenaeus vannamei* is off white or translucent-white to greenish-white, body with bluish hue and minute pigmentation. Its pleopods appear white. Body is much more slippery than *P. monodon* and is difficult to hold firmly. In live specimens, body being translucent, the normal curved alimentary tract containing feed matter is clearly visible from outside when held with fingers.

P. monodon requires at least 135-140 days farming period attaining marketable size (30-35gm), *L. vannamei* attain marketable size in 105 days. Its growth has been found to be uniform within 10ppt to 40ppt salinity in brackishwater farm ponds, and takes less time to grow to market size. In West Bengal conditions, *L. vannamei* grows normally in 10-24ppt salinity with a stocking density of 60-90nos./sq.mt and harvested at 20-25gm size; FCR is lower at 1.2. Larval survivability rate is 50-60% in nursery ponds, which is more in comparison to *P. monodon*. It is a column feeder and females have open thelycum structure.

BENEFITS OF FARMING

In India, coastal brackishwater aquaculture was historically focused mainly on tiger shrimp *Penaeus monodon* farming but production issues, economic loss and disease (particularly WSSV outbreak) led to the introduction of SPF (Specific Pathogen Free) *L. vannamei* in 2009 by Coastal Aquaculture Authority of India (CAA). The merits are its fast growth, perceived low incidence of native diseases and less susceptible to the same, higher availability of genetically-selected viral-pathogen-free domesticated broodstock, high larval survival, stronger adaptability to low salinity, better tolerance to ammonia and nitrite toxicity, availability of SPF domesticated strains and culture feasibility over a wide salinity range with possibility of high density farming (Liao and Chien, 2011; Jana, 2014). In India, it has been possible to reach *L. vannamei* production levels of 10-12tonnes/ha/crop in 3-4 months (Jayaraman, 2017).

L. vannamei Farming in Purba Medinipur

Many areas in southern fringes of Purba Medinipur district *of West Bengal* have already emerged and developed for modified-extensive and semi-intensive shrimp culture practice. Here we will find brackishwater shrimp culture farms in 16-17 Community Development Blocks out of total 25 in the district. Shrimp culture is one of the leading economic activities in this district. Its southern part has a coastline of about 80km; these areas are influenced by Haldi River, Rasulpur River and Hooghly River. These areas are also connected by Orissa coast canal, Pichhaboni canal/river,

Ramnagar canal, Kalinagar canal (at Marishda village), Bamunia canal, Mandarmoni canal, Contai canal, Raja khal and other small canals of perennial brackish water. These rivers and canals are connected directly or indirectly with Bay of Bengal from where required amount of favourable water are available for shrimp culture. Most of the shrimp farming activity, particularly for water supply, depends on these creeks/canals/rivers. The dynamic and potential estuarine river system and canal system in Purba Medinipur provides considerable scope for brackishwater shrimp culture.

In last few years, professional shrimp farmers in many coastal states of India have shifted to the culture practice of this alternative species *L. vannamei*, owing to its afore-mentioned superior aquaculture traits compared with *P. monodon*. *The scenario is no exception in Purba Medinipur district*. Culture of *L. vannamei* species has been started here since 2012. There has been a change over of black tiger shrimp cultivating farms to *P. vannamei* culture in WB and Odisha (Source: Annual Report of Avanti Feeds Ltd 2016-2017). *L. vannamei* farm ponds in Purba Medinipur district accounts for highest production level of this economically-important shrimp in our country (Courtesy: Sri Prakash Chandra Behera, Business Head, Aqua Division, PVS Group, Vijayawada, India).

VISITED FARM SITE

Soula beach and landing centre is located at a distance of 10km from Contai town in Purba Medinipur district, at the terminal end of Contai - Soula Road running parallel and adjacent to Contai canal. The *L. vannamei* culture farm visited by authors, namely Rajashree Aquaculture Farm is located at about 500mt from Soula beach. Its address is: Vill. Thakurchak/ Soula, PS Junput Coastal Area, Gram Panchayat Nayaput under Contai-I Development Block. Proprietor of the farm Sri Sukhendu Pradhan, an amicable person, aged 48 and resident of Nachinda village is personally known to second author. Even in his absence, authors were entertained at farm site by two experienced farm workers/farm technicians, who take care of entire pond management practices meticulously and responsible for proper growth of *L. vannamei* under culture. Additionally there are eighteen supporting workers.

This *L. vannamei* farm was established in 2015, land lease document was prepared, payment cleared and subsequently started functioning in 2016. It covers a total water-spread area of 3.6 hectare (900 decimal), that includes seventeen earthen grow-out culture ponds (each of 1800-2500sq.mt in area), one nursery pond and one reservoir pond each of 1000sq.mt in area. Brackishwater is supplied in the farm from nearby Pichhaboni canal and Baisa canal. The nursery pond and reservoir (reserve tank) complex is protected on all four sides by a layer of nursery green shade net, erected at 9 feet in height. Over every pond, top structures have been set up as lines of thread, and used as 'bird fence network' to prevent fish poaching by birds. A bucketful of potassium permanganate solution was found at the entry gate of nursery pond - reservoir pond complex, which is a hygiene measure and aimed at washing hands and legs with it before entering. Farm implements are washed in it before use in nursery pond. Both these ponds have been lined with HDPE plastic impermeable black geomembrane sheet, including embankments and slope region, which serve as 'crab fence', besides having other usefulness.

AIR BLOWER

Regularly 20% water exchange is done in nursery pond, where no aquaculture products neither dolomite are used. Those are used in reservoir pond, where the water is treated and let into nursery after thirty days. In addition to three paddle-wheel aerator device in nursery pond, 5nos. of spirally coiled perforated rubber tube based 'electric air blower' aeration system have been maintained at five positions over HDPE sheet on pond bottom to enhance and maintain ideal dissolved oxygen concentration. Initially air is conveyed from a Roots Blower (having high motor power, high pressure and air capacity) to all five structures *via* common pipeline; subsequently air is pushed into water through perforated tubes and 2mm small bubbles are created.

MANAGEMENT PRACTICES

In nursery pond, SPF *L. vannamei* PL-8/PL-10 stage, 6-7mm size are stocked at 12 lakh in 1000sq.mt area and reared for about 30 days. The seeds are bought at Rs 0.60/- / piece in oxygenated polythene bags, by aerial route/flight service from a Chennai-based hatchery registered by CAA, owned by M/s. C. P. Aquaculture (India) Pvt. Ltd., where SPF *L. vannamei* broodstock is imported for seed production. (Note: From hatching, *L. vannamei* takes about 21 days to reach PL-12 stage). Post-larvae are nursed to a larger size (PL-30 or first juvenile), those are harvested on 26th-32nd day at 1-2gm size (22-24mm) for stocking in grow-out ponds, where *L. vannamei* are reared for 80-85 days. After catering to the grow-out ponds, when 1-2gm stage are found excess after being stocked therein, those are allowed to remain in nursery pond. On the day of visit (towards the end of culture season), authors found 12-15gm stage of *L. vannamei* being propagated to marketable size in nursery pond, where the density is 125nos./sq.mt. The 6-7mm stage will be stocked here again in February-March of next year.

Two crops/two cycles of *L. vannamei* are regularly produced per year; first during February-March to June and again during July to October. Winter months are avoided. Water column is 5.0 feet in grow-out ponds, water exchange is generally not done. Since pH of brackishwater ponds in Thakurchak village is 6.5-6.6, agri-limestone powder is used in ponds in routinewise manner. Commercially available aquaculture products like ammonia adsorber, mineral mix ('MagKCal mix') enriched with trace minerals, multi-strain soil and water probiotics, nutrient mixture are used in culture ponds judiciously in recommended dose. Drying and tilling of pond bottom, treatment with LSP, soil scrapping (3 inches) are done at the end of one crop. Necessary conditioning of pond water with aquaculture products is done before *L. vannamei* PL-30 stocking. Inlet canals in ponds and reservoir are dried and cleaned from time to time.

About farmed shrimp production, we were informed that in the previous crop, total 33000kg (33 tonnes) marketable-sized *L. vannamei* have been harvested at 28-30gm size from grow-out ponds covering 2.2 hectare area in 110 days period (including growth period in nursery pond). Those were sold at Rs 380-480/- / kg. Farm produce packed with ice are handed over to reputed shrimp processing plants in southern West Bengal and Odisha.

FEEDING

In this farm, from day of stocking, growing *L. vannamei* in grow-out ponds are fed five times in 24 hours till evening time; successively at 5.30am, 8.30am, 11.30am, 2.30pm and at 5.30pm. In every pond, after 90 minutes from every installment feeding, amount of feed in check tray is observed and pond aeration devices are not operated during this 90 min period. Aeration is commenced from 90th minute and operated for the next 90 minutes till time of application of the next installment feed. From 7.00pm till 5.30am of next morning, *L. vannamei* are not fed, all aerators are kept in continuing operation in full phase in every pond. In this farm, sinking type pelleted feed (2mm dia) having brand name 'Penaeus vannamei Prawn feed 7704S BLANCA', marketed by Charoen Pokphand aquatics feed Malaysia, is used for *L. vannamei*.

Calculation of amount of feed to be provided is done accordingly: on the 60th day of culture in grow-out pond (including nursery phase), average body weight (ABW) of growing *L. vannamei* generally has been found to be 12gm. In such a situation, in each of 0.2 hectare ponds, the biomass is 1200kg {(12 × 100000)gm; stocking density 500000nos./ha} and in 24 hours, total 35-40kg feed will be applied for *L. vannamei* at this stage. This amount is divided equally for the five installments. On the 15gm stage of ABW, in each of 0.2 hectare ponds, the biomass become 1500kg and in 24 hours, total 55kg feed will be applied. If 9kg feed needs to be applied per installment in 24 hours in each pond, an amount of 36gm is kept in check tray, i.e., 4gm check tray feed for every kg feed in pond. During the entire period of grow-out culture, a minimum of 2gm (to begin with) and upto 7gm feed is kept in check tray every time in every pond in this farm. Growing *L. vannamei* intakes less feed during moulting phase. On each and every time, feed is broadcasted from feed sacks over entire water surface evenly, using the indigenous stout thermocol float {(1.5 × 1.5) sq.mt in area, 1 foot thick} and rope fitted at one embankment and connected across to other, to gently cruise through water.

AERATION AND OTHER FEATURES

In every pond, 2 numbers of paddle-wheel type (1 HP each, four paddle wheels) and 2 spiral aerators (2 HP each) have been installed near to four corners. A combined spiral-paddle wheel aerator model costs Rs. 30,000/-; it causes aeration and feeble water flow/water current in pond simultaneously. It is installed in few ponds. Spiral aerator oxygenates pond water column more effectively than paddle wheel aerator; the latter is responsible for causing water current also. *P. vannamei* have a schooling behavior and usually swim on water currents formed by aerators. The shrimp has a minimum dissolved oxygen requirement of greater than 3ppm. Aerators are placed at proper positions to facilitate proper water circulation. According to a published literature, 8 HP of aeration is required for each 1,00,000nos. *L. vannamei* seed stocked.

Hydrogen peroxide aqueous solution (imported grade) is used as 'soil purifier' directly at pond bottom in culture ponds at 30-40lit / ha in conditions when bottom soil turns black and unhygienic. It helps in oxidation of soil organic matter. Workers have experienced that in *L. vannamei* ponds where molluscan population is more at bottom, more nutrients (KCl, $MgCl_2$) have to be supplied externally in the form of submerged bags having fine pores. Dinoflagellate bloom was observed in one culture pond, but it does not have any negative impact on shrimp growth, farm workers mentioned. In 0.18-0.25ha grow-out ponds, 1,00,000nos. *L. vannamei* PL-30 is stocked per pond. In this farm, stocking density of 50nos./sq.mt is maintained in grow-out ponds, but it can be increased to 80nos./sq.mt, farm technicians mentioned. Salinity in ponds ranges in between 12-15ppt. We had a view of 40-50 samples of *L. vannamei* of size 12-15gm under culture in ponds, caught using cast net.

END NOTE

Farm technicians mentioned that farmed *Penaeus monodon* are normally fed four times in 24 hours at 6 hour interval, with 25% of the daily amount applied in morning hours, 20% in afternoon, 30% in evening and rest 25% at night; but for *L. vannamei*, this procedure is not followed at all. There are some scattered reports from *L. vannamei* farmers in other areas of Purba Medinipur district about disease problems seldom observed in the shrimp, which are white faecal disease/syndrome (caused by the bacterium *Microsporidia* sp.), white muscle disease and black gill disease. High Quality Protein Binder, immunoboosters and other feed supplements, those having growth promotion and disease prevention effects, are added in daily feed and fed to *L. vannamei*. Use of products having calcium and magnesium minerals helps to get rid of white muscle disease.

In Purba Medinipur conditions, the final *L. vannamei* production/harvest rate from most ponds ranges from 12 tonne to 24 tonne/hectare/crop, depending stocking density, growth rate and percentage of survivals (Behera, 2016). Survival of shrimp in all ponds ranges from 74.8-84.4%. To maintain correct pH level in grow-out ponds, application (twice weekly) of dolomite at 80kg/ha at night and gypsum at 81kg/ha during daytime after 20 days of culture and upto end of the crop gives good result in *P. vannamei* culture (Palanikumar *et al.*, 2011). As done in this farm, workers finish out last meal of a day within 6.00pm and start running aerators from 7.00pm to next morning 5.30am. This method has given good result in maintaining oxygen level of more than 3ppm in ponds at night.

In this *L. vannamei* farm that we visited, every precaution is taken; sufficient aeration is provided to avoid dissolved oxygen stress and susceptibility to diseases, balanced mineral profiles are maintained to encourage proper moulting and healthy growth of the shrimp, feeding schedule is maintained strictly in every pond. High standards are maintained here. In terms of management protocols and production level, its eminence is in same level to other successfully-functioning *L. vannamei* farms in this district that are relatively old in existence.

A *L. vannamei* grow-out pond

Aerators in operation in farm

Authors at the farm site

Authors with farm technicians

Observation of fed in check tray

The check tray

Combined paddle-wheel and spiral aerator

Conventional paddle-wheel aerator

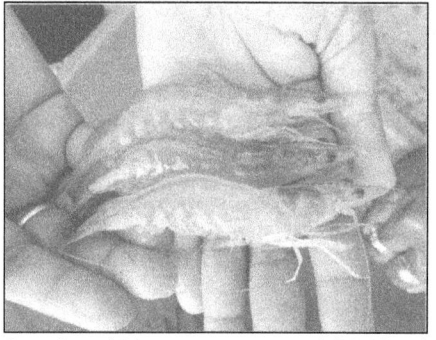
Samples of *Litopenaeus vannamei* (12-15gm)

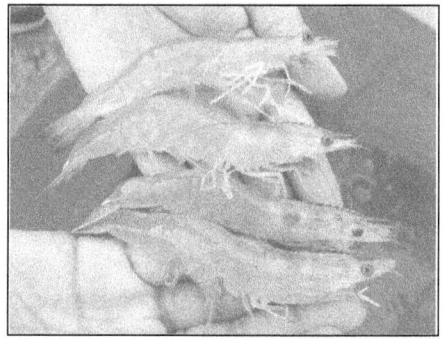
L. vannamei another view

Supplementary feed for *L. vannamei*

L. vannamei feed in bulk

Method of broadcasting feed in pond

New model of paddle wheel aerator

Spiral aerator in operation

Feed for *L. vannamei*

The nursery pond

Another view of nursery pond

Root Blower – motor and pipeline

Basic structure of spirally-coiled air blower

DR V.G. JHINGRAN – A GREAT FISHERY SCIENTIST

Dr Vishwa Gopal Jhingran (Dr V.G. Jhingran), a noted scientist and administrator, is the only Indian fishery and aquaculture scientist till date to be awarded the Indian civilian honour Padmashri from Government of India. He was one of the pioneers of modern fisheries and aquaculture in India, worked extensively and had been one of the outstanding leaders of the science and practice of both capture and culture fisheries as well as introducer of pioneering techniques. In January 1991, Dr Jhingran finalised the preface to the Third edition and acknowledgements for the Third edition of his epochal Book 'Fish and Fisheries of India', and died on 15th in the same month at the age of seventy-one. Year 2016 happened to be the twenty-fifth death anniversary of legendary Dr Jhingran.

The ICAR-Central Institute of Freshwater Aquaculture, presently located at Bhubaneswar, had its beginnings in the Central Inland Fisheries Research Sub-station (as Pond Culture Division of CIFRI) established at Cuttack in 1949, under the erstwhile Central Inland Fisheries Research Institute. The contributions of Late Dr B.S. Bhimachar, Late Dr V.G. Jhingran and Late Dr A.V. Natarajan, the past Directors of CIFRI as well as those of Dr K.H. Alikunhi, Dr. H.L. Chaudhuri, Dr V. Ramachandran, Dr M.T. Philipose, Dr R.D. Chakrabarti, who led the Sub-station at Cuttack paved way for establishment of the Freshwater Aquaculture Research and Training Centre in Bhubaneswar in 1976. Dr Jhingran had great influence in it. Dr V.G. Jhingran was born in June 1919 in Jharkhand, did his MSc in Zoology from Benaras Hindu University in 1941. He completed his Doctoral research (Ph.D.) in 1948 in Fishery Biology from Stanford University, California, USA. He joined the ICAR-Central Inland Fisheries Research Institute, Barrackpore in 1948 as Scientific Officer and rose to the position of Director in 1966 (Vass *et al.*, 2007).

On his retirement from the institute on June 30, 1979, Dr Jhingran joined the Food and Agricultural Organisation of the United Nations (FAO) as Chief Technical Advisor at the African Regional Aquaculture Centre, Nigeria, and held the position till June 1981. More recently, Dr Jhingran served as Consultant/Advisor on aquaculture and fisheries to Asian Development Bank, Indian Agricultural Universities and industrial enterprises in India. Dr Jhingran participated and represented India in various international meetings and forums, held under the auspices of such august bodies as Royal Society of London, Indo-Pacific Fisheries Council, UNDP/FAO. He chaired the 17th session of the FAO/IPFC symposium on 'Development and Utilization of Inland Fishery Resources', held at Colombo in October 1976, and also the Technical Committee on Inland Fisheries set up by the Government of India. He was the President of the Zoology, Entomology and Fisheries section of 66th Indian Science Congress, held at Hyderabad in 1979 and delivered his Presidential address on 'Need for ecological orientation to the management of inland fisheries resources'.

Dr Jhingran contributed over one hundred papers on fisheries published in periodicals of international repute such as Nature, J. Fish. Res. Bull. Canada, Proc. Indo-Pacif. Fish. Counc., J. Bombay Nat. Hist. Soc., Proc. Indian Nat. Acad. Sci., etc., contributed a chapter in Book 'Coastal Aquaculture in Indo-Pacific Region', published by Fishing News Ltd., London in 1972. He received Rafi Ahmed Kidwai Award (gold medal) from ICAR in January 1976, which was for the biennium 1972-'73, for his outstanding contribution in the field of fish culture. It was awarded to him by Sri Jagjivan Ram, then Union Minister of Agriculture. His work on composite fish culture in freshwater ponds and on freshwater prawn farming and mullet culture in brackishwaters have been of immense practical importance and represented major breakthrough in inland aquaculture in India.

Dr Jhingran also contributed in the propagation of *Cirrhinus mrigala* and to studies on age and growth of this Indian major carp. He contributed in large-scale fish tagging operations in Chilka Lake in Odisha; his pioneering work on the problem of depletion of fisheries of Chilka Lake led to the formulation of clear-cut measures for developing fisheries of the lake. Dr Jhingran received the prestigious National Award 'Padmasree' in April 1977 from Sri B. D. Jatti, the then Acting President of India; it was a recognition of his contributions towards development of aquaculture in India through a process innovatively termed by him as 'aquaplosion', as aquatic-counterpart to 'green revolution' in agriculture. He also received the Ichthyological Society of India gold medal in 1979 and the Chandrakala Hora Medal in 1982. Dr V. G. Jhingran became Fellow of the National Academy of Sciences of India in 1969, Fellow of The Zoological Society of India, Bodh Gaya in 1970, and was the founder President of Inland Fisheries Society of India, Barrackpore. Dr Jhingran was responsible for formulating several coordinated research projects in inland fisheries, which helped boost India's fish production in experimental pond culture from 600kg/ha/year to 6000kg/ha/year.

THE BOOK 'FISH AND FISHERIES OF INDIA'

As of 1991, the book 'Fish and Fisheries of India', authored by Dr V. G. Jhingran, continued to remain the only comprehensive treatise on the fisheries of the country, whose coverage is extensive. Dr Jhingran had painstakingly blended into an integrated whole a great mass of scientific knowledge accumulated over decades. His involvement with the problems of fish and fisheries for over thirty years provided considerable background for writing this treatise.

The First Edition of the massive scientific treatise 'Fish and Fisheries of India', was published in 1975. The book was widely acclaimed immediately upon its publication and quickly established itself as an essential in the field of Indian fishery and aquatic biology. Its second edition was brought out in 1982. The demand for the book had been so persistent that first edition and second edition of it have to be reprinted several times. The revised and enlarged Third edition, published by Hindustan Publishing Corporation (India), Delhi, in 1991, had been enriched with added information and encompassing within itself the entire gamut of capture and culture fisheries management; it is invaluable for readers, such as planners, scientists, PhD researchers and technologists working in the field of fisheries, BSc and MSc students of aquatic biology, be it fisheries (BFSc and MFSc) or limnology, entrepreneurs of marine products, commercial fishermen, freshwater and brackishwater fish farmers and biologists. Various statistics in the field of capture fisheries as well as export of marine products was updated in it. Management of *beel* fisheries of north-eastern part of India, fish feeds and their formulation, fish genetics, integrated aquaculture with agriculture, fisheries education in India, management of Indian EEZ, role of satellite imagery in fishery development - many features were added in it. This Book is considered as Bible to MFSc students and PhD researchers/young scientists in fisheries and inland aquaculture, it is the reference text of all students of inland aquaculture.

Dr Jhingran's permanent residence was at: 132, Indira Nagar Colony, DehraDun, Uttar Pradesh. The newly modified auditorium hall at ICAR-Central Institute of Freshwater Aquaculture has been named as "Dr V. G. Jhingran Auditorium Hall". Dr Jhingran's wife Kiran gave up her brilliant career in vocal classical Indian music. According to youngerly distinguished fishery expert Late Prof. H. P. C. Shetty (who died in November 2015), former Director of Instruction, College of Fisheries, Mangalore and former FAO expert: "Dr V. G. Jhingran was an extremely hardworking scientist with a vision. His book 'Fish and Fisheries of India' made him a household name in India; fish farmers across India came to know him because of his book. He was not the one to sit back and relax, and was 'workaholic' till his very end". We pay heartfelt homage and humble tribute to this illustrious person.

Padmasree Dr. V.G. Jhingran   Dr. Jhingran receiving Padmasree Award

REFERENCES

Behera, P.C. (2016): Management Practice of Vannamei Shrimp Culture Ponds with High Stocking Density and Zero Water Exchange in Purba Medinipur District of WB, India, in Relation to Growth, Survivals and Water Quality; *https://en.engormix.com/aquaculture/articles*

Jana, T.S. (2014): Comparative Study on Environmental Impact, Cultural Aspects, Productivity and Return on Investment of *Penaeus monodon* and *Litopenaeus vannamei* in East Midnapore, West Bengal, *MFSc Thesis Submitted to WBUAFS, Kolkata*: 1-118.

Jayaraman, R. (2017): Sustainable Coastal Aquaculture in India, *Aquaculture Asia*, 21(2): 21-23.

Liao, I.C. and Chien, Y.H. (2011): The Pacific White Shrimp *Litopenaeus vannamei* in Asia: The World's most Widely Cultured Alien Crustacean, In: *Invading Nature - Springer Series in Invasion Ecology*, 6.

Palanikumar, P., Velmurugan, S. and Citarasu, T. (2011): Factors Influencing in Success of *Penaeus vannamei* Culture, *Aquaculture Asia*, 16(1): 10-16.

Vass, K.K., Suresh, V.R. and Bhowmick, U. (2007): Reminiscence – CIFRI 1947 to 2007, *ICAR-Central Inland Fisheries Research Institute Publication*: 1-153.

Pages: 154-184
Eco-tourism, Environmental Problems and Sustainable Development
Edited by: Dr. Soubam Premchandra Singh; Dr. Ashok K. Rathoure
Dr. Pawan Kumar 'Bharti'
ISBN: 978-93-86841-57-5
Edition: 2018
Published by: Discovery Publishing House Pvt. Ltd., New Delhi (India)

An Overview on Biomedical and Biodental Waste Management

Dr. Sheela Kumar Gujjari
Dr. Pragyan Mohanty
Dr. Anil Kumar Gujjari

ABSTRACT

As dental practitioners it is necessary to recognize that some of the materials and procedures that are used to provide dental health services may present challenges to the environment. Realizing this, appropriate measures have to be taken to minimize the production of these wastes and their potential environmental effects as well as their proper disposal. This review article identifies some of the common wastes produced by dental offices as well as common biomedical wastes, ways undertaken to manage them and future methods that should be undertaken. And provides practical suggestions for reducing the impact of dentistry as a profession on the environment.

Recent times have marked an increased awareness of individuals towards general as well as oral health. This buoyancy in healthcare sector has led to tremendous increase in the quantity of waste generated by hospitals, clinics and other establishments. These health care generated wastes are termed as "biomedical wastes" (BMW). It carries a high potential for infection and injury in comparison to any other type of waste. Its improper handling may result in serious public health consequences along with a significant impact on the environment.

Department of Periodontology, JSS Dental College and Hospital, Mysuru - 570 015, Karnataka (India)

According to various statistical surveys quantity of healthcare waste produced in a typical developing country is predominated by a wide range of factors and may range from 0.5 to 2.5 kg per bed per day. For example, India generates around 500 tons of biomedical wastes every day (1). Increase in the generation capacity along with improper disposal methods to combat the increase, insufficient physical resources and lack of adequate research on medical waste management further worsens the situation.

In order to achieve a well balanced overall health, maintenance of oral health becomes a key in the process. Dentistry which encompasses practices to promote and enhance oral health and well-being, requires a wide range of materials and equipment which generate large amount of hazardous wastes. Hence the waste produced in dental hospitals as well as various dental clinics become a part of "biomedical waste". Even if the amount is small, when not managed properly, these wastes can be detrimental to both the dentist as well as the environment.

INTRODUCTION

Hospital is a complex institution which provides specialized treatments to maintain health of an individual. Hence highly hazardous and toxic wastes are generated from these establishments. Improper or inadequate treatment of these wastes before disposal accentuates the growth of various pathogenic organisms which can contaminate other nonhazardous/non-toxic municipal waste. The waste handlers when come in contact with these are most affected, as they rummage through all kinds of poisonous material. Therefore a rigorous regime of segregation of waste at source as well as judicious planning and management of waste disposal system can reduce the risk proportionately. This can be achieved by proper training of health care establishment personnel at all levels coupled with sustained motivation.

Of the many biomedical wastes, the wastes generated from dental hospitals and clinics and their management are the least explored ones. Dental practices produce large amounts of waste which are mostly contaminated with infected body fluids and involves the usage of various materials such as silver amalgam and various chemical solvents which contains various toxic elements which are easily released into the biosphere through atmospheric gases as a result of incineration of these wastes or direct disposal into the water streams through the dental practice sewage system and evacuation system. Even if dentists generate only a small amount of the total medical waste, the quantity of waste generated is equally important. A lesser amount of biomedical waste means lower burden on waste disposal work but a more efficacious waste disposal system.

BIOMEDICAL WASTE MANAGEMENT WASTE SCENARIO IN INDIA

Of the total waste generated from healthcare sector only a small amount of waste accounting to around 15% is considered lethal and becomes hazardous and toxic in nature for the public when mixed with the municipal waste general. Hence this non general biomedical waste becomes a matter of concern and can be a serious threat to the community as well as the environment if not segregated and disposed of adequately.

Economically, India has been accounted as an emerging country marked by significant urbanization and industrialization. This economic growth has resulted in increased waste generation per person. Despite significant development in social, economic and environmental status, the waste disposal systems especially of the biomedical waste in India have remained relatively unchanged. According to the Associated Chambers of Commerce and Industry (ASSOCHAM) predictions, "India will generate 130 million tonnes of e-waste by 2018 from the current 93.5 million tonnes in 2016. And by 2020, India is expected to generate 260 million tonnes of e-waste".

India being one of the populous countries of the world, recent increase in awareness amongst individuals towards healthcare has resulted in growth in the health sector scenario. With a marked growth the amount of waste generation has also increased drastically. Hence effective management of these waste pose a challenge for the densely populated areas in order to maintain a desired ecological balance.

Researchers have shown that about 30% of the total injections administered each year were done using reused or improperly sterilized medical equipment, and about 10 percent of healthcare institutions sell these used syringes to the waste pickers. A research showed that the population which lives within 3km distance from old incinerators, saw an increase of risk in contracting cancer by 3.5 percent(10). Hence construction and maintenance of a proper waste disposal system should be supported by appropriate rules and regulations which should be abided by diligently.

BIO-MEDICAL WASTE RULES (1998)

For adequate and efficient waste disposal The Ministry of Environment and Forests notified the "Bio-Medical Waste (management and handling) rules in July 1998.

In accordance with these Rules, it is the duty of every "occupier" i.e. a person who has the control over the institution and or its premises, to take all necessary steps to ensure that waste generated is handled without any adverse effect to human health and environment.(5)

Further amendments were made by the Central Government and published the Bio-medical Waste Management Rules, 2016 dated 28th March, 2016 which stipulated duties of the "Occupier" or "Operator" of a Common Bio-medical Waste Treatment Facility as well as the identified authorities. According to these rules, every occupier or operator handling bio-medical waste, irrespective of the quantity is required to obtain authorisation from the respective prescribed authority i.e. State Pollution Control Board and Pollution Control Committee, as the case may be.(7)

The occupier ensures pre-treatment of the laboratory waste, microbiological waste, blood samples and blood bags through disinfection or sterilisation on-site in the manner as prescribed. Occupier provides training, immunisation, health check-up and occupational safety to all its health-care workers (HCWs). The major accidents are also reported to the prescribed authority and in the annual report. The occupier establishes a system to review and monitor the activities related to BMWM a committee. The occupier and CBMWTDF are liable for damages caused to environment or public due to improper handling BMW under section 5 and section 15 of Act.

Rules has been expanded to include vaccination camps, blood donation camps, first aid rooms of schools, forensic laboratories, medical colleges, research laboratories, household BMWs and other such camps/programmes, any other health-care activity related to any system of medicine.

Emission standards and equipment standards, effluent, pits are delineated. For traceability of the BMW, bar coding and GPS are introduced.

Emphasis has been laid on accident reporting, records and website related to BMW. In the final disposal technologies, sustainable, eco-friendly (plasma pyrolysis), green technologies, newer technology, waste to energy options and recycling (authorised recyclers) are included.

Even after a long time of implementation and amendments in the law most of hospitals in India still fail to abide the mentioned guidelines and fail to achieve the desired standards for the biomedical waste management. According to a report by the INCLEN Programme Evaluation Network (IPEN), 18 to 64 percent of hospitals and healthcare institutions do not use the satisfactory methods for biomedical waste management (BMW). This can be due to insufficient amount of resources required for BMW or lack of awareness among the healthcare officials or due to use of poor disposal method.

Dentistry is a branch of medical sciences which comes in direct contact with the body fluids. Even the smallest dental treatment involves contamination with saliva. Although the waste generated from these practices may account for least in amount but they are the most contaminated ones. The disposal of the dental waste usually involves incineration which results in formation of highly toxic gases which has a great effect on the ecosystem. Hence proper disposal of this small amount of waste can have a great impact on the ecosystem.

INTERNATIONAL AGREEMENTS AND CONVENTIONS (10)

1. The Basel Convention

It regulates the transboundary movements of hazardous and other wastes under the "prior informed consent" as per national or domestic legislation to prevent and punish illegal traffic in hazardous and other wastes.

2. The Stockholm Convention, 2006

It is a global treaty to protect human health and the environment from POPs. POPs are polychlorinated dibenzo-p-dioxins and dibenzofurans that are stable and are widely distributed, accumulate in the fatty tissue and are toxic to humans and wildlife. It is essential to reduce or eliminate releases of POPs by incinerators and other combustion processes through best available techniques (BAT) guidelines and promote best environmental practices (BEP) for new incinerators within 4 years. The training, collection, transport, source reduction, segregation, resource recovery and recycling are BEP. The BAT guidelines for BMW incinerators and waste water require to achieve air emission levels of dioxins and furans no higher than 0.1 ng I-TEQ/Nm3 and aims at alternative technologies.

3. AARHUS Convention of The United Nations Economic Commission for Europe, 1998

This convention focuses on access to information, public participation in decision-making and aims at access to justice in environmental matters and rights.

4. The International Solid Waste Association

It is an independent, international and non-profit making association and aims to promote and develop sustainable and professional waste management worldwide.

5. WHO Guidance

The WHO policy paper suggests that government organisations adopt recycling, polyvinyl chloride (PVC)-free medical devices, risk assessment and sustainable technologies to promote environmentally sound management of BMW.

VARIOUS STUDIES ON BIOMEDICAL WASTE MANAGEMENT IN INDIA

Various studies have been carried out in different states of India to gather knowledge regarding the various waste disposal system followed as well as to evaluate the awareness among the personnel's about waste and its disposal.

1. From 2009-2012 a cross sectional audit was carried out by L.Joseph on biomedical waste, segregation and awareness of the hospital common waste in the hospital.

   Conclusion: The study concluded that periodic training and emphasis on policies implementation is necessary for optimizing the compliances to the effective segregation. Involvement of hospital administration plays a vital role in creating policies efficiently.

2. Asif Choudhary and Deepika Stathia carried a study at Gandhinagar hospital, Jammu where they monitored various samples of biomedical waste generated from the hospital about 3 months.

Conclusion: Concluded that the average solid waste generated per bed per day was 632.04 g of which almost 61.28 g is biodegradable and rest is non-biodegradable. Biomedical waste treatment in the hospital involves the collection by the sweepers then disposing in the community dustbins. Thus the waste was not disposed off in an efficient and secure method.

3. The INCLEN programme evaluates network study group New Delhi formed a situational analysis and prediction about performances in 25 districts from 20 states in India. The health facilities were assigned into one of the three categories (Red, Yellow, Green) based on their cumulative median score.

    Result: The result of analysis depicts that about 85 percent of primary, 60 percent of secondary and 54 percent of tertiary healthcare institutions falls under the red category. The study emphasised on the urgent need of greater commitment towards BMW Management policies.

4. Dr. Anjali Acharya [4] studied the impact of the biomedical waste on the environment of Pune city. A survey was conducted in 10 hospitals of the Pune city

    Result: More than 55% of employees were unaware about the adequate collection and treatment methods of biomedical waste. Nearly 62% respondents of survey do not find it a serious issue and approximately 45% of users were ignorant.

5. Vijay Krishna depicted the scenario of biomedical waste management in Varanasi city (U.P)

    Conclusion: Biomedical waste treatment is generated by a private organization, Centre for Pollution Control (CPC) works very effectively. There are a number of guidelines for management of infectious waste from medical institutions. CPC is responsible for collection, segregation and treatment of the waste in best suitable manners along with the documenting at every step of treatment.

6. A study was conducted by Ramandeep S Narang *et al* among 160 dental professionals and auxiliary staff in a dental hospital/clinics in Amritsar, India to determine awareness of biomedical waste (BMW) management policies and practices and to inform the development of future policies for effective implementation of BMW rules.

    Conclusion: There was a lack of awareness on most aspects of BMW management among dental auxiliary staff in the dental hospital/clinics in Amritsar and a lack of awareness on some aspects among dentists who work in the hospital/clinics. The results provided the hospital authorities with data upon which they can develop a strategy for improving BMW management.

7. In a systematic review by Kapoor D et al on the knowledge and awareness among various dental teaching institutions in India regarding biomedical waste management it was concluded that the knowledge and awareness level of subjects was inadequate and there was a considerable variation in practice and management regarding BMW. Hence there is a great need for training programmes in dental teaching institutions in India.

More studies should be conducted among various levels of personnel in order to create awareness among health care professionals as well the authorities of the hospitals towards proper disposal of Biomedical waste and its management. It will also act as a stepping stone towards development of new rules and amendments in the existing ones for better functioning.

BIOMEDICAL WASTE MANAGEMENT IN KARNATAKA

According to MOEF (The Ministry of Environment & Forests, India), 2011 Karnataka was the highest BMW generator at 62,241 kg/day, followed by Uttar Pradesh (44,392 kg), Maharashtra (40,197 kg) and Kerala (32,884 kg). Karnataka is the worst offender as a sizeable portion of this waste (18,270 kg/day) does not get disposed of scientifically, and probably gets mixed with other municipal waste. The MOEF indicate a total of 4,05,702 kg of BMW is generated every day in the country as a whole, of which only 2,91,983 kg is disposed. The figure shows that 1,13,719 kg/day of waste is left unattended which more often re-enters the system.

States	BMW Generated (kg/day)	BMW Disposal (kg/day)
Karnataka	62,241	43,971
Uttar Pradesh	44,392	42,237
Maharashtra	40,197	40,197
Kerala	32,884	29,438
West Bengal	23,571	12,472
Total	4,05,702	2,91,983

Source: http://indiatoday.intoday.in/story/disposed-medical-waste-karnataka-deadlyvirus/1/158691.html

Bangalore is one of the top destinations in India for medical education. This cosmopolitan city has become a prominent health care destination for people from developed as well as developing countries. With its infrastructure and massive development, management of hospital waste becomes need of the hour. Although several initiatives have been undertakento manage hospital waste in the city, there still exists a missing links that has serious implications for both human health and urban ecology of Bangalore (12)

Various studies have been conducted to evaluate the waste management in Bangalore only.
1. Study by Pruthvish *et al* (1997) estimated the quantum of waste generated in Bangalore at 1,32,500 kg/day and put the quantum of health care waste in that at 5,100 kg/day (Gaur, 1995) (12)
2. Another study in the Nagarbhavi ward of Bangalore city conducted Manasi K *et al* identified 27 sources as BMW generators of which 4 were dental sources. In general there was a lack of proper waste disposal and awareness amongst them.

Other studies conducted in Karnataka state:
1. A study by Madhu Narendra *et al.* on 'Assessment of Biomedical waste of various hospitals in Mysore city Karnataka, India' highlighted the issue of lack of knowledge and awareness regarding legislations on bio-medical waste management even among qualified hospital personnel. (12)
2. A study by Shivaraju HP *et al* on Healthcare waste management and practices: in Kodagu District of Karnataka concluded that there were inappropriate practices in segregation, collection and transportation as well as major drawbacks in their infrastructures and facilities. Lack of knowledge, low awareness, and guilty attitudes in healthcare workers was also reported. (13)

WHAT IS BIOMEDICAL WASTE?

According to the Bio-medical Waste Rules 1998 of India, biomedical waste (= Biodental waste) is defined as "Any solid, fluid or liquid waste, including its container and any intermediate product, which is generated during the diagnosis, treatment or immunization of human beings or animals, in research pertaining there to, or in the production or testing of biological and the animal waste from slaughter houses or any other like establishments."(2)

CLASSIFICATION OF BIOMEDICAL/DENTAL WASTE

The World Health Organization (WHO) has broadly classified medical waste into eight categories:
- General Waste
- Pathological
- Radioactive
- Chemical
- Infectious to potentially infectious waste
- Sharps
- Pharmaceuticals
- Pressurized containers

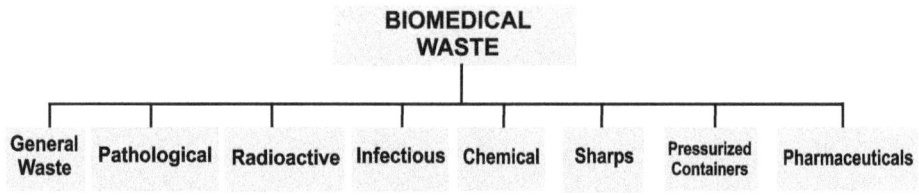

Fig. 8.1

TYPES OF WASTE GENERATED IN DENTISTRY (8):

The waste generated in dentistry can be further divided into:
- Biomedical waste- Non anatomic waste & Anatomic waste, sharps.
- Silver containing waste-used fixer solution and unused x-ray films.
- Lead containing wastes-lead aprons and lead foils inside the x-ray films.
- Mercury containing wastes-element mercury, scrap amalgam.
- Chemicals, disinfectants and sterilizing agents.

Numerous products that are used in dentistry can be classified as hazardous waste. There are certain limits on what can be discharged down the drain or discarded into landfill. It may not always be that a hazardous waste immediately requires disposal. Certain substitution methods are devised which entails segregation of waste products before disposal thereby providing a time leeway. These biological substances that pose a threat to the health of living organisms, primarily humans are termed as "BIOHAZARDS".

BIOHAZARD AND DENTISTRY

Dental health care workers are constantly in an exposure to multitude of pathogenic organisms by default as a part of occupational hazard. While carrying out any dental procedure, dental health care workers are constantly exposed to saliva, microorganism, blood and other body fluids. Hence, dental health care professionals are subjected to potential infection from needle stick injury, direct transcutaneous transfusion from infected blood products and indirectly through skin and bruises. This kind of infection can lead to an array of contiguous diseases ranging from infections to HIV, Hepatitis B, Tuberculosis and Pneumonia. This necessitates an increased awareness about various biohazards associated with dentistry and training of health care worker towards proper waste management of these biohazards and its disposal. Thus, training and education of health care professionals can increase adherence to infection control measures in dental clinics and hospitals.

CLASSIFICATION OF BIOHAZARDS

Bio hazardous agents are classified for transportation by UN number

- Category A, UN 2814 – Infectious substance, affecting humans: An infectious substance in a form capable of causing permanent disability or life-threatening or fatal disease in otherwise healthy humans or animals when exposure to it occurs.
- Category A, UN 2900 – Infectious substance, affecting animals (only): An infectious substance that is not in a form generally capable of causing permanent disability or life-threatening or fatal disease in otherwise healthy humans and animals when exposure to them occurs.
- Category B, UN 3373 – Biological substance transported for diagnostic or investigative purposes.
- Regulated Medical Waste, UN 3291 – Waste or reusable material derived from medical treatment of an animal or human, or from biomedical research, which includes the production and testing.

LEVELS OF BIOHAZARD

The United States' Centres for Disease Control and Prevention (CDC) categorized various diseases in levels of biohazard

Level 1 being minimum risk and Level 4 being extreme risk.

Laboratories and other facilities are categorized as BSL (Biosafety Level) 1-4 or as P1 through P4 for short (Pathogen or Protection Level).

Biohazard Level 1: Precautions against the bio hazardous materials in question are minimal, most likely involving gloves and some sort of facial protection. Usually, contaminated materials are left in open (but separately indicated) waste receptacles. Decontamination procedures for this level are similar in most respects to modern precautions against everyday viruses (i.e.: washing one's hands with anti-bacterial soap, washing all exposed surfaces of the lab with disinfectants, etc). In a lab environment, all materials used for cell and/or bacteria cultures are decontaminated via autoclave.

Dental point of view: For any evaluation of the oral cavity gloves are a necessity. It is mandatory to use antibacterial soaps and solvents before and after treatment for washing hands. Should wear surgical masks and protective eyewear or chin-length plastic face shields during dental procedures in which splashing or spattering of blood, saliva, or gingival fluids is likely. Rubber dams, high-speed evacuation and proper patient positioning, when appropriate, should be utilized to minimize generation of droplets and spatter.

Biohazard Level 2: Bacteria and viruses that cause only mild disease to humans, or are difficult to contract via aerosol in a lab setting.

"Routine diagnostic work with clinical specimens can be done safely at Biosafety Level 2, using Biosafety Level 2 practices and procedures.

Research work (including co-cultivation, virus replication studies, or manipulations involving concentrated virus) can be done in a BSL-2 (P2) facility, using BSL-3 practices and procedures.

Virus production activities, including virus concentrations, require a BSL-3 (P3) facility and use of BSL-3 practices and procedures"

Dental point of view: Blood and saliva should be thoroughly and carefully cleaned from material that has been used in the mouth (e.g., impression materials, bite registration), especially before polishing and grinding intra-oral devices. Contaminated materials, impressions, and intra-oral devices should also be cleaned and disinfected before being handled in the dental laboratory and before they are placed in the patient's mouth.

Biohazard Level 3: Bacteria and viruses that can cause severe to fatal disease in humans, but for which vaccines or other treatments exist.

Dental point of view: Dental health care professionals are subjected highly susceptible to get infected with Hepatitis B infection from needle stick injury, direct transcutaneous transfusion from infected blood products and indirectly through skin and bruises. Hence dentists should be more cautious in handling patients with infectious diseases and should take the necessary vaccine before handling them.

Biohazard Level 4: Viruses and bacteria that cause severe to fatal disease in humans, and for which vaccines or other treatments are not available. When dealing with biological hazards at this level the use of a Hazmat suit and a self-contained oxygen supply is mandatory.

The entrance and exit of a Level Four biolab will contain multiple showers, a vacuum room, an ultraviolet light room, autonomous detection system, and other safety precautions designed to destroy all traces of the biohazard.

Multiple airlocks are employed and are electronically secured to prevent both doors opening at the same time.

All air and water service going to and coming from a Biosafety Level 4 (P4) lab will undergo similar decontamination procedures to eliminate the possibility of an accidental release.

Dental point of view: Diseases without vaccination such as HIV, when handling such patients proper barrier methods should be followed such as double gloves, masks, protective eyewear, gowns, and waterproof aprons. Dental equipment and surfaces that are difficult to disinfect (e.g., light handles or X-ray-unit heads) and that may become contaminated should be wrapped with impervious-backed paper, aluminium foil, or clear plastic wrap. The coverings should be removed and discarded, and clean coverings should be put in place after use with each patient.

HAZARDOUS EFFECT OF BIOMEDICAL/DENTAL WASTES: (14)

The pollutants from biomedical waste that affects the environmental balance and can cause damage can be classified into biological, chemical and radioactive. These biomedical wastes affects the air, water as well as the soil.

Air Pollution

Air pollution can be caused in both indoors and outdoors atmosphere. Biomedical waste that is generated by air pollution can been classified in three types namely-Biological, Chemical and radioactive.

In-door Air Pollution

Pathogens present in the waste can enter and remain in the air for a long period in the form of

spores or as pathogens .Segregation of waste, pre-treatment at source can reduce this problem to a certain extent. The indoor air pollution caused due to chemicals from poor ventilation can cause diseases like Sick Building Syndrome (SBS). Proper building design and well-maintained air conditioners can reduce the SBS. Chemicals should be utilized as per prescribed norms.

Out-door Air Pollution

Outdoor air pollution can be caused by pathogens. The biomedical waste without pre-treatment when transported outside the institution or dumped in open areas, the pathogens can enter into the atmosphere. Chemical pollutants that cause outdoor air pollution have two major sources-open burning and incinerators.

- Open burning of bio-medical waste is the most harmful practice. When the gases are inhaled it can cause respiratory diseases. The design parameters and maintenance of such treatment and disposal technology should be as per the prescribed standards. (Bdour 2004).

  Radioactive Emissions

Research and radio-immunoassay activities generate small amount of radioactive gas. Gaseous radioactive material should be evacuated directly to the outside. The use of such device requires maintenance of the trapped and monitoring of the off-gas (Malviga 1999).

Water Pollution

The liquid waste generated when let into sewers can lead to water pollution, if not treated properly (Rao, 1995; Rao & Garg, 1994). There are instances where dioxins are reported from water bodies near incinerator plants. Dioxins enter the water body from the air (Chitins *et al*, 2000; Ravikant *et al*, 2002; Saini & Dadhwal 1995)

Radioactive Effluent

Radioactive waste in liquid form can come from chemical or biological research, from body organ imaging, from decontamination of radioactive spills, from patient's urine and from scintillation liquids used in radioimmunoassay. Under normal circumstances, urine and faeces can be handled as no radioactive waste so long as the patient's room is routinely monitored for radioactive contamination (Patil & Pokhrel, 2004; Shah *et al*, 2001).

Land Pollution

Soil pollution from bio-medical waste is caused due to infectious waste, discarded medicines, chemicals used in treatment and ash and other waste generated during treatment processes. Heavy metals such as cadmium, lead, mercury etc.,which are present in the waste will get absorbed by plants and can then enter the food chain. Nitrates and phosphates present in leachates from landfills are also pollutants. Excessive amounts of trace nutrient elements and other elements including heavy metals in soil are harmful to crops and to the animals and human beings (Mehta 1998).

According to WHO (November, 2015):

- 85% of the total waste generated is general and non-hazardous waste.
- Remaining 15% is hazardous material that may be infectious, toxic or radioactive.
- Around 16 billion injections every year are administered worldwide, but not all of the needles and syringes are disposed properly.
- Health-care waste constitutes of harmful pathogens that can infect patients, health workers and the general public. Infectious wastes include items that are contaminated with body fluids such as blood and blood products, used gloves, cultures and stocks of infectious agents, wound dressings, discarded diagnostic samples, swabs, bandages and disposal medical devices.
- Certain wastes are incinerated which produces toxic air pollutants as emissions.

Hospitals, dental clinics, laboratories, research centres, mortuary, autopsy centres, blood banks and collection services are major sources of health-care waste.

High-income countries generate on average up to 0.5 kg of hazardous waste per bed per day; while low-income countries generate on average 0.2 kg. However, health-care waste is often not separated into hazardous or non-hazardous wastes in low-income countries making the real quantity of hazardous waste much higher. (WHO, 2015)

ENVIRONMENTAL IMPACT

Treatment and disposal of healthcare waste indirectly affect the ecosystem balance by releasing of pathogens and toxic pollutants into the environment.

- Improper construction of the landfills can predispose to contamination of drinking water thereby resulting in spread of infectious water-borne diseases.
- Waste handlers are at occupational risks if the disposal facilities are not well designed, run, or maintained.
- Incineration of waste is the most common method exercised for waste disposal. Inadequate incineration or incineration of unsuitable materials results in the release of pollutants into the air and ash residues. Incinerated materials generate dioxins and furans, which are human carcinogens and are associated with a range of adverse health effects. Incineration of heavy metals or materials with high metal content (in particular lead, mercury and cadmium) can lead to the spread of toxic metals in the environment.

  From environmental point of view prevention and recycling of waste reduces greenhouse gases associated with these activities by reducing methane emissions, saving energy, and increasing forest carbon sequestration thereby in turn contributing in prevention of climate change
- Only modern incinerators operating at 850-1100 °C and fitted with special gas-cleaning equipment are able to comply with the international emission standards for dioxins and furans.

HAZARD TO GENERAL PUBLIC

Bio-medical waste adversely affects the general health when proper disposal techniques are not followed. Simply dumping of bio-medical waste in municipal dustbins, open spaces, water bodies etc., leads to the spread of diseases. Emissions from incinerators and open burning leads to exposure to harmful gases containing dixon and furans which can cause cancer and respiratory diseases

INVERTED WASTE PYRAMID FOR SOLID WASTE MANAGEMENT (6)

According to an article by Hari Srinivas, urban solid wastes are managed by a hierarchy where the broad top is landfill (Macrosolution) were waste is least treated causing maximum impact on the environment.

At the narrow botton is waste management at individual level (microsolution), at the source of waste generation which has minimum effect on the environment. Ranging between these two extremes are the other nodes of waste disposal ranging from incineration to recycle and reuse.

This hierarchy of waste disposal is denoted in the form of inverted pyramid.

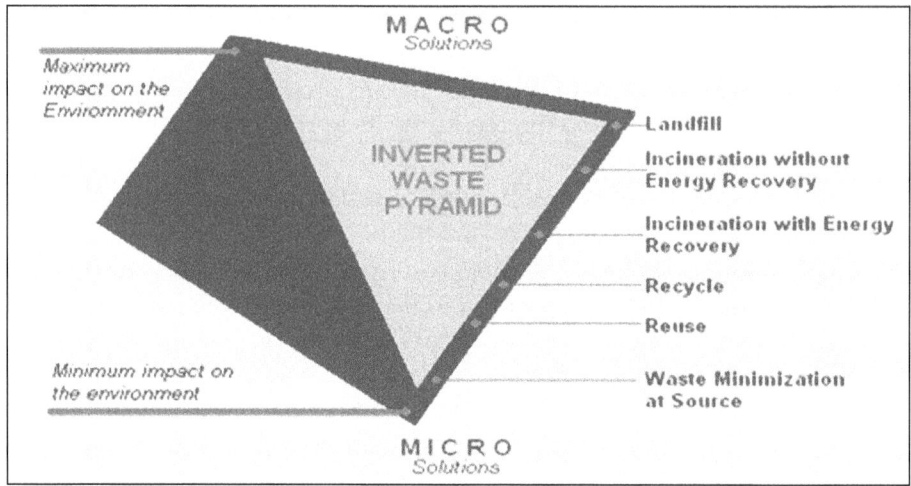

Fig. 8.2: The inverted pyramid of solid waste management *(Hari Srinivas)*

NEED OF BIOMEDICAL/DENTAL WASTE MANAGEMENT

Inadequate BMW management causes environmental pollution, unpleasant smell, growth and multiplication of vectors that may lead to the transmission of diseases ranging from typhoid, cholera, hepatitis to acquired immune deficiency syndrome (AIDS) through injuries(needle prick injury) from contaminated syringes and needles.(3)

It is important to prevent spread of communicable diseases through water and items contaminated with blood, body fluids or contaminated organs. In hospitals, rag pickers who sort out the garbage are at a risk of getting tetanus and human immunodeficiency virus (HIV) infections. The recycling of disposable syringes, needles, intravenous (IV) sets, and other articles like glass bottles without proper sterilization are responsible for hepatitis, HIV, and other viral diseases.

It becomes the primary responsibility of health administrators to manage hospital waste in a safer and eco-friendly manner.(3)

Given below are the reasons which enlist the need for the management of hospital waste:

1. Sharps and materials contaminated with blood and other body fluids generated in dental offices and clinics, if improperly managed, can expose patients, practitioners and waste handlers to cross-transmission of blood-borne pathogens, including hepatitis B, hepatitis C and HIV and other opportunistic pathogens.
2. Nosocomial infections in patients due to poor infection control practices and poor waste management.

3. Risk of infection outside the hospital for waste handlers and scavengers and at times, for the general public living in the vicinity of hospitals.
4. Risks associated with hazardous chemicals and drugs to the persons handling wastes at all levels.
5. "Disposable" being repacked and sold by unscrupulous elements without even being washed.
6. Drugs that have been disposed of, being repacked, and sold off to unsuspecting buyers.
7. The risk of air, water, and soil pollution directly due to waste, or due to defective incineration emissions and ash.(4)

WHAT IS BIOMEDICAL/DENTAL WASTE MANAGEMENT?

Hospital waste management means management of the waste produced by hospitals using techniques that will check the spread of diseases.

In 1998, Biomedical Waste (Management and Handling) Rules were introduced in India to garner the attention of health care professionals, patients and waste handlers towards proper waste disposal techniques.

Objectives of Biomedical/Dental Waste Management:

1. Prevent transmission of disease between various groups of people i.e health care professional, patients and waste handlers.
2. Prevent injury to health care worker those handle the biomedical waste or are in support services that monitor the disposal of waste.
3. In general prevent to cytotoxic and genotoxic effects of biomedical wastes.
4. To establish a well designed and applied waste management system thereby helping in effective and efficient waste disposal
5. Lastly, to establish a well balanced ecosystem by achieving the above mentioned objectives.

BIOMEDICAL WASTE MANAGEMENT PROCESS

The various steps involved in biomedical waste management can be broadly divided into:

1. Handling
2. Segregation
3. Mutilation
4. Disinfection
5. Storage
6. Transportation
7. Final disposal

For effective management and reduction of biomedical waste segregation (separation) and identification of the waste are the vital steps.

The most appropriate way of identifying the categories of biomedical waste is by sorting the waste into colour coded plastic bags or containers.

CATEGORIZATION OF BIOMEDICAL WASTES

Category	Waste Category	Treatment/Disposal
(1)	(2)	(3)
Cat. No. 1	Human Anatomical Waste (human tissues, organs, body parts)	Incineration/deep burial
Cat. No. 2	Animal Waste Animal tissues, organs, Body parts carcasses, bleeding parts, fluid, blood and experimental animals used in research, waste generated by veterinary hospitals/colleges, discharge from hospitals, animal houses)	Incineration/deep burial
Cat. No. 3	Microbiology & Biotechnology waste (wastes from laboratory cultures, stocks or specimens of micro-organisms live or attenuated vaccines, human and animal cell culture used in research and infectious agents from research and industrial laboratories, wastes from production of biological, toxins, dishes and devices used for transfer of cultures)	Local autoclaving/waving/ incineration
Cat. No. 4	Waste Sharps (needles, syringes, scalpels blades, glass etc. that may cause puncture and cuts. This includes both used & unused sharps)	Disinfections (chemical treatment autoclaving/micro waving and mutilation shredding
Cat. No. 5	Discarded Medicines and Cytotoxic drugs (wastes comprising of outdated, contaminated and discarded medicines)	Incineration/destruction & drugs disposal in secured landfills
Cat. No. 6	Soiled Waste (Items contaminated with blood and body fluids including cotton, dressings, soiled plaster casts, line beddings, other material contaminated withblood)	Incineration/autoclaving microwaving
Cat. No. 7	Solid Waste (waste generated from disposable items other than the waste sharps such as tubing, catheters, intravenous sets etc.)	Disinfections by chemical treatment waving & mutilation shredding

(Contd...)

(1)	(2)	(3)
Cat. No. 8	Liquid Waste (waste generated from laboratory & washing, cleaning, house-keeping and disinfecting activities)	Disinfections by chemical treatment and discharge into drain.
Cat. No. 9	Incineration Ash (ash from incineration of any bio-medical waste)	Disposal in municipal landfill
Cat. No. 10	Chemical Waste (chemicals used in production of biological, chemicals, used in disinfect ion, as insecticides, etc.)	Chemical treatment discharge into drain for liquid & secured landfill for solids

Note:
a. There will be no chemical pre-treatment before incineration. Chlorinated plastics shall not be incinerated.
b. Deep burial shall be an option available only in towns with population less than half a million and in rural areas.
c. Chemical treatment using at least one per cent hypochlorite solution or any other equivalent chemical regent. It must be ensured that chemical treatment ensures disinfection.
d. Mutilation/shredding must be such that it prevents unauthorized reuse.

Table 8.1: Color coding and type of container for disposal of bio-medical waste

Color Coding	Type of Container - I Waste Category	Treatment Options as per Categorisation
Yellow	Plastic bag Cat. 1, Cat. 2, and Cat. 3, Cat. 6.	Incineration/deep burial
Red	Disinfected container/plastic bag Cat. 3, Cat.6, Cat.7.	Autoclaving/Microwaving Chemical Treatment
Blue/White Translucent	Plastic bag/puncture proof Cat. 4, Cat. 7.Container	Autoclaving/Microwaving Chemical Treatment and destruction/shredding
Black	Plastic bag Cat. 5 and Cat. 9 and Cat. 10. (solid)	Disposal in secured landfill

Notes:
- Colour coding of waste categories with treatment options as defined in Table 8.1, shall be selected depending on treatment option chosen, which shall are specified in Table 8.1.
- Waste collection bags for waste types needing incineration shall not be made of chlorinated plastics.
- Category 8 do not require containers/bags
- Category 3 if disinfected locally need not be put in Containers/bags.

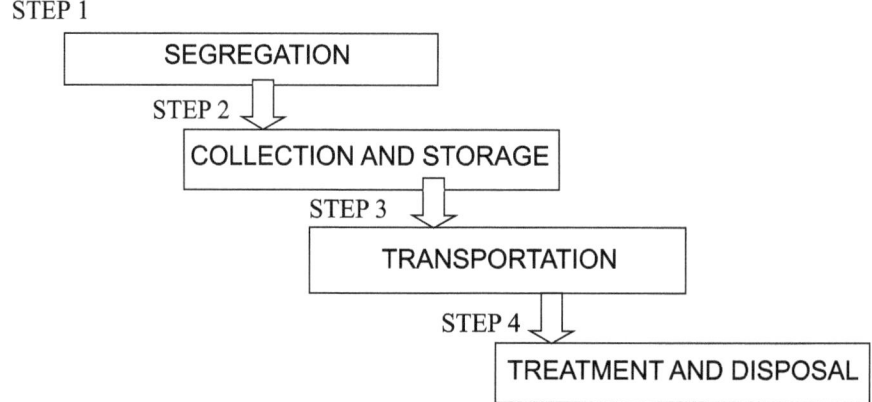

Steps of Biomedical Waste Management

WASTE SEGREGATION

Waste identification is an important tool, but waste segregation becomes the main stay in waste management. According to the above mentioned table waste should be first categorised followed by disposal into the appropriate containers. The use of colour coding and labelling of hazardous waste containers provides great assistance in waste separation.

WASTE ACCUMULATION AND STORAGE

Waste accumulation and storage occurs between the point of waste generation and site of waste treatment and disposal.

- No untreated BMW should be stored beyond 48 hours.
- If necessary to store beyond 48 hours, the authorized person must take permission of the prescribed authority.
- The authorized person should ensure that waste does not adversely affect human health and environment.

WASTE TRANSPORTATION

When medical waste is not treated onsite, the untreated waste must be transported from the generation site to another site for treatment and disposal.

Within the hospital:

- Waste routes should be designated and separate time should be earmarked for BMW to reduce chances of its mixing with general waste.
- Dedicated wheeled trolleys are used and they should be cleaned and disinfected in case of any spillage.
- Trolleys should not have any sharp edges and should be easy to clean.

Outside the hospital:

- BMW shall be transported only in vehicles authorized by competent authority as specified by government.

WASTE TREATMENT

Treatment is mainly required to disinfect or decontaminate the waste, right at the site of generation so that it is no longer hazardous.

WASTE DISPOSAL

The waste disposal methods vary in their capabilities, cost, and impacts on the environment.

The various disposal methods include incineration, autoclaving, chemical methods, thermal methods (low and high), ionizing radiation process, deep burial and microwaving.

BIOMEDICAL/DENTAL WASTE DISINFECTION:

Disinfection of the biomedical waste during its treatment is divided into four levels.

Level 1: Low Level Disinfectants In this level most of the vegetative bacteria, fungi and some viruses become inactive, but micro bacteria and bacterial spores remains active. Therefore a treatment method of this level is considered inadequate.

Level 2: Intermediate Level Disinfectant This type of treatment methods includes inactivating all the micro bacteria, viruses and fungi and vegetative bacteria, although the bacterial spores remains active.

Level 3: High Level Disinfectants At least log and reduction of bacterial spores of either B subtious or B stearothermophilus is included so as to achieve a high level disinfection. A 4log10 reduction is considered equal to about 99.99 percent reduction of bacterial spores.

Level 4: Sterilization This level is achieved by at least 6log reduction in spores of B stearothermophilus.

BIOMEDICAL WASTE MANAGEMENT TECHNIQUES

1. **Autoclaving:** This is a thermal process in which waste comes in direct contact with steam in a controlled manner for disinfecting the waste for a sufficient duration. For easy treatment and for safety during operation, the horizontal system is preferred, specially designed for treatment purpose. According to a research, for effective inactivation of microorganisms and bacterial spores, for a small amount of waste, a 121°C temperature is required for 60 minutes

    Uses: Autoclaving is typically used for sterilizing the reusable medical equipments.

    Limitation: Autoclaves allow treatment for only limited quantities of the waste and release harmful gases.

2. **Microwave Irradiation:** In microwave irradiation method, the inactivation of microbial is done by using the heating effect of electromagnet rays. The frequency of these rays lies between 300 and 300,000 MHz. Most of the microorganisms gets destroyed a frequency of about 2450 MHz.

   Uses: Microwave irradiation method is used for disinfecting a variety of biomedical waste.

   Limitation: It is not used for the treatment of cytotoxic, hazardous or radioactive waste. Contaminated animal caresses, body parts and human organs are also excluded.

3. **Chemical methods:** Chemical disinfecting was previously used to kill microorganisms on medical equipments, but now it is also used for biomedical waste treatment. Chemicals are inactivate or kill pathogens thereby chemical treatment disinfects rather than sterilization. Sodium Hypochlorite, Fenton Reagent, and Hydrogen peroxide are the most commonly used chemicals for this method.

   Uses: Most useful for the treatment of liquid biomedical waste such as urine, blood, stools, or for hospital sewage.

   Limitation: Relatively high capital and operational cost. Also, some microbes may become resistant to some disinfectants.

4. **Solar Disinfection:** This method uses the thermal effect of solar rays for disinfecting the biomedical waste. 7 log reduction in amount of viable bacteria, when a box type solar cooker is used to disinfect the waste.

   Uses: It can be used as a low cost technique for the countries which cannot afford costly treatment methods.

   Limitation: It cannot be used for the treatment of cytotoxic, hazardous or radioactive waste.

BIODENTAL WASTES

A number of hazardous wastes are associated with dentistry which when disposed improperly, can cause harm to the environment. These include chemical solutions, lead foil film backing, mercury, scrap dental amalgam, fluorescent tubes and batteries. If liquid hazardous wastes are discharged into the through the evacuation system into the sewer, they potentially impact the wastewater treatment plant, and/or pass through the treatment plant into various water bodies. Alternatively, if materials are disposed of in the trash, they may eventually contaminate the soil, ground water, or create a public health problem.

Hence it necessitates the need to educate the doctors, dental nurses, paramedical staff and associated members of the hazards and ill effects of Biodental Waste; the "know how" to treat dental Waste and its corresponding disposal attributing to Biodental Waste Management.

OVERVIEW OF MERCURY USED IN DENTISTRY

Around the world dental amalgam is the most commonly used filling material for decayed teeth. Often referred to as "silver fillings" all dental amalgams consist of 45-55% metallic mercury. It is a well suggested fact that mercury is neurotoxin that can cause harm to humans, especially children, pregnant women, and foetuses. Further, the use of dental amalgam results in substantial quantities of toxic mercury released annually into the environment. Once in the environment, mercury pollution damages animals, plants, and the entire ecosystem, while creating "hotspots that last for centuries."

It has been revealed that critical issues for health related safety arises when mercury exists in either liquid or vapour form as it can be absorbed through the alveoli in the lungs at 80% efficiency and through the gastrointestinal tract at efficiencies of 0.01% for elemental, 7% for inorganic and 95 to 98% for organic.

Types of Amalgam Waste Generated at Dental Clinics:

- **Non-contact amalgam (scrap)** is excess mix leftover at the end of a dental procedure.
- **Elemental mercury vapour** is released from dental amalgam alloy
- **Contact amalgam** is amalgam that has been in contact with the patient.
  Example: Extracted teeth with amalgam restorations, carving scrap collected, scrap left on instruments and matrix bands and amalgam captured by chair side traps, filters, or screens.
- **Amalgam separators** that comply with ISO 11 143 capture over 95% of amalgam waste but also trap other treatment debris.
- **Chair side traps** capture amalgam waste during amalgam placement or removal procedures (traps from dental units dedicated strictly to hygiene may be placed in the general waste).
- **Vacuum pump filters** or traps contain amalgam sludge and water.
- **Amalgam sludge** is the mixture of liquid and solid material collected within vacuum pump filters or other amalgam capture devices.
- **Empty amalgam capsules** are the individually dosed containers left over after mixing precapsulated dental amalgam.

WAYS DENTAL AMALGAM POLLUTES THE ENVIRONMENT

1. Wastewater from dental offices

Mercury that is released into the waterlines are dangerous because wastewater treatment facilities are designed to process human waste and not heavy metals. Thus, the mercury from dental discharges is separated out into sludge or biosolids. The sludge is usually incinerated, which releases mercury pollution into the atmosphere, and the biosolids are often used as fertilizer, which contaminates soil with mercury.

2. Human waste

Researchers have shown that amalgam fillings contribute to mercury levels in saliva, urine, and faeces and patients with dental amalgam excrete more than ten times more mercury in their faeces than those without mercury fillings. A study in Sweden in 1994, when researchers suggested that mercury was being released to their country's environment annually as a result of dental mercury excretion in faeces and urine. (15) Considering that dental mercury is released in faeces and urine, and methyl mercury (such as that taken in from fish consumption), is also released in faeces and urine, the impact of human waste containing various forms of mercury is a contributing factor in water pollution.

3. Cremation and burial

A 2013 assessment on mercury from UNEP reported: "Global emissions from use of mercury in dental amalgam resulting from cremation of human remains are estimated at 3.6 (0.9 – 11.9) tonnes in 2010."(16). Cremation of bodies with amalgam fillings adds to air emissions and deposition onto land and into waterways

4. Mercury Vapour

Mercury present in the amalgam is discharged into waste streams via the dental office vacuum-pump system. This system also discharges large quantities of air, either into the atmosphere exterior to the office building or into the sewer system.

WAYS TO COMBAT MERCURY RISKS CAUSED BY DENTAL AMALGAM:

1. Amalgam Separators

Amalgam separators reduce the amount of mercury discharge in wastewater from dental offices. Amalgam separators are devices designed to capture amalgam particles from dental office wastewater through sedimentation, filtration, centrifugation, or a combination of these mechanisms. Some separators may also use ion exchange technology to remove mercury from wastewater.

It should also be remembered that amalgam separators only contribute to solving the problem of dental mercury in wastewater and not the additional burdens placed by amalgam fillings on the environment and human health.

2. Alternatives to Amalgam as a Filling Material

Alternatives to amalgam include composite resin, glass ionomer, porcelain, and gold, among other options. Most consumers choose direct composite fillings because the white coloring matches the tooth better and the cost is considered moderate.

3. Safe Removal of Existing Amalgam Fillings

Unsafe amalgam removal process releases mercury vapour and particles that can be harmful to the patient, the dentist, the dental staff, and the environment.

IAOMT has developed new safety recommendations Safe Mercury Amalgam Removal Technique (SMART) for removal of existing dental mercury amalgam fillings. It includes use of masks, water irrigation, and high volume suction by supplementing these conventional strategies with a number of additional protective measures.

4. Educating Dentists

Some dentists have already stopped using amalgam; while others require training in mercury-free dentistry [dentistry that does not place any new mercury amalgam fillings]. Since some countries have banned or drastically reduced the use of dental mercury, their dental schools shed light upon how to make a successful transition away from amalgam.

Elemental Mercury Waste Management:
- Unused elemental mercury should be stored in tightly sealed container.
- Certified waste carrier should be contacted for recycling or disposal.
- "Mercury spill kit" should be used if you have a spill of elemental mercury.
- Reacting unused elemental mercury with silver alloy to form scrap amalgam.
- Donot place elemental mercury in the garbageand also elemental mercury should not be washed down the drain.

Scrap Amalgam Management: (17)
- MercontainerTM (Sponge type) is appropriate to store the scrap amalgam. Empty amalgam capsules can be disposed in the garbage due to non-hazardous in nature.
- Using an ISO 11143 compliant amalgam separator on the suction lines is suitable for removing over 95% of the contact amalgam before diffusing in the sewer system.
- Disposable suction traps on your dental units should be changed weekly. Always use gloves, mask, and glasses while cleaning the suction traps. Disposable trap should be placed into a properly labelled container of Merconvap TM solution for proper disposal. After filling it, a certified waste carrier should be contacted for recycling or disposal of it.

Amalgam Capsules Management:
- Different sizes of amalgam capsules should be stored.

- Empty amalgam capsules as well as capsules that cannot be emptied should be placed in a wide mouth airtight container that is marker "Amalgam Capsule Waste for Recycling"
- The container lid should be tightly sealed and sent for recycling once when filled.

LINE CLEANERS

Non bleach non chlorine containing line cleaners will minimize amalgam dissolution.

Best Management Practices for Amalgam Waste

Do	Don't
Do use precapsulated allows and stock a variety of capsule sizes	Don't use bulk mercury
Do recyle used disposable amalgam capsules	Don't put used disposable amalgam capsules in biohazard containers, infectious waste containers (red bags) or regular garbage
Do salvage, store and recycle non-contact amalgam (scrap amalgam)	Don't put non-contact amalgam waste in biohazard containers, infectious waste containers (red bags) or regular garbage
Do salvage (contact) amalgam pieces from restorations after removal and recyle the amalgam waste	Don't put contact amalgam waste in biohazard containers, infectious waste containers (red bags) or regular garbage
Do use chair-side traps, vacuum pump filters and amalgam separators to retain amalgam and recyele their contents	Don't rinse devices containing amalgam over drains or sinks
Do recycle teeth that contain amalgam restorations. (Note: Ask your recycler whether or not extracted teeth with amalgam restorations require disinfection)	Don't dispose of extracted teech that contain amalgam restorations in biohazard containers, infectious waste containers (red bags), sharps containers or regular garbage.
Do manage amalgam waste through recycling as much as possible	Don't flush amalgam waste down to drain or toilet
Do use line cleaners that minimize dissolution of amalgam	Don't use bleach or chlorine–containing cleaners to flush wastewater lines

American Dental Association. Best management practices for amalgam waste. October 2007.

SILVER CONTAINING DENTAL WASTES

Silver is another heavy metal that can enter water system via improper disposal of dental office waste. Silver is a component of dental amalgam as well as present in the form of silver thiosulfate in radiographic fixer (a solution normally used in the processing of dental radiographs) presents a greater environmental concern. Some forms of silver are more toxic than others; for example, silver thiosulfate is less toxic than free silver ions.

Used radiographic fixer must not be washed down the drain. The best way to manage silver waste is through recovery and recycling.

Undeveloped X-ray films contain a high level of silver and must be treated as hazardous waste. Unused films should be accumulated in an approved container for recycling by the disposal company.

Minimize film purchase by using a digital x-ray unit.

Dentists can install in-house silver recovery units to salvage the silver themselves.

Lead-containing Wastes:
- The lead foil inside X-ray packets and lead aprons contain toxin that can result in contamination of soil and groundwater in landfill areas after disposal.
- Lead foils can be managed by collecting lead foil packets in a marked container, once container is full, a certified waste carrier should dispose it off for recycling .lead foil packets should not be thrown into the regular garbage.
- Unwanted lead aprons should be disposed of by certified waste carrier.

BIOMEDICAL WASTES IN DENTAL OFFICE

It includes blood-soaked gauze, tissues and syringes but not extracted teeth. Non-sharp biomedical waste products should be stored in a yellow bag labelled with a biohazard symbol. Sharps (i.e., syringes, suture needles) should not be included in the bagged general or biomedical waste, but should be stored in a puncture-resistant, leak-proof, properly labelled container until collection and incineration.

MUTILATION

Mutilation should be strictly practiced; it is recommended for disposable needles and other sharp wastes. Mutilated needles and other sharp wastes may be kept in puncture proof containers with 1% Sodium Hypochlorite solution for primary disinfection and after every 2 days the solution should be changed.

CHEMICALS, DISINFECTANTS, AND STERILIZING AGENTS

Staff should be trained in Workplace Hazardous Materials Information System (WHMIS) for the handling of materials. Steam or dry heat can be use to sterilize dental instruments, whenever it's possible.

Non-chlorinated plastic containers (not PVC) should be preferred to decrease environmental impacts and placed in the solid waste stream.

Halogenated sterilants have a detrimental effect on environment.

Ignitable sterilants should not be poured down the drain as they have potency to explode.

HCHO sterilants should also not be disposed down the drain.

Directly pouring of sterilant into a septic system may significantly disrupt the bacteria which normally breakdown wastes.(18)

GENERAL OFFICE WASTE

This review attempts to focus on the larger issues relating to the environmental impact of dentistry, dental staff can also implement a variety of other practices to make the dental office more environmental friendly. Purchase of products with minimal packaging and use of reusable plastic containers (e.g., for cleaning and disinfecting solutions) can reduce general waste production.

Products made from recycled or partly recycled materials can also be used e.g., cotton rolls, paper towels.

Energy-efficient lighting and temperature regulation can limit office energy use.

Single-spaced printing and use of both sides of pages can decrease the amount of paper used in the dental office.

Various components of a bio medical dental waste management protocol[20]

Steps to be followed for thorough dental BMW management:

- Identify the applicable regulations, accreditation standards, and guidelines in the dentist's country, state and municipality for the management of biomedical waste
- Based on central, state and local regulations, dentists or health care facilities should develop protocols for biomedical waste management that address the following aspects, if applicable
- Definition of dental waste
- Identification of dental waste
- Identification of materials that can be recycled
- Segregation of dental waste from other waste
- Segregation of materials that can be recycled
- Containerization as per appropriate guidelines
- Labelling when needed
- Storage
- Transportation
- Recycling
- Disposal
- Education
- Record keeping
- Develop and conduct an educational program for dental staff
- Educate patients involved in home health care/dental care about appropriate disposal of bio hazardous waste
- Verify appropriate implementation of the program
- Regularly evaluate the program and update if required

The proposed simplified biomedical waste segregation scheme for dental clinics

Red Bag	Yellow Bag	Blue Bag	Black Bag
Disposable Injection syringes, IV set without needle Saline bottles Plastic suction tips Toothbrushes, denture brushes Disposable plastic/fiber instruments Plastic/rubber tubes Rubber lids of any vial Used plastic drapes.	Anything contaminated by blood or body fluids Body parts Any item which have been in contact with the patient Bandages, cottonTeeth (with/without fillings but without amalgam fillings) Dressings and swabs Disposables such as gloves, aprons, masks, drapes, contaminated wipes, throat packs Discarded crowns, bridges and cast partial dentures Waxes, gutta purcha points, absorbent points Disposable impression trays with impression material Acrylic partial dentures, complete dentures, denture teeth Plaster/stone casts Cheek retractors, tongue depressors, wedges Rubber dam material Plastic X ray pouches (outer covering) Catheters (after draining) Unwanted laboratory specimens Suture materials without needle.	Glass bottlesBroken glass Discarded medicines Antiseptics, disinfectants (not contaminated by body fluids) Used or unused drug vials Cartridges and ampoules.	Used or unused sharps Needles without syringes Scalpel blades Metal objects Metal matrix bands Broken metal instrument tips Burs Endodontic files, broaches, reamers, spreaders, silver points Orthodontic metal brackets, wires,bands Suture needles Broken/discarded ultrasonic tips Metallic bars, clasps from partial dentures Metal lids of vials All metallic dental implants related material Xray.

Clinical Relevance to General Dentistry:
- Dental practices/hospitals produce a lot of biomedical waste (BMW)
- There are no specific guidelines for management of BMW in dental settings
- The nature of BMW generated in dental practices is somewhat different as compared to that of medical settings
- There is a grave need for educating dentists as well as access to BMW services

NEWER METHODOLOGIES TO DISPOSE BIOMEDICAL WASTES: (8)

Emerging technologies include plasma pyrolysis, alkaline hydrolysis, superheated steam, ozone and promession.

Plasma pyrolysis

An ionised gas in the plasma state is used to convert electrical energy to temperatures of several thousand degrees using plasma torches or electrodes with minimal or no air. It is used to break down pathological waste, infectious, plastic, hazardous chemical or pharmaceutical wastes. It is safe, eco-friendly, has energy recovery and has negligible harmful emissions of dioxins and furans. Production of clean alloyed slag which could be used in construction material and value added products such as metals. Its disadvantages include large initial investment costs, carbon dioxide pollution, large electrical energy input, and highly corrosive plasma flame leading to frequent maintenance.

Ozone (O_3) can be used for especially pharmaceutical waste, water and air treatment. It is a strong oxidizer and breaks down to a more stable form (O_2). Ozone systems require shredders and mixers to expose the waste to the bactericidal agent. Regular tests should be conducted to ensure that the microbial inactivation standard is met.

Promession

It includes freeze-drying using liquid nitrogen and mechanical vibration to disintegrate cadavers into powder before burial. The process speeds up decomposition, reduces both mass and volume and allows the recovery of metal parts.

Alkaline hydrolysis

It is a process that converts body parts, specimens and cadavers into a decontaminated aqueous solution and destroys fixatives, hazardous chemicals and waste contaminated by prion. After the waste is loaded in the basket and into the hermetically sealed tank, alkali is added along with water at temperature of 127°C or higher and stirred. After digestion time of 6-8 h, by-products include mineral constituents of bones and teeth, solution of amino acids, sugars, soaps and salts. It can also destroy chemotherapeutic or cytotoxic agents and aldehydes (such as formaldehyde and glutaraldehyde)

Nanotechnology

It is used to cleanse environmental air to improve indoor quality air and includes a photo catalyst with wide spectrum of light and is bactericidal and fungicidal. It utilises the energy from light to generate hydroxyl species and superoxide anion (O_2^-) which decompose and oxidise toxic pollutants to carbon dioxide and water.

Photocatalysis

It is a novel technology for disinfection and decontamination of hospital waste water which utilises solar energy or ultraviolet rays to disinfect microbes and decontaminate antibiotic from waste water at the point of origin. It is efficient and affordable technology.

Membrane bioreactors

It combines the biological-activated sludge process with a membrane filtration step for sludge water separation. Various types of membrane bioreactor (MBRs) are available such as aerobic MBR, anaerobic MBR, organic pollutant MBR.

Other emerging technologies for destruction of BMW include gas-phase chemical reduction, base-catalysed decomposition, supercritical water oxidation, sodium reduction, verification, superheated steam reforming, Fe-TAML/peroxide treatment (pharmaceutical waste), biodegradation (using mealworm or bacteria to eat plastics), mechanochemical treatment, sonic technology, electrochemical technologies, solvated electron technology and phytotechnology. These emerging technologies are not ready for routine application to health-care waste

CONCLUSION

As dental practitioners, we must recognize that some of the materials and procedures we use to provide dental health services may present challenges to the environment. Realizing this, we can begin to take measures to minimize the production of these wastes and their potential environmental effects. As health practitioners, we should be concerned with promoting not only human health and well-being but also that of the environment.

A proactive approach will allow our profession to succeed in an era of increased public environmental concern and environmentally protective legislation. It is not only our legal obligation to provide dental services that benefit the public at minimal expense to the environment, but also our moral and ethical obligation.

REFERENCES

1. Agarwal B, Kumar M, Agarwal S, Singh A, Shekhar A. Bio Medical Waste and Dentistry. Journal of Oral Health and Community Dentistry 2011;5(3): 153-5.
2. Thirumala S. Study of Bio-medical Waste Generation and Management in Various Hospitals in Davangere City of Karnataka, India. Nitte University Journal of Health Science. 2013; 3(3): 22-4.

3. Ministry of Environment and Forests Notification New Delhi, 20th July, 1998.
4. Hari Srinivas-The Inverted Pyramid of Solid Waste Management- (http://www.gdrc.org/uem/waste/inverted-pyramid.html)
5. Published In The Gazette Of India, Extraordinary, Part II, Section 3, Sub-Section (I)] Government of India Ministry of Environment, Forest and Climate Change Notification, New Delhi, The 28th March, 2016.
6. Harender Singh[1], Dj Bhaskar[2], Deepak R Dalai[3], Rahila Rehman[4], Mohsin Khan[5] Dental Biomedical Waste Management.
7. Acharya DB, Singh M. The Book of Hospital Waste Management. Minerva Press, New Delhi, 2000; 15: 47-48.
8. Malini R Capoor[1], Kumar Tapas Bhowmik[2] Current Perspectives on Biomedical Waste Management: Rules, Conventions and Treatment Technologies.
9. Kirti Mishra[1], Anurag Sharma[2], Sarita[1], Shahnaz Ayub[2] A Study: Biomedical Waste Management in India.
10. S Manasi K S Umamani N Latha Biomedical Waste Management: Issues and Concerns - A Ward Level Study of Bangalore City.
11. Harikaranahalli Puttaiah- Harikaranahalli Puttaiah-Shivaraju Shivaraju[1], Behzad Shahmoradi[2] Healthcare Waste Management and Practices: A Case Study in Kodagu District, Karnataka, India.
12. Management of Biomedical Waste in India and other Countries: A Review.
13. B. Ramesh Babu*, A.K. Parande, R. Rajalakshmi, P. Suriyakala, M. Volga. Central Electrochemical Research Institute, Karaikudi - 630 006, Tamilnadu, India. Received July 29, 2008; Accepted March 16, 2009.
14. Kao RT, Dault S, Pichay T. Understanding the Mercury Reduction Issue: The Impact of Mercury on the Environment and Human Health. *J Calif Dent Assoc.* 2004; 32(7): 574-79.
15. A Comprehensive Review of the Toxic Effects of Mercury in Dental Amalgam Fillings on the Environment and Human Health The International Academy of Oral Medicine and Toxicology (www.iaomt.org) 2016 update.
16. Hiltz M[1]. The Environmental Impact of Dentistry- J Can Dent Assoc. 2007 Feb; 73(1): 59-62.
17. Bhaskar Agarwal[1], Mohit Kumar[2], Srishti Agarwal[3], Ajay Singh[4], Abhinav Shekhar[5] Bio Medical Waste and Dentistry; Johcd.org,September 2011; 5(3)(153-155)
18. Palanisamy Pasupathi*, Sivaraman Sindhu, Babu Shankar Ponnusha, Athimoolam Ambika Biomedical Waste Management for Health Care Industry Int J Biol Med Res. 2011; 2(1): 472-486.
19. B. Ramesh Babu*, A.K. Parande, R. Rajalakshmi, P. Suriyakala, M. Volga Management of Biomedical Waste in India and other Countries: A Review J. Int. Environmental Application & Science, Vol. 4 (1): 65-78 (2009).
20. Widmer AF, Frei R. Decontamination, Disinfection, Sterilization. In: Versalovic J, Carroll KC, Funke G, Jorgensen JH, Landry ML, Warnock DW, Editors. Manual of Clinical Microbiology. 10th ed., Wahington DC, USA: ASM Press; 2011. p. 143-73.
21. Rutala WA, Weber DJ and the Healthcare Infection Control Practices Advisory Committee (HICPAC). Guideline for Disinfection and Sterilization in Healthcare Facilities. Atlanta: Centres for Disease Control; 2008.
22. American Dental Association. Best Management Practices for Amalgam Waste. October 2007.

Pages: 185-212

Eco-tourism, Environmental Problems and Sustainable Development
Edited by: Dr. Soubam Premchandra Singh; Dr. Ashok K. Rathoure
Dr. Pawan Kumar 'Bharti'
ISBN: 978-93-86841-57-5
Edition: 2018
Published by: Discovery Publishing House Pvt. Ltd., New Delhi (India)

Photo Degradation of Surfactants towards Pollution Free Society and Environment

Dr. Swati Sharma
Dr. Rashmi Sharma
Dr. Arun Kumar Sharma

ABSTRACT

Photocatalysis has attracted the attention of scientific community all over the world due to its multifarious applications in various fields like energy, environment, technology, waste water treatment, pollution control etc. by large number of publication of papers and reviews in last three decades.

Exact information about Photodegradation of the Copper (II) Soaps plays a vital role in its selection in specific phenomena such as foaming, wetting, detergency, emulsification etc and also in their use as herbicides, fungicides, pesticides and insecticides. The work will provide significant information towards green & safe chemistry.

It is the prime objective of environmental education to make people aware about the importance of protection and conservation of our environment because indiscriminate release of various pollutants such as surfactants in the environment has created a new facet in the environment pollution.

Photodegradation has been considered in many reaction of biological, synthetic and industrial importance where energy received from sun can be better utilized for converting the pollutants into less toxic or almost harmless materials.

Department of Chemistry, S.P.C. Govt. College Ajmer - 305 001 Rajasthan (India)

The Present Work Highlights:

1. Synthesis of Copper (II) soaps derived from Saturated fatty acids i.e. Stearic and Palmitic acid, Edible Oils i.e. Mustard and Soyabean oil and Non-edible oils i.e. Neem and Karanj.
2. Spectral Studies (IR and NMR) have been carried out to understand the structure insight of the Copper (II) soaps.
3. Photocatalytic Degradation of Copper (II) soaps of saturated fatty acids, Edible and Non-edible oil was carried out in the presence of semiconductor (ZnO).
4. Photocatalytic Degradation of Copper (II) Soaps was studied Spectrophotometrically in non aqueous and non polar solvent Benzene. The effect of various parameters such as concentration of soap, amount of semiconductor, effect of light intensity & the effect of polarity of solvent (methanol) on the rate of photocatalytic degradation have been observed.

INTRODUCTION

There are a number of methods to control the environmental pollution, but photochemical reactions played a very important role for the treatment of pollutants. It is the prime objective of environment education to make people aware about the importance of protection and conservation of our environment because indiscriminate release of various pollutants in the environment leads to serious health hazards[1]. Photochemistry plays a significant role in many reactions of biological, synthetic and industrial importance in which energy received from sun can be better utilized for converting the pollutants into less toxic materials[2].

As we all are aware that photosynthesis is a natural photochemical reaction has been known since prehistoric time, which utilizes a part of solar energy input on this planet. This photochemical reaction consumes a very little amount (0.023%) of solar insolation and even then, it is enough to feed the whole world as far as fuels, food grains and other edible material are concerned. The process of photosynthesis keeps a control on increasing amount of CO_2 in the atmosphere thus keeping the global warming under control.

A kind of pollution, which has emerged in last few years, is the surfactant or detergent pollution. As it is a well known fact that detergent do not prefer biodegradable pathways and on the other hand, the chemical degradation of the surfactant will add a new member in the list of existing types of pollution[3]. Thus photocatalytic technique may prove to be faster and more economical than the traditional techniques of treating these types of pollutants. The importance of these types of research is increasing recently and has become a subject of major public health concern and scientific interest.

PHOTOCATALYSIS PHENOMENON

In ancient time, sun was the only natural source of energy. In due course of time, the nature developed perfection in utilizing light energy for driving some photochemical reactions and thus provided a way for the self-propagation of life. Photocatalyst is defined as a species, which induces some photochemical reactions and the term photocatalysis is used for those chemical reaction which occurs in the presence of light and a photocatalyst. In this type of chemical reaction, an electron-hole pair is generated on exposing a photocatalyst to light. This electron can be used for reducing a substrate whereas the hole may be utilized for oxidation[4].

A photocatalyst is basically a semiconductor. The energy difference between the conduction band (Lowest Unoccupied Molecular Orbital, LUMO) and valence band (Highest Occupied Molecular Orbital, HOMO) is called a band gap. This shown in figure 9.1.

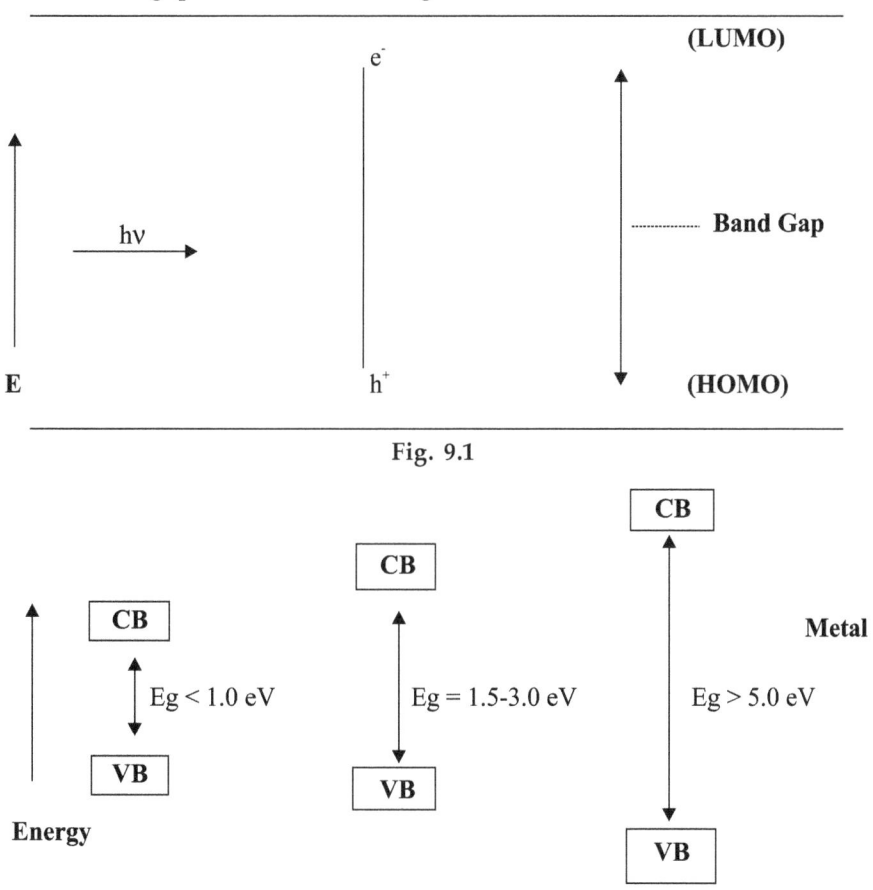

Fig. 9.1

Fig. 9.2

On the basis of the band gap (Eg), Insulators, Conductors and Semiconductors are defined[4] as follow figure 9.2.

Insulator: When the energy gap between the conduction band and valence band is larger enough [Eg> 5.0eV], there is negligible or no flow of electrons, than the material is called an insulator.

Conductor: When the energy gap between the conduction band and valence band is much less [Eg< 1.0 eV], there is a smooth flow of electron from the valence band to the conduction band, even under ordinary Conditions. Such a substance is known as conductor e.g. metals.

Semiconductor: Semiconductors on the other hand have a band gap of medium order [Eg = 1.5-3.0 eV]. They show conducting behavior only under certain specified conditions like exposure to light or at elevated temperature etc.

In order for photocatalysis to proceed, the semiconductor should absorb energy equal to or more than its band gap. The importance of photocatalysis lies in the fact that by choosing a photocatalyst (semiconductor) of desired band gap, one can drive the reaction in the desired direction, as photocatalyst provides oxidation as well as reduction environment simultaneously.

The band gaps of various semiconductors[4] are given in table 9.1.

Table 9.1: Band gaps of different semiconductors

Semiconductor	Band gap (eV at 300K)
ZnS (Wurtzite)	3.91
ZnS (Zinc Blende)	3.54
SiO_2	3.60
TiO_2	3.20
ZnO	3.03
CdS	2.42
Fe_2O_3	2.20
CdO	2.10

PHOTOCATALYTIC REACTIONS

The chemical reactions that occur in the presence of semiconductor and light are collectively termed as photocatalytic reactions. The photocatalytic reactions can be classified into two categories:

Homogeneous Photocatalysis

If both, the semiconductor and the reactant are in the same phases and then such reactions are named as homogeneous photocatalysis.

Heterogeneous Photocatalysis

If the reactant and semiconductor both are in different phases, then such reactions are termed as heterogeneous photocatalytic reactions.

Photochemistry using semiconductor nanoclusters is involved in a group of waste treatment methods called Advanced Oxidation Processes (AOPs) such as photofenton, photocatalysis and sonolysis. Extensive research in photocatalysis resulted in various applications based on the use of semiconductors. Zinc Oxide is an attractive semiconductor for numerous applications[5] because of its hardness, chemical stability, optical transparency, large excitation energy and piezoelectric properties. Mansilla and Villasnov[6] investigated photodegradation of kraft – black liquor using platinum-impregnated ZnO and reported complete discoloration after 60 min U.V. irradiation. Photocatalytic reactions of xylidineponceau on semiconducting zinc oxide powder were reported by Sharma et al[7]. It has been reported that ZnO shows better activity than TiO_2 in the photodegradation of some dyes in aqueous solutions since it can absorb more light quanta[8]. Use of ZnO in photobleaching of brilliant green and iron (II) oxide in photobleaching of some dyes (malachite green, crystal violet and methylene blue), have been reported by Ameta et al[9-10]. However, ZnO undergoes photocorrosion under U.V. light illumination, which results in a decrease of its photocatalytic activity in aqueous media [11-12].

Photocatalytic degradation of textile dyeing waste water using TiO_2 and ZnO has been reported by Hussein et al[13]. Photobleaching of rose bengal has been studied by Sharma et al[14]. The Photocatalytic degradation of $CHCl_3$, $CHBr_3$, CCl_4 and CCl_3COOH was investigated by Choi and Hoffmann[15] in aqueous TiO_2 suspension. Munoz et al[16] reported that the oxygen was produced under U.V. light in the aqueous suspension of ZnO Containing Hg (II), Ag(I) and CrO_4^{-2} ions. The reduction of Cu (II) ions in aqueous suspension of ZnO under U.V. illumination was investigated by Domenech and Prieto[17]. Hema et al[18] studied the ZnO catalyzed photooxidation of aniline by molecular oxygen and final product was identified as azobenzene.

Dodd et al[19] synthesized nanosized ZnO particles by mechanical milling, heat treatment and washing. It was observed that the photocatalytic activity was maximum, when particle size was around 33nm, may be due to an increase in the charge carriers recombination rate. Sirtori etal[20] studied the photocatalytic degradation of aqueous solution of camphor using TiO_2 and ZnO Photocatalysts.

The oxidation of organic substrates like Isopropanol[21], Phenol[22], Acetanilides[23], etc. over ZnO was also studied. Yanagida[24] et al used nanocrystallineZnS for photooxidation of organic compounds. Chakrabarti and Dutta[25] used ZnO for photodegradation of methylene blue and Eyosin Y. A reduction in Chemical Oxygen Demand (COD) and removal of colour was achieved in this Case. The degradation of salicylic acid, aniline and ethanol of using TiO_2 was investigated by Kawaguchi[26]. Chung et al[27] studied the photochemistry of methanol adsorbed on powdered TiO_2. The photocatalytic activity of commercial ZnO powder has been studied by Sakthivel et al[28] and the results were compared with TiO_2.

Photodegradation of orange-G over ZnO in presence of surfactant was studied by Ameta et al[29]. Photooxidation of acetic acid by oxygen in presence of TiO_2 and dissolved copper ions has been investigated by Bideau et al[30]. Park and Kim[31] reported the photocatalyticdecomposition of carboxylic acid derivatives in presence of semiconductors, whereas Miyoshi et al[32] have studied the light induced decomposition of saturated carboxylic acid on iron oxide incorporated clay suspended in aqueous solution. Gulati etal[33] used ZnO particulate system in photo bleaching of toludine blue.

Carson and Mayo[34] observed the oxidation of 1, 2 diphenylcyclopropane on illuminated ZnO in the presence of air. Conley et al[35] demonstrated direct assembly and integration of ZnO nanobridges into working device on silica over insulator substrates. Ye et al[36] reported synthesis of ZnO nanoplatelets as thin as 10nm, which shows higher efficiency in photodegradation of dyes than ZnO nanorods. Kosanic[37] studied photodegradation of of oxalic acid in the presence of O_2 over TiO_2 powder dispersed in aqueous solution. Photocatalytic process using TiO_2 and coupled semiconductor in the photodegradation reaction of 4-chlorophenol was investigated by Lo et al[38]. Photoelectrochemical reduction of cupric ions under U.V. light irradiation in $CuSO_4$, methanol and TiO_2 system has been investigated by Wang and Van[39]. Hidaka[40] studied the photodegradation of surfactants over the semiconductor.

Sirtori et al[41] studied heterogeneous photocatalytic degradation of aqueous solution of camphor using TiO_2 and ZnO photocatalysts in the presence of U.V. light. Koca and Sachin[42] reported the photocatalytic hydrogen production by direct sunlight from sulfite/sulfide solution using CdS/ZnS. Khodja et al[43] reported that the degradation of 2- phenyl phenol (used as fungicide) can be catalyzed by TiO_2 and ZnO.

The visible light induced photodegradation of organic pollutants on dye adsorbed TiO_2 surface was investigated by Chatterjee and Mehta[44]. Karunakaran et al[45] used TiO_2 as a photocatalyst for oxidation of aniline. Parakh et al[46] reported photocatalytic oxidation of sulphite to sulphate ions over CdS. Dong et al[47] studied the fabrication and characterization of ZnS hollow nanoclusters in micelle system. A large shift in U.V.-Visible spectrum suggests that the hollow nanoclusters have quantum confinement effect. Li and Haneda[48] synthesized ZnO powder with different morphologies by alkali precipitation, organo-zinc hydrolysis and spray pyrolysis.

A direct evidence for the participation of extrinsic surface sites in the enhancement of photocatalytic activity of luminescent ZnS catalyst was reported Anpo et al[49]. CdS (as a sensitizer) is highly efficient for the photocleavage of water[50, 51] due to the tendency of CdS to undergo photoanodic corrosion.

Photochemical and photocatalytic degradation of an azo dye in an aqueous solution by U.V. irradiation was reported by Dasilva and Faria[52], whereas Senthikumar[53] reported photodegradation of a textile dye catalyzed by sol-gel derived nanocrystalline TiO_2 via ultrasonic irradiation. Banerjee et al[54] proposed a smart technique for fabrication over ZnO. Gehlot et al[55] observed interaction of methyl orange with cationic micelles and its effect on photochemistry of dye. Rao et al[56] carried out the photocatalytic degradation of crystal violet over semiconducting ZnO powder suspended in aqueous solution. Navarro et al[57] used ZnO as a catalyst for the production of hydrogen by the partial oxidation of methanol. Some experiments on the sensitization of ZnO by means of electrochemical cell technique were carried out by Hauffe et al[58].

Zinc oxide was prepared by homogeneous hydrolysis with thioacetamide. Its photocatalytic activity and destruction of warfare agent was studied by Houskova et al[59]. Pauporte and Rathousaky[60] used electrodeposited mesoporous ZnO thin films an efficient photocatalyst for the degradation of dye pollutants. Photocatalytic oxidation of alcohols over CdS was studied by Jain et al[61]. Baxi et al[62] used iron (III) oxide as photocatalyst for oxidation of adipic acid.

Kinetic studies on degradation of the oxirane ring of epoxidisedkaranj oil have been observed by Goud et al[63]. Vora et al[64] used ZnO to observe degradation kinetics of 2, 4- dinitroaniline. Enhanced photodegradation of methylene blue using $ZnFe_2O_4$/MWCNT composite synthesized by hydrothermal method was studied by Singhal et al[65]. Photodegradation of phenol by Advanced Oxidation Process under U.V. irradiation using TiO_2 was studied by Nickeslat et al[66]. Verma et al[67] reported the photodegradation of azo dye acid red-18 (ponceau 4R) using methylene blue immobilized resin dawex-11. A comparison of TiO_2 with periwinkle and snail shell's powder as photocatalyst by the photocatalytic degradation of chlorobenzene in aqueous solution was investigated recently by Oghenejoboh et al[68].Photodegradation of paracetamol using degussa TiO_2 was studied by Desale et al[69]. Aliabadi and Abyar[70] used titanium dioxide net for the degradation of acrylonitrile.

Ramazol red was degraded in presence of ZnO photocatalyst by Sivakumar et al[71]. Xie et al[72] observed photoassisted degradation of dyes in the presence of Fe^{III} and H_2O_2 under visible light. Photocatalytic mineralization of methylene blue using buoyant TiO_2 coated polystyrene beads has been studied by Fabiyi and Shelton[73]. The photocatalytic removal of bacterial pollutants from drinking water was carried out by Dunlop et al[74] while Sokmen and Ozkan[75] investigated the effect of inorganic anion on the photocatalytic discoloration of textile waste water with modified titania. Doong et al[76] coupled CdS with TiO_2 for 2-chloro phenol degradation under U.V. irradiation. In their study both CdS and TiO_2 could be exited. The combination of the 2 semiconductors showed better charge separation. Keller and Garin[77] observed that photocatalytic oxidation of methyl ethyl ketone (MEK) were increased by coupling TiO_2 and WO_3 and SiC.

Photocatalytic oxidation of 2-propanol over CdS was investigated by Green and Rudhan[78]. Davis and Huang[79] observed the effect of CdS characteristics on the photocatalytic oxidation of thioacetamide. Photocatalytic oxidation of ethanol was reported by Jain et al[80] and Belouson et al[81]. Yamagata et al[82] observed the photocatalytic degradation of alcohols on TiO_2.

Ameta et al[83] have extensively reviewed the field of photocatalytic reactions. One electron reduction of organic dyes such as thiazine, oxazine, squaraine and methyl orange as well as viologen and fullerene have also been carried out in presence of various colloidal semiconductors[84].

Nefedov[85] observed the possible use of photocatalytic materials for phonogram and sound track recording. Photocatalysis has also been used for degradation of pesticides like atrazine[86] and as a bactericide for spectrococci[87] while Nehra et al[88] made use of irradiated titania semiconductor photocatalyst slurries in aqueous media for photooxidative degradation of the pesticide permethrin.

Photocatalysis provides a promising solution to the problem to release of wide ranging volatile organic compounds, many of which pose hazardous environmental threats[89-90].

AN OVERVIEW OF NATURAL FATS AND OILS

Oils and fats are invaluable for human dietary regimen. They are not only a concentrated source of energy but also sources of essential fatty acids which in turn act as building blocks for fats and oils. The edible vegetable oils are a rich source of fatty acids which have diverse application in various fields of industries like textiles, paints, cosmetics, food and pharmaceuticals both in their natural form and derivatives.

Natural fats are mixtures of mixed glycosides in which the three fatty acids etherifying glycerol differ from each other[91-96]. The available analysis of natural fats is usually based on an analysis of fatty acids rather than the actual mixed glycerides, which occur in the natural products. A complete description of a fatty acid molecule most include the length of their carbon chain, the number of double bonds and also the exact position of double bonds.

The simplest fatty acids are referred to as saturated fatty acids. They have no unsaturated linkage and cannot be altered by hydrogenation or halogenation. When double bonds were present, fatty acids are said to be unsaturated – monounsaturated (MUFA) if only one double bond is present, and polyunsaturated (PUFA) if they have two or more double bonds, generally separated by a single methylene group.

Non-edible Oils

The Neem tree is a member of Mahogany family, meliaceae, it is today known by the botanical name *AzadirachtaIndica*. Multitude of uses and remedies include all the parts of the Neem tree[96-97].

The Neem Oil is a major non wood product of Neem. The oil is greenish yellow to brown in color with fixed acrid bitter taste having disagreeable odour. The oil contains 0.427 percent sulphur. The quantity of sulphur is reduced to 0.109 percent if the oil is agitated with alcohol.

The oil is used in skin diseases, ulcers, rheumatism, laprosy, sprain metritis, ear trouble, dental and gum troubles and asthma. It exhibits antiseptic, antimicrobial and antifertility activities. Oil contains nimbidin and nimbin as active principles. Nimbidin is toxic to parasitic nematodes, antidiabetic, analgesic, antipyretic, antihelminthic and antifungal. Nimbin is antipyretic. Other constituents present in the oil are Nimbinin, Nimbanliol, Tiglic acid, Gedunin, Meldenin, Salannin, Azadirone, Vepinin, Nimbinene and Salannol possess insecticidal property. This oil is most important for commercial point of view. The oil yield is sometimes as high as 50 percent of the weight of kernel.

Oil can be converted to "polyol" which may find use as a rocked propellant fuel in place of polypropylene glycol. It can also be used in textile and rubber industry. Organic compounds of oil are being used with advantage to tan raw hides and skins.

Various Neem extracts are known to act on various insects as the bodies of these insects absorb the Neem compounds as if they were the real hormones. It works in the following ways.

- Disrupting of inhibiting the development of eggs, larvae or pupae.
- Blocking the moulting of larvae or nymphs.
- Repelling larvae and adults.
- Deterring females from laying eggs.
- Sterilizing adults.
- Deterring feedings.

Some other remedies of Neem oil include, aids preventative, inhibits allergic reactions, reduced tumors and cancers, reduced insulin requirement in diabetes, kills external parasites, reduced elevated heart rates and high blood pressure, toxic to the herpes virus and effective insect repellent etc.

Like Neem tree, Karanj is primarily valued for its seeds leaves, shade and ornamental value [96-102]. Its botanical name is *Pongamia Pinnata*. Pongam tree is of family leguminosae.

The oil known as "Pongam oil" is used for leather, dressing, soap and candle-making, lubrications and illumination. It is applied in scabies, rheumatism, hepes and leucoderma and also given as stomachic and cholagogue. Non fatty portion of oil contains active principles karanjin (1.25%) and pongamol (0.85%).

Biodiesel was pepared from crude oil of *Pongamia Pinnata* and *AzadirachtaIndica* by trans-esterification with methanol in presence of KOH as catalyst[103-104].

Edible Oils

Mustard tree is a member of Brassicaceae family. The mustard oil has distinctive pungent taste. Oil can be produced from black mustard (*Brassica nigra*) brown mustard (*Brassica junsia*) and white mustard (*Brassica hirta*). The characteristic pungent flavor of mustard oil is due to allylisothiocyanate. Mustard oil is a fatty vegetable oil extracted from the mustard Seeds. Being edible oil, it is widely used for cooking. It has been used in ayurveda since times immemorial due to its healing and medicinal properties and is considered beneficial for hair, skin and body. Mustard oil is considered healthy as it is devoid trans-fats, is low in saturated fats and has a high content of mono-unsaturated fats and poly-unsaturated fatty acids. Thus it offers an array of health benefits as increases appetite, powerful stimulant for digestion, reduces risk of cancer, relieves cold and cough joint pain. Oil has got an antibacterial, antifungal and anti-inflammatory action as well.

Soyabean oil is a vegetable oil extracted from seeds of the Soyabean (*Glycine max*). It is one of the most widely consumed cooking oil.

Soyabean oil is a drying oil, which means that it will slowly harden upon exposure to air, forming a flexible, transparent and water proof solid. Because of this property, it is used in some printing ink and oil paint formulations. Soyabean oil is also used as fixative for insect repellents.

SIGNIFICANCE OF SURFACTANTS

Surfactants or surface active agents are materials that tend not only to accumulate at surfaces but also by their presence, change the properties of surfaces. Generally they are active at interfaces which can be between solid/liq, liq/liq or liq/gas pair of phases.

The surfactant molecule is typically composed of a strongly hydrophobic (water hating) as well as hydrophilic (water loving) moiety i.e. it share the property of amphipathy[105]. Hydrophobic end is non-polar and hydrophilic a polar therefore the molecule has partially both properties and has a dual nature. The hydrophilic portion (often includes anions or cations) of the surfactant monomer is referred to as the "head" of the molecule. The hydrophobic part is typically an elongated hydrocarbon chain, referred to as the tail of the molecule therefore surfactant monomer is illustrated as a tadpole with a head and a tail.

On the basis of charged carried by the polar head group surfactants are classified as anionic, cationic and non-ionic or amphoteric[106].

Surfactants are capable to lower the interfacial tension and therefore used as emulsifiers, detergents, dispersing agents, foaming agents, wetting agents, penetrating agent etc. surfactants are used as wood preventative water proofing and repelling agent eg fish net protection and in various industries of rubber, paints and varnishes[107-108].

COPPER METAL

Group - IB

Atomic Number - 29

Natural Isotopes - ^{63}Cu (69.1%), ^{65}Cu (30.9%)

Copper has a single s-electron outside the filled 4d shell but cannot be classed in Group-I, as it has little in common with the alkalies except formed stoichiometries in the +1 oxidation state because ten d- electrons are rather ineffective in shielding the outer s- electron from the coulomb field of the nucleus.

First ionization potential of Cu is higher than that of the alkalies since the electrons of the d- shell are also involved in metal binding the heat of sublimation and the melting point of copper are also higher than those of alkalies. These factors are responsible for the more noble character of copper and the effect is to make the compounds more covalent and to give them higher lattice energies.

The charge +2 is common in Copper. The d^9 arrangement of Cu^{+2} give rise to square arrangement in which two ligands are attached by little longer bonds, above and below the plane of the other four around the metal atom or to distorted octahedral arrangements. The enthalpy of hydration of Cu^{+2} suggests that the dispositive ion is much more stable in aqueous solution. Copper form numerous complex compounds in which compound with Cu (I) the characteristic Co-ordination number are 2,3 and 4 which for Cu (II) are 4 and 6.

Copper has a wide diversity of uses in electrical refrigeration, heavy industries, powder metallurgy and communications. Much of the Copper produced is utilized in various alloys. Copper (II) complexes have been found as medicinally important in the treatment of many diseases including cancer [109-110].

Many compound of copper are employed as pesticides either alone as Cu (I) oxide and Cu(II) sulphate or in mixtures as for eg.cupronil containing

35% Cu II carbonate hydroxide and 15% Zinc N,N-dimethyldithiocarbamate. The fungicide cuprozen which contains 37.5% Cu (II) chloride hydroxide and 15% Zineb (Zinc ethylene-bis-dithiocarbamate), Bordeaux-mixture a fungicide prepared by reacting Cu (II) sulphate with hydrated lime and burgundy mixture a fungicide similar to bordeaux mixture but containing Na_2CO_3 instead of lime[1].

Reed reviewed the methods of preparation of copper soaps described by several workers[111-113].

STRUCTURE SOLUBILITY AND MICELLAR PROPERTIES OF SURFACTANTS

One of the most characteristic properties of amphiphilic molecules is their capacity to aggregate in solutions. Of course the aggregation process depends on the amphiphillic species and the condition of the system in which they are dissolved. In solution, there is tendency for grouping of molecules in which "like is associated with like". The abrupt change in many physicochemical properties is seen in aqueous solutions of amphiphillic molecules or surfactants with long hydrophobic chains, when a specific concentration is exceeded and is attributed to the formation of oriented colloidal aggregates. The narrow concentration range (over which these changes occur) has been called the critical micelle concentration (cmc) [114-115]. It depends on such factors like chain length, structure of surface-active agents, the presence of additives, the temperature and the nature of solvents. The effect of temperature and electrolytes on the solubilization and cmc has been studied by Kolthoff and Striecks[116].

The structure of micellar aggregates has been a matter of discussion[117], Mc-Bain proposed the presence of molecular aggregates in soap solutions on the basis of unusual changes in electrical conductivity observed with changing in soap concentration. He also suggested the lamellar and spherical forms co-exist[118]. A simple form of micelle, recognized by Hartley was consisting of spherical aggregates[119]. It is however, a very mobile structure and on dilution of the solution it dissociates extremely rapidly.

X-ray studies by Harpins *et al* suggested the sandwich/lamellar model[120]. Later Debye and Anacker[121] proposed that micelles are rod shaped rather than spherical or disc like.

Many colloid chemical behaviour of copper (II) soap surfactant in non-aqueous mixture of varying compositions has been investigated by Mehrotra and Mehta *et al*[122-123], using viscometric and allied parameters. A number of solvents have been used to understand the micellar features of Copper (II) soaps by viscosity, surface tension, parachor and electrical conductance. Membrane incorporating heavy metal soaps has been used to determine the concentration of surface - active ion by measuring membrane potential.

Malik [124-125], Popov [126] and Mehrotra [127] carried out the versatility of colorimetric and polarographic method for the determination of the metal content is copper soaps. Gilmour [128] suggested a covalent chelate structure for copper laurate, based on magnetic measurements. Simultaneously Satake, Kishita and Martin [129-134] examined structure of copper stearate, oleate and their complexes.

Viscometric studies at various temperature apparent molar volume, ultrasound, and surface tension and anti-fungal activities related with micellar features of copper soaps in various organic solvents have been studied by Sharma *et al* [135]. Sherwani and Sharma[136] have evaluated various parameters pertaining to micellar characteristics like density, apparent molar volume of copper soaps derived from various edible oils. Elaine, Gerald and Robert [137] investigated the theoretical and experimental studies of the electronic states of cobalt (II) stearate and dimeric copper (II) stearate.

Viscometric behaviour and micellization of complexes of copper (II) stearate with N-donor heterocylic dyes was studies by Mathur *et al*[138]. Synthesis and characterization of anti-fungal agents containing copper (II) soaps of edible and non edible oils were studied by Sharma *et al* [139-140]. Studies at CMC, solute-solvent and solute-solute interactions of copper (II) soaps derived from edible oils in methanol-benzene system at 303 K were studied by Sherwani *et al* [141]. Viscometric behaviour and micellar studies of biodegradable organometallic complexes in binary solvent system and studies of solute-solvent interactions and applications of copper palmitate with 2-amino benzothioazole were studied by Mathur *et al*[142-143].

Higher fatty acids were estimated by measuring the optical density of copper soap in $CHCl_3$. The dipole moment of copper oleate in benzene was investigated by Benerjee and Palit[144]. Fisel[145] described the formation of the complex in electro-chromatographic analysis of soaps in presence of bases. Kaufman [146] and Fisel[147] reported solid green complex of copper and oleic acid. Malik [148-149] reported polarographic behaviour of copper soap in pyridine o-toludine and dioxane. The molar susceptibility temperature variation of hydrated copper acetate soaps was studied and it was concluded that curie and weiss law are not obeyed by copper soaps [150-153].

Schulman and Riely[154], with the help of X-ray diffraction propounded the concept that the structure of copper (II) soaps consists of closely packed uniform water sphere in oil or oil in water. It is pointed out by Anacker[155] that the molecular weight obtained for soap solutions is incompatible with the assumption of a spherical micelle. According to Mc-Bain and Johnson[156], the spherical micellar concept is totally inadequate to account for the solubilization of hydrocarbons.

Matuura[157] investigated the IR spectra and X-ray diffraction patterns of copper oleate. Various other workers have studied different spectral techniques like IR, ESR, NMR and magnetic moment studies of various complexes containing copper so as to determine their geometrical and structural aspects[158-160].

Thermal stability and various kinetic parameters of edible vegetable oils were explained by Souza[161] and Zhang[162] *et al*. It was established from T.G.A. curves that the thermal decomposition of edible oils takes place in three steps corresponding to the thermal degradation of polyunsaturated, monounsaturated and saturated fatty acids respectively. The various kinetic parameters included energy of activation, order of reactions and pre exponential factors done by various other workers [163-169].

Various other scientists have done thermal analysis of various alkaline earth and transition soaps of fatty acids like laurate, caprate, caprylate, palmitate and stearate [170-174]. Mattielo[175] used copper soaps as driers for the preparation of paints, varnishes and other protective coating. It was observed that the addition of copper soaps to fuel oil reduced the smoke and fumes of burning oil and thus it helps in controlling pollution[176].

Leyland and Stanford[167], Pederson[168] and Gebhardt[169] pointed out that the oxidation of natural rubber increases rapidly by the addition of copper stearate. The thermal degradation of polypropylene containing copper stearate was explained by Osawa and Matuzaki[177]. Satake and Matuura[178] examined the structure of copper stearate, oleate and their complexes by magnetic susceptibility measurements and observed that copper oleate takes a binuclear structure similar to that of copper stearate.

Tsuboi[179] prepared copper stearate by treating the acid with the hydroxide in presence of ammonia at elevated temperature and it was observed by Brauner[180] that the presence of basic nitrogen compounds permits the rapid and total reaction between the metal and the acid. The formation of the complexes of copper distearate and dipalmitate with amines were described by Fisel[181]. Goldfein[182] *et al* studied the effect of copper stearate on the kineties and mechanism of bulk polymerisation of methyl mathcrylate.

The decomposition of ethyl diazoacetate in presence of copper stearate in cyclohexane was studied by Dyaknov *et al*[183] and it was observed by Maizus, Skibida and Emanuel[184] that no free radical was formed in the decomposition of hydrogen peroxide in presence of copper stearate. Tulupov and Gagarina[185] pointed out that the hydrogenation of cyclohexane in presence of copper stearate is a pressure dependent. Grant[186] studied the NMR spectra of copper stearate[187].

The effectiveness of copper soaps as fungicides, bactericides, herbicides and insecticides were studied by many coworkers [188]. Copper stearate, copper oleate and copper abietate (from resins) are employed mainly for root-proofing textile ropes etc.

A moderately concentrated aqueous soap solution is able to take into thermodyanamically stable solution, various organic compounds that in the absence of show only small solubility in water. This phenomenon was termed as "solubilization" by Mc-Bain and co-workers[189-191]. The phenomenon of solubilization was first discovered by Gad[192].

VonHann[193], Lindan[194] and Winsor[195] studied the similarity between hydrotropy and solubilization. Solubilization of silver stearate by non-ionic surfactants in organic solvents was studied by Jain and Singh[196]. The solubility of copper stearate in water and benzene at 25°C was determined by Dobry[197], Nobel, Scalane and Eisher[198] determined the solubility of copper soaps of wool wax acid in non-aqueous solvents, Matuura and Nagasue[199] explained the chemical behaviour of copper stearate and oleate in dioxane and pyridine.

Nelson and Pink[200] concluded (on the basis of solubility measurementstaken at different temperatures) that copper laurate aggregates in toluene, but the association effect is reduced in iso-butyl alcohol. Mehrotra and Rai et al[201] and Mehta et al[202] confirmed the dimeric nature of copper soaps in chloroform and benzene with the determination of the molecular weights by ebullioscopically. Nobel, Scalane and Wood et al[203] studied the solubility of cupric laurate and stearate in CCl_4.

Varkonyi and Sz'ell[204] studied the water repellency of copper (II) soaps and it was observed that treating the heavy fabrics with copper naphthenate formed water proofing and water repellant coating [205]. It was observed by Zahradniuk et al[206] that copper (II) soaps were more effective for protection of stored sugar beets.

Bartleson and Hughes [207] used copper (II) soaps in lubricants, which were stable to oxidative deterioration. To decrease water and tear or drawing dies, lubricant containing copper (II) soap was observed to be more effective[208].

Atkins[108] suggested copper oleate, copper resinate, copper naphthenate, mixed copper (II) soap containing stearate, with oleate, palmitate with laurate are the copper (II) soaps used in preservation of fishing nets, canvas and also wood These soaps are used with coal tar for better effect.

SIGNIFICANCE AND APPLICATIONS OF PRESENT WORK

In the last two decades, Photocatalysis has attracted the attention of scientific community all over the world due to its multifarious applications in various fields like energy, environment, technology, waste water treatment, pollution control etc. Heterogeneous photocatalysis using semiconductor particles is one of the most active fields of research to degrade large number of organic and inorganic pollutants present in the environment.

Although a lot of work has been carried out in the field of photocatalysis but no work has been reported by the photodegradation of copper surfactants.

The extensive use of surfactants has created a new problem in environmental pollution, because surfactants are either slowly biodegradable or these do not biodegrade at all, therefore photocatatytic degradation provides a promising solution to this problem.

In the present investigation, photocatalytic degradation of copper soaps derived from saturated fatty acids (copper stearate and copper palmitate), Copper soaps of edible and non edible oils have been carried out. Photodegradation of copper soaps was studied spectrophotometrically in non aqueous and non polar solvent benzene using zinc oxides as semiconductor. The effect of various parameters such as concentration of soap, amount of semiconductor, effect of light intensity, effect of polarity of the solvent etc, on the rate of degradation has been observed.

Survey of the literature reveals that copper soaps of fatty acids are having great biological, pharmaceutical, industrial and analytical applications. These types of large molecules cannot be metabolized rapidly by micro-organisms naturally. Thus if macromolecules were dissected into smaller plural entities by radiation, they would not persist in the environment for a long period and becomes ecofriendly.

SYNTHESIS

All chemicals used were of LR/AR grade. Copper (II) soaps were prepared using direct metathesis. The copper soaps of saturated fatty acids (Stearic and Palmitic acid) were prepared by mixing acid with alcohol and adding saturated solution of KOH. Addition of saturated $CuSO_4$ solution to the above solution formed a blue colored soap i. e. Copper Stearate and Copper Palmitate. On the other hand the non-edible oils i.e. Neem (*Azadirachtaindica*) and Karanj (*Pongamia Pinnata*) and edible oils i.e. Mustard (*Brassica juncea*) and Soyabean (*Glycine max*) were refluxed with 2N KOH solution and alcohol for about 4 hrs. The neutralization of excess KOH was done by addition of 0.5 N HCl. Saturated solution of copper sulphate was then added to it for converting neutralized soap into their corresponding copper (II) soap.

The copper (II) soaps obtained were filtered, washed with warm water followed by alcohol at 50 C and recrystallized with hot benzene.

The fatty acid composition of edible and non-edible oils was confirmed through GLC of their methyl esters. The formation of the copper (II) soaps was confirmed by IR and NMR techniques. The metal copper was analyzed by standard procedures (Iodometry). Average molecular weight of the soaps was calculated by saponification equivalent value (S.E.) and saponification value (S.V.) of the oil. S.E. may be taken as an average molecular weight of oil. S.E. value was determined by experiment and from these values; average molecular weights of copper (II) soaps were calculated.

The Copper (II) soaps taken for studies have been synthesized are abbreviated as follows:

- **From saturated fatty acids:**
  1. Copper (II) soap of Stearic acid CS
  2. Copper (II) soap of Palmitic acid CP
- **From edible oils:**
  1. Copper (II) soap of Mustard oil CMu
  2. Copper (II) soap of Soyabean oil CSo
- **From non-edible oils:**
  1. Copper (II) soap of Neem oil CNm
  2. Copper (II) soap of Pongamia oil CPm

SPECTROSCOPIC STUDIES

IR Spectral Studies

The absorption band observed at ~ 2918 cm^{-1} corresponds to asymmetric stretching vibration of methyl and methylene group, whereas symmetric stretching vibration of the group occurred at lower frequency i.e. ~ 2850 cm^{-1}. The absorption band at ~ 1610 cm^{-1} and ~ 1217 cm^{-1} are due to carboxylate ion COO^-, C-O antisymmetric and symmetric stretching respectively in CS, CP, CMu, CSo, CNm and CPm soaps. In unsaturated fatty acids, the band appearing at ~ 3010 cm^{-1} corresponds to olefinic =C-H stretching in CMu, CSo, CNm and CPm soaps. Copper oxygen (Cu-O) stretching bands were observed nearly at ~ 490 cm^{-1}. These bands confirm the formation of soaps.

NMR Spectral Studies

The proton NMR spectra of copper (II) soaps show signals for $-CH_3$ protons attached to $-CH_2$-R group at 0.9 δ and $-CH_2$ protons attached to $-CH_2$-R group show signal at 1.2 δ. Other signals observed between 2.0 δ to 2.1 δ are due to $-CH_2$ attached to one C=C bond. Vinylic proton gives signal around 5.5 δ in CMu, CSo, CNm and CPm soaps. All the above peaks are due to long chain fatty acid content "R" of the soap molecule [(R-COO)$_2$Cu].

PHOTODEGRADATION

Copper (II) soaps derived from Stearic and Palmitic acid, from edible oils (mustard and soyabean) and non- edible oils (Neem and karanj) were used in the present investigation. All the solutions were prepared in hot benzene. Degradation was observed upon addition of ZnO to the soap solution. Irradiation was carried out with a 200 W tungsten lamp. Light intensity was varied with the help of solarimeter (CEL India, Model SM 201). The progress of the photocatalyticreaction was observed by taking absorbance at regular time intervals using U.V.–visible spectrophotometer (Systronics Model 106).

The photocatalytic degradation of the soaps were observed at λ_{max} = 420 nm. The optical density (O.D.) decreases with increasing time. The rate of degradation is favorably affected by ZnO. A plot of 2 + log O.D. (absorbance) versus time was linear and hence, this reaction follows pseudo-first order kinetics. The rate constants of this reaction were determined by the expression:

$$k = 2.303 \times \text{slope}$$

(a) Effect of concentration of soap

The effect of soap concentration was observed by taking different concentration of soaps. The rate of photocatalytic degradation of soap was found to increase with increasing concentration and further increase in the soap concentration resulted in a decrease in the rate of degradation.

(b) Effect of amount of semiconductor

The amount of semiconductor (ZnO) may also affect the photocatalytic degradation of soaps and hence, different amounts of photocatalysts were used. It was observed that initially, the rate of degradation of soaps increases with an increase in the amount of semiconductor, but it becomes virtually constant after a certain amount of ZnO.

(c) Effect of light intensity

To observe the effect of light intensity on the photocatalytic degradation of soaps, the distance between the light source and the exposed surface area was varied. The data indicate that the rate of photocatalytic degradation was found to increase with increasing light intensity and then rate of reaction decreases with further increase in the light intensity.

(d) Effect of solvent

The rate of photocatalytic degradation of soap is also affected by the change in solvent. The percentage of methonol was varied from 20% to 80% to observe the solvent effect. It was observed that the rate of degradation continuously decreases with increase in the concentration of methanol.

MECHANISM

A tentative mechanism for the photocatalytic degradation may be proposed as:

$$SC \xrightarrow{h\nu} SC^* \quad \ldots (1)$$

$$SC^* \longrightarrow SC\,[h^+\,(VB)] + e^-\,(CB) \quad \ldots (2)$$

$$h^+ + ZnO \longrightarrow O + Zn^+ \quad \ldots (3)$$

$$e^- + Zn^+ \longrightarrow Zn \quad \ldots (4)$$

$$e^- + O_2 \longrightarrow O_2^{\cdot -} \quad \ldots (5)$$

$$h^+ + O_2^- \longrightarrow O_2 \quad \ldots\ldots (6)$$
$$Zn + O_2 \longrightarrow ZnO + O \quad \ldots\ldots (7)$$
$$ZnO \longrightarrow Zn + \tfrac{1}{2} O_2 \quad \ldots\ldots (8)$$
$$^1Soap_0 \xrightarrow{h\nu} {}^1Soap_1 \quad \ldots\ldots (9)$$
$$^1Soap_1 \xrightarrow{ISC} {}^3Soap_1 \quad \ldots\ldots (10)$$
$$^3Soap_1 + O \longrightarrow \text{Products [epoxides]} \quad \ldots\ldots (11)$$
$$Cu^{+2} + e^- \longrightarrow Cu^+ \quad \ldots\ldots (12)$$

- Initially on exposure to light the semiconductor (SC) will be excited to give SC*, the excited state of semiconductor. This excited state will provide an electron in the conduction band (CB) and a hole in the valence band (VB)[1]. The hole in the valence band may react with ZnO to produce atomic oxygen and Zn^+, while electron in the conduction band reduces the Zn^+ ion to Zn and this electron may be utilized by atmospheric oxygen to give superoxide anion radical[1]. This radical may react with h^+ and form atmospheric oxygen. This oxygen molecule may utilized by Zn to regenerate the semiconductor.

- When the solution of soap in the benzene was exposed to light in the presence of a semiconductor, the soap molecule may be first excited to its first excited singlet state. These excited molecules are transferred to corresponding triplet state through Inter System Crossing (ISC)[1] and then it reacts with atomic oxygen (which is produced in above steps) to give products.

- IR spectral studies of degraded soap molecule suggests that the peak at 1620 cm^{-1} due to >C = C< stretching has been clearly disappears which may be attributed to the fact that double bond reacts with available atmospheric oxygen to form epoxide as product.

- IR, NMR and thermal studies also support the proposed mechanism in which >C = C< site present in all the natural oil segment of the soap molecules reacts/breaks/degrades first and the soap derived from natural oils degrade comparatively faster than saturated segment of stearate and palmitate soaps.

- The discoloration of the soap solution also suggests that some of the Cu^{2+} ion of the soap may reduce to Cu^+ or Cu^o to some extent during the process of degradation by trapping photogenerated electron in the system.

- The literature survey reveals that the presence of oxygen may also affect the photodegradation of soap molecule as the main oxidation products of the esters are keto or hydroxy compounds.

- Several mechanism of C-C bond fission is there in the oxidation. In α -mechanism only one C-C bond is broken to form C_m and C_{n-m} products, while in β mechanism, two C-C bonds are broken in the β-position to form C_m, C_{n-m-1}, CO_2 etc. The α and β mechanisms of C-C bond scission may be regarded as a result of peroxy radical isomerisation to form labile dihydroperoxide.

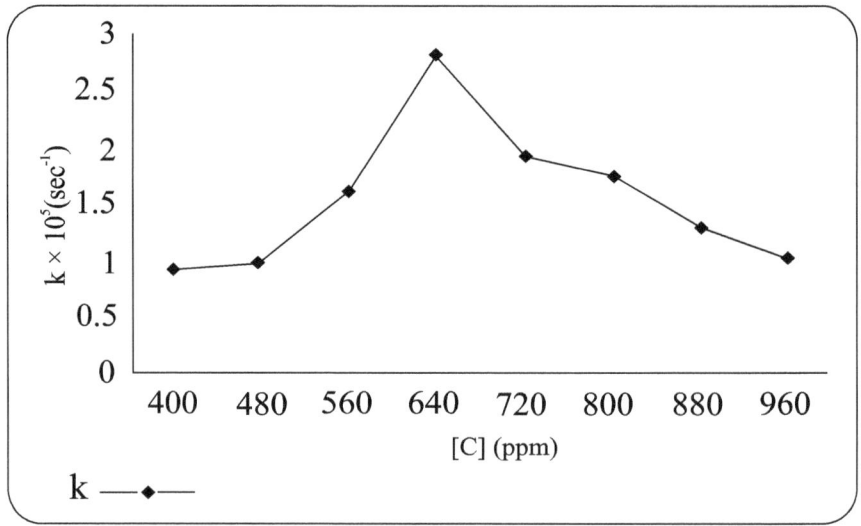

Fig. 9.3: Effect of concentration of copper stearate

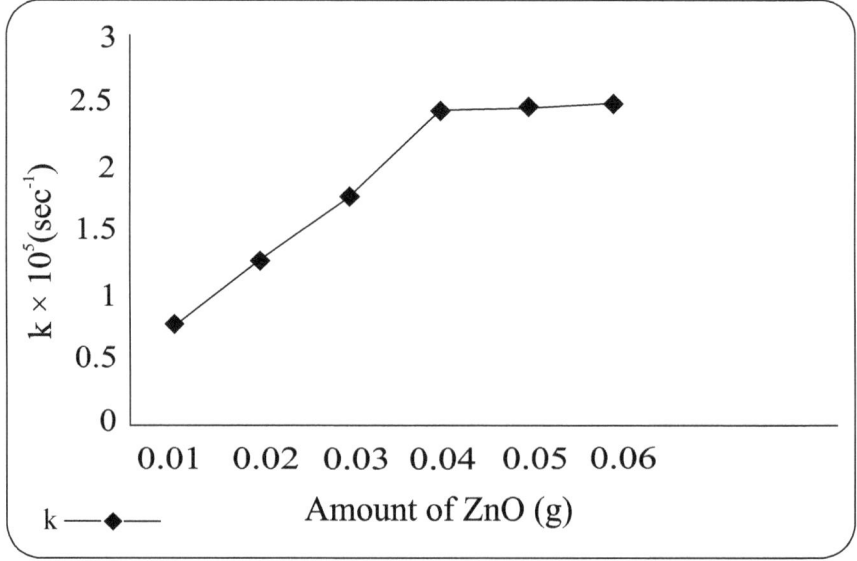

Fig. 9.4: Effect of amount of semiconductor (ZnO) on Copper stearate

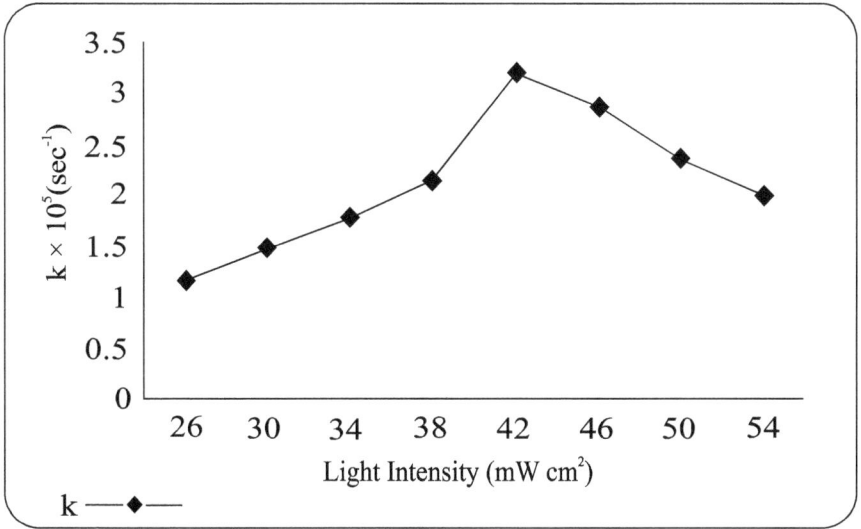

Fig. 9.5: Effect of light intensity on copper stearate

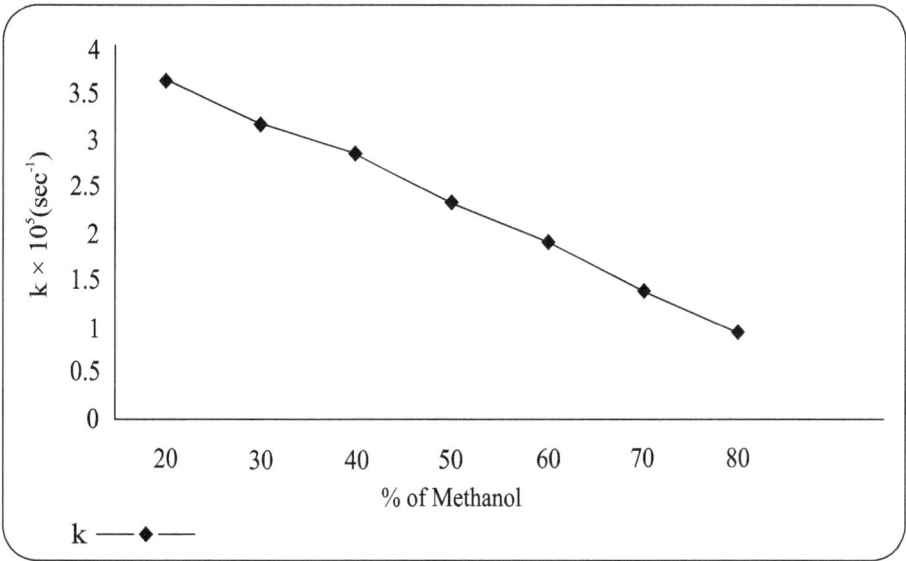

Fig. 9.6: Effect of solvent on copper stearate

CONCLUSION

The present study suggests that the rate of photocatalytic degradation increases, by increase in the concentration of soap to a certain limit and then continuously decreases. Rate of degradation also increases when the amount of semiconductor was increased and further, the rate becomes constant; thus, an optimum quantity of semiconductor is required. It is also observed that degradation increases with light intensity to a limit and then decreases on further increasing the light intensity. The effect of polar solvent inhibits the rate of degradation.

It was observed from these data that the rate of photocatalytic degradation of Cu (II) soaps derived from edible oils is higher than the degradation of Cu (II) soaps of non-edible and Cu (II) soaps of saturated fatty acids. The order of degradation is:

Cu (II) soaps of edible oils > Cu (II) soaps of non edible oils > Cu (II) soaps of saturated fatty acids.

All the studies suggest that as the photocatalytic degradation is faster in soaps derived from edible oils and non-edible oils, the products such oleo chemicals, agrochemicals, detergents, pesticides, insecticides etc. should be preferably made by using of natural fatty acids obtained from natural sources instead of Stearic and Palmitic type pure long chain saturated fatty acids.

The above studies will provide significant information regarding pollution control due to use of metallic soaps.

REFERENCES

1. Filov V.A., Bandman A.L."*Harmfull Chemical* Substances" EillsHorwood Ltd., Eng. 1, (1988), 66.
2. Sachdeva D., Parashar B. and Sharma V.K. *Int. J. Chem. Sci.*, Bhardwaj S., Punjabi P.B. 8(2), (2010), 1321-1328.
3. Ameta S.C. *J. Indian Chem. Soc.* 79, (2002), 305-307.
4. Benzamin S. *Ph.D. Thesis M.L.S. University, Udaipur, Rajasthan, India* (2008).
5. Kurtz M., Bauer N., Buscher C., Wilmer H., Hinrichsen O., Becker R., Rabe S., Merz K., Driess M., Fischer R.A. and Muhler M. *Catal. Lett.* 92, (2004), 49.
6. Mansilla H.D. and Villasnov J. *J. Photochem. Photobiol.* 78A, (1994), 267.
7. Sharma A., Rao P., Mathur R.P. and Ameta S.C., *J. Photochem. Photobiol.* 86A, (1995), 197.
8. Sakthivel S., Neppolian B., Shankar M.V., Arabindoo B., Palanichamy M. and Murugesan V. *Sol. Energy Mater. Sol.Cells* 77, (2003), 65.
9. Sharma A., Sharma B., Mathur R.P. and Ameta S.C. *Poll. Res.* 20(3), (2001), 419-423.
10. Ameta R., Vardia J., Punjabi P.B. and Ameta S.C. *Indian J. Chem. Tech.* 13, (2006), 114.
11. Hariharan C. *Appl. Catal. A. Gen.* 304, (2006), 55.
12. Spathis P. and Poulios I. *Corrosion Sci.* 37, (1995), 673.
13. Attia Abbas J., KadhimSalih H. and Hussein Falah H. *E - Journal of Chemistry* 5(2), (2008), 219-223.
14. Sharma A., Sharma R., Rathore S.S. and Ameta S.C. *J. Indian Chem. Soc.*79, (2002), 929-931.
15. Choi W. and Hoffmann M.R. *Environ. Sci. Technol.* 31, (1997), 99.
16. Munoz J., Domenech J. and Andres M. *J. Electeochim. Acta.* 32, (1987), 773.
17. Domenech J. and Prieto A. *J. ElectrochimActa.* 31, (1986), 1317.

18. Hema M.A., Ramakrishna V. and Kuriacose J.C. *Indian J. Chem.* 15B, (1977), 947.
19. Dodd A., Mikinley A., Saunders M. and Tsuzuki T. *J. nanoparticles Research* 8, (2006), 43.
20. Sirtori C., Altvater P.K., Freitas A.M. de and Peralta and Zamora P.G. *J. Hazard. Mater.* 129, (2006), 110.
21. Kuriacose J.C. and Markhan, M.C. *J. Catal.* 1, (1962), 498.
22. Markham M.C., Hannan M.C. and Evans S.W. *J. Am. Chem. Soc.* 76, (1954), 820.
23. Markham M.C., Kuriacose J.C., Marco J.A.D. and Giaquint C. *J. Phy. Chem.* 66, (1962), 932.
24. Yanagida S., Kawakami H., Midori Y., Kizumoto H., Pac C. and Wada Y. *Bull. Chem. Soc. Japan* 68, (1995), 1811.
25. Chakrabarty S. and Dutta B.K. *J. Hazard Mater.* 112, (2004), 269.
26. Kawaguchi H. *Environ. Techno. Lett.* 5, (1984), 471.
27. Chung C.C., Chen C.C. and Lin J.L. *J. Phy. Chem.* 103B, (1999), 2439.
28. Sakthivel S., Neppolian B., Shankan M.V., Arabindo B., Palanichamy M. and Murugesan V. *Solar Energy Material Solar Cells* 77, (2003), 65.
29. Ameta R., Jain S., Bhatt C.V. and Ameta S.C. *Rev. Rourn. Chim.* 45, (2000), 49.
30. Bindeau M., Claudel B., Faure L. and Kazouan H. *J. Photochem. Photobiol.* 61A, (1991), 269.
31. Park K.H. and Kim J.H. *Bull. Kor. Chem. Soc.* 12, (1991), 438.
32. Miyoshi H., Mori H. and Yoneyama H. *Langmuir* 7, (1991), 503.
33. Gulati S., Heetawala F., Sharma V.K. and Ameta S.C. *Poll. Res.* 22, (2005), 213.
34. Carson P.A. and Mayo P.D. *Can. J. Chem.* 65, (1977), 976.
35. Conley J.F., Streiker L. and Ono Y. *App. Phy. Letts.* 87, (2005), 223114.
36. Ye C., Bando Y., Shen G. andGolberg D. *J. Phy. Chem.* 110, (2006), 15146.
37. Kosanic M.M. *J. Photochem. Photobiol.* 119A, (1988), 119.
38. Lo S.C., Lin C.F., Wu C.H. and Hsieh P.H. *J. Hazard Mater.* 114, (2004), 183.
39. Wang Y.Y. and Van C.C. *J. Photochem. Photobiol.* 84A, (1994), 195.
40. Hidaka H. *Proc. Indian Acad. Sci.* (Chem. Sci.) 110, (1993), 215.
41. Sirtori C., Altvater K., De Freitas A.M. and Peralta – Zamora P.G. *J. Hazard Mater.* 129, (2006), 105.
42. Koka K. and Sahin M. *Int. J. Hydrogen Energy* 27, (2002), 363.
43. Khodja A.A., Sehili T., Pilichowski J.F. and Boule P. *J. Photochem. Photobiol.* 741A, (2001), 231.
44. Chatterjee D. and Mehta A. *J. Photochem. Photobiol.* 153A, (2002), 199.
45. Karunakaran C., Sethivelan S. and Karuthapandion *J. Photochem. Photobiol.* 172A, (2005), 207.
46. Parakh M., Aliz.,Vardia J. and Ameta S.C. *Res. J. Chem. Environ.* 2, (1998), 49.
47. Dong W., Chu Y., Yang F., LiU Y. and Lu J. *Chem. Letts.* 34, (2005), 1254.
48. Li D. and Haneda H. *Chemosphere* 51, (2003), 129.
49. Anpo M., Matsumoto A. and Kodama S. *J. Chem. Soc. Chem. Commun* B, (1987), 1038.
50. Borgarellom E., Kalyansundaram K., Duonghon D. and Gratzel M. *Anew. Chem. Int. Ed. Engl.* 20, (1981), 987.
51. Taquikhan M.M., Bhardwaj R.C. and Jadhav C.M *J. Chem. Soc. Chem. Commun* (1985) 1690.
52. Dasilva G. and Faria J.L. *J.Photochem. Photobiol* 172A, (2005), 121.

53. Senthikumar S., Parkodi K. and Vidyalakshmi P. *J. Photochem. Photobiol* 170A, (2005), 225.
54. Banerjee A., Ranamohan R. and Patani M.S. *Mater. Res. Bulletin* 36, (2001), 1259.
55. Gehlot M.H., Ferriera M. and Neumann M.G. *J. Photochem. Photobiol* 87A, (1995), 55.
56. Rao P., Patel G., Sharma S.L. and Ameta S.C. *J. Toxicol. Environ. Chem.* 60, (1997), 155.
57. Navarro R.M., Pena M.A. and Fierro J.L.G. *J. Catal.* 212, (2003), 112.
58. Hauffe H., Danzmann H.J., Pusch H., Range J. and Volz H. *J. Elecrochem. Soc.* 117, (1970), 993.
59. Houskova V., Stengl V., Bakardjieva S., Murafa N., Kalendova A. and Oplustil F. *J. Phy. Chem. A* 111, (2007), 4215.
60. Pauporte T. and Rathousky J. *J. Phy. Chem. C* 111, (2007), 7639.
61. Jain S. and Ameta S.C. 5(2), (2007), 496-504. *Int. J. Chem. Sci.*
62. Baxi V. Kataria P., Ameta R. and Punjabi P.B. *Int. J. Chem. Sci.* 2(4), (2004), 537-542.
63. Goud V.V., Patwardhan A.V. and Pradhan N.C. *Int. J. Chem. Sci.* 5(4), (2007), 1533-1540.
64. Vora J.J., Chauhan S.K., Parmar K.C., Vasava S.B. Sharma S. and Patel J.A. *Int. J. Chem. Sci.* 7(2), (2009), 1286-1294.
65. Singhal S., Sharma R., Singh C. and Bansal S. *Indian J. Mater. Sci.* 2013, (2013), 1-6.
66. Nickeslat A., Amin M.M., Izanloo H., Fatehizadeh A. and Mousavi S.M. *J. of Environ. and Public Health* 2013, (2013), ID 815310.
67. Meena R.C., Verma V. and Disha *Int. Res. J. Environ. Sci.* 2(12), (2013), 35-41.
68. Oghenejoboh K.M., Aisien F.A. and Ihoeghian N. *British J. Appl. Sci. and Technol.* 4(5), (2014), 808-822.
69. Desale A., Kamble S.P. and Deosarkar M.P. *Int. J. of Chem. and Phy. Sci.* 2, (2013), 140-148.
70. Aliabadi M. and Abyar Aliyeh *J. Bio. and Environ. Sci.* 3(12), (2013), 36-42.
71. Sivakumar T., Shanthi K., Guru S.P.S., Srividya B., Kiruthinga P.S. and Rahunathan R. *Asian J. Microbiol. Biotech. Environ. Sci.* (1999), 3.
72. Xie Y.D., Chen F., He J.J., Zhao J.C. and Wang H. *J. Photochem. Photobiol. (A)* 104, (2000), 235.
73. Fabiyi M.E. and Shelton R.L. *J. Photochem. Photobiol. (A)* 132, (2000), 121.
74. Dunlop P.S.M., Oyme J.A., Manga N. and Eggins B.R. *J. Photochem. Photobiol.* 148A, (2002), 355.
75. Sokmen M. and Ozkan A. *J. Photochem. Photobiol.* 147B, (2002), 77.
76. Doong R.A., Chen C.H., Maithreepala R.A. and Chang S.M. *Water Res.* 35, (2001), 2873.
77. Keller V. and Garin F. *Catal. Commun* 4, (2003), 377.
78. Green K.J. and Rudhan R. *J. Chem. Soc.* 88, (1992), 3599.
79. Davis A.P. and Huang C.P. *The ACS J. Surf. Colloids* 7, (1991), 709.
80. Jian C., Oizing Z., Jiliang He and Chem. Yu *TaiyangnengZuebau* 7, (1986), 878.
81. Bolousou V.M., Kashuba E.V. and Lyashenko L.V. *Ukr. Khim. Zh. SSSR.* 54, (1988), 1042.
82. Yamagata S., Bada R. and Fujishima A. *Bull. Chem. Soc. Japan* 62, (1989), 1004.
83. Ameta S.C., Chaudhary R., Ameta R. and Vardia J. *J. Indian Chem. Soc.* 80, (2003), 257.
84. Kamat P.V. *Progr. React. Kinetic.* 19, (1994), 277.
85. Nefedov V.N., Kuzmina E.A., Yu Martynov I., Mashtalir N.N., Kisilitra P.P. and Barachevskii V.A. *Ir. Vses. Kihifotointa* 69, (1985).

86. Pelizzetti E., Minero C., Pramauro E., Barbini M., Maurino V. and Tosata M. *Chem. Industr.* 69, (1987), 88.
87. Toshiyuki H., Yunji J., Yoshio N., Onada K. and Morioka Y. *Koku. Eis. Gok. Tass.* 87, (1987), 520.
88. Nehra K., Zhao J., Serpone W. and Pelizzetti E. *J. Photochem. Photobiol.* 64A, (1992), 2.
89. Serpone N. and Pelizzetti E. *Photocatalysis* Wiley, (1989).
90. Linsebigler A.L., Lu G. and Yates J.T. *J. Chem. Soc. Rev.* 95, (1995), 735.
91. Gunston F.D. "*An Introduction to the* Chemistry of Fats and Fatty Acids". Chapmann and Hall Ltd., London (1950).
92. Playfair L. *Ann.*, 37, (1841), 152.
93. Fremy E. *Ann.*, 36, (1840), 44.
94. Voelcker A. *Ann.*, 64, (1848), 342.
95. Noller C.R. *J. Am. Chem. Soc.*56, (1934), 156.
96. Tyagi P.D. *Non Conventional Vegetable Oils*, (1991).
97. Srivastava R. *Neem and Pest Management* (2001).
98. Sacc *Ann.,* 51, (1844), 213.
99. Hilditch T.P. *J. Soc. Chem. Ind.* 58, (1934), 233.
100. Raphael R.A. *Nature*, 165, (1950), 235.
101. Shinowara G.Y. *J. Biol. Chem.* 134, (1940), 331.
102. Arens C.L. *et. al. Biochem. J.* 37, (1943), I.
103. Azam M., Mohibbe, Waris A. and Nahar N.M. *Biomass and Bioenergy* 29, (2005), 293-302.
104. Karmee S.K. and Chadha A. *Bioresource Technology* 96(13), (2005), 1425-1426.
105. Mukherji P. and Meysels K.J. *Natl. Stand. Ref. Data. Ser.* (U.S. Natl. Bur. Stand) No. 36, (1971).
106. Moroi Y. "*Micelles: Theortical and Applied Aspects" Springer* (2005).
107. Jurij J., Hostynek H. and Oward I. *Maibach Taylor and Formics* 5, (2006), 16.
108. Atkins W.R.G. "*The Preservation of Fishing Nets by Treament with Copper Soaps and other substances"* Part 3, (1936), 627-641.
109. Sorenson R.J. *J. Chem. Br.* 16, (1984), 1110.
110. Orvig C. and Abrahams M.J. *Chem. Rev.* 99, (1999), 2201. 1, (1988), 66.
111. Reed P.D. *J. Am. Perfumer Aromat.* 76(3), (1961), 49-50.
112. Koeing A.E. *J. Am. Chem. Soc.* 36, (1914), 951.
113. Levy J. *Fatty Acids: Their Ind. Appl.* (1968), 200-20.
114. Mahapatra B.B. and Ray Paspa *J. Indian Chem. Soc.* 79, (2002), 536.
115. Mahapatra B.B. and Mishra R.R. *J. Indian Chem. Soc.* 78, (2001), 395.
116. Kolthoff I.M. and Striecks W. *J. Phy. Colloid. Chem.* 52, (1948), 915 ;53, (1949), 424.
117. Mc. Bain J.W. *Trans Faraday Soc.* 9, (1913), 99.
118. Mc. Bain J.W. *Colloid Chemistry, Theoretical and Applied (J. Alexander Ed.) Reinhold New York*, (1944).
119. Hartle G.S. *Aqueous Solutions of Paraffin Chain Salts, Hermann, Paris*, (1936).
120. Mattoon R.H., Stearns R.S. and Harpins W.D. *J. Phy. Chem.* 15, (1947), 209.
121. Debye P. and Anacker E.W. *J. Phy. Colloid Chem.* 5, (1951), 644.
122. Mehrotra K.N., Mehta V.P. and Nagar T.N. *J. Prakt. Chem. Bd.* (1970), 312.

123. Mehrotra K.N., Jain and M. *Indian J. Chem.* 31(A), (1992), 452-6.
124. Malik W.U. and Ahemad S.I. *J. Polarog. Soc.* 12(2), (1966), 50-58.
125. Malik W.U. and Haque R. *J. Analyt. Chem.* 189, (1962), 179.
126. Popov A., Yanishlieva N. and Iuanova B. *Maslo-Sapuena Prom. Byal.* 6(4), (1967), 13-19.
127. Mehrotra K.N., Mehta V.P. and Nagar T.N. *J. Fur. Prakt. Chemic. Bed.* 313, Heft 4, (1971), 607-13.
128. Gilmour A. and Pink R.C. *J. Indian Chem. Soc.* (1953), 2198.
129. Satake I. and Matuura R. *Mem. Fac. Sci. Kyushu Univ. Ser.* C_5 (1962), 13-20.
130. Kishita M., Inoue M. and Kubo M. *Nippon Kagaku Kaishi* 84, (1963), 758.
131. Martin R.L. and Waterman H. *J. Indian Chem. Soc.* (1957), 2545-51.
132. Mehrotra R.C. and Raj A.K. *J. Inorg. Nucl. Chem. Soc.* 21(3/4), (1961), 311.
133. Kokot R. and Martin R.L. *Inorg. Chem.* 3(9), (1964), 1306.
134. Martin R. and Whitelay A. *J. Indian Chem. Soc.* (1952), 1394.
135. Sharma R., Saxena M. and Acharya S. *J. Indian Chem. Soc.* 89, (2012), 585-592.
136. Sherwani M.R.K., Sharma R., Gangwal A. and Bhutra R. *Indian J. Chem.* 42A, (2003), 2527-2530.
137. Elanine Hart, Gerald R. Van Hecke and Robert C. Cave *Department of Chemistry Harvey Mudd.College Clarmont*, CA 91711, U.S.A.
138. Mathur N., Ojha K.G., Imran A. and Pooja S. *Tenside Surf. Det.* 1, (2009), 24-30.
139. Sharma R., Tank P., Saxena M., Bhutra R. and Ojha K.G. *Tenside Surf. Det.* 2, (2008), 87-91.
140. Sharma R. and Khan S. *Tenside Surf. Det.* 3, (2009), 145-151.
141. Sharma R., Saxena M., Bhutra R., Tank P. and Sherwani M.R.K. *Int. J. Chem. Sci.* 6(2), (2008), 839-849.
142. Mathur N., Bargotya S. and Mathur R. *Res. J. Pham. Bio. and Chem. Sci.* 5(2), (2014), 989-997.
143. Mathur N. *J. Curr. Chem. Pharm. Sci.* 1(1), (2011), 37-51.
144. Banerjee B.C. and Palit S.R. *J. Indian Chem. Soc.* 27, (1950), 385.
145. Fisel S. *ZhurNeorgKhim* 5, (1955), 1090.
146. Kaufman H.P. and Lissling *Fette U. Seiler* 55, (1953), 90-95.
147. Fisel S. *Acad, rep, Popular Romain FilialolajiStudicCareetaxi Stiint*, 7(2), (1956), 13-17.
148. Malik W.U. and Haque R. *J. Am. Oil Chemists Soc.* 41(6), (1964), 168.
149. Malik W.U. and Ahemad S.I. *Indian J. Chem.* 2(4), (1964), 168.
150. Guha B.C. *Proc. Roy. Soc. A* 206, (1951), 353.
151. Foex G. and Karantases J. *Compt. Rend.* 237, (1953), 982.
152. Figgis B.N. and Martin R.L. *J. Indian Chem. Soc.* 35, (1956), 37.
153. Herron R.C. and Pink R.C. *J. Indian Chem. Soc.* (1953), 2198.
154. Schulman J.H. and Riley D.P. *J. Colloid Sci.* 3, (1948), 383.
155. Anacker E.W. *J. Colloid Sci.* 8, (1953), 402.
156. Mc. Bain J.W. and Johnson K.E. *J. Am. Chem. Soc.* 66, (1944), 9.
157. Matuura R. *Nippon Kagaku Kaishi* 82, (1961), 1624.
158. Manhas B.S., Kalia S.B. and Sardana A.K. *J. Indian Chem. Soc.* 83, (2006), 652.
159. Reddy R.K., Reddy K.M. and Mahendra K.N. *Indian J. Chem.* 45A, (2006), 858.

160. Sharma V.K. and Shrivastava S. *Indian J. Chem.* 45A, (2006), 1368.
161. Souza A.G., Santos J.C.O., Conceicao M.M., Dantas Silva M.C. and Prasad S. *Brazillian J. Chem. Engg.* 21(2), (2004), 265.
162. Zhang Q., Saleh A.S.M., Chen J., Sun P. and Shen Q. *J. Thermal Anal. Colorimetry* 115(1), (2014), 19-29.
163. Santos J.C.O., Santos A.V., Souza A.G., Prasad S. and Santos I.M.G. *J. Food Science* 67(4), (2002), 1393.
164. Tank P. *Ph.D. Thesis* M.D.S. University, Ajmer, *India*, (2007).
165. Reddy K.H., Reddy P.S. and Bahu P.R. *Transition Met. Chem.* 25, (2004), 154.
166. Kriza A., Spinu C. and Plemiceanu M. *J. Indian Chem. Soc.* 76, (2000), 82.
167. Leyland B.N. and Stanford R.L. *Trans Inst. Rubber Ind.* 35, (1959), 25.
168. Pedersen L.H. *Acta. Chem. Scand.* 4, (1950), 487.
169. Gabhardt H.L. *Foundary* (1946), 74, 110, 198, 200, 202, 204, 206.
170. Rasheed A. and Bhobe R.A. *J. Indian Chem Soc.* 53, (1976), 442.
171. Kambe H., Ozania T., Onoue M. and Igarashi S. *Bull. Chem. Soc. Jpn.* 35, (1962), 81.
172. Mehrotra K.N., Saroha S.P.S. and Kachhwaha R. *Tenside Surf. Det.* 18(1), (1981), 28.
173. Mehta V.P., Heda L.C. and Gupta R. *Asian J. Chem.* 4(4), (1992), 791.
174. Adeoson S.O. *J. Therm. Anal.* 14(3), (1978), 235.
175. Mattiello J.J. "*Protective and Decorative* Coatings" Wiley, Newyork, Vol. 1, (1941).
176. Esso Research and Engg. Co. *Fr.* I 381, (CI.C. 109), (1964), 305, 381.
177. Osawa Z. and Matuzaki K. *Kagyo Kagaku Zasshi, Japan* 68(3), (1965), 570-3.
178. Satake I. and Matuura R. *Kolloid – Z* 176, (1961), 31-8.
179. Tsuboi T. *Japan* Feb. 8, (1955), 1366.
180. Brauner C.O. *U.S.* 2 April 12, (1949), 466, 925.
181. Fisel S. *Acad. rep. Popular Romaine FilialolasiStudicCareetaxiStiint*; 7(2), (1956), 13-17; 6(3/4), (1955), 295-326.
182. Goldfein M.D., Stepukhovich *Vysokomol, Soedin, Ser.* A.D. and CheptSov. A. 9(12), (1961), 2641-6.
183. Dyakonov I.A., Vitenberg A.G. and Komendantov *Zhur. Org. Khim.* 1(7), (1964), 1183-8.
184. Maizus Z.K., Skibida I.P. and Emanuel *Doklady. Akad. Nauk.* S.S.S.R. 164(2), (1965), 374-7.
185. Tulupov V.A. and Gagarina M.I. *Zhur. Khim. Fiz.* 38(6), (1964), 1695-8.
186. Grant R.F. *Can. J. Chem.* 42(4), (1964), 951.
187. Mehta V.P., Hasan M., Mathur S.P. and Rai G.L. *Tenside Surf. Det.* 16, (1979), 2.
188. Singh H., Srivastava U.K., Shukla S.N. and Upadhyaya M.K. *Indian J. Chem.* 31A, (1992), 472.
189. Mc. Bain J.W. and Morrill R.C. Jr. *J. Am. Chem. Soc.* 63, (1941), 670.
190. Mc. Bain J.W. and Green A.A. *J. Am. Chem. Soc.* 68, (1946), 1731.
191. Mc. Bain J.W. and Laing M.F. *J. Am. Chem. Soc.* 58, (1936), 2610.
192. Gad *Arch. Anat. Physiol.* 181, (1978).
193. Von Hann F.V. *Kolloid* 2, (1932), 62, 202.
194. Lindan G. *Naturwiss* 20, (1932), 396.

195. Winsor P.A. *Trans Faraday Soc.* 44, (1948), 376, 382, 387, 390.
196. Jain A.K. and Singh R.P.B. *J. Colloid Interface Sci.* 77(1), (1980), 274.
197. Dobry A. *J. Phy. Chem.* 58, (1950), 576.
198. Nobel R.W., Scalan T.J. and Eisher *J. Am. Oil Chem. Soc.* 35, (1962), 31-2.
199. Matuura R. and Nagasue K. *Mem. Fac. Sci. Kyusha* Univ. Ser. C_3, (1958), 49-54.
200. Nelson S.M. Pink R.C. *J. Indian Chem. Soc.* (1952), 1744.
201. Mehrotra R.C. and Rai A.K. *J, Inorg. Nucl. Chem.* 21(3/4), (1961), 311.
202. Mehta V.P., Hasan M. and Mathur R.P. *An. Quin.* 74, (1978), 1016.
203. Wood J.A., Angela B. and Mc Donald H.A. *Tenside Surf. Det.* 24(3), (1987), 146-50.
204. Varkonyi B. and Sz'ell T. *Acta. Univ. Szagadiensis Acta. Phys. et. Chem.* 5, (1959), 73.
205. Duren Fabric Chemisch B.H. *Ger.* 1, 062, (1959), 664.
206. Zahradniuk J., Schmidt L. and Havranek A. *ListyCukrov* 83(9), (Czech), (1967), 193-7.
207. Bartleson D.J. and Hughes C.E. *U.S.* 2, (1951), 542, 560.
208. Yokouldev V.M., Pershina N.Y., Bekrenev A.N. and Masalkina *Polytechnic Ins. Samara U.S.S.R.*, Su1, (CI CIO MI 73/00), (1992), 715-835 Appl. – 4, 084, 08 Jan (1990), 747.

Pages: 213-225

Eco-tourism, Environmental Problems and Sustainable Development
Edited by: Dr. Soubam Premchandra Singh; Dr. Ashok K. Rathoure
  Dr. Pawan Kumar 'Bharti'
ISBN: 978-93-86841-57-5
Edition: 2018
Published by: Discovery Publishing House Pvt. Ltd., New Delhi (India)

A Review on Adsorbent Nature of Graphene/Metal Oxide Composites for Water Remediation Technology

Rabinarayan Panigrahi[1]
Dr. Ranjan Kumar Pradhan[2]
Dr. Manas Ranjan Senapati[3]

ABSTRACT

Recent works have shown that Graphene/metal oxide composites can perform multiple roles including adsorbents and antimicrobial agents making them an effective agent against all major water pollutants including organic molecules, heavy metal ions and water borne pathogens, respectively. This review concludes with a summary on the role of graphene based materials in removal of pollutants from water and some proposed strategies for designing of highly efficient multifunctional Graphene/metal oxide composites for water remediation. This article presents a comprehensive review on the application of Graphene/metal oxide composites in water treatment and their role as adsorbent in water remediation. The current state of the art in Graphene/metal oxide composites for water purification and also provide a comprehensive analysis of the nature of interaction of these composites with various types of pollutants. A brief perspective on the challenges and new directions in the area is also provided for researchers interested in designing advanced water

---

[1] PGT Chemistry, KIIT International School, Bhubaneswar (India)
[2] Deputy Advisor, NITI Aayog, Government of India
[3] Professor & Head Dept. of Chemistry, Trident Academy of Technology, Bhubaneswar - 751 024 (India)

treatment strategies using graphene based advanced materials. Recently, numerous studies devoted to utilization of self assembled metal oxides nonmaterial on graphene and reduced graphene oxide for removal of different water pollutants have been reported. This review aims of extending information related to the utilization of metal oxide/graphene composite for water remediation and evaluation of their activity against different types of waterborne pollutants. This desalination approach offers some unique features which gives it an edge over other existing techniques such as high energy efficiency, environmentally benign nature and no secondary waste generation during the process.

INTRODUCTION

Adsorption is one of the most exploited phenomenons for the desalination of water. As compared to other water treatment practices, it offers several advantages such as the ease of performance, no harmful generation of by products during the course of treatment and above all, it can remove nearly all types of pollutants from waste water.[6] especially, for the removal of toxic heavy Metal ions adsorption is the preferred approach, as the metal ions cannot be degraded by photo-catalysis or any other chemical reaction. The two dimensional atomic chicken-wire structure of graphene[7] can serve as a mesh containing pores of ne size for removal of pollutants from water. Also, as a prerequisite, graphene exhibits a much higher theoretical surface area than activated carbon and thus can act as an efficient adsorbent. In addition to unprecedented surface area, graphene and its oxide derivative, graphene oxide, also provides freedom of introduction of functionalities[8] which can favor selective adsorption of pollutants. The combination of graphene with the metal oxide extends the life time of the adsorbent material by acting as support material which inhibits leaching of ne metal oxides particles into the treated water. Until now, graphene has been explored as an adsorbent for the removal of various dyes,[9-11] heavy metal ions[12] and other aromatic pollutants. Besides the application of pristine graphene as an adsorbent, graphene modified with surfactant,[13] nanomaterials, polymers and biomolecules have also been explored as adsorbents and are found to be exhibit excellent adsorption efficiency. Presence of active groups such as carbonyl, epoxy and hydroxyl groups on the surface of graphene oxide enables it to interact with a wide variety of molecules and thus can undergo surface modification. Moreover, these entangled active groups of graphene oxide can also bind to the heavy metal ions present in the solution via surface complexation so it can also be used to extract ions from solution.[14] Graphene oxide is highly acidic in nature therefore can readily adsorb basic molecules and cations. The incorporation of metal oxide nanoparticles on graphene limits their re-stacking and aggregation, thereby enhancing the surface area of the composite.[15,16]. While incredible strides in science and technology have indeed raised the quality and standard of the human life and health, it has nevertheless brought about a multitude of problems as well. Among them, water pollution and contamination is one of the biggest and the most alarming problems that demands formidable and effective solutions.

ABOUT GRAPHENE

The first reported synthesis of the proclaimed "miracle material" by Novoselov et al.[2] in 2004 garnered immense interest among researchers resulting in an inundation of studies devoted to various aspects of graphene in last few years. Path breaking discoveries of sp² hybridised carbon derivatives such as C_{60}: buckministerfullerene, carbon nanotubes and graphene[2] at pivotal moments in time have ensured that the research has forayed into new directions and pathways. In the family of carbon nanomaterials, graphene seems to be the one with the mostpotential due to its outstanding physical, chemical and electronic properties. Graphene, is a two dimensional material having single layer of sp² network of carbon atoms, is considered as the thinnest and hardest material known so far.[2-4] Graphene inherently displays a large number of intriguing and peculiar properties such as high room temperature charge carrier mobility (100 000 cm^2 V^{-1} s^{-1}), theoretically large surface area (2630 m^2 g^{-1}), optical transparency, excellent mechanical strength (2.4 - 0.4 TPa), high thermal conductivity (2000 to 5000 W m K^{-1}) and capacity of sustaining large electrical current density (10^8 A cm^{-2}).

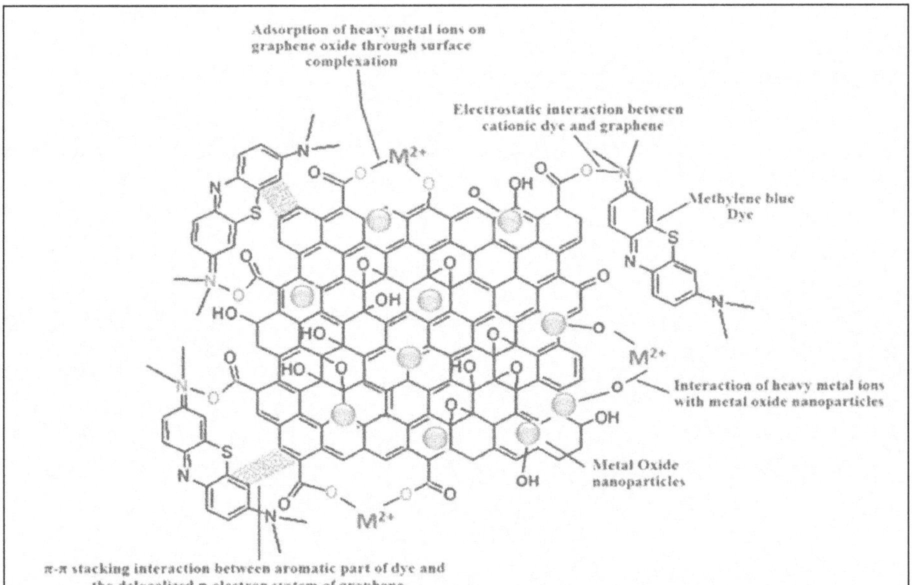

Fig. 10.1: Different types of interactions in involved in the adsorption of pollutants on metal oxide/graphene oxide

Modes of interaction of graphene/metal oxide composite with different type of pollutants are shown in figure 10.1.

MECHANISM OF ADSORPTION

As discussed earlier, nanomaterials posses a higher surface to volume ratio and hence a composite of graphene with nanomaterials potentially acquires much enhanced surface area, thereby increasing the adsorption efficiency. Apart from adsorption, capacitive deionization has also been extensively explored for the desalination of water. The combination of graphene with the metal oxide extends the life time of the adsorbent material by acting as support material which inhibits leaching of ne metal oxides particles into the treated water. The incorporation of metal oxide nanoparticles on graphene limits their re-stacking and aggregation, thereby enhancing the surface area of the composite.[15,16] At the same time, in situ growth of metal oxide nanoparticles on graphene results in less agglomeration among particles as graphene sheets acts as building blocks for the nanoparticles growth and keeps them in dispersed form. Furthermore, the functional groups and defect sites of graphene act as the nucleation and growth sites for nanoparticles. The amalgamation of graphene with metal oxide renders mechanical strength to the composite and increases the robustness of the adsorbent. The work also discusses the possible mechanisms involved in degradation of different pollutants by metal oxide/graphene composite. In light of the increasing concerns related to issue of water pollution, the search of new and more effective water treatment strategies is highly desirable and we believe that this review can provide a comprehensive current state-of-the-art in the area and will prove helpful in designing new water treatment strategies by building upon the current strategies. Theoretically, graphene exhibits a very high surface area (2600 m^2 g^{-1}) which makes it an attractive alternative against the more traditional adsorbents, such as activated and mesoporous carbons. To this effect, graphene and its derivatives have been explored as adsorbents for the removal of pollutants.[17-22] The adsorption efficiency of the graphene can be greatly enhanced by making a composite of it with other nanomaterials.

FE_3O_4 ADSORBED ON GRAPHENE

The hybrids of graphene with magnetic nanomaterials such as Fe_3O_4 have been extensively exploited for removal of pollutants from water[23-25]. Fe_3O_4 is one of the most frequently used materials for water purification due to its high biocompatibility which ensures safety and also the magnetic properties which makes it easy to collect post treatment. Chandra etal.[27] used a magnetite reduced graphene oxide (M-RGO) composite for the removal of Arsenic ions and also studied the effect of pH on the adsorption efficiency of the hybrid material. It was observed that the adsorption efficiency is highly dependent on the pH values. After the adsorption, the Fe_3O_4 graphene composite can be easily separated out from the solution via the use of a magnet. However, in continuous flow systems, the poor stability and the ease of further oxidation to Fe_2O_3 a-Fe_2O_3 and g-Fe_2O_3 are proving to be the major hurdles for its application.[27] These difficulties can potentially be overcome by incorporating the Fe_3O_4 nanoparticles in a graphene matrix. Besides the adsorption of heavy metal ions, adsorption of organic pollutants[26,32] on metal oxide/graphene composite has also been investigated. He et al.[33] prepared Fe_3O_4 graphene composite having covalent binding between Fe_3O_4 and gra-phene. The surface of Fe_3O_4 was modified with tetraethyl orthosilicate and (3-aminopropyl) triethoxysilane (APTES), to attach active amino groups on to the surface of Fe_3O_4. Furthermore, these active amino groups entangled on the surface of Fe_3O_4 were exposed to carboxylic group present on the surface of graphene oxide resulting in the formation of covalent bonds. The as prepared Fe_3O_4/graphene composite exhibited excellent adsorption capacities of nearly 190.14 and 140.79 mg g^{-1} for methylene blue and neutral red, respectively. Wang etal.[26] reported on the speedy adsorption of organic dye, fuchsine, on the magnetic nanocomposites, wherein, nearly 96% of the dye got adsorbed within 10 minutes. This quick adsorption of fuchsine was attributed to two different types of interaction between graphene and dye molecules, including: (i) VanderWaals interactions between the aromatic backbone of the dye molecule and the hexagonally packed carbon atoms, and (ii) p–p stacking interaction among aromatic part of the dye and the delocalized p-electron system of graphene.

EFFECT OF PH IN ADSORPTION

When the pH of the solution was less than the point of zero charge (pH_{pzc}), M-RGO got charged positively thereby, attracting more As (V) anions and leading to an accelerated adsorption of As (V) anions. As the pH of the solution was increased beyond the pH_{pzc} positive charge on M-RGO got reduced but the anionic charge kept increasing due to As (III) anions leading to an increase in adsorption. This is suggestive of the fact that, unlike the adsorption of As (V), the adsorption of As (III) ions on M-RGO is due to surface complexation instead of electrostatic interactions. Lu and co-workers[23] too studied the effect of pH on adsorption of Co (II) on magnetite graphene hybrid. A steady increase in adsorption is observed with an increase of pH from 3 to 6, but the rate of adsorption increased abruptly within the pH range of 6–8.5 and retains high sorption concentration on increasing pH > 8.5. A study by Zhu et al.[29] showed that the removal of the chromium ions by magnetic graphene composite is highly dependent on pH and the composite shows a complete removal of Cr (IV) in acidic pH (1–3). At acidic pH the concentration of $HCrO_4^-$ ions which have higher tendency for adsorption on the composite was dominant over

CrO_4^{2-}. The decreased uptake of Cr (VI) species by the composite on raising pH from acidic to basic was attributed to the increased concentration of OH- ions on the surface of composite, competing with the chromium ions for the available adsorption sites on the composite surface. Similarly, highly acidic solution can also impede the sorption ability of the composite because at high acidic pH, the concentration of hydrogen ions which can compete with the metal ions for the active sites available, exceeds, and can limit the uptake of metal ions by composite.[30,31]. Sun et al.[34] demonstrated excellent removal efficiency for Rhodamine B (91%) and malachite green (94%) dyes. For these systems, the crucial parameters affecting the performance of the composites were the loading of Fe_3O_4 in the composite and the pH of the solution. An increase in the loading of Fe_3O_4 in composite beyond a certain amount caused a drop in the performance, due to a reduction in the exposed surface area of composite. Luo etal.[37] used magnetic Fe_3O_4/graphene composite for the extraction of six sulfonamides from the water and also optimized various parameters such as pH, graphene content and extraction time.

Optimal extraction conditions to achieve maximum efficiency were found to be pH 3, graphene 0.3 mg and an extraction time of 4 min. Wu and co-workers[25] employed graphene based magnetic nanocomposite for the pre-concentration of few carbamate pesticides in environmental water sample. The magnetic graphene composite exhibited good adsorptive ability, strong magnetism and could be reused up to twelve times without any significant loss in sorption capacity. In an another study by Zhao et al.,[36] magnetic graphene as an adsorbent in the solid phase extraction procedure for the enrichment of some triazine herbicides in water samples was employed.

METAL OXIDES OTHER THAN FE_3O_4 ADSORBED ON GRAPHENE

Other metal oxides such as SiO_2, ZnO, MnO_2, $CoFe_2O_4$ (ref. 35) and ZrO_2 (ref. 38) have also been hybridized with graphene to formulate adsorbents. For large scale application of composites as adsorbents; the selectivity of the adsorbent towards targeted adsorbate is highly desirable. The SiO_2/graphene composites prepared by Hao et al.,[15] exhibited excellent selectivity for Pb(II) ions out of several available divalent ions such as Cu^{2+}, Ni^{2+}, Co^{2+}, Cd^{2+} and Cr^{3+}. However, an enhancement in the ionic strength of the solution by adding salts such as KNO_3 suppressed the adsorption efficiency of the composite, as these salts compete with the metal ions for the available adsorption sites on the surface of composites. Lee and Yang[39] studied the effect of hydrothermal treatment period on the adsorption efficiency of the TiO_2 blossoms/graphene composite for the removal of Zn^{2+}, Cd^{2+} and Pb^{2+} ions. Zong and co-workers[38] obtained ZrO_2 functionalized graphite oxide by prostrating method and employed it as a sorbent material for the removal of phosphate ions. Again, the adsorption capacity of phosphate ions on ZrO_2 functionalized graphite oxide was found to be highly dependent on the pH values and diminished on increasing the pH value from 2–12 and attained its maximum at a pH value of 2.03. This reduction in the adsorption capacity on increasing pH was explained on the basis of variation in the extent of various types of interaction between phosphate ions and ZrO_2/graphene composite including electrostatic interaction, ion-exchange and acid base interaction.

Li et al.[40] reported defluoridation of aqueous solution using manganese oxide coated graphene oxide and also studied the effect of different parameters such as pH, adsorbent dose, contact time and temperature on adsorption behavior of composite. Manganese oxide/graphene oxide composite exhibited maximum adsorption efficiency at pH 5.5. On increasing the adsorbent dosage from 5 to 65 mg per 50 mL, the adsorption percentage was also enhanced from 6 to 45%. Nanocomposite of hydrated zirconium oxide with graphene oxide prepared by Luo et al. show excellent adsorption capacities 95.15 and 84.89 mg g^{-1} for As (III) and As(V) ions, respectively. These values were nearly 3.54 and 4.64 times higher than pristine ZrO(OH)$_2$ nanoparticles. An increase in adsorbent dosage enhanced the adsorbent percentage, but reduced the overall adsorption capacity, as the increase in the dosage beyond the threshold amount resulted in unsaturated reactive sites, lower surface area and increased diffusion path length. On the other hand, at lower dosage all active sites got occupied by the adsorbate, thereby enhancing the adsorption capacity. However, it should be noted that the mechanism involved in the adsorption of heavy metal ions on graphene supported metal oxide nanoparticles is not clear and under investigation. Ren et al[41] have performed a detailed characterization study of MnO_2/graphene samples before and after adsorption of copper and lead ions on it. Fig. 10.2 shows suggested mechanism involved in adsorption of Cu (II) and Pb (II) ions on d-MnO_2/graphene. The d-MnO_2/graphene showed excellent cycling as well and it was observed that the material can be used for at least four times, without any significant loss in the sorption ability. Recently, Their results revealed that initially, the protonation of functional group may take place and surface oxygen of different groups C–OH, Mn–OH or –COOH groups, which can behave as Lewis acid and forms tetradentate monodentate complexes with Cu (II) and Pb(II) ions which are lewis base in nature. Ren et al.[41] studied the adsorption of nickel ions on graphene/d-MnO_2 nanocomposite and noticed a significant effect of temperature upon extent of sorption of nickel ions on the nanocomposites. On increasing the reaction temperature from 298 K to 318 K, the adsorption capacity of graphene nanosheets/d-MnO_2 composite was enhanced from 46.55 to 60.01 mg g^{-1}. The adsorption capacity of the graphene/d-MnO_2 composite was observed to be 1.5 and 15 times higher than for d-MnO_2 and graphene nanosheets respectively.

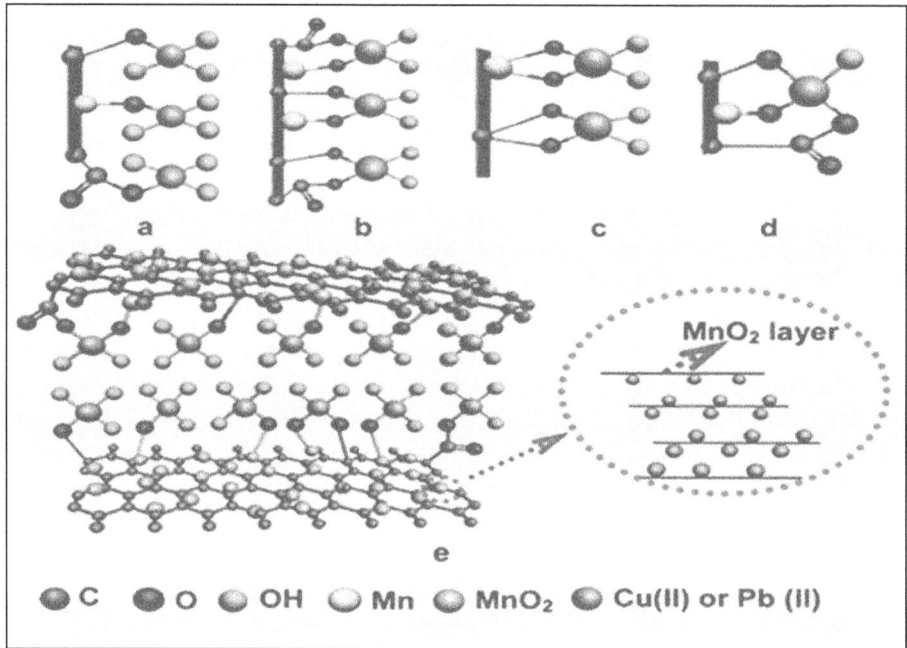

Fig. 10.2: Possible tetradentate configurations after Cu(II) and Pb(II) sorption: (a) monodentate, (b) bidentate mononuclear, (c) bidentate binuclear, (d) multidentate, and (e) proposed tetradentate monodentate complexes on GNS/MnO$_2$ surface and MnO$_2$ layer in actual solution. (REF-1)

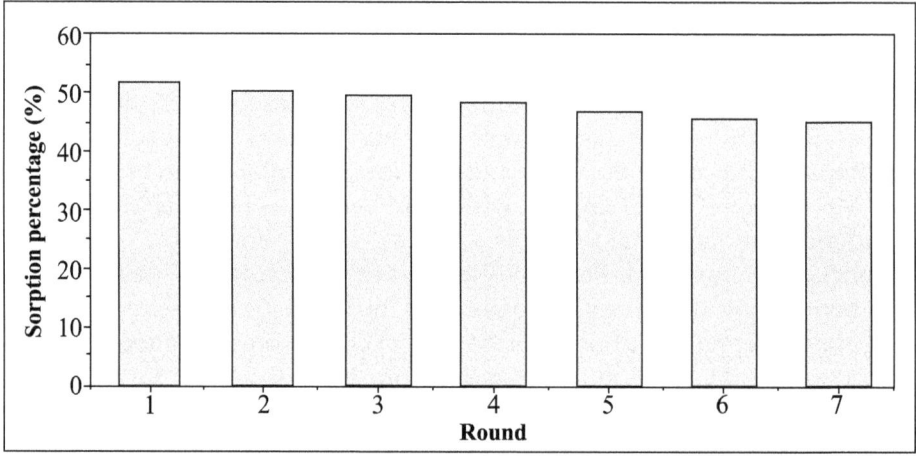

Fig. 10.3: Recycled efficiency of Fe3O4/GO in the removal of U(VI). T ¼293 K, pH ¼ 5.5 _ 0.1, CU(VI)initial ¼ 1.12 _ 10_4 mol L_1, m V_1 ¼ 0.3 gL_1, I ¼ 0.01 mol L_1 KNO$_3$

Figure 10.3 shows the variation of the sorption efficiency upon multiple regeneration rounds for the removal of U(IV) by Fe_3O_4/GO.[24] It can be clearly observed that the regenerated Fe_3O_4/GO maintained good sorption efficiency.

HOW TO IMPROVE ADSORPTION EFFICIENCY?

Ample studies have reported on the reduction in the adsorption capacity of the composites upon an increase in the amount of metal oxide beyond a critical limit. Since metal oxides are comparatively heavy and posses lower surface area to weight ratio as compared to graphene, so an inordinate increase in the amount of metal oxide in the composites, results in a reduction of the adsorption capacity. An increase in the pH value can enhance the concentration of hydroxyl groups on the surface which can hinder adsorption of metal ions; on the other hand, highly acidic pH can increase the concentration of H⁺ ion in the solution which compete with metal ions for the sorption sites available on the adsorbent so maintaining a pH at which both performance retarding side reactions can be prevented is highly desirable. The adsorption capacity of the materials for heavy metal ions, organic molecules such as dyes and other pollutants is highly dependent on the pH value and hence maintaining a pH which favors adsorption is absolutely crucial. Some heavy metal ions such as chromium and arsenic form different metastable species at different pH levels and out of these various metastable species few may acquire compatibility and can be easily adsorbed on adsorbent which increases the adsorption capacity of the composite. As adsorption is a superficial phenomenon, hence, the surface properties of the adsorbent play very important role in deciding its sorption ability. It has been found that presence of active groups such as –COOH and –OH on to the surface of the graphene contributes signi cantly to its sorption capacity by forming complexes with metal ions. Therefore, an enhancement in the number of active groups on the surface increases sorption capacity. Furthermore, the surface of graphene can be modified with some other groups such as $-NH_2$, which can readily combine with the metal ions in the solution. Not only the functionalities present on the surface of the support interact with the metal ions, but the functional groups on the semiconductor nanoparticles also interact with the metal ions of pollutant.

Hence, synergistic effects can be expected in the case of dual functionalized catalyst and support, for example functionalized semiconductor nanoparticles on reduced graphene oxide (which retains some –OH and –COOH and –C–O–C– groups even after reduction). A good adsorbent should not only be quick in adsorption of pollutants but should also exhibit speedy and complete desorption of pollutants during regeneration, for it to be reused. Ease of regeneration of adsorbent decides its wide scale applicability. The desorption of pollutants can be carried out by adjusting the pH of the solution to a value which impedes adsorption. Replacement of metal ions by H^+ ions through acid treatment can be another way to regenerate the absorbent. For organic pollutants, such as dyes and pesticides, regeneration can be carried out by simply washing composite with a solvent to dissolve away the pollutants. Heat treatment can also be an attractive option for regeneration of the adsorbent if adsorbent is stable at higher temperatures. Along with a high activity, the durability is an important issue which needs to be resolved to provide real life applications for metal oxide/graphene based adsorbents. Loose physical adhesion or weak and labile bonding between metal oxide and graphene can result in the leaching of metal oxide in to the treated water which can not only reduce the life time of the adsorbent but also can cause cross contamination of the water. Thus, the strength of bonding between metal oxide and graphene is a matter of great concern and synthesis route, reaction conditions and nature of reactants, which can facilitate affirm bonding between the metal oxide and graphene must be chosen. Surface of the metal oxide and graphene can be modified with functional groups which can help in attaining tight binding between metal oxide and graphene. The removal of the adsorbent, post water treatment, from the purified water remains a considerable issue with traditional adsorbents. The introduction of magnetic adsorbent materials in composites makes them easier to be separated from the purified water; thus providing an edge to the magnetic metal oxide containing composite on nonmagnetic metal oxides. After completion of adsorption, magnetic adsorbent can easily be recovered from the treated water using an external magnet, which eliminates the risk of cross contamination.

CONCLUSION

This review can be an input to the sum of efforts for understanding various phenomenon and properties related to the metal oxide/grapheme composite particularly for those which are important from the point of view of water treatment. This review can be an input to the sum of efforts for understanding various phenomenon and properties related to the metal oxide/grapheme composite particularly for those which are important from the point of view of water treatment. It was concluded that graphene oxide (GO) sheets serves as scaffold for the cell surface attachment and proliferation. Graphene oxide (GO) lms also did not exhibit any cytotoxic effects on the mammalian cells, which gives an edge to graphene over carbon nanotubes which have been found to be toxic at different concentrations.[42,43] It was suggested that the introduction of contaminants in to the graphene oxide films during preparation might be a reason behind the observed antimicrobial activity of the graphene reported in various studies. Therefore a preparation method which can yield pure and quality graphene material is highly desired to completely and fully understand antimicrobial activity of graphene. Apart from selection of preparation method for graphene, investigations to find out minimum inhibitory concentration (MIC) and suitable dosage amount of graphene for antimicrobial applications is also very much important. The unique properties of graphene, in conjunction with size-dependent properties of nanomaterials induces further functionalities to the composites such as high adsorption capacity, extended light absorption range and improved charge separation properties along with high stability. The features which graphene endows to the composite and role of it in improving photo catalytic activity, adsorptive and antimicrobial activity of composite. The technology for synthesis of high quality graphene is not fully mature, and the precise control on the final product in terms of purity, control of defects and defect sites, number of layers and re-aggregation is yet to be established. The micro, nanoporosity of the structures along with the high surface area of graphene lends itself for high adsorption capabilities of heavy metal ions, organic dyes and possible hydrocarbon spills. Developing water treatment technologies based on metal oxide/graphene composite will be an interesting but difficult task for researchers since still there are few questions answers of which yet to be nd out such as what will the eventual fate of these composite and to what extent these technologies and materials are environment friendly?

This means recycling and disposal of these expired composites is also a big challenge. Strategies for recycling and disposal of used composites will develop concurrently along with their application in household water purification devises to avoid waste generation. Development of methods for the formation of composites of graphene with metal oxides without losing surface area of graphene significantly is also a major challenge in the designing of metal oxides/graphene composites based adsorbents. Adsorbents developed using metal oxide/graphene composites will have to compete with the activated carbons in term of cost and popularity. Few studies mentioned in this article have reported that metal oxide/graphene based composite can be utilized for selective adsorption of ions which is needed to be further investigate to design adsorbents which can have selectivity towards specifications.

REFERENCES

1. R.K Upadhyay, N. Soin & S.S Roy, RAC Adv. 2014, 4, 3823-3851.
2. K.S. Novoselov, A.K. Geim, S. Morozov, D. Jiang, Y. Zhang, S. Dubonos, I. Grigorieva and A. Firsov, Science, 2004, 306, 666-669.
3. C. Lee, X. Wei, J.W. Kysar and J. Hone, Science, 2008, 321, 385-388.
4. Y. Zheng, N. Wei, Z. Fan, L. Xu and Z. Huang, Nanotechnology, 2011, 22, 405701.
5. A.K. Geim and A.H. MacDonald, Phys. Today, 2007, 60, 35-41.

6. S. Wang, H. Sun, H. Ang and M. Tad´e, Chem. Eng. J., 2013, 226, 336-347.
7. J. Theron, J. Walker and T. Cloete, Crit. Rev. Microbiol., 2008, 34, 43-69.
8. D.R. Dreyer, S. Park, C.W. Bielawski and R.S. Ruoff, Chem. Soc. Rev., 2010, 39, 228-240.
9. A. Farghali, M. Bahgat, W. El Rouby and M. Khedr, J. Alloys Compd., 2012, 555, 193-200.
10. T. Wu, X. Cai, S. Tan, H. Li, J. Liu and W. Yang, Chem. Eng. J., 2011, 173, 144-149.
11. D. Zhang, L. Fu, L. Liao, B. Dai, R. Zou and C. Zhang, Electrochim. Acta, 2012, 75, 71-79.
12. Z.-H. Huang, X. Zheng, W. Lv, M. Wang, Q.-H. Yang and F. Kang, Langmuir, 2011, 27, 7558-7562.
13. Y. Wu, H. Luo, H. Wang, C. Wang, J. Zhang and Z. Zhang, J. Colloid Interface Sci., 2013, 394, 183-191.
14. G. Zhao, J. Li, X. Ren, C. Chen and X. Wang, Environ. Sci. Technol., 2011, 45, 10454-10462.
15. L. Hao, H. Song, L. Zhang, X. Wan, Y. Tang and Y. Lv, J. Colloid Interface Sci., 2012, 369, 381-387.
16. G. Williams, B. Seger and P.V. Kamat, ACS Nano, 2008, 2, 1487-1491.
17. G.K. Ramesha, A. Vijaya Kumara, H.B. Muralidhara and S. Sampath, J. Colloid Interface Sci., 2011, 361, 270-277.
18. J.N. Tiwari, K. Mahesh, N.H. Le, K.C. Kemp, R. Timilsina, R.N. Tiwari and K.S. Kim, Carbon, 2013, 56, 173-182.
19. 227 Z. Li, F. Chen, L. Yuan, Y. Liu, Y. Zhao, Z. Chai and W. Shi,Chem. Eng. J., 2012, 210, 539-546.
20. S. Bai, X. Shen, G. Zhu, A. Yuan, J. Zhang, Z. Ji and D. Qiu, Carbon, 2013, 60, 157-168.
21. O.G. Apul, Q. Wang, Y. Zhou and T. Karanl, Water Res., 2013, 47, 1648-1654.
22. Z. Pei, L. Li, L. Sun, S. Zhang, X.-q. Shan, S. Yang and B. Wen, Carbon, 2013, 51, 156-163.
23. W. Lu, Y. Wu, J. Chen and Y. Yang, Cryst Eng Comm, 2013, DOI: 10.1039/c3ce41833b.
24. 237 P. Zong, S. Wang, Y. Zhao, H. Wang, H. Pan and C. He, Chem. Eng. J., 2013, 220, 45-52.
25. Q. Wu, G. Zhao, C. Feng, C. Wang and Z. Wang, J. Chromatogr., A, 2011, 1218, 7936-7942.
26. C. Wang, C. Feng, Y. Gao, X. Ma, Q. Wu and Z. Wang, Chem. Eng. J., 2011, 173, 92-97.
27. V. Chandra, J. Park, Y. Chun, J.W. Lee, I.-C. Hwang and K.S. Kim, ACS Nano, 2010, 4, 3979-3986.
28. M. Liu, C. Chen, J. Hu, X. Wu and X. Wang, J. Phys. Chem. C, 2011, 115, 25234-25240.
29. J. Zhu, S. Wei, H. Gu, S.B. Rapole, Q. Wang, Z. Luo,N. Haldolaarachchige, D.P. Young and Z. Guo, Environ.Sci. Technol., 2012, 46, 977-985.
30. B. Aly¨uz and S. Veli, J. Hazard. Mater., 2009, 167, 482-488.
31. A.-H.Chen, S.-C.Liu, C.-Y.Chen and C.-Y. Chen, J. Hazard. Mater., 2008, 154, 184-191.
32. X. Yang, J. Li, T. Wen, X. Ren, Y. Huang and X. Wang, Colloids Surf., A, 2013, 422, 118-125.
33. F. He, J. Fan, D. Ma, L. Zhang, C. Leung and H.L. Chan,Carbon, 2010, 48, 3139-3144.
34. H. Sun, L. Cao and L. Lu, Nano Res., 2011, 4, 550-562.
35. N. Li, M. Zheng, X. Chang, G. Ji, H. Lu, L. Xue, L. Pan and J. Cao, J. Solid State Chem., 2011, 184, 953-958.

36. G. Zhao, S. Song, C. Wang, Q. Wu and Z. Wang, Anal. Chim. Acta, 2011, 708, 155-159.
37. Y.-B.Luo, Z.-G. Shi, Q. Gao and Y.-Q. Feng, J. Chromatogr., A, 2011, 1218, 1353-1358.
38. E. Zong, D. Wei, H. Wan, S. Zheng, Z. Xu and D. Zhu, Chem.Eng. J., 2013, 221, 193-203.
39. Y.-C. Lee and J.-W. Yang, J. Ind. Eng. Chem., 2012, 18, 1178-1185.
40. Y. Li, Q. Du, J. Wang, T. Liu, J. Sun, Y. Wang, Z. Wang, Y. Xiaand L. Xia, J. Fluorine Chem., 2013, 148, 67-73.
41. Y. Ren, N. Yan, Q. Wen, Z. Fan, T. Wei, M. Zhang and J. Ma, Chem. Eng. J., 2011, 175, 1-7.
42. G. Jia, H. Wang, L. Yan, X. Wang, R. Pei, T. Yan, Y. Zhao and X. Guo, Environ. Sci. Technol., 2005, 39, 1378-1383.
43. H. Wang, J. Wang, X. Deng, H. Sun, Z. Shi, Z. Gu, Y. Liu andY. Zhaoc, J. Nanosci. Nanotechnol., 2004, 4, 1019-1024.

Pages: 226-245

Eco-tourism, Environmental Problems and Sustainable Development
Edited by: Dr. Soubam Premchandra Singh; Dr. Ashok K. Rathoure
Dr. Pawan Kumar 'Bharti'
ISBN: 978-93-86841-57-5
Edition: 2018
Published by: Discovery Publishing House Pvt. Ltd., New Delhi (India)

Present Status and Future Strategies of Wood Preservation Industry

Bandana Dhiman
Bhupender Dutt

INTRODUCTION

Wood is a prominent constructional material because its low cost and availability in various forms and sizes, together with such properties as relatively great strength with respect to weight, ease of shaping and fastening, low heat conductivity and sound–deadening quality, have made it is outstanding building material from the time of first settlers' down to present. Due to its biological origin, it is one of the most complex constructions materials and its strength and durability have become of paramount importance in the general construction field. Relatively easy to fabricate into beams, columns, and roof systems using simple hand tools. It has affinity for moisture and this can lead to biological deterioration caused by insects and decay fungi. The various organization and individual interested in furthering the use of forest products have done much in recent year to increase the serviceability of wood and the resultant economy in its utilization.

Biological damage to wood and wood products is mainly caused by the mould, stain, decay fungi, and insects such as beetles and termites and development of low environmental impact technologies for the elimination of biological damage is one of the vital goals of wood protection industry (Freitag *et al.*, 1991). Protection against these organisms is generally realized

---

Wood Science and Technology, Department of Forest Products, College of Forestry Dr. Y.S. Parmar, UHF, Nauni, Solan (H.P.) (India)

by drying or chemical treatment of wood products. Although relatively low-toxic chemicals are presently used as wood protectants, public concerns remain about the use of these chemicals (Byrne, 1998).

What is preservation?

It is an art of protection of wood against any factor whatsoever that may damage and ultimately destroy it. In practical sense it refers to improvement of wood natural durability by treatment with chemicals. It is an outstanding practice to improve the serviceability of wood by chemical treatment under condition that favours early deterioration by decay.

Many chemicals are used to enhance the durability of wood and wood-derived products that are very important in our life. Such chemicals are copper, chromium, arsenate, zinc etc. Though these preservatives are useful to protect wood from biodeterioration, but environmental toxicity is also related with them. These chemicals are harmful for many species for our biodiversity including animals, plants, beneficial microbes, nematodes, invertebrates etc.

Shortage in supply of durable wood species has resulted in increase in the use of plantation grown timber species. In order to enhance the service life of plantation grown non-durable species, preservative treatment become necessary. (Tripathi *et al.*, 2009)

Naturally Rot-resistant Woods

These species are resistant to decay in their natural state, due to high levels of organic chemicals called *extractives*, mainly polyphenols. Extractives are chemicals that are deposited in the heartwood of certain tree species as they convert sapwood to heartwood. Some rot-resistant woods are:

- Ironbark (*Eucalyptus* Spp.)
- Totara (*Podocarpus totara*)
- Kauri (*Agathis australis*)
- Coast redwood (*Sequoia sempervirens*)
- Western red cedar (*Thuja plicata*)

Natural durability of individual wood species against biotic factors depends mainly on the chemical structure and amount of extractives present (Jelokava & Sindler, 2001). Wood extractives are made up of numerous components that can be isolated from wood using non polar and polar solvents. Higher the proportion of extractives, the greater the durability of the heartwood (Hillis, 1978). Extractives (oils, tannins, and resins) toxic to biological organisms are thought to be the primary mechanism by whereby wood naturally resists attack. As a tree grows, the cells in the central rings die to create heartwood. Water and nutrients cease to flow through the heartwood, and extractives collect and concentrate in the heartwood. For this reason, the Building code permits only an occasional piece of naturally durable lumber to have a very small amount of sapwood.

Decay of wood is caused by digestive action of enzymes secreted by the fungal hyphae resulting loss of both timber production and uses of wood. Cellulose hydrolysis is achieved by endoglucanases and cellobiohydrolases, collectively termed cellulases. Hydrolysis of hemicellulose, a mixed polymer, occurs via the action of hydrolytic xylanases, mananases and possibly other hydrolases with broad substrate specificity (Eaton & Hale, 1993). The mineralization of lignin involves two peroxidases, lignin peroxidase and Mn-dependant peroxidase, and a polyphenoloxidase, laccase, collectively known as lignin-modifying enzymes (LME's). These enzymes catalyze production of highly reactive radicals which oxidize phenolic and non-phenolic lignin components (Pointing, 2001).

There are wood species that are naturally resistant to bio-deterioration agents. The resistance is mainly due to the accumulation of extractives in the heartwood some of which are decay inhibitors (Kityo and Plumptre, 1997). It is these extractives which render the heartwood poisonous to wood destroying organisms. Haygreen and Bowyer (1996) and Milton (1995) noted that the chemical composition and amount of extractives in wood is highly variable within and between tree species and can range from 2-15% of wood weight.

The question that needs to be asked is 'Can naturally occurring extractives be used to enhance the durability of those wood species in which these extractives are lacking?' Hillis (1978) and Laver (1978) observed that extractives from bark and wood have the potential to replace synthetic wood preservatives. Investigation revealed that extractives could protect wood effectively at laboratory scale. Majority of vascular plants are potential source of anti-microbial agents (Tripathi *et al.*, 1978). Condensed tannins are natural preservatives and antifungal agents found in high concentrations in the bark and wood of some tree species (Zucker, 1983). It has also been postulated that wood extractives can protect heartwood via at least three different mechanisms, namely fungicidal activity, free radical scavenging/ antioxidation and metal chelation (Schultz & Nicholas, 2000).

The use of treated wood has declined from historical highs. Because concrete and steel have greater load bearing capacity, few wharves and other large structures are currently being constructed on wood pilings. In particular, concrete pilings are cost-competitive with treated wood pilings over the long-term and are competing in these markets. The other major uses of treated wood, such as railroad ties, highway sign posts and utility poles, generally only interact with the aquatic environment during flooding or through improper disposal of construction or demolition debris. Yet, despite the overall decline in treated wood use, many instances continue to arise where project proponents wish to use treated wood.

Types of Wood Preservatives

Oil-Type Preservatives
- Creosote
- Pentachlorophenol
- Copper Naphthenate
- Oxine Copper (Copper-8-Quinolinolate)
- IPBC and Insecticides

Waterborne Preservatives
- Chromated Copper Arsenate (CCA)
- Ammoniacal Copper Zinc Arsenate (ACZA)
- Alkaline Copper Quaternary (ACQ) Compounds
- Copper Azoles (CBA-A and CA-B)
- Borates
- Other Waterborne Preservatives

Preservatives which are no longer available commercially
- Ammoniacal Copper Arsenate (ACA)
- Acid Copper Chromate (ACC)
- Ammoniacal Copper Citrate (CC)

Oil-Type Preservatives

Oil-type preservatives cause no appreciable strength loss because they do not chemically react with wood cell wall components. However, treatment with oil-type preservatives can adversely affect strength if extreme in-retort seasoning parameters are used (for example, Boultonizing, steaming, or vapor drying conditions) or if excessive temperatures or pressures are used during the treating process. They are not usually used for applications that involve frequent contact with human skin or inside dwellings because they may be visually oily or oily to touch, or have a strong odor.

Waterborne Preservatives

Waterborne preservative treatments can reduce the mechanical properties of wood. Treatment standards include specific processing requirements intended to prevent or limit strength reductions resulting from the chemicals and the waterborne preservative treatment process. They have become more widely used in recent years because the treated wood has a dry, paintable surface and no odor. The most common of these preservatives has been Chromated Copper Arsenate (CCA). Wood treated with CCA, commonly called green treated.

Primary objective of preservative treatment is to increase the life of material in service, thus decreasing the ultimate cost of the product and avoiding the need of frequent replacement in permanent construction. Therefore wood is treated with a chemical preservative or synthetic chemical fungicide to prevent damage by these aggressive biodeteriogens (Craig *et al.*, 2001), which have negative impacts on human health and environment.

Development in Wood Preservation from History

The history of humankind is closely intertwined with wood utilization. Some of the earliest uses of wood were for fuel for heating and cooking. Even today, this accounts for the highest demand and use of wood in many developing countries. A period of significant advances in industrial processing occurred during the Industrial Revolution. Among these advances in the United States was the construction of trans-continental railroads, which created the need for crossties and switch ties.

As industrial technology advanced, wood was used more frequently in exterior structural applications. Wood species that did not possess inherent decay resistance properties failed in service due to biological attack, creating a need for preservative-treated wood. Several historical treatises on wood preservation can be found in the literature (Hunt and Garratt, 1967).

References uttered that the use of Bitumen by ancient Egyptians about 2000-4000 years back to preserve their coffin and wooden dowel pin. Garlic boiled in vinegar to preserve wood from attack by worm. Wood and bamboo can be buried in mud to help protect it from insects and decay. This practice is used widely in Vietnam to build farm houses consisting of a wooden structural frame, a bamboo roof frame, and bamboo with mud mixed with rice hay for the walls. While wood in contact with soil will generally decompose more quickly than wood not in contact with soil, it is possible that the predominantly clay soils prevalent in Vietnam provide a degree of mechanical protection against insect attack which compensates for the accelerated rate of decay.

- In the 1700s, Mercuric chloride and Copper sulfate were first recommended.
- Zinc chloride was recommended as wood preservative in 1815.
- Use of coal-tar creosote, which was patented in 1836 by Franz Moll.
- Copper naphthenate has been used as a wood preservative in 1889 (in Germany).
- In 1928 Pentachlorophenol formed by the reaction of chlorine on phenol by W. Iwanowski and J. Turski.
- In 1929 L.P. Curtin patented the use of chlorine derivatives of coal-tar acids.
- In 1938 CCA (copper chromate arsenate) was accentuated and patented by Kamesam.

Three forms were standardized by AWPA: type A in 1953, type B in 1964, and type C in 1969, with type C dominating the market place today. The three types differ in their ratio of Cu:Cr:As.
- A major arsenical preservative, ammoniacal copper arsenate (ACA), was standardized in 1950

Another historically important preservative is pentachlorophenol (C_6Cl_5OH), which is a crystalline chemical compound formed by the reaction of chlorine on phenol. It is widely used oil borne preservative. During 1928 W. Iwanowski and J. Turski, discovered the use of di-, tri-, and polychlorinated phenols for wood-preserving purposes. In 1929 in the United States, L.P. Curtin patented the use of "chlorine derivatives of coal-tar acids of higher molecular weight than the cresols" expressing a preference for chlorinated phenols. The production of chlorinated phenols in the United States for wood preserving experiments did not begin until about 1930 (Hunt and Garratt, 1967).

Beginning of wood preservation on scientific lines: Wood preservation as a science was developed by the British Navy to protect its ships from dry rot. About 1832 Kyan (chemist), the British admiralty medical chief Sir William Burnett and a coal tar expert Bethel, developed processes for the impregnation of wood. Kyan used mercuric chloride, Burnett used zinc chloride for dipping timber in a solution and for timber treatment Bethel use creosote under pressure.

In India wood preservation on scientific and modern basis was introduced by Sir Ralph Pearson of the Indian forest service in year 1908. He did valuable pioneer work during the course of his service at Dehradun and entitled as Father of wood preservation of India.

Economic Value of Wood Preservation: Treatment of the timber ensures a service life three times as long as that of untreated wood. The economic value of wood preservation is convincingly demonstrated by the extended service life.

Examples of wood preservation practices:
- Untreated railway sleepers may last 5 to 6 years but treated sleepers for 20 to 25 years.
- Untreated transmission poles may stand for about 4 to 6 years, properly impregnated poles for 30 years.

Impacts of use of CCA-treated Wood on Health and Environment

Copper, chromium and arsenic are natural constituents of the earth's crust and copper and chromium are essential micronutrients for many life forms (Brooks, 1993). The principal use is as a constituent of metal alloys, but other major uses are as a base for the manufacture of fungicides and for pigments. It is also of interest to note that estimates that each year, volcanoes contribute 7,000 tonnes of arsenic to the global environment, approximately half the amount used annually in CCA preservatives.

The arsenic in CCA is a known human carcinogen and has been linked to nervous system damage and birth defects. About 138 million pounds of CCA are used to treat wood each year.

(U.S. EPA. Integrated Risk Information System (IRIS) on Arsenic). These synthetic chemicals are expensive and often harmful to the workers and the environment. These preservatives are not readily degraded to harmless products and are not easy to detoxify. The copper based preservatives are also poor inhibitors of mould (Arango *et al.*, 2005) and are very costly.

Three commercially available non-arsenical systems appear poised to replace CCA for residential applications: alkaline copper quat (ACQ), amine copper azole (CA), and copper bis-(N-cyclohexyldiazeniumdioxy) (Cu-HDO or copper xyligen). Excellent technical discussions of the newer preservative systems and their properties and applications can be found in the literature. (Nicholas and Shultz 1995, Goodell *et al.* 2003).

Many toxic chemicals are used in wood preservation and wood processing industry. These chemicals are harmful for many species for our biodiversity including plants, beneficial microbes, nematodes, invertebrates, etc. So, scientists are working on biological preservative having no harmful effect on biodiversity.

Since the use of heavy metal-based wood preservatives such as chromated copper arsenate (CCA) was voluntarily withdrawn from housing markets in the U.S., research has been focused on developing new user friendly wood preservatives to protect wood against fungi, mould and insects (Kartal *et al.*,2004).

Environmental Concerns with CCA Alternatives

Environmental and health concerns have been raised over the use of CCA-treated wood. It is likely that CCA alternatives will circumvent some of these concerns simply because they do not contain arsenic. Because they have been developed relatively recently or have been used infrequently, only limited research has been conducted on their potential leaching and environmental impact. Much available data have been obtained using small samples that accelerate leaching and allow more rapid comparisons between preservative formulations. Although useful as a comparative tool, leaching rates derived from small samples should not be directly extrapolated to commodity size material. Leaching from wood treated with water-based preservatives is also dependent on completion of fixation reactions. The active ingredients of various waterborne wood preservatives (copper, chromium, arsenic and zinc) are initially water soluble in the treating solution but become resistant to leaching when placed into the wood.

Pentachlorophenol: PCP is an organochlorine compound used as a pesticide and a disinfectant. This chemical is not uncommon in the aquatic environment and is extremely toxic to fish. Expose to penta concentrations of only a few parts per billion can cause death within minutes for many species of salmon and trout.

First produced in the 1930s, it was marketed under many trade names. It can be found in two forms: PCP itself or as the sodium salt of PCP, which dissolves easily in water. (United States Environmental Protection Agency, 2006). PCP has been used as a herbicide, insecticide, fungicide, algaecide, and disinfectant and as an ingredient in antifouling paint. Some applications were in agricultural seeds (for non food uses), leather, masonry, wood preservation, cooling tower water, rope, and paper mills. Its use has declined due to its high toxicity and slow biodegradation.

Chromated Copper Arsenate (CCA): CCA treated wood also known as Wolmanized wood, is used on decks, fences and playground equipment to prevent wood decay. This Web site provides the current regulatory status, as well as technical and general information regarding the handling, use, and potential hazards associated with CCA-treated wood.

Creosote - a wood preservative used for commercial purposes only; it has no registered residential uses. Creosote is obtained from high temperature distillation of coal tar. It is used as a fungicide, insecticide, miticide, and sporicide to protect wood, primarily utility poles and railroad ties. EPA is currently reassessing creosote as part of its ongoing reregistration program. Three of the classes of chemicals found in coal tar creosote that are known to cause harmful health effects are polycyclic aromatic hydrocarbons (PAHs), phenol, and cresols. Creosote is made up of about 75-85 percent PAHs and several of them are known to cause cancer.

FUTURE STRATEGIES

Many chemicals are used today to enhance the durability of wood and wood-derived products that are very important in our life. Such chemicals are copper, chromium, arsenate, zinc etc. Though these preservatives are useful to protect wood from biodeterioration, but environmental toxicity is also related with them.

In recent decades, public attention to the environmental issues of utilization of metal containing wood preservatives and the disposal problem of chemically treated wood have received interest in the oldest approach to wood protection using natural extract derrived from plants or microorganism (Evans, 2003). The use of biological mean have greater advantages over the use of chemical for degradation because biotechnological synthesized product are less toxic and environmental friendly(Liu *et al.*, 1998). As result various environment friendly treatment or naturally durable plant species are being evaluated (Yalinkilic *et al.*,1998).

Challenges in Developing New Wood Preservatives

In today's society we have become accustomed to rapidly developing and changing products in most residential commodities. Consumers and regulators sometimes seem frustrated that the wood preservation community does not rapidly produce a wide selection of effective replacements for CCA. Unfortunately, it currently takes many years to bring a new wood preservative to market. A formulation must meet several important criteria to be an effective wood preservative. The first challenge is identification of a combination of active ingredients that will provide long-term protection against a wide range of organisms that damage wood. In addition to decay fungi, the preservative must protect against attack by termites, carpenter ants, beetles, and other insects. Even within decay fungi there is a range of species and strains that differ in chemical tolerance. The preservative must also resist detoxification by non-wood-attacking fungi and bacteria.

These requirements preclude the use of compounds that have a very narrow or specific toxicity to only one type of organism. A wood preservative needs some degree of broad spectrum efficacy, which is in direct conflict with the goal of identifying environmentally friendly compounds. Because a wood preservative must protect against a range of organisms while simultaneously resisting environmental degradation, it has proven difficult to develop reliable methods of accelerating evaluation of preservatives. The chemical wood preservative that have been banned or limited for some application in some European countries, U.S. and Japan is (CCA). (Kartal *et al*., 2004)

The screening of plant extracts and plant products for antimicrobial activity has shown that higher plants represent a potential source of novel antibiotic prototypes (Afolayan, 2003). It is also reported that the antifungal properties of poisonous plant extract from *Nerium oleander* L. can make it effective wood preservative (Goktas O *et al*., 2007).

Higher tropical plants can produce diverse anti-microbe and anti-insect substances (Downum *et al*., 1993; Lis-Balchin *et al*., 1996; Nakamura *et al*., 1996). Substances such as flavonoids, alkaloids, and terpenoids are the secondary metabolites produced by the plants as chemical defense against pests and diseases attacks. It is estimated only 10% of these tropical plants have been investigated for their pesticidal activity. Teak is one of these plants which produce secondary metabolic products containing phenolic compounds.

Natural products from plants such as *Ageratum conyzoides, Ficus retusa, Lavandula pubescens, Lawsonia alba* etc. have been evaluated and found to have great potentials as novel fungicide sources for controlling pathogenic fungi (Salih A. Bazaid *et al*., 2010).

Clark *et al.* (1990) reported that hexane and methanol extracts of *Juniperus Virginiana* heartwood and needles had antifungal and antibacterial activity. Essential oil are generally perceived as safer alternative to synthetic pesticides and recently Duringer *et al.* (2010) reported heartwood extracts of Port Orford cedar posed little to no risk to aquatic organisms.

The plants tested were *Calatropis, Datura, Ocimum, Ricinus* and *Thidax*. Among the plant parts tested, extracts of roots and flowers were found to be effective in inhibiting sporulation and growth of fungi. Bandara and Wijayagunasekeya (1988) evaluated three rhizomatous herbs, i.e. *Acorus calamus* (Araceae), *Zingiber zerumbet* and *Curcuma longa* (Zingiberaceae) for their antifungal activity against *Cladosporium* sp., *Btryodiplodia theobromae, Fusarium solani, Phytophthora infestans, Pythium* sp., and *Pyricularia oryzae*. Their results revealed that extracts of *A. calamus* and *Z. zerumbet* had profound effect on growth of all fungi tested.

Arthrinium phaeospermum is one of the causal agent of wood decay of *A. falcataria*. The infection by this fungus reduces the durability and quality of wood (Novianto, 2009). Synthetic chemical fungicides has been used as preservatives to control this wood decay however, an increase in the awareness on the negative impacts of these chemicals particularly on human health and environment has made this preservative unsuitable. Many chemical wood preservatives have been prohibited for use on wood (Priadi, 2005). Exploration of the higher plants to produce wood preservative agents that are environmentally friendly and safe to the human health is necessary.

Reddy *et al.* (2009) tested the antifungal activity of phyto-extracts and plant oils of several plant species such as *Azadirachta indica, Allium cepa, Allium sativum. Tegetes erecta, Aloe barbadensis, Eucalyptus globulus* against the growth of *Cercospora moricola* Cooke, the causal agent of leaf spot of Mulberry (*Morus alba* L.). Highest mycelial growth inhibition (72.59%) was recorded in *Eucalyptus globulus* at 10% concentration. Plant oils viz., *Madhuca indica* oil (3%), *Cymbopogon citratus* oil (0.05%) and neem oil (3%) also inhibited the mycelial growth of the fungus with 75.73%, 73.22% and 24.44% inhibition respectively, when compared to control. The antifungal activity of aqueous, petroleum ether, benzene, chloroform, methanol and ethanol extracts and alkaloid extract of *Prosopis juliflora* leaves (Mimosaceae) was evaluated for antifungal activity by poisoned agar technique against *Alternaria alternata* a causal organism of brown spot of tobacco. Aqueous extract recorded highly significant antifungal activity at 24% concentration.

Leaf extract of *Dalbergia sissoo* was found to have toxicity towards fungi and some soil microbes. Acetone extractive of 3.0% concentration was found best in resisting the decay fungi. Another aspect of the work was to determine the effect of biological preservative to protect wood from deterioration, which is supposed to have no harmful effects on biodiversity. Natural extracts of Rosewood leaves have been purified using different solvents and treat them to see the effect against wood decay fungi. It was revealed that neem extract is a source of biological preservative (Dhyani *et al.*, 2005). They used acetone, ethyl alcohol and methyl alcohol extract of neem leaves to inhibit the growth of *Poria menticola* (a brown rot) and *Polyporus versicolor* (a white rot).

It was also proved from this experiment that leaf extract of *Dalbergia sissoo* has also potentiality to be used as biological preservative. So that it can be used extensively for commercial wood preservation. That can expose a new window in wood preservation industry and this is a technique, which have no environmental toxicity.

Another work of Sethy *et al.* (2005) proved that alcoholic extract from the heartwood of *Dalbergia latifolia* have the potentiality to protect wood decay fungi. It this work, it was revealed that at 0.5% retention level, treated rubber blocks exposed to fungus showed a weight loss of 15% as compared to 57% in control blocks. A positive correlation was found between fungal decay resistance and retention of the extract. Majority of vascular plants are potential source of anti-microbial agents (Tripathi *et al.*, 1978).

Taylor *et al.*, (2006) suggested that the methanol-soluble extractives of *Thuja plicata* and *Chamaecyparis nootkatensis* play an important role in heartwood resistance to attack by *Coptotermes formosanus* and *Postia placenta*. They further noted that methanol soluble extractives of the heartwood of those tree species were positively correlated with both termite and decay resistance.

The potential use of extract derived from herbaceous plants, seed or fruit wastes, so called essential oil, to protect wood against degrading fungi and insect has received much attention worldwide (Vanneste *et al.*, 2002)

Experiment has showed that 3.0% concentration of acetone as solvent with leaf extract of *Dalbergia sissoo* showed best result in inhibiting the attack of soil fungi and bacteria. It cause 22%weight loss in wood after treatment. (Ahmad Humayan *et al.*, 2007)

Lyon *et al.*, (2007) reported that a combination of boric acid with linseed oil has good potential for increasing boron retention, reducing leachability and improving efficacy of the product against termites. Mackeen *et al.*, (1997) showed the broad screening of antinematode activity of some native plant extracts against the pine wood nematode (*Bursaphelenchus xylophilus*).

Astiti (1998) found that the water extract of teak leaf obviously inhibited the growth of *Monilia* sp., the cause of wood decay. The methanol crude extract of the leaf of *Tectona grandis* at concentration 5 mg ml-1 inhibited the sporulation of *Alternaria cajani* and *Helminthosporium* sp. by 86.8% and 90.0%, respectively (Shalini and Srivastava, 2008). The methanol extract of teak leaf significantly inhibited the fungal radial growth, total biomass and sporulation of *A. phaeospermum*, the causal agent of wood decay of *A. falcataria*. This extract can be considered as one of the alternatives to chemical wood preservatives for controlling the wood decay on *A. falcataria*. A further study is needed to isolate and identify the active compounds that are responsible for antifungal activity against *A. phaeospermum*.

Devi (2013) investigated that the leaf extract of *Parthenium* and Chauhan (2013) studied that fruit extract of *Melia azedarach* L. at different concentration *i.e.* 0.25, 0.50, 1.00, 1.50 and 2.00 percent inhibit the fungus growth as well as increased the dimensional stability of three wood species *i.e. Bombax ceiba* L., *Celtis australis* L and *Pinus roxburghii* Sargent. Dhiman (2014) extended this same study to find the effect of growth of Polyporus fungus on given wood species by using root extract of *Acorus calamus* (bach). It was found that fungus growth inhibit with increase in root extract concentration which act as bio-preservative.

One of the methanol extract of *Acorus calamus* containing â-asarone fraction showed high antifungal activity against *Microsporam gypsemum* and *Trichopyton rubrum*; also with antifungal activity with crude dichloromethane extract of *Acorus calamus* L. rhizome (Vohora *et al.*, 1990 & Mukherjee *et al.*, 2007). Indian calamus oil contains high amount of â-asarone (77.7%) and 6.8% á-asarone. Acorenone (20.9%) and isocalamendiol (12.8%) were dominant in the rhizomes. (Radušiene *et al.*, 2007). The investigated fraction is an antimicrobial guided one of methanol extract of *A. calamus* containing â-asarone as a major component (Phongpaichit *et al.*, 2005).

AN EXPERIMENT STUDY

Study on the Effect of *Acorus calamus* L. Rhizome Extract on the Growth of Wood Rotting Fungus on Treated Wood Samples

Acorus calamus is a perennial wetland plant of Acoraceae family. It is commonly known as "bach" or "ugragandha" in India. Roots, rhizomes and leaves have been used in the Indian systems of traditional medicine for hundreds of years. This plant has insecticidal properties (Perrett, Sheena & Whit field, 1995).

Sweet flag (Bach)

Rhizome

Wood samples: *Pinus roxburghii* Sargent, *Celtis australis* L. and *Bombax ceiba* L. of size 5cm × 2.5cm × 2.5cm + 0.25cm × 0.15cm × 0.15cm (longitudinally × radially × tangentially)

Extract Treatment Method

Samples were dipped in 0.25%, 0.5%, 1%, 1.5% and 2% (w/v) *Acorus calamus* L. extract solution for 72 hours. The samples meant for control were dipped in distilled water. After dipping treatment specimens were first dried in air and then dried at 105-+2°C to constant weight.

Isolation and Identification of Fungus

An isolated pure culture of Polyporus fungus was revived from preserved fungus. The isolated fungus was transferred to the agar slants and purified by hyphal tip technique. The purified fungal culture was again transferred to Petri plates containing malt agar medium and kept for incubation at 25 + 1°C for routine work. The identification of the isolated fungus was made with the help of standard literature and appropriate standard keys (Waterhouse, 1963; Waterhouse, 1970; Ho, 1982)

Media Preparation

For the growth of fungus malt agar solid media was prepared directly by adding 2 per cent of malt and 2.5 per cent of agar in 1000 ml distilled water. About 100 ml of the medium was poured in air tight glass jars of 500 ml and autoclaved at 15 lb pressure per square inch (psi) for 20 minutes. Each treatment was replicated three times aseptically and allowed to solidify.

The glass jars were inoculated with culture bits (5 mm) cut from 10 days old vigorously growing culture and the inoculated glass jars were incubated at 25 + 1°C. Wood samples were sterilized by keeping them under UV light in Laminar Air Flow for 20 minutes prior to fungus decay tests. All instruments used under LAF were sterilized with alcohol then with spirit lamp to avoid contamination and for better results.

Observations Recorded: The following observations were recorded to study the effect of extract on growth of fungus:

(i) Disease Severity

Per cent severity was calculated according to McKinney (1923).

$$\text{Disease severity} = \frac{\text{Sum of all disease rating}}{\text{Total number of rating} \times \text{maximum disease grade}} \times 100$$

The following scale was used for recording the disease severity:

Numerical Ratings	% Surface Coverage	Description
0	0	No surface coverage
1	0-25	Very less surface coverage
2	26-50	Less surface coverage
3	51-75	Moderate surface coverage
4	>76	Large surface coverage

(ii) **Per cent fungus growth inhibition**

Per cent growth inhibition (Vincent, 1947) was calculated as:

$$I = \frac{C-T}{C} \times 100$$

Where,

I = Per cent growth inhibition
C = Per cent fungus colonization in control
T = Per cent fungus colonization in treated wood

Results

Effect of *A. calamus* L. rhizome extract on fungus colonization on treated and untreated wood

Treatments	Fungus Growth Index (%)			Fungus Growth Inhibition (%)		
	P. roxburghii (S_1)	C. australis (S_2)	B. ceiba (S_3)	P. roxburghii (S_1)	C. australis (S_2)	B. ceiba (S_3)
T_1 (0.25%)	83.33	100.00	91.67	16.67	0.00	8.33
T_2 (0.50%)	75.00	91.67	83.33	25.00	8.33	16.67
T_3 (1.00%)	58.33	75.00	75.00	41.67	25.00	25.00
T_4 (1.50%)	50.00	66.67	41.67	50.00	33.33	58.33
T_5 (2.00%)	25.00	33.33	33.33	75.00	66.67	66.67
T_6 (Control)	100.00	100.00	100.00	0.00	0.00	0.00

Polyporus fungus colonization has been decreased with increase in *A. calamus* rhizome extract concentration i.e. 2.00 per cent concentration have minimum fungus colonization as compared to 0.25 per cent concentration.

Fungal Biotechnology

Enhanced permeability of spruce by fungi modification: Aspiration of bordered pits in Norway spruce wood is the main reason why the treatability with preservatives is greatly inhibited for increasing the durability against micro-organisms. If this restriction could be overcome wood could be treated more effectively. For this purpose Norway spruce wood is exposed to the white-rot fungus *Physisporinus vitreous* that selectively degrades the pit membranes, without altering the mechanical properties of wood. At present we are undertaking studies to optimize conditions under which the colonization of wood by the fungus is improved with the objective to upscale our patented procedure as a biotechnological method for industrial purpose.

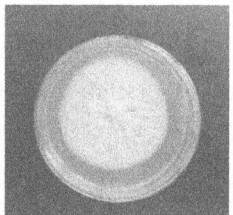   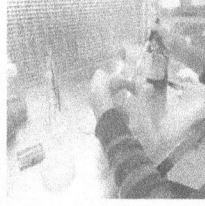   

Polyporus spp.   Fungus inoculation   Agar Media

Pinus roxburghii Sargent

Celtis australis L.

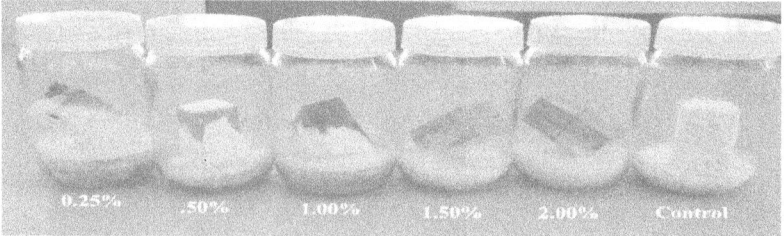

Bombax ceiba L.

Fungus testing on different wood samples

CONCLUSION

The future for wood preservation looks very bright indeed. Various new wood substitutes for solid treated wood like wood-plastic composites, oriented strand board (OSB), laminated veneer lumber (LVL), and parallel strand lumber (PSL). Modern wood preservation is barely two centuries old. Wood, being the most versatile building material that has ever been utilized, will continue to need protection from degrading agencies. Significant growth in this industry has been seen in every single decade since Bethell originally impregnated timber with creosote in the 1830s.

The treated wood industry is undergoing a major transition as CCA is replaced in most residential applications. CCA alternatives have been developed and are becoming more widely available. The alternatives rely heavily on copper as the primary biocide, with a range of co-biocides to help protect against copper-tolerant organisms. Studies indicate that the CCA alternatives do release measurable quantities of copper and co-biocide into the environment. However, these components have lower mammalian toxicity than does arsenic, and they are less likely to raise concerns about environmental impacts. As the treated wood industry evolves, it is likely that a wider range of types and retentions of wood preservatives will become available, with the treatment more closely tailored to a specific type of construction application.

The use of newer process technologies holds promise for new wood preservatives, and breaks ground for modern advances in commercial production plants, and innovation in research opportunities. There is an increasing need to educate the consumer regarding new wood-treating chemistries and new products.

As shortage in supply of durable species becomes the cause of plantation of non-durable species which are more susceptible to wood destroying agencies. Therefore, in order to enhance the service life of non-durable species, preservative treatments become necessary. Wood preservatives such as chromated copper arsenate (CCA) have been banned or limited for some applications in some European countries, the United States, and Japan. Now, natural plants extractives to protect wood against wood degrading fungi and insects has been one of the possible approach for developing new wood preservatives. Therefore numbers of non durable plant species are grown. If these species are treated with ecofriendly preservatives, their use as timber can be enhanced without any harm to nature.

Anoher Lignin which is considered as a residue in pulp and paper production processes, being mainly used as fuel in the recovery boiler for energy generation. However, more valuable uses of lignin could be developed for several interesting applications such as bio-preservative activity. The antioxidant potential of lignin and the fungicide were analyzed. The analyzed lignin showed neutralization and inhibition activities (antioxidant capacity). e.g, Eucalyptus organosolv lignin.

REFERENCES

Afolayan, A.J. (2003): Extracts from the Shoots of *Arctotis artotoides* Inhibit the Growth of Bacteria and Fungi, *Pharm. Biol.*, 14: 22-25.

Ahmad Humayan Kabir and M. Firoz Alam. (2007): Reduction of Environmental Toxicity Through Eco-friendly Wood Biopreservative Department of Botany, University of Rajshahi, Bangladesh.

Astiti, N.P.A. (1998): Effectiveness Water Wxtract of the Leaf of *Tectona grandis* L.f against the Growth of *Monilia* sp. Jurnal Biologi Udayana 2: 1-12.

Bandara, J.M.R.S. and Wijayagunasekera. (1988): Antifungal Activity of some Rhizomatous Plant Extracts. In Abstract Papers of the 5th International Congress of Plant Pathology, Kyoto, Japan.

Barnes, R.A., Gerber, N.N. (1955): The Antifungal Agent from Osage Orange Wood. *J. Am. Chem. Soc,* 77 (12): 3259-3262.

Bazaid, S.A. and Nehal, S.E. (2010): Assessment of the Bioregulatory Activity of the Leaf Juices of Higher Plants in Al-Taif, Saudi Arabia against *Fusarium solani, Phytopthora* spp. and *Rhizoctonia solani*. *Arch. Phytopathol. Plant Protec*, 43(11): 1064-1071.

Byrne, A. (1998): Chemical Control of Biological Stain: Past, Present and Future. In: Proc. of Biology and Prevention of Sap Stain. Forest Products Soc. Madison, WI, pp. 63-69.

Brooks, K.M. (2005): Literature Review, Computer Model and Assessment of the Potential Environmental Risks Associated with Creosote Treated Wood Products Used in Aquatic Environments. Prepared for the Western Wood Preservers Institute. April 23, 1995. 137 p.

Chauhan, K. (2013): Studies on Wood Characteristics using Fruit Extract of *Melia azedarach* L. as a Wood Biopreservative. M.Sc. Thesis, Dr. Y.S. Parmar University of Horticulture and Forestry, Nauni (Solan) 85 p.

Craig, J.B., Rodney, A.E. and Thorp, C.H. (2001): Effects of Chromated Copper Arsenate (CCA) Wood Preservative on Early Fouling Community Formation. *Marine Pollution Bulletin*, 42(11): 1103-1113.

Clark, A.M., McChesney, J.D., and Adam, R.P. (1990): Antimicrobial Properties of Heartwood Bark/Sapwood and Leaves of *Juniperus species, Phytotherapy Research,* 4(1): 15-19.

Devi, N. (2013): Studies on Wood Characteristics using *Ageratum conyzoides* L. extract as a Wood Biopreservative. M.Sc. Thesis, Dr. Y.S. Parmar University of Horticulture and Forestry, Nauni (Solan) 77 p.

Dhiman, B. (2014): Studies on Wood Characteristics using Rhizome Extract of *Acorus calamus* L. (sweetflag) as a Wood Biopreservative. M.Sc. Thesis, Dr. Y.S. Parmar University of Horticulture and Forestry, Nauni (Solan) 76 p.

Dhyani, S., Tripathi, S. and Jain, V. K. (2005): Neem Leaves, a Potential Source for Protection of Hardwood against Wood Decaying Fungus. *International Research Group on Wood Preservation,* IRG/WP: 05-30370.

Downum, K.R., Romeo, J.T. and Sataford, H.A. (1993): Phytochemical Potential of Tropical Plants. Plenum Press, New York.

Duringer, J.M., Swan, L.R., Walker, D.B. and Craig, A.M. (2010): Acute Aquatic Toxicity of *Juniperu occidentalis* Foliage and Port Orford cedar (*chamaecyparis lawsoniana*) Heartwood Oils, *Environment Monitoring and Assessment*, 170(1-4): 585-598.

Evans, P. (2003): Emerging Technologies in Wood Protection, *Forest Products Journal*, 53(1): 14-22.

Eaton, R.A. and Hale, M.D.C. (1993): *Wood: Decay, Pests and Protection*. Chapman & Hall, London, 1: 479-519.

Freitage, M., Morrell, J.J. and Bruce A. (1991): Biological Protection of Wood: Status and Prospects, *Biodeterioration* Abstracts, 5: 1-13.

Fiege, H., Voges, H.-M., Hamamoto, T., Umemura, S., Iwata, T., Miki, H., Fujita, Y. Buysch, H.-J., Garbe, D., and Paulus, W. (2000): "Phenol Derivatives". *Ullmann's Encyclopedia of Industrial Chemistry* (Weinheim: Wiley-VCH).

Gupta, P., Dev, I. (1999): Studies on the Fungal Toxicity of Sal (*Shorea robusta*) Heartwood Extractives. *J. TDA* (India), 45 (1-2): 16-24.

Goktas, O., Mammadov, R., Baysal, E., Duru, M.E., Ozen, E. and Colak, A.M. (2007): Application of Extracts from Poisonous Plant, *Nerium oleander* L. as a Wood Preservative, *Af. J. Biotech.* 6(17): 2003-2003.

Haygreen, J. G. and Bowyer, J. L. (1996): *Forest Products and Wood Science*: Anintroduction, 3rd Ed: 198-199, Lowa State University press, Ames, Lowa.

Hillis, W. E. (1978): Extractives. Special Paper, 8th World Forestry Congress. Djakarta. WORLD BANK. Forestry Sector Policy Paper, World Bank, Washington, D.C.

Ho, H.H. (1982): Affinity Groups Among Plant Pathogenic Species of *Phytopthora* in Culture, *Mycopathologia*, 79: 141-146.

Hunt, G.M. and Garratt, G.A. (1967): Wood Preservation. Third. ed. The American Forestry Series. McGraw–Hill, New York.

Kartal, S.N., Imamura, Y., Tsuchiya, F., Ohsata, K. (2004): Preliminary Evaluation of Fungicidal and Termicidal Activities of Filtrate from Biomass Slurry Fuel Production, *Bioresour Technol*, 95(1): 41-47.

Kartal, S.N., Dorau, B.F., Lebow, S.T. and Green, F. (2004): Effects of Inorganic Ions on Leachability of Wood Preserving N, N-hydroxynaphthalaiflide (NHA). *Forest Product Journal*, 54: 80-84.

Kityo, P.W. and Plumptre, R.A. (1997): The Uganda Timbers users Handbook. A Guide to Better Timber use, Common Wealth Secretariat, London.

Laver, M.L. (1978): Chemicals from Bark. Special Paper, 8th World Forestry Congress. Djakarta. WORLD BANK. Forestry Sector Policy Paper. World Bank, Washington, D.C.

Lis-Balchin, M., Dean, S. and Hart, S. (1996): Bioactivity of New Zealand Medicinal Plant Essential Oils, *Acta Horticulturae* 426: 13-29.

Liu, C.Z, Wang, Y.C., Ouyang, F., Ye, H.C. and Li, G.F. (1998): Production of Artemisimin by Hairy Root Culture of *Artemissia annua* L.in bioreactor, *Biotechnol. Lett.* 20(3): 265-268.

Lyon, F., Thevenon, M.F., Hwang, W.J., Imamura, Y., Gril, J. and Pizzi, A. (2007). Effect of an Oil Heat Treatment on the Leachability and Biological Resistance of Boric Acid Impregnated Wood, *Ann. For. Sci*, 64: 673-678.

Mackeen, M.M., Ali, M.A., Abdullah, M.A., Nasir, R.M., Mat, N.B., Abdul, R.R. and Kawazu, K. (1997): Antinematodal Activity of some Malaysian Plant Extracts against the Pine Wood Nematode, *Bursaphelenchus xylophilus*, *Pestic. Sci*, 51: 165-170.

Milton, F.T. (1995): The Preservation of Wood. A Self Study Manual for Wood Treaters, Minnesota Extension Service, University of Minnesota Collage of Natural Resources.

Nakamura, Y.K., Matsuo, T., Shimoi, K. and Nakamura, Y. (1996): Methyl Methane Thiosulfonate in Homogenates of Cruciferae and Liliaceae Vegetables. *Bio. Biotech. Biochem*, 60: 1439-1443.

Nicholas, D.D. and Shultz, T.P. (1995): Biocides that have Potential as Wood Preservatives: An Overview. *In*: Wood Preservation in the '90s and Beyond. Proc. 7308. Forest Prod. Soc., Madison, WI. pp. 169-179.

Novianto. (2009): Factors Affecting the Wood Decay during Preservation Cited 2010 January 31.

Parrett, Sheena and Whit Field. (1995): Antihelmithic and Pestcidal Activity of Acorus, *Annal of Plant Protection Sciences,* 20(2): 452p.

Phongpaichit, S., Pujenjob, N., Rukachaisirikul, V. and Ongsakul, M. (2005): Antimicrobial Activities of the Crude Methanol Extract of *Acorus calamus* Linn. Songklanakarin, *J. Sci. Technol,* 27(2): 517-523.

Pointing, S.B. (2001): Feasibility of Bioremediation by White-rot Fungi, *Applied Microbiology and Biotechnology*, 57: 20-33.

Priadi, T. (2005): Wood Decay by Fungi and the Control Strategy, Scientific Paper, School of Postgraduate Bogor Agricultural University, Bogor Indonesia (in Indonesian Language).

Raduiene, J., Judentiene, A., Peèiulyte, D. and Janulis, V. (2007): *Plant Genetic Resources: Characterization and Utilization,* 5: 37p.

Reddy, R.G., Nirmala, R.S. and Ramanamma, C.H. (2009): Efficacy of Phytoextracts and Oils of Certain Medicinal Plants against *Cercospora moricola* Cooke of Mulberry (*Morus alba* L.) Leaf Spot, *Journal of Biopesticides,* 2: 77-83.

Salih, A., Bazaid and Nehal, S.E. (2010): Assessment of the Bioregulatory Activity of the Leaf Juices of Higher Plants in Al-Taif, Saudi Arabia against *Fusarium solani, Phytopthora* spp. and *Rhizoctonia solani,* Archives of Phytopathology and Plant Protection, 43(11); 1064-1071.

Schultz, T.P. and Nicholas, D.D. (2000): Naturally durable Heartwood: Evidence for a Proposed Dual defensive function of the extractives, *Phytochemistry,* 54: 47-52.

Sethy, A.K., Nagaveni, H.C., Mohan, S., Chandrashekar, K.T. (2005): Fungal Decay Resistance of Rubber Wood Treated with Heartwood Extract of Rosewood, *International Research Group on Wood Preservation,* Document No. IRG/WP: 05-30367.

Taylor, A.M., Gartner, B.L., Morrell, J.J. and Tsunoda, K. (2006): Effects of Heartwood Extractive Fractions of *Thuja plicata* and *Chamaecyparis nootkatensis* on Wood Degradation by Termites or Fungi, *J. Wood Sci,* 52: 147-153.

Tripathy, R.D., Srivastava, D. and Dixit, S.N. (1978): Lawsone, an Antifungal Antibiotic from Leaves of *Lawsonia inermis*: Its Action on Pathogen and Host Plant, *Ind. Jour. Mycol Plant Pathol*, 81: 89-90.

Tripathi, S., Bagga, J.K., Jain, V.K. (2005): Preliminary Studies on ZiBOC- A Potential Eco-friendly Wood Preservative. *International Research Group on Wood Preservation,* Document No. IRG/WP: 05-30372.

Tripathi, S., Rawat, K., Dhayani, S. and Pant, H. (2009). Potential of *Lantana camara* L. Weed against Wood Destroying Fungi, *The Indian Forester,* 135(3): 403-411.

U.S. EPA. Integrated Risk Information System on Arsenic, Inorganic American Wood Preservers Institute. (1996): "The 1995 Wood Preserving Industry Protection Statistical Report." p. 12.

Vanneste, J.L., R A Hill, S.J. Kay. Farrell, and P.T. Holland (2002): Biological Control Agent. 106(2): 228-23.

Vincent, J.M. 1(947): Distortion of Fungal Hyphae in the Presence of Certain Inhibitors. *Nature,* 150: 850p.

Vohra, S.B., Shah, S.A. and Dandia, P.C. (1990): Central Nervous System Studies on an Ethanol Extracts of *A. Calamus* Rhizomes, *Journal of Ethnopharmacology,* 28: 53-62.

Waterhouse, G.M. (1963): Key to the Species of *Phytopthora* de Bary, *Mycological Paper* (CMI) 92: 1-22.

Waterhouse, G.M. (1970): The Genus *Phytopthora* de Bary, *Mycological Paper* (CMI). 122: 1-59.

Yalinklic, M. K., Imamura, Y., Takahashi, M., kayayciouglu, H., Nemli, G., Demirci, Z., Ozdemir, T. (1998): Biological, Physical and Mechanical Properties of Particleboard Manufacture from Waste Tea Leaves, *Int Biodegradation,* 41(1): 75-84.

Zucker, W.V. (1983): Tannins: Does Structure Determine Function? An Ecological Perspective, *Am. Nat.,* 121: 335-365.

Application of Biotechnological Tools for Characterization and Management of Seed Borne Diseases

Richa Chauhan

Plant disease management is one of the biggest challenges in intensive crop production systems. It is estimated that pests and diseases cause an annual loss of about 30% in developing countries. A major cause of this loss are the disease. India, about 20% of the production including post harvest products, valued at 12-15 billion US dollars, is lost to diseases. Effective disease management practices are thus important to enhanced food security, sustainability and stable trade. Widespread adoption of high yielding disease resistance varieties (host-plant resistance) is the most important strategy of minimizing the losses caused due to pathogen. In the past, conventional plant breeders in close collaboration with plant pathologists, have successful in management of diseases to a considerable extent. However, success in disease management through plant breeding largely depends on access to useful genes for disease resistance. The new tools of molecular biology and biotechnology will allow many more plant diseases to be managed by breeding because of the loss of regeneration to assure safety. This approach is expected to be ecologically sustainable, economically affordable and socially acceptable.

Pulses and oilseeds are very important for Indian economy. Hence, this is increasing emphasis on these crops for enhancing their productivity. The unrestricted movement and exchange of germplasm is vital to progress

---

Assistant Professor, Chamanlal Mahavidhyalay, Landhaura, Roorkee (Uttarakhand) (India)

in crop improvement programs, but such movement must not at any time jeopardize crops by spreading pest or disease. Hence, high priority should be given for management of seed borne diseases.

The tools and techniques of molecular biology and biotechnology which can be used for characterization and management of seed borne discussed are as follows:

BIOTECHNOLOGICAL TOOLS AND TECHNIQUES

(a) DNA Molecular Marker

The DNA molecular marker can be used to detect variation in both coding and non coding regions of the genome. The main characteristic of DNA marker are dominant expression, infinite number, phenotypically neutral having no epistatic and development effects. DNA markers can be used to develop saturated linkage map of important crop. This will facilitate tagging of resistant genes to molecular markers. Subsequently marker assisted selection can be performed to select disease resistant plants.

(b) Molecular Diagnosis and Characterization

Considerable progress has been made over the last few years in the development of DNA-based techniques for detection of micro-organisms. Identification of plant pathogens involving extraction of nucleic acid comparison by RFLP and RAPD PCR analysis is now in many cases, a routine procedure of great value to plant pathologists is development of PCR tests which allow detection of very low levels of pathogen DNA extracted from host plants.

Advantages:
- Targets the genome of the pathogen
- A wide range of detection and amplification techniques is available
- Very sensitive.

Disadvantage:
- Specialized facilities are generally require.
- Skill based required is high
- Nucleotide sequence information is generally needed.

Some of the techniques required for molecular diagnosis and characterization of pathogens and genome mapping of crop plants are discussed briefly.

1. Polymerase Chain Reaction (PCR)
- The PCR test amplifies a region of DNA (usually a few hundred base pairs) in positive samples. The DNA can then be visualized on a gel. The presence or absence of the DNA band indicates a positive or negative result respectively.

- PCR is now used widely in many fields including detection of human pathogens enterovirses and environmental organisms.
- PCR is relatively easy to perform compared to many other molecular techniques and can be applied to a wide variety of plant pathogens and pests including viruses, fungi, bacteria and nematodes.
- For the development of successful species or strain specific PCR tests. It is essential to identify DNA sequence that are unique or characteristic for those species or strains.
- Amplification of DNA can be based on different types of DNA sequences:
  - Internal transcribed spacer regions of the r-DNA gene block.
  - Repetitive target sequences.
  - Non-repetitive target sequences.
- The PCR can also be adopted in number of different types of tests
  - Reverse transcription PCR (RT-PCR)
  - Immunocapture PCR
  - Multiplex PCR

2. Restriction Fragment Length Polymorphism (RFLP)

- Restriction fragment length polymorphisms can be used to discriminate between organisms.
- Organisms are distinguished by differences in the DNA restriction patterns when cut with enzymes.
- RFLP analysis can be combined with the use of specific DNA probes for the detection of a pathogen. This often provides a more sensitive and specific tests.

RFLP can be defined as variation in length in DNA fragment produced by digestion of the DNA sample with restriction endonuclease which is revealed after probing colonel DNA sequences to specific regions of eukaryotic genome.

If RFLP markers tightly linked to resistant gene are available, the plants can be screened at the seedling stage itself for the particular RFLP marker. Some pest/diseases affect the crop at flowering/post flowering stage and RFLP markers permit as to screen for resistant against them in early stage without waiting till the appropriate stage of the crop and without waiting for the infection to occur.

3. Random Amplified Polymorphism DNA (RAPD)

A standard procedure for the identification of polymorphism based on PCR has been enveloped William *et al.* (1990). RAPD sequence (marker) are based on the use of single short (10-mers) synthetic oligonucleotide primers. PCR amplification involves the use of two oligonucleotide primers, repeated cycle of heat denaturation of the DNA, annealing of the primers to their complimentary sequences. The primers flanking the hyper variable regions are designed and used to amplify that specific regions.

RFLP and RAPD involves the establishment of linkage association between these markers and trait of interest in a segregation population and both can be used to map the trait of interest.

4. Amplified Fragment Length Polymorphism (AFLP)

AFLP marker is produced when restriction site differences exist between two DNA sources. One of the strength of AFLP's is the sheer number of marker produced per assay (Thomas *et al.*, 1995, Vos *et al.*, 1995). The complexity (number of fragments) of AFLP fingerprints can be manipulated by increasing or decreasing the number of selective bases and changing base composition (Zabeau, 1993). AFLP analysis is a rapid and efficient method for producing DNA fingerprints and genetic mapping (Zabeau, 1993).

(c) DNA Fingerprinting

- DNA fingerprinting uses short oligonucleotide primers (usually 10 mt long) of arbitrary sequences in a PCR reaction with the target genomic DNA segments are amplified and fractionated on a gel to reveal a characteristic profiles vary between genetically distinct individuals.
- DNA fingerprinting is useful for identifying minor genetic variations between closely related pathogens (for example it can distinguish strains or pathovars of a pathogen).

DNA Fingerprinting of Pathogen – Ascochyta Rabiei as a Case Study

Program for disease control and resistance breeding depend on the reliable identification and characterization of pathogen (pathotypes and population). A classical biological pathotyping technique, using a set of different host genotypes, is laborious, time consuming required strict standardization of test conditions. A reliable characterization of the genetic make up of different strains, their levels of pathogenicity, their extent of variability, geographical distribution and their genotype and phenotypic interaction(s) with the host plant is, therefore very difficult to achieve by means of biological pathotyping.

In order to characterized Ascochyta blight of chickpea, two innovative approaches to differentiate between various A. rabiei isolate were introduced. The first approach is using a DNA fingerprinting technique that is based on the detection of hypervariable restriction fragment length polymorphism (RFLPs) in the fungal genome. DNA fingerprinting relies on the presence of a particular class of repetitive DNA in the fungal genome.

This class consists of short motifs which are tendamly arranged to form long, more or less homogenous, arrays. Two characteristics qualify this kind of sequence for DNA fingerprinting. First, the tandem repeats are dispersed throughout the genome (multilocus appearance). Second, the tendamly arranged repetitions exhibit a high degree of polymorphisms, mainly resulting from different copy numbers of the basic motifs. To detect the polymorphism, P^{32}- endlabeled oligonucleotide probes (radio active) have been used in the past. Presently non-radioactive DNA fingerprinting using digoxigen in labeled probes are being used. It was successfully demonstrated that non-radioactive DNA fingerprinting of A. rabiei can be as successful and as informative as the radioactive procedures. Results also confirmed the findings that isolate 1, 2, 3 and 4 an definitely different using the enzyme/probe combination Hinf I/$(GATA)_4$ whereas isolate 3 and 5 as well as isolates 4 and 6 share an identical fingerprinting pattern. Since this method avoids the use of radioactivity, it is easier to be adopted in many laboratories.

In a second approach genomic DNA of the six isolates was amplified using oligoxynuceotide primers and the taq DNA polymerase (nm radioactive). Since the target sequences for the primers used are randomly dispersed throughout the genome, the technique is called RAPD (random amplified polymorphic DNA). The results showed that the amplification fingerprints generated with single primers or primer combination detect either no variation or little variation. The duplex primer approach allows discriminating power of the RFLP technique. Once this is achieved, RAPD will be superior over RFLP because of substantial saving in costs and time needed for DNA pathotyping of Ascochyta rabiei isolates.

(d) Recombinant DNA Technology

The techniques of inserting genes across species and genetic barriers is termed as r- DNA technology because it involves making incision in DNA of recipient, inserting spliced DNA pieces from a donor biological species, and finally regaining a single functional DNA macromolecule. The process of *in vitro* recombination and transfer into foreign host involves mainly four steps namely:

1. Gene isolate and identification
2. Splicing of foreign DNA in to the vector
3. Insertion and maintenance of the recombinant plasmid in a host
4. Selection of desired clone.

r- DNA technique has been used to generate transgenic plants resistant to insect, pest, fungal, bacterial and viral disease to identify disease resistance genes and to generate improved strains of biocontrol agents. Progress has been made to develop transgenic crop plant possessing resistance to several fungal and viral diseases using several strategies.

(e) Cell/Tissue Culture based Technique

Plant tissue culture is known to be capable of introducing genetic and epigenetic changes in cultured cells which result in differences among the regenerated plants. Where possible, epigenetic variation can be eliminated by taking seeds from the newly transformed plants but unwanted genetic variation may need to be eliminated by backcrossing the transgenic plants to another plant, which would often be the original non transgenic genotypes.

Tissue culture techniques that have been found to be useful are micropropagation, somaclonal variation for production of disease – free planting material, cell culture techniques for selection of improved cell lines and embryo rescue techniques to introgression traits for disease resistance from wild relatives.

1. Somaclonal Variation

Plant regenerated from somatic cell in culture are known as somaclone. Variation among these clones is referred as somaclone variation. Early blight resistance clones of particular potato cultivar could only be identified by inoculating leaves of regenerated plants with toxin derived from Alternaria solani, the early blight fungus. The ability to make changes in only a few genes indicates the usefulness of somaclone variation for the development of disease resistant varieties.

2. Cell Line Selection

Use of culture filtrate and toxic metabolites in the production of the disease resistant plants:

Variation can be introduced into cultured cells by exposing the cells to sublethal concentration of fungal culture filtrate and toxin metabolites. These metabolites might contain toxic principles too. Selection of toxin resistant plant tissue and cell cultures offers a practical means of generating novel disease resistant plant (Brettell *et al.*, 1979). This technique has been used to develop varieties resistant to crop pathogens. The relationship between reaction of calli and reaction of the same genotypes as complete plants can be very close when the toxic compound responsible for the virulence is used to detect sensitive individuals at the early development stage.

3. Wide Hybridization

Transfer of characters from wild to cultivated genepool are easily done by wide hybridization. However, presence of strong incompatibility barriers restrict the gene flow from one species to another species. In this method mainly transfer of those characters which are resistant and tolerant to diseases and pests can done through use of techniques of embryo/ovule/endosperm/ovary culture.

STRATEGIES FOR DISEASE/PEST MANAGEMENT
1. Disease Resistance

One of the main bottleneck of conventional breeding programme for developing resistant varieties of crop plant, is unavailability of suitable resistant genes. In addition, disease resistance is lost due to the evaluation of new forms of pathogens. Genetic engineering offers opportunity to develop treansgenics having resistant genes both from related and unrelated sources.

(a) Fungal disease

Recently a lot of efforts have been made to identify and isolate genes which after transfer may render viable resistance to fungual diseases. The major strategies involves transfer of race-cultivar-specific resistance traits from related crop species. However, the resulting transgenic plants will remain susceptible to other races of pathogen. Furthermore, the large scale growth of the newly developed fungus-resistant cultivars is likely to lead to the evolution of new virulent races, and the cultivation of crops as monoculture will promote rapid epidemic outbreak. However, the pathogen inducible simultaneous expression in transgenic plants of specific resistance gene, together with the corresponding virulence gene, has the potential to result in broad range, nonspecific pathogen resistance.

Another strategy is to develop transgenic with genes producing antifungal proteins e.g. chitinase and β- 1,3 glucanases. These antifungal enzymes catalyze the hydrolysis of chitin and β- 1,3 glucan, both major components of cell wall of many fungi. Through the breakdown of these components, the two hydrolysis are through to inhibit fungal growth. Four classes (I to IV) of the plant endochitinase have been described, of which at least three are present in tobacco. Three major classes (I-III) of β- 1,3 endochitinase are found in plant species. The class I hydrolyses are localized in plant vacuole and are potent inhibitors of growth *in vitro* of many fungi. The combination of class I β- 1,3 glucanase, both in quantities insufficient to show an effect by themselves, results in very strong antifungal activity, indicating that these hydrolyses, results in very strong antifungal activity, act synergistically. In contrast, class II hydrolyses, which are very homologous to the class I hydrolyses but which are localized extracellular, are not antifungal either alone are in combination with other proteins. It is not yet established whether hydrolyses class III and IV exhibit fungal growth- inhibiting activities *in vitro*. The tobacco genes encoding class I hydrolyses are constitutively expressed in the roots and the lower leaves.

Still tobacco plant is susceptible to the fungal root pathogen *R. solani*. On introduction of a cauliflower mosaic virus 35S promoter- driven class I endochitinase gene in tobacco, the transgenic plants constitutively expressing the gene showed an enhanced resistance to *R. solani*. Apparently, a certain basal level of an antifungal endochitinase is not sufficient to protect plants against antifungal endochitinase is not sufficient to protect plants against fungi, whereas elevated levels may lead to enhanced resistance. In contrast, it has been found that the constitutive expression in *N. cylvestris* of a tobacco class I chitinase gene under the control of cauliflower mosaic virus 35S promoter did not alter the susceptibility of the transgenic plants to the fungal leaf pathogen *C. nicotiana,* despite the fact that *Cercospora spp.* are sensitive to chitinases *in vitro*. This could indicate results obtain *in vitro* are difficult to extrapolate *in vivo* or that the *in vitro* antifungal proteins are not localized at the preferred site of action in the transgenic plants. To target vacuolar antifungal proteins out of action in the transgenic plants. To target vacuolar antifungual proteins out of the cell, both a class I chitinase and a class I β- 1,3 glucanase gene have been modified. In transgenic plants expressing either of the two modified genes, the two hydrolyses were found extracellulary. Both targeted proteins retained their fungal growth inhibiting activities and together they still showed synergy in the inhibition of fungal growth *in vitro*. The transgenic plants have not yet been tested for resistance against *C. nicotiana*. Besides, there are other antifungal protein like osmotic, lectin, thionins which can be modified and targeted to extracellular places. Yet another strategy is to use the plants ability to produce phytoalexins as in many cases correlation have been found between the concentration of phytoalexins and resistance to specific pathogens. In addition many other new concepts have been developed to obtain broad range pathogen resistance and these concepts will be worked out further in the next few years. Undoubtedly, increasing knowledge of molecular level basis of both pathogencity and resistance will lead to the development of new strategies in future. Somaclonal variation is a possible source of fungal resistance.

(b) **Viral diseases**

Genetic engineering for virus resistance is one of the major success stories in plant biotechnology. New sources of antiviral transgene that confer effective resistance in plants continue to be discovered. It has been known for some time that the infection of host by a wild virus strain (the inducer) protects the plant from the super infection by a second, more virulent but related virus (the challenger). This phenomenon has been coined cross-protection, but its mechanism of action has not been deciphered yet. One hypothesis stresses the importance of the presence of the inducer RNA (the replicated genome of the wild virus) in the host cell, which hybridizes to the challenger's RNA and prevents either its replication or translation into protein. Cross protection might also be a consequence of successful computation of the inducer virus for receptors at the plant cell surface, so that the challenger will not recognize the potential host. Yet another theory capitalizes on the abundance of coat proteins in the infected cell, normally used for the assembly of viral RNA into infective particles, now assemble with the incoming RNA of the challenger virus and prevents its replication. As a consequence, the super infection is impossible or delayed or insufficient. The coat protein gene of the model virus TMV (tobacco mosaic virus) was, isolated as a cDNA copy, inserted into a plant transformation vector tighter with appropriate promoter and polyadenylation signals, transformed into tobacco cells and constitutively expressed. Plant regenerated from the cells or otherwise normal, were either not infected or the disease symptoms developed more slowly than in control plants. Since this initial report, genetically engineered cross protection mediated by viral coat proteins has been successfully applied a wide spectrum of plant viruses belonging to different virus groups. The strategy has been shown to be effective under field conditions and against mixed infection by two different viruses. Moreover, heterogonous infection from related virus has been reportedly observed. Though the mechanism of coat protein-mediated cross- protection in transgenic plants is still unclear, and several lines of evidence points to additional mechanisms that work independently of coat protein accumulation. It should be kept in mind, however, that the acquired tolerance can in some cases be overcome by an increased concentration of the virus, or the presence or the naked RNA in the inoculum.

The possibility of engineering resistance using viral genes other than the coat protein gene has also been extensively investigated. These include genes coding for function such as (i) the RNA-dependent RNA polymerase or replicase protein involved in virus replication, (ii) viral protein involved in cell to cell movement and (iii) viral protease involved in processing polyprotein gene products. However, it has not yet been definitively established whether the RNA transcript or the protein products of the transgenic plays the active role in resistance. There are several reports of similar replicase- mediated resistance to different viruses : PVX (Potato virus X), Pea early browing virus, CMV (Cucumber mosaic virus) and CyRSV.

FUTURE PROSPECTS

The review of work on biotechnological aspects of management of seed borne diseases of pulses and oilseeds indicates that most of the approaches are still largely at experimental or pre- technological stage. Application of DNA fingerprinting in diagnosis, molecular characterization and classification of strain/pathotypes and disease management through host plant resistance using biotechnological tools in next few years will establish the utility of these techniques in plant disease management. Considering that seed borne diseases of pulses and oilseeds are the major constraint in enhancing the productivity of pulses and oilseeds, it is to be expected that conventional and biotechnological approaches will find increasing applications in the future. Environmental concerns and to minimize the use of fungicide and pesticides would further demand development of pest and disease resistant cultivars. The cost benefit ratio and availability of resources for the more resource intensive biotechnological tools will ultimately determine their use.

REFERENCES

Brettell, R.I.S. and Ingram, D.S. (1979). Tissue Culture in the Production of Novel Disease Resistant Crop Plants. Biol. Rev., 54: 329-345.

Zabeau, M. (1993). Selective Resistriction Fragment Amplification: A General method for DNA Fingerprinting. Europian Patent Application. 0-534-858-A1.

Singh, N.P., Weigand, F. and Kahl, Gunter (1994). Molecular Characterization and Detection of Genetic Variability in Ascochyta rabiei of chickpea. International Conference on DNA Finger Printing held from 13-16 Dec., 1994 at Hyderabad.

Vos, P., Hogers, R., Bleeker, M., Reijans, M., Van de Lee, T., Hornes, M., Frijters, A., Pot, J., Peleman, J., Kuiper, M. and Zabeau, M. (1995). AFLP: A New Technique for DNA Fingerprinting. Nuclic Acids Res. 23: 4407-4414.

Thomas, C.M., Vos, P., Zabeau, M., Jones, D.A., Norcott, K.A., Chadwick, B.P.. and Jones, J.D.G. (1995). Identification of AFLP Markers Tightly Linked to the Tomato Cf-9 Gene for Resistance to Claosporium Julvum. Plant Journal. 8: 785-794.

Pages: 256-271
Eco-tourism, Environmental Problems and Sustainable Development
Edited by: Dr. Soubam Premchandra Singh; Dr. Ashok K. Rathoure
Dr. Pawan Kumar 'Bharti'
ISBN: 978-93-86841-57-5
Edition: 2018
Published by: Discovery Publishing House Pvt. Ltd., New Delhi (India)

Role of Agriculture in National Development with Special Reference to India

Prasann Kumar

ABSTARCT

Few Indian commercial crops–such as Cotton, indicia, opium, wheat, and rice–made it to the global market under the British rule in India. The second half of the 19th century saw some increase in land under cultivation and agricultural production expanded at an average rate of about 1% per year by the late 19th century. An Indian began by 9000 BC as a result of early cultivation of plants, and domestication of crops and animals. Settled life soon followed with implements and techniques being developed for agriculture. Double monsoons led to two harvests being reaped in one year. Indian products soon reached the world via existing trading networks and foreign crops were introduced to India. Plants and animals–considered essential to their survival by the Indians–came to be worshiped and venerated.

Key words: Agriculture, Biotic, Crop, Diffusion, Monsoons

INTRODUCTION

Indians began in 9000 BC as a result of early cultivation of plants, and domestication of crops and animals. Settled life soon followed with implements and techniques being developed for agriculture. Double monsoons led to two harvests being reaped in one year. Indian products soon reached the world via existing trading networks and foreign crops

---

Assistant Professor, Department of Agronomy, School of Agriculture, Lovely Professional Univesity, Jalandhar - 144 411 (Punjab) (India)

were introduced to India. Plants and animals–considered essential to their survival by the Indians–came to be worshiped and venerated. Excavations, legends and remote sensing tests reveal that agriculture is 10,000 years old. Women by their intrinsic insight first observed that plants come up from seeds.Men concentrated on hunting and gathering during that time. Women were the pioneers for cultivating useful plants from the wild flora. They dug out edible roots and rhizomes and buried the small ones for subsequent harvests. They used animal meat as main food and their skin for clothing. The middle ages saw irrigation channels reach a new level of sophistication in India and Indian crops affecting the economies of other regions of the world. Land and water management systems were developed with an aim of providing uniform growth. Despite some stagnation during the later modern era the independent Republic of India was able to develop a comprehensive agricultural programme

- Food is the very essential for the survival of any living organisms.
- It is the source of energy for carrying its metabolic process.
- But the food produced by the naturally is not enough to meet all the needs, to meet the needs the of the growing population there is a need to produce the food other than what nature gifted us.
- The production of crops and rearing livestock for the economic purpose is called agriculture.
- Agriculture helps to meet the basic needs of human and their civilization by providing food, clothing.
- Hence, agriculture is the most important enterprise in the world. It is a production unit where the free gifts of nature, namely land, light, air, temperature and rain water etc.
- The term agriculture is derived from Latin which means culturing the land.
- When we split the term agriculture into two ager and cultura.
- Ager refers to land and culture means culturing.
- It is a science and art producing the crops and livestock for economic purposes.
- Agriculture is not only the crops it also includes dairying, horticulture, and livestock breeding.
- Animals such as the ox, sheep, goat and chicken are reared in the farms for its meat and eggs.

Irrigation was developed in the Indus Valley Civilization by around 4500 BC. The size and prosperity of the Indus civilization grew as a result of this innovation, which eventually led to more planned settlements making use of drains and sewers. Sophisticated irrigation and water storage systems were developed by the Indus Valley Civilization, including artificial reservoirs at Girnar dated to 3000 BC, the archaeological evidence of an animal-drawn plow dates back to 2500 BC in the Indus Valley Civilization. Outside of the Indus Valley area of influence there are 2 regions with distinct agricultures dating back to around 2800-1500. These are the Deccan Plateau and an area within the modern states of Orissa and Bihar.The construction of waterworks and aspects of water technology in India is described in Arabic and Persian works. The diffusion of Indian and Persian irrigation technologies gave rise to an irrigation system which brought about economic growth and growth of material culture. Agricultural 'zones' were broadly divided into those producing rice, wheat or millets (Figure 13.1).

Fig. 13.1: Indus valley civilization
Source: Based on Review of Literature

EMPHASIS ON AGRICULTURAL HISTROY

Few Indian commercial crops–such as Cotton, indicia, opium, wheat, and rice–made it to the global market under the British rule in India. The second half of the 19th century saw some increase in land under cultivation and agricultural production expanded at an average rate of about 1% per year by the late 19th century. Due to extensive irrigation by canal networks Punjab, Narmada valley, and Andhra Pradesh became centers of agrarian reforms. From 1891 to 1946, the annual growth rate of all crop output was 0.4%, and food-grain output was practically stagnant. There were significant regional and intercrop differences, however, non-food crops doing better than food crops. Among food crops, by far the most important source of stagnation was rice. Bengal had below-average growth rates in both food and non-food crop output, whereas Punjab and Madras were the least stagnant regions. In the interwar period, population growth accelerated while food output decelerated, leading to declining availability of food per head. The crisis was most acute in Bengal, where food output declined at an annual rate of about 0.7% from 1921 to 1946, when the population grew at an annual rate of about 1%.

- On 15-08-1947 India got its independent from the British rule
- By that time there was a severe crisis for food in India as all our resources were plundered by the British
- And moreover during the British rule the emphasis is more given to the cash crops rather than the food grains
- Cash crops such as rubber, tea, coffee, cotton and sugar cane was hugely encouraged by the British as they can use to as the raw materials in various industries
- This led to a shortage of food grains in India
- In fact, many famines caused by these illicit acts done by the British like the great Bengal famine
- After independence the importance is more given to the food crops such as the wheat and rice
- After our constitution came into the act five year plans started
- The first five year plan was on agriculture and industries
- Government of India privatized the agriculture and made income generated by the agriculture as nontaxable income
- During the early 70's green revolution was started for the saturation of grain and hunger free India

GREEN REVOLUTION AND ATTAINING SATURATION

The Green Revolution in India was a period when agriculture in India increased due to improved method & technology. The Green Revolution allowed developing countries, like India, to overcome poor agricultural productivity. It started in India in the early 1960s and led to an increase in food grain production, especially in Punjab, Haryana and Uttar Pradesh during the early phase. The main development was higher-yielding varieties of wheat, which were developed by many scientists, including Indian geneticist M.S. Swaminathan, American agronomist Dr. Norman Borlaug, and others. The Indian Council of Agricultural Research also claims credit for Udit Singhal for developing rust resistant strains of wheat.

The introduction of high-yielding varieties(HYV) of seeds and the increased quality of fertilizers and irrigation technique led to the increase in production to make the country self-sufficient in food grains, thus improving agriculture in India. The methods adopted included the use of high-yielding varieties (HYVs) of seeds with modern farming methods.

The production of wheat has produced the best results in fueling self-sufficiency of India. Along with high-yielding seeds and irrigation facilities, the enthusiasm of farmers mobilized the idea of the agricultural revolution. Due to the rise in the use of chemical pesticides and fertilizers there was a negative effect on the soil and the land such as land degradation (Figures 13.2 & 13.3).

Fig. 13.2: **Schematic diagram of changing in climate**
Source: Based on Review of Literature

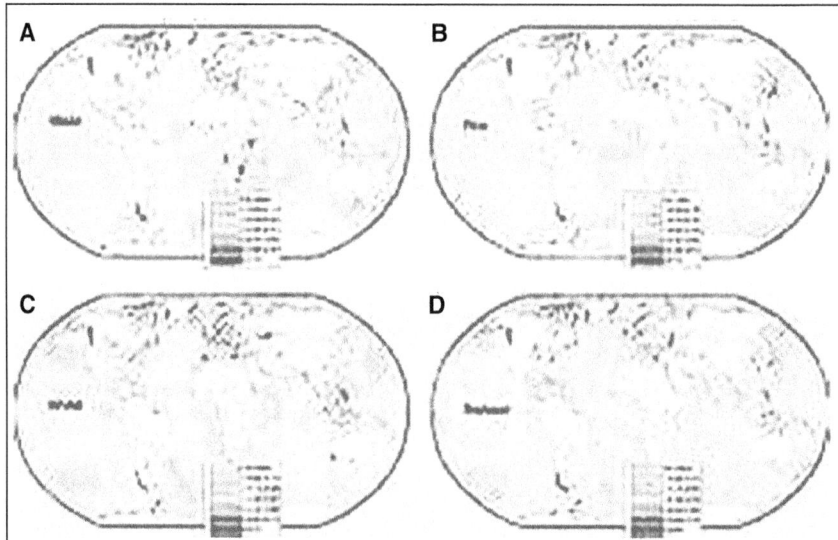

Fig. 13.3: **Wheat production in world**
Source: Based on Review of Literature

- Although the agriculture as main aspect in the five year plan was implemented for three consecutive times there was a short supply of food grains in India in late 60's.
- During the tenure of Indira Gandhi the crisis reached to the peaks.
- India started importing rice from Japan and China, that's the first time ever in history of worlds a country with 12 perennial rivers importing food grains.
- The government of India started several research institutes and deployed many scientists in the field as the counter measure.
- Dr MS Swaminathan (Father of Green Revolution) succeeded in the gene mutation of the Mexican variety wheat.
- This gave birth to the green revolution in India.
- Punjab region was selected for growing wheat, within a short time we have attained a saturation of grains.
- The yield was raised around six tons per a hectare, which was a phenomenal growth.

WORDS DELIVERED BY MS SWAMINATHAN

The future belongs to those nations which have grains not guns. You can withstand every other sanction not the sanction which deny the food. Food stands first in the hierarchy of needs of mankind, if a man dies of hunger, of hunger that's a social shame (Figures 13.4 & 13.5).

Fig. 13.4: MS Swaminathan
Source: Based on Review of Literature

Fig. 13.5: **Agriculture is the backbone of the country**
Source: Based on the Review of Literature

- Agriculture is the backbone of this country
- It plays a vast role not only in the development, but also in governing the country
- The country is not its brick and mortar, but merely its people, for the sustenance we need food
- Particularly in countries like India to feed 1.2 billion people there should be toil more than the words
- It provides food grains to millions of people
- India has a plurality in every aspect including the foods

India is an agricultural country. About seventy percent of our population depends on agriculture. One third of our National income comes from agriculture. Our economy is based on agriculture. The development of agriculture has much to do with the economic welfare of our country.As India is an agricultural country so it's very important to take care of the agricultural resources, farmers, land and other agricultural related issues. Problems with these issues will directly be reflected in the yield of the crops and the production scales. The present role of Indian agriculture to increase the economy of a country is discussed below:

1. Agriculture contributes to the national income
2. It also produces employment to people in a large scale
3. It provides raw materials to the industry
4. Contributes man power to industry

    5. Purchasing power
    6. Capital formation
    7. Foreign exchange

- Agriculture contributes 13.5% of national income in the year 2013
- In the year 2003 the contribution was 23% and when India got independence it was 56%
- But the major income to a country should come from taxes such as revenue, in developed countries like us and the UK the contribution of agriculture is less than 5%
- The Indian economy is not so advanced but in the near future we will develop (After seeing the statistics)
- Although the income gained by the farmer is non taxable he ought to pay the other taxes like GST and other value added taxes like every other citizen of this county

Employment generation

- More than half of the population in our country lives in villages
- Employment generation of all citizens is a tough task without agriculture
- More than 55% of the Indian population are involved in the agriculture activities like farming, animal husbandry, fishing, beekeeping etc.
- This helps Indian economy phenomenally
- No wonder India has the third largest economy in the world
- But the problem is Indian youth are showing more interest in vocational courses rather than agriculture this somewhat destabilizes the balance and other side of the coin is 800 million people of this country earns less than $1 a day, most of the agriculture laborers don't get enough pay.

Foreign exchange

- India has really increased its production, from the ship to the mouth we attained an over saturating point where we are exporting.
- India is exporting the grains and raw material to the other country by means if air and water.
- India exported $38 billion worth of agricultural products in the year 2015.
- The foreign exchange Indian economy is also improved.

Raw materials to industry

- Agriculture and the industries are interdependent.

- The fertilizers and seeds produced by the industry are needed for agriculture and industries need raw materials from the farm.
- Raw materials such as tea leaves, coffee beans, jute, cotton, sugarcane, oil seeds to the industry.
- The industries process these raw materials and finished product is sent to market for the consumers.
- The interdependency is getting stronger as the economy is growing.

Increasing purchasing power
- Agriculture provides purchasing power not only to those directly engaged in it, but to others also whoare in the industries and services. When farmers earn more they also spend more. In the process, they create new markets and new opportunities for hundreds of blacksmiths, carpenters, masons, weavers, pressers, transporters and countless others.
- Thus, there are many industries, the prosperity and employment which are dependent upon the purchasing power of the agricultural population. Hence, it is concluded that besides purchasing food fornon-agricultural workers and raw materials for consumer industries, it has created demand for a greatmany new industries, which, in turn, have provided high and well paid employment.
- This existing role of agriculture in the Indian economy points out the necessity for the development of Indian agriculture to the fullest extent possible as the prosperity of agriculture largely stands for the prosperity of the Economy.

Capital formation
- Capital formation includes the building of the houses and land development etc.
- Before the independence the capital formation from agriculture is not up to the mark
- The British imposed high tax rates on the Indian farmers (above 45%) thus there was no chance of the capital formation those days.
- After independence the taxes were reduced and the modern farming techniques were adopted this increased the capital formation and helped in the economic development of India.
- **Instability:** Agriculture in India is largely dependent on the monsoon. As a result, production of food-grains fluctuates year after year. A year of abundant output of cereals is often followed by a year of acute shortage.

Fig. 13.6: Cultivation of crops
Source: Based on Review of Literature

- **Cropping pattern:** the crops that are grown in India are divided into broad categories: food crops and non food crops. While the former comprise food grains, sugarcane and other beverages, the latter includes different kinds of fibers and oilseeds. In recent years there has occurred a fall in agricultural production mainly due to fall in the output of non-food articles. Moreover Rabi production has become as important as Kharif production in the late 1990s. In 1999-2000, for example, of the total grain production of 209 million tones, Rabi accounted for 104 million. Tones. This indicates a structural change in agricultural production (Figure 13.7).

Fig. 13.7: Cropping pattern of crops
Source: Based on Review of Literature

- **Land Ownership:** It is believed that large parcels of land in India are owned by a- relatively small section of the rich farmers, landlords and money-lenders, while the vast majority of farmers owns very little amount of land, or no land at all. Moreover, most holdings are small and uneconomic. So the advantages of large-scale farming cannot be derived and cost per unit with 'uneconomic' holdings is high, output per hectare is hectare is low. As a result,the peasants cannot generate sufficient marketable surplus. So they are not only poor, but are often in debt (Figure 13.8).

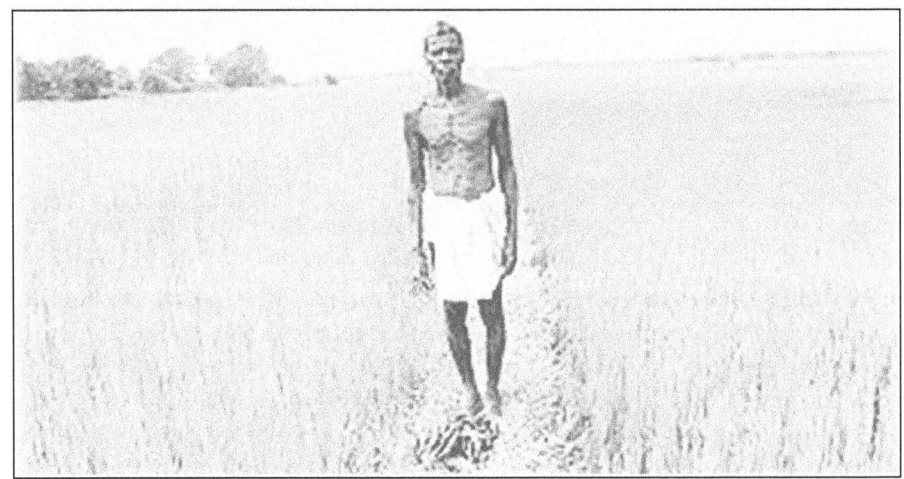

Fig. 13.8: Land ownership of the farmer
Source: Based on Review of Literature

- **Subdivision and Fragmentation of Holding:** Due to the growth of population and the break-down of the joint family system, there has occurred continuous sub-division of agricultural land into smaller and smaller plots. At times small farmers are forced to sell a portion of their land to repay their debt. This creates further sub-division of land. Such sub-division and fragmentation make the efficient use of land virtually impossible and add to the difficulties of increasing capital equipment on the farm. All these factors account for the low productivity of Indian agriculture.

- **Land Tenure:** The land tenure system of India is also far from perfect. In the pre-independence period, most tenants suffered from insecurity of tenancy. They could be evicted any time. However, various steps have been taken after independence to provide security of tenancy.

- **Conditions of agricultural Laborers**: The conditions of most agricultural laborers in India are far from satisfactory. There is also the problem of surplus labor or disguised unemployment. This pushes the wage rates below the sub-sistence levels (Figure 13.9).

Fig. 13.9: Conditions of agricultural laborers
Source: Based on the Review of Literature

- **Inadequate use of manures and fertilizers:** Inadequate use of manures like cow-dung or vegetable refuge and chemical fertilizers makes Indian agriculture much less productive than Japanese or Chinese agriculture.
- **The use of poor quality seeds:** In India, not much use has been made of improved varieties of seeds. The main cereals (rice, millets and pulses) are still growing chiefly with unimproved seeds (Figure 13.10).

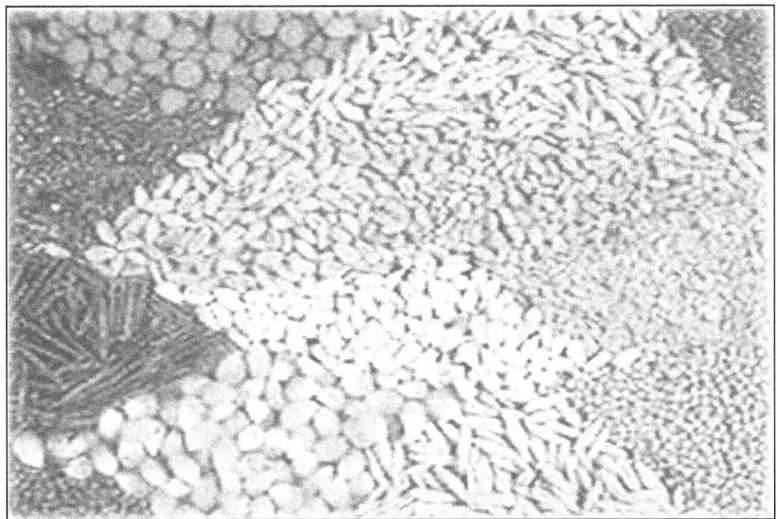

Fig. 13.10: Use of the poor quality seeds
Source: Based on Review and Literature

- **Inadequate use of efficient farm equipment:** The methods of cultivation in most areas of India are still primitive. Most farmers continue to use native plough and other accessories. However, the problem is not shortage of one of modern machinery. The real problem is that the units of cultivation are too small to permit the use of such machinery (Figure 13.11).

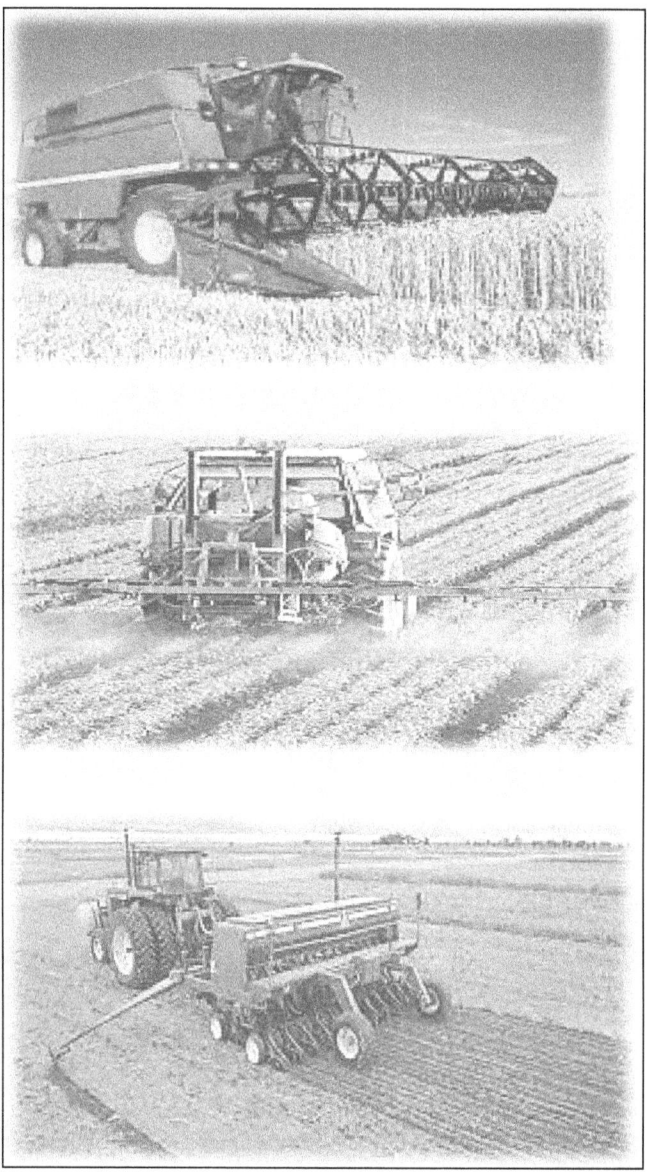

Fig. 13.11: Efficient farm equipments
Source: Based on Review of Literature

Proper arrangement of water supply should be done to avoid the acute shortage of crops due to instability of monsoon. The reallocation of holdings, which are fragmented, the creation of farms which comprise only one or a few parcels in place of the multitude of patches formerly in the possession of each peasant should be done.Solution to land ownership problem is Co-operative farming in which the farmers pool their resources and share the profit. Government of India established the National Seeds Corporation (NSC) in 1963 and the State Farmers Corporation of India (SFCI) in 1969. Thirteen State Seed Corporations (SSCs) were also established to augment the supply of improved seeds to the farmers (Figure 13.12).

Fig. 13.12: Forage and vegetable seeds
Source: Based on the Review of Literature

High Yielding Variety Program (HYVP) was launched in 1966-67 as a major thrust plan to increase the production of food grains in the country. In order to maintain the quality of the fertilizers, 52 fertilizer quality control laboratories have been set up in different parts of the country. In addition, there is one Central Fertilizer Quality Control and Training Institute in Faridabad with its three regional centers in Mumbai, Kolkata and Chennai. Also to avoid the losses due to inappropriate storage facilities, the government has setup many rural storage centers where grains can be safely kept (Figure 13.13).

Fig. 13.13: **High yielding variety**
Source: Based on Review and Literature

As agriculture plays a very vital role in our country's economy, then losses in the agricultural produce will adversely affect the nation's economy. Farmers are our real heroes who work so hard just to feed the country and improve the nation's economy. Therefore, it's a prime responsibility to take care of them and the whole agricultural system in order to protect our country from acute scarcity of food and resources. Many steps have been taken by our government to improve the agriculture sector due to which many of the farmers are benefiting along with overcoming up to the losses in agriculture.

CONCLUSION

Although the status of Indian agriculture raised comparatively well fromthe past, there is a need to increase in the production. New farming techniques should be brought to India like rain guns and harvest machines. Irrigation facilities should be well developed. Soil tests should be conducted and the remedies should be suggested. Skilled laborer should be employed. Educating farmers are very necessary for the growth in agriculture sector. The youth drain should be stopped, and attracting educated youngsters into the field is indispensable. Banks should provide interest free loans to farmers for encouraging them to farm. Equal pay for men and women attracts more woman laborer to work in the farms. The proper wage rate should be given to the farmlaborers. Unless these changes take place in the agriculture country economic growth rate would never reach to 9%, if 9% growth is attained in near future India stands one among the developed countries of the world.

REFERENCES

www.edugree.com
www.mssrf.org
www.yourarticlelibrary.com
www.economicsdiscussion.net
www.importantindia.com

Index

A

AARHUS Convention of the United Nations Economic Commission for Europe, 158
Acorus calamus, 237
Ageratum conyzoides, 234
AIDS, 168
Allium cepa, 235
Alovera sp., 113
Arabian sea, 111
Arachis hypogaea, 98
ASSOCHAM, 156
Avicennia, 99
Ayurveda, 30
Azadirachta indica, 193, 194

B

Basel Convention, 157
Beeswax, 73
Biodiversity of Senchal Wildlife Sanctuary, 34
Biomedical and biodental waste management, 154-184
    biodental wastes, 174
    biohazard and dentistry, 162
    biomedical waste management
        in Karnataka, 160-161
        process, 169-170
        techniques, 173-174
        waste scenario in India, 155-156
    bio-medical waste rules (1998), 156-157
    biomedical wastes in dental office, 179
    biomedical/dental waste disinfection, 173
    categorization of biomedical wastes, 170-172
    chemicals, disinfectants, and sterilizing agents, 179
    classification of
        biohazards, 163
        biomedical/dental waste, 161-162
    environmental impact, 167
    general office waste, 180-182
    hazard to general public, 167
    hazardous effect of biomedical/dental wastes, 165
        air pollution, 165
        in-door air pollution, 165
        land pollution, 166
        out-door air pollution, 165
        radioactive effluent, 166
        water pollution, 165
    international agreements and conventions, 157-158
    introduction, 155
    inverted waste pyramid for solid waste management (6), 167-168
    levels of biohazard, 163-164
    line cleaners, 178
    mutilation, 179
    need of biomedical/dental waste management, 168-169
    newer methodologies to dispose biomedical wastes: (8), 182-183
    objectives of biomedical/dental waste management, 169
    other studies conducted in Karnataka state, 161
    overview of mercury used in dentistry, 175

silver containing dental wastes, 178-179
types of waste generated in dentistry (8), 162
various studies on biomedical waste management in India, 158-160
waste
    accumulation and storage, 172
    disposal, 173
    segregation, 172
    transportation, 172-173
    treatment, 173
ways dental amalgam pollutes the environment, 175-176
ways to combat mercury risks caused by dental amalgam, 176-178
what is biomedical waste, 161
what is biomedical/dental waste management, 169

BMWs, 157
Brassica juncea, 200
British Navy, 231
Buddhal temple, 43
Buddhist Monastery, 34

C

CCA, 232
Ceriops, 99
Chandra, Himadri, 141
Characterization and management of seed borne diseases, 246-255
    biotechnological tools and techniques, 247-251
    cell/tissue culture based technique, 251
    DNA fingerprinting, 249-250
    DNA molecular marker, 247
    future prospects, 254-255
    molecular diagnosis and characterization, 247-249
    recombinant DNA technology, 250
    strategies for disease/pest management, 252-254
Chauhan, Richa, 246

Cirrhinus mrigala, 151
COD, 189
Costa Rica, 31
Crocodile Park, 33
Cultural Aspects, 20
Curcuma longa, 235

D

Development of Women and Children in Rural Areas (DWCRA), 62
Dhiman, Bandana, 226
District Rural Development Agencies (DRDA), 63
DNA, 247
Dubare Elephant Camp, 15
Dutt, Bhupender, 226

E

Ecological status, 89-122
    data collection and literature, 90-91
    faunal biodiversity of study area, 103-111
    introduction, 89-90
    marine environment study by NIO, 111-112
    marine national park and marine sanctuary eco-sensitive zone, Jamnagar, 99-103
    methodology, 90
    Pindara jetty in Kalyanpur taluka, Dwarka, Gujarat, 89-122
    planktonic and benthic habitat, 116-119
    results and discussion, 91
        cultivated plants in study area, 98-99
        observations, 91-98
        status of the forest, their category in study area, 99
    sediment quality, 113-116
    study area and study period, 90
Economic Aspects, 20
Eco-tourism, 1, 2
Esakkimuthu, M., 56

F

FAO, 150
FAO/IPFC symposium, 150
Ficus retusa, 234
Fish and Fisheries of India, 150
Flora and Fauna Angling/Fishing Adventure, 49
Focused Group Discussion, 36

G

Gandhi, Mahatma, 59, 72
GATS, 32
GDP, 7, 57
Gemmaria sp., 114
GHG, 3
Ghosh, Subrato, 141
Global warming, 133
Goddess Durga, 30
Gouri Shankar mandir, 30
Government of India, 28, 61
Greater Spotted Pelican, 115
Green revolution, 151, 259
GST, 263
Gujjari, Anil Kumar, 154
Gujjari, Sheela Kumar, 154
Gulf of Kachchh, 99
Gulf of Mannar, 75

H

Hibiscus rosa-sinensis (China rose), 99
HIV, 162, 164, 168
HYVP, 259, 269

I

IGAU, 37
Impact of poor environmental sanitation, 123-140
    aims of the study, 125
    background of the study, 124
    definition of some terms, 125
    discussion and analysis of result, 135-137
    introduction, 124
    justification of the study, 125
    literature review, 126
        concept of environmental sanitation, 127
        consequences of poor environmental sanitation, 129-133
        how to handle environmental problem, 133-134
        important of environmental sanitation, 134
        introduction, 126
        problem of environmental sanitation in Nigeria, 128-129
        sanitation in colonial/northern Nigeria, 127
        scope of environmental sanitation, 126-127
    materials, 134
    methodology, 134-135
    methods of data
        analysis, 135
        collection, 135
    population of the study, 135
    recommendation, 140
    scope and delimitation of the study, 125
    statement of the problem, 125
    study area, 135
INCLEN Programme Evaluation Network (IPEN), 157
Indian bees (Apis cerana indica), 66
Indian Ocean, 75
Indian Tourism Development Corporation (ITDC), 28
Indus Valley Civilization, 257
Integrated Rural Development Programme (IRDP), 61
International Solid Waste Association, 158
Introduction, 1-5
IPCC Fifth Assessment Report, 4
Italian bees (Apis mellifera), 66

J

Jatropa Carcass, 29

K

Kalchuri dynasty, 30
Kameswari, VLV, 56
Kanger Valley National Park, 30
Karanj, 200
Karl Pearson formula, 78
Kazaure, Mustapha Bashir, 123
Kerala, 28
Khadi and Village Industries Commission (KVIC), 66
Kharif season, 48
Kodagu, Karnataka India, 6-25
Krishi Vigyan Kendra, 86
Kumar, Prasann, 256

L

L. vannamei, 142
Laminar Air Flow, 238
Litopenaeus vannamei, 141-153

M

Madhya Pradesh, 30
Madikeri Fort, 14
Madras Presidency, 73
Maharashtra, 33, 58
Management practices in *Litopenaeus vannamei* farming in coastal, 141-153
   aeration and other features, 146
   air blower, 144
   benefits of farming, 142
   distinguishing features of L. vannamei, 141-142
   end note, 146-149
   feeding, 145-146
   Fish and Fisheries of India, 151-152
   Jhingran, Dr. V.G., 150-151
   L. vannamei farming in Purba Medinipur, 142-143
   management practices, 144-145
   visited farm site, 143-144
Marine National Park and Sanctuary, 99
Marthandam Beekeeping Society, 78
Mohanty, Pragyan, 154
Mother Nature, 28
MUFA, 193
Mustard, 200
Mythological scripts, 30

N

Nagarahole National Park, 14
National Horticultural Board (NHB), 71
National Parks, 29
National Seeds Corporation (NSC) in 1963, 269
Nature Conservancy, 2
New Millennium, 59, 72
NGOs, 63, 71, 86
NHB, 86
NOAA, 3
Non-governmental organizations, 38

P

P. monodon, 142
Panigrahi, Rabinarayan, 213
Pearson correlation coefficient, 19
Pelecanus philippensis, 115
Photo degradation of surfactants, 185-212
   copper metal, 195-196
   heterogeneous photocatalysis, 189-192
   homogeneous photocatalysis, 188
   introduction, 186
   mechanism, 202-205
   overview of natural fats and oils, 192-193
      edible oils, 194
      non-edible oils, 193-194
   photo degradation, 201-202
   photocatalysis phenomenon, 187-188
   photocatalytic reactions, 188
   significance and applications of present work, 199-200

significance of surfactants, 194-195
spectroscopic studies, 201
structure solubility and Micellar properties of surfactants, 196-199
synthesis, 200-201

Pindara Jetty, 90

Pinna bicolar, 114

Pollination, 73

Pollution free society and environment, 185-212

Pongamia pinnata, 200

PRA, 36

Pradhan, Ranjan Kumar, 213

PUFA, 193

Purba Medinipur, West Bengal, 141-153

PVC, 158

R

Ramchurjee, Charles V., 6

Ramchurjee, Nichola A., 6

Ramgarh forest hill, 30

Random Rural Appraisal (RRA), 36

Rathoure, Ashok Kumar, 89

Residents satisfaction to eco-tourism impacts and their attitudes and opinions, 6-25
awareness of the respondents to standards of living and eco-tourism plans and development, 16-19
correlation between independent variables- Pearson product-moment correlation, 19-21
economic impacts of eco-tourism, 9
environmental impacts of eco-tourism, 10-12
introduction, 7-8
method, 12
results and discussion, 15
profile of the respondents, 15-16
social and cultural impacts of eco-tourism, 9-10
study area, 12-13
tourism on Kodagu, 13-15

Review on adsorbent nature of graphene/metal oxide composites for water remediation technology, 213-225
about graphene, 215-216
effect of pH in adsorption, 217-218
FE_3O_4 adsorbed on graphene, 216-217
how to improve adsorption efficiency, 221-222
introduction, 214-215
mechanism of adsorption, 216
metal oxides other than FE_3O_4 adsorbed on graphene, 218-221

Rhizopora, 99

River Haldi, 142
Kaveri, 15
Lakshmanatirtha, 14

RNA, 254

Role of agriculture in national development with special reference to India, 256-271
introduction, 256-258
emphasis on agricultural history, 258-259
green revolution and attaining saturation, 259-261
words delivered by MS Swaminathan, 261-270

Role of Conservation Research and Education Centers in growing Nature-based Tourism, 32

Rosella Montana, 114

Rural entrepreneurship, 56-88
agricultural land holding pattern in India, 58-59
beekeeping in India, 65-67
concept of entrepreneur and entrepreneurship, 63-65
conceptualisation of entrepreneurial potential, 69-72
constraints experienced by beekeepers, 83-86
entrepreneurial potential of beekeepers, 81-82
entrepreneurship

and economic development, 59-61
development programmes in India, 61-63
extent of adoption of scientific beekeeping technologies by beekeepers, 80-81
introduction, 57-58
profile and communication characteristics of beekeepers, 79-80
relationship between
    extent of adoption of scientific beekeeping technologies and entrepreneurial potential of beekeepers, 82
    socio-economic and communication characteristics of beekeepers and their entrepreneurial potential, 82
research data collection tools and techniques, 78
research locale of the study, 75-76
research methodology, 73
research research design, 78
research selection of
    blocks, 76
    respondents, 78
    villages, 76-77
research statistical tools, 78-79
research universe of the study, 73-75
results and discussion, 79
sustainable beekeeping practices in Indian context, 72-73
theories of entrepreneurship, 67-69

S

Safe Mercury Amalgam Removal Technique (SMART), 177
Sarbhanja, 34
SC/ST, 39, 61
Scarcity of food and resources, 270
Scheme for Training and Employment Programme (STEP), 62
Scotland of India, 14

Sea Customs Act 1878, 90
Senapati, Manas Ranjan, 213
Sharma, Arun Kumar, 185
Sharma, Rashmi, 185
Sharma, Swati, 185
Shimla of Chhattisgarh, 34
SHM, 86
Shuwarin Kiyawa, Nigeria, 123-140
Sick Building Syndrome (SBS), 165
Singh, Chandrahas, 26
Singh, Nandkumar, 26
Social Aspects, 20
Socio-environmental survey of Mainpat, 26-55
    agricultures, 37
    discussions, 48-49
        demography of study site, 48
        status of eco-tourism management and development in study site, 48-49
    eco-tourism
        in India, 28-29
        places in Chhattisgarh, 29-30
    geography, 35-36
    history, 35
    important eco-tourism places in Sarguja district, 30-31
    introduction, 26
    land, 38
    material and methodologists, 36
    method of data collection, 38-39
    need of the study, 31
    objective, 31
    place to visit in Mainpat, 34-35
    recommendations, 49-50
    relationship between eco-tourism and sustainable tourism, 26-28
    result and discussion, 39-48
    review literature, 31-34
    soil, 38

some general information of Mainpat, 36-37

study area, 34

suggestions, 50-53

to assess the future prospects of eco-tourism in study site, 49

Soyabean (*Glycine max*), 200

Standard of Living, 20

State Horticultural Mission (SHM), 71

Stockholm Convention, 2006, 158

Strategies of wood preservation, 226-245

    challenges in developing new wood preservatives, 234-237

    development in wood preservation from history, 230-231

    environmental concerns with CCA alternatives, 232-233

    experiment study, 237-238

    extract treatment method, 238

    future strategies, 233

    impacts of use of CCA-treated wood on health and environment, 231-232

    introduction, 226-227

    isolation and identification of fungus, 238

    media preparation, 238-239

    naturally rot-resistant woods, 227-228

    oil-type preservatives, 229

    results, 239

        effect of A. calamus L. rhizome extract on fungal colonization on treated and untreated wood, 239

        fungal biotechnology, 239-240

    types of wood preservatives, 229

    waterborne preservatives, 229-230

    what is preservation, 227

Sultan, Tipu, 14

Swaminathan, MS, 261-270

Swarnajayanti Gram Swarozgar Yojana (SGSY), 62

T

Tectona grandis, 236

TFC, 28

The Protestant Ethic and Spirit of Capitalism, 67

Thenmala, 28

Tibetan camp, 34

Tibetan refugees, 35

Tiger of Mysore, 14

Tourism, 10

    industry, 28

Training of Rural Youth for Self-Employment (TRYSEM), 62

Triticum aestivum, 98

U

United Nations Statistical Commission, 28

W

Water pollution, 133

Weather and Accommodation facilities, 43

WHO, 126, 158, 161

    Guidance, 158

Wild Life Protection Act, 1972, 33

Wildlife Sanctuary, 14

World Conservation Union, 2

World Summit on sustainable tourism (2002), 32

WTO, 28, 32

Z

Zingiber zerumbet, 235

Lightning Source UK Ltd.
Milton Keynes UK
UKHW032215020621
384820UK00002B/6